Fundamentals of Strategic Management

RAGHAVAN PARTHASARTHY

City University of New York, Baruch College

Houghton Mifflin Company   Boston   New York

To my family.
—R.P.

Publisher: George Hoffman
Associate Sponsoring Editor: Joanne Dauksewicz
Editorial Assistant: Amy Galvin
Project Editor: Shelley Dickerson
Editorial Assistant: Sarah Driver
Senior Art/Design Coordinator: Jill Haber
Composition Buyer: Chuck Dutton
Associate Manufacturing Buyer: Brian Pieragostini
Executive Marketing Manager: Steven Mikels
Marketing Specialist: Lisa E. Boden

Cover Image: © Michael Simpson/Getty Images

Printed in the U.S.A.

Library of Congress Control Number: 2005936320

Student Edition (use for ordering) –
ISBN 13: 978-0-618-42759-8
ISBN 10: 0-618-42759-7

Exam Copy –
ISBN 13: 978-0-618-73226-5
ISBN 10: 0-618-73226-8

1 2 3 4 5 6 7 8 9–EB–09 08 07 06 05

Brief Contents

Contents

PART THREE Strategic Choice 97

PART FOUR   Strategy Implementation 191

Preface

"What causes a business to succeed?" This essential question forms the basis of discussion in each chapter of *Fundamentals of Strategic Management,* providing students with a solid grounding in strategic management theory by emphasizing strategy in practice. Written especially for the undergraduate student, this clear and uncomplicated approach to strategic management will engage and encourage students who may have little or no business experience and often find complicated theoretical discussion cumbersome and intimidating. The brevity of the text also allows instructors and students to move more quickly beyond conceptual understanding to practical applications of theory through case discussions or strategic management simulations.

Concise texts on strategic management, like this one, are already on the market. What differentiates this text from others is the level at which it is written and the supporting features that accompany it. Following are some of its highlights:

- The text is written in a simple, engaging, and conversational style. It avoids complex sentences and unnecessary verbiage. Ideas in each chapter are clearly developed to enable students to quickly grasp and internalize them.

- Key terms are defined and explained in jargon-free language. Concepts are illustrated with examples from well-known companies, such as Nike, PepsiCo, and Wal-Mart.

- The text takes a hands-on, application-driven approach by providing models that the students can readily use to perform critical analyses (e.g., industry analysis, internal analysis of a firm).

- Each chapter opens with a vignette, written in an anecdotal fashion, and the theme of the vignette is well-integrated with the chapter material.

- Each chapter ends with a simple summary that offers a good review tool for students.

- Each chapter includes projects and application exercises designed to involve students on an experiential level.

- The text material is comprehensively integrated through the use of two running cases appearing at the end of chapters. The Southwest Airlines case integrates the material presented in chapters 1–5; and the PepsiCo case integrates the material presented in chapters 6–10.

Organization of the Text

This book follows a traditional sequencing of topics. It contains 10 chapters, grouped into five parts. Part One describes the strategic management process and the context within which it occurs – business mission, stakeholders, corporate governance, and social responsibility issues. Part Two explains the impact of the external and internal environments on company performance and discusses the frameworks commonly used to assess industry conditions and firm competencies. Part Three examines the strategic choices available to a firm at the business, corporate, international, and functional levels to realize the company's mission and vision. Part Four covers strategy implementation and organizational structure mechanisms to implement strategies. Part Five discusses strategic control and explains how firms evaluate their long-term performance.

Pedagogical Features

In writing this text, I have kept the needs of instructors and students in mind. Following are some of the pedagogical features of this text that I believe should be helpful in effectively teaching and learning strategic management at a fundamental level:

- Chapter opening vignettes, written in an anecdote-like fashion, provide an excellent organizing theme to start the day's lecture, explain chapter concepts, and facilitate application-oriented learning.
- "Strategy in Practice" inserts help explain strategic management applications and create short case scenarios for class discussion.
- A chapter-ending running case allows the instructor to explain strategic management concepts and issues in an integrated manner.
- Key terms are highlighted and defined in simple language. The text also includes a comprehensive glossary of key terms.
- Chapter-ending exercises include research projects designed to serve as excellent source material for term assignments.

Instructor Supplements

A variety of ancillary materials are designed to assist the instructor in the classroom.

HMXChange Case Database. The perfect solution for those who want to vary case content each semester, the HMXChange Case Database offers a customized casebook designed to suit the needs of your particular course. As an added convenience, all casebook(s) content is retained online, making it easy to return to the case database at your convenience to review new cases, make alternations to current casebooks, and obtain reorder information easily from any computer with an Internet connection.

Online Instructor's Resource Manual. An instructor's manual provides a chapter summary, objectives, and a thorough lecture outline for each chapter. In addition, teaching tips and guidelines for the end-of-chapter projects are included as well as complete answers to the end-of-chapter discussion questions. Comprehensive teaching notes for the two running cases on Southwest Airlines and PepsiCo are also provided.

Test Bank. The test bank includes true-false, multiple-choice, and essay questions for each chapter in the textbook. Complete answers, with page references, are provided for all questions.

Online Teaching Center. The Online Teaching Center provides instructors with lecture notes, answers to end-of-chapter questions, teaching notes for the end-of-chapter cases, and basic and premium PowerPoint slides that can be downloaded for classroom use.

HMTesting.   The computerized version of the Test Bank allows instructors to select, edit, and add questions, or generate randomly selected questions to produce a test master for easy duplication. Online testing and gradebook functions allow instructors to administer tests via their local area network or the World Wide Web, set up classes, record grades from tests or assignments, analyze grades, and compile class and individual statistics. This program can be used on both PC and Macintosh computers.

Videos.   The video package highlights real-world companies and corresponds with the concepts and topics highlighted in the text. The video guide provides teaching notes to help prepare for each video and to provide in-class discussion ideas.

PowerPoint.   This classroom presentation package (downloadable from the Web) comes in basic and premium versions, including over 25 slides per chapter combining clear, concise text and art to create a total presentation package. Instructors who have access to PowerPoint can edit slides to customize them for their presentations. Slides can also be printed as lecture notes for class distribution. In addition to slides covering textbook content, the premium version of the program provides examples and data that supplement what is in the text. These slides come with additional notes for instructors.

Call-in test service.   This service lets instructors select items from the Test Bank and call our toll-free faculty services number (800-733-1717) to order printed tests.

Student Supplements

Online Study Center.   This especially rich resource for students includes Internet links that allow students to further explore strategic management issues and resources, a flashcard glossary, and ACE self-study questions.

Online Strategic Management Simulation.   *Micromatic* is a business simulation game designed for use in both graduate and undergraduate Business Policy/ Strategic Management courses. In addition, many businesses have used *Micromatic* for management development training. Because of the number and type of decisions the student users must make, *Micromatic* is classified as a medium to complex simulation exercise. Both the student and the instructor can quickly and easily learn *Micromatic.* Users like *Micromatic* for both the excitement the game generates and the authors' service for the game.

Wall Street Journal Subscription Offer.   A *Wall Street Journal* offer is available with this textbook. Students whose instructors have adopted *WSJ* with *Fundamentals of Strategic Management* will receive, shrink-wrapped with their book, a registration card for the 10-week print and online subscription to the *WSJ.* Students must fill out and return the registration card found in the text to initiate the subscription privileges. The text package will also include a copy of the *Wall Street Journal Student Subscriber Handbook,* which explains how to use both print and online versions of the newspaper. This is only sold as a package with new textbooks. *WSJ* subscriptions cannot be sold as a stand-alone item.

Acknowledgements

This textbook could not have been accomplished without the help and generous support of others. I am forever indebted to my wife Jan for her love, forbearance, and for single-handedly managing the household while I was busy writing this book.

I am grateful to my son and daughter for their words of love, support, and encouragement. Heartfelt thanks are due to my colleagues at the Zicklin School of Business and elsewhere who freely shared their ideas with me, helping me to continuously refine my thinking and understanding of strategic management. Most importantly, I am deeply obliged to those professionals at Houghton Mifflin who provided me with an unstinting support that was necessary to transform my manuscript into a finished product. Special thanks go to George Hoffman, Publisher; Lisé Johnson, Senior Sponsoring Editor; Joanne Dauksewicz, Associate Sponsoring Editor; Steve Mikels, Executive Marketing Manager; and Shelley Dickerson, Project Editor. Immense thanks also are also due to the following reviewers whose comments and suggestions helped me in no small a manner:

A.D. Amar, *Seton Hall University*
Suzanne Clinton, *Cameron University*
Robert D'Intino, *Rowan University*
Sanjay Goel, *University of Minnesota, Duluth*
Leslie Haugen, *University of St. Thomas*
John Humphreys, *Eastern New Mexico University*
Deborah Johnson, *Franklin University*
Kamalesh Kumar, *University of Michigan, Dearborn*
Edwin Leonard, *Indiana University-Purdue University*
William Lundstrom, *Cleveland State University*
Randall Martin, *Florida International University*
Richard Martinez, *Baylor University*
David Olson, *California State University, Bakersfield*
James Pappas, *Oklahoma State University*
Lori Paris, *California State University, Fresno*
Tara Radin, *Hofstra University*
William Ritchie, *Florida Gulf Coast University*
John Ross, *Texas State University*
Thomas Sgritta, *University of North Carolina at Charlotte*
Bing-Sheng Teng, *George Washington University*
Mike Wakefield, *Colorado State University, Pueblo*
Garland Wiggs, *Radford University*

About the Author

Raghavan Parthasarthy teaches at the Zicklin School of Business, Baruch College (City University of New York), where he also received his PhD in 1991. A recipient of Baruch's Best Doctoral Dissertation Award, he has taught graduate- and undergraduate-level courses at the Stern School of Business of New York University. Dr. Parthasarthy focuses his research and writing on Corporate Strategy, Competitive Strategy, and Strategic Management of Technology and Innovation. His scholarly work has appeared in the *Academy of Management Review, Strategic Management Journal,* and *Journal of Engineering and High Technology Management,* among others. He is also a principal partner at Strategy Consulting Group, in which capacity he has advised AT&T, Ford Motor Company, BSNL (India), Punjab Agro Industries Corporation, and the State Government of Punjab (India) on strategy initiatives.

Part One

The Strategic Management Context

Overview of Strategic Management

CHAPTER OBJECTIVES

After reading this chapter, you should be able to:

- Define strategic management and discuss its importance for a firm's competitive success and sustained profitability

- Define strategy and describe alternative definitions of strategy

- Discuss how strategy creates competitive advantage necessary for sustained profitability

- Define a successful firm and describe how to measure a firm's success

- Describe the strategic management process, the steps involved in this process, and alternative models of strategy formulation

- Define strategic leadership and explain how it is essential for a firm's long-term success

Opening Case

Kodak was once the most popular and respected brand of photographic films. Eastman Kodak began business in 1901 in New Jersey, and by the 1950s it was a household name. George Eastman's invention, which made it possible to record images on a film (as opposed to the traditional glass plates), had revolutionized photography, thrusting his company to instant fame. By designing an easy-to-use portable camera for his film, Eastman popularized photography among the masses. Kodak grew rapidly, aided by the novelty of its products, continuous innovation such as color film, and the absence of competition. Worldwide expansion through production and marketing operations in other countries soon catapulted Kodak to its position as a global leader in the film business. By the early 1990s, Kodak, a giant corporation with over 100,000 employees, was a blue-chip company with gross sales of $20 billion.

It all changed for Mama Kodak, as the firm is affectionately known, when competition in the form of Fuji Photo Film Company of Japan came knocking at its doors. Using the latest manufacturing technologies, Fuji cut the production cost of photographic film without lowering image quality and competed on price, snatching Kodak's customers rapidly. By the 1970s, Fuji was a potent competitor in the U.S. and international markets, limiting Kodak's ability to raise prices on its signature product, the roll film. But a more severe blow to Kodak came in 1981, when Sony introduced a digital camera that stored images on a computer chip. By eliminating the need for film, the digital camera seriously threatened Kodak's very survival. Suddenly, a world without film emerged as a possibility.

Kodak responded to these competitive threats by diversifying into other businesses and reducing its dependency on the film business. During the 1980s and 1990s Kodak moved haphazardly in and out of several unrelated businesses. In 1988, the company acquired a pharmaceutical business—an industry in which it had very little knowledge—only to sell it in 1994 when the acquisition proved unprofitable. It entered the office copier business, but intense competition in that industry soon forced Kodak to sell that business too. Kodak then introduced a 35-mm camera but was late to market and the market ignored it. It developed a disposable camera but delayed marketing the camera, thus losing opportunities. Bad acquisitions, failed innovations, and lethargic responses to competitive threats exacted their toll on Kodak's gross income. From an all-time high of $20 billion in 1992, Kodak's sales plummeted to $13.5 billion in 2004. To cut its losses, the company restructured itself several times, each time reducing its workforce sizably. In 2004, Kodak's employee strength was 50,000—a mere half of what it had been a decade earlier.

The photographic film business remains Kodak's mainstay, representing 70 percent of its sales income. But each year the market for film is shrinking, making Kodak a leader in a declining industry. Although Kodak had plans to enter the digital camera market as early as Sony, the company hesitated, fearing the entry would cannibalize its film business. It finally moved in, long after many others did, through a series of acquisitions that cost over $4 billion. Its investments have yet to pay off, partly because the demand for digital photography is still emerging. Even when demand does emerge in full force, Kodak may not be able to secure a commanding market share because of its late arrival in a field in which Sony and Canon are well-established players. In the meantime, for each digital camera Kodak sells, it sacrifices film sales on which it has a higher gross margin. As a result, most Wall Street analysts are not optimistic about Eastman Kodak's future. For the first time in its one-hundred-year history, they are recommending that investors stay away from its stock.[1]

How do we explain what caused Kodak's troubles? Could Kodak have prevented its failures? Kodak's history tells us that the company was not always aware, or in control, of its industry environment. It drifted with the environment, reacting to change as it occurred rather than anticipating change or influencing it. As a result, Kodak allowed competition and alternative technology easy access into its territory. As a leader in the photo film business, Kodak should have prevented competitor entry by frequently improving its technology. It should have developed new technologies that would have set the standards for competing in the photographic industry in its favor. Instead, Kodak failed to pioneer new technologies, moved in late when such technologies emerged, and let new entrants take control in setting alternative technology standards. This inability to *strategically manage* its business—anticipating change and taking actions to influence environmental conditions in its favor—brought Kodak to its present state.

Kodak is hardly the only firm that got into trouble because of its failure to monitor change and strategically manage its environment. In recent memory, General Motors, Sears, and IBM paid a price for similar negligence.[2] During the 1970s, General Motors was the leader in U.S. auto sales with more than 50 percent market share, but by 2005 this share had dropped to a paltry 26 percent, hardly sufficient to keep the firm profitable.[3] General Motors had surrendered much of its business to foreign auto firms by failing to prevent their entry into the United States and by not anticipating and responding in time to a growing consumer demand for small, fuel-efficient, high quality cars.[4] For eighty years, Sears was the world leader in retailing but lost its preeminent position due to a lack of industry awareness and adaptation. During the 1980s and 1990s, Sears never clearly understood the changes occurring in the retail industry, reacting to rather than anticipating them, and allowing the more vigilant and well-prepared Wal-Mart to overtake it.[5] In November 2004, a financially troubled Sears was acquired by an equally troubled Kmart for $11 billion.[6] Until the early 1990s, IBM was the dominant force in the computing industry. It was fully complacent about the mainframe technology and its hold on that technology, and so it virtually ignored changes occurring in the field of information processing. By then, minicomputers and server technologies had entered the industry and made inroads into IBM's sales and market position. IBM may never again be as dominant a force in the information processing industry as it once was.[7]

In industries where General Motors, Sears, and IBM lost ground, Toyota, Wal-Mart, Dell, and Hewlett-Packard gained prominence. Business history is filled with similar examples of firms not succeeding at all or succeeding but failing to retain their success. As a student of business management you certainly would want to know the reasons why firms succeed or fail. What characteristics separate successful firms from unsuccessful ones? How do firms like Wal-Mart emerge as leaders of an industry and remain leaders while others in the same industry, such as Kmart or Sears struggle just to stay in business? How do firms like Southwest Airlines continually earn superior profits even under hostile industry conditions when their peers, such as United Airlines, languish? While you may find detailed answers to these and similar questions in different parts of this book, what we will say here, in a nutshell, should serve as a comprehensive answer to such questions. *Successful firms manage their activities strategically: they not only manage their internal resources competently but also monitor and proactively manage their industry or competitive environment.* Let us examine this statement closely:

- Competent management of internal resources gives birth to unique capabilities—for example, ability to innovate frequently.
- Proactive management of the industry environment assures a firm a favorable market position.
- Together, unique capabilities and a favorable market position endow a firm with the competitive advantages it needs for long-term success.

Strategy in Practice 1.1 describes how Intel, the leading maker of microprocessors, strategically manages its internal resources and the industry environment to stay ahead of competition.

This book is about *strategic management* and how it creates *competitive advantage for long-term success*. This chapter does the following:

- provides a broad description of *strategic management* that subsequent chapters will examine in detail
- defines *strategy* and explains how it creates *competitive advantage*
- describes competitive advantage and how it is essential for a firm's long-term success
- defines a *successful firm*
- describes how managers formulate and implement strategies
- illustrates the specific strategies that managers employ at different levels of a firm to create the competitive advantages necessary for long-term success

What Is Strategic Management?

Strategic management refers to a series of long-term decisions and actions taken by managers in which they select and implement strategies. The purpose of these strategies is to build the firm's strengths through market positioning and/or accumulation of internal resources that will give the firm an advantage over rivals. In a nutshell, gaining and sustaining competitive advantage by formulating and implementing appropriate strategies describes strategic management.

Traditionally, managers sought competitive advantages by efficiently managing the firm's internal resources. Simple markets and stable industries allowed them to focus only on the firm's internal resources and activities when aiming for competitive advantages. Markets and industries are no longer simple or stable; they have become differentiated and dynamic, and many are global in size. New industries and new market segments emerge almost overnight due to dramatically changing technologies, while established industries and segments disappear just as quickly. Small firms aided by radical innovations and global market opportunities, rapidly emerge as dominant firms, while established firms lose markets/customers and disappear just as rapidly. Differentiated markets, dynamic technologies, and globalization of businesses have altered both the nature of competition and how firms compete. In the new situation, traditional techniques that focus solely on the efficient management of internal resources are not only archaic but also insufficient for competitive success. Today's business environment requires firms to gain sustainable competitive advantages by actively managing their external environment, side by side with internal resources.

Strategy in PRACTICE 1.1

HOW INTEL MANAGES ITS INTERNAL RESOURCES AND EXTERNAL ENVIRONMENT STRATEGICALLY FOR SUPERIOR PERFORMANCE

Intel makes microprocessors using patented technology. A leader in the semiconductor industry, Intel commands a 75 percent market share for microprocessors and maintains a dominating presence throughout the computer industry. In 2004, its gross revenues were $34 billion, ten times larger than those of its nearest rival, Advanced Micro Devices. During the same year, its market capitalization was greater than that of the Big Three U.S. automakers combined. Undoubtedly, Intel is a truly successful firm. In its thirty-five-year existence, the company has transformed itself into a semiconductor giant and the most profitable chip manufacturer in the world. How did Intel do it? Academicians and researchers unanimously say that through carefully positioning itself in its market, controlling industry forces, and by deploying internal resources in pursuit of technological innovation and market-share goals, Intel has gained enduring competitive advantages resulting in superior company performance.

From its very inception in 1968 Intel's management of internal resources has been guided by two goals: (a) to develop and commercialize unique semiconductor technologies and (b) to continuously enhance those invented technologies. Development of unique technologies was intended to give the firm proprietary products, leading to technological leadership and pioneering advantages. Continuous enhancement of such technologies was intended to prevent competitive imitation, thereby allowing Intel to retain its leadership position. By making massive R&D investments and competently managing its intellectual resources, Intel emerged as a highly knowledgeable firm in the

semiconductor and electronics-components manufacturing business. This knowledge helped Intel to invent several proprietary products—the microprocessor being just one of them. The microprocessor is a unique technology that virtually set the standard for building personal computers, thereby paving the way for Intel to dominate the PC industry from the outset. And, by continuously enhancing its microprocessor architecture, Intel has made it difficult for rivals to achieve competitive parity.

Intel has proactively managed its external environment, achieving a dominant market position and preventing rival forces from gaining an upper hand. To begin with, it freely licensed its microprocessor technology to competitors. This had the twin effects of popularizing Intel's design architecture while discouraging rivals from developing competing versions of microprocessors. Second, to keep competitors weak, Intel frequently launched patent infringement suits against them. Some of these suits were aimed at former employees and PC manufacturers so as to prevent them from becoming Intel's future rivals. Third, to make consumers associate its name with quality and insist on Intel's processor inside the PC, the company employed a branding strategy. The "Intel Inside" slogan was designed to encourage PC buyers to focus on the processor inside, rather than the PC maker's name on the box, when they made purchasing decisions.

Source: T. Jackson, *Inside Intel: Andy Grove and the Rise of the World's Most Powerful Chip Company* (New York: Penguin Books, 1997); R. A. Burgelman, *Strategy Is Destiny* (New York: The Free Press, 2002); Intel Corporation, *Annual Report*, 2003.

Examples of environmental management include barring entry of new competitors into the market, controlling suppliers and customers, restricting rival firms from becoming too powerful, or altering industry conditions in a way that favors a firm.[8] When managing internal resources, the aim is to develop core competencies that not only give a firm superior capability in current and future operations but will also allow the firm to disrupt rivals' capabilities.[9] *The process of managing both the external environment and internal resources in ways that create sustainable advantages over competition is called strategic management.*

Strategy is the source of competitive advantage, and is fundamental for business success. When well-conceived and executed, strategy creates the competitive advantage the firm needs to outperform rivals. Clearly, an understanding of both *strategy* and *competitive advantage* is essential before we can proceed to understand strategic management in detail.

What Is Strategy?

There is no single, universally accepted definition of the term **strategy**.[10] Several definitions exist and each is relevant under certain conditions and in certain contexts.[11] Some writers define it as a deliberately designed *plan* to achieve a firm's ends.[12] By this definition, a firm systematically considers several alternatives for attaining its long-term goals and selects an alternative that best fits its needs. It then rigidly implements this alternative through an elaborate series of decisions and actions in which it allocates resources to tasks and monitors results. Others define strategy as decisions and actions that align a firm's strengths to industry opportunities and threats.[13] In this sense, strategy is a *process* in which a firm continuously adapts to external conditions so as to be the fittest for its environment. (Remember Darwin's theory that adaptive species survive and succeed?). Yet, for others, strategy is a *pattern* in a stream of decisions[14] —that is, strategy is what a firm consistently does. Thus, a firm that consistently promotes its brand and sells its products only through upscale stores is said to be using a differentiation strategy. And for some others, strategy is a "ploy"—a maneuver intended to outwit, confuse, or fool the enemy.[15]

Military science, where the strategy concept originated, defines strategy from a *positional* perspective: the way troops are arranged and placed on the battlefield to secure an advantage over the enemy.[16] Imagine a small army positioning its troops on the top of a hill to gain an advantage over a larger enemy. Since there can be several troop formations, each arrangement is based on a strategy aimed at achieving a certain military goal. Some management scholars have modeled their definition of strategy for a firm on this positioning approach, which might include building a strong market position by erecting large-scale production and distribution facilities or occupying and defending a niche segment.[17]

In this text, we will use a simple definition proposed by some,[18] but with a slight modification: *strategy is a set of decisions and actions that managers make and take to attain superior company performance relative to rivals.* This definition implicitly assumes that hurdles exist in the path to superior company performance. In the absence of hurdles, there would be no need for a strategy. Hurdles arise from the actions of rival firms competing for the same goal. The aim of strategy, therefore, is to equip a firm with the strengths it needs to overcome hurdles. Strategy does this by guiding managers to allocate resources in a way that would endow the firm with an advantage over rivals—a strong market position, and exceptional internal capabilities—leading to superior company performance. For example, in an industry where the pricing power of firms is low, managers may allocate marketing resources to the product so as to position it as a premium brand (known as differentiation strategy— for example, Rolex). When effective, a strong market position gives the firm a pricing advantage—the ability to charge a higher price even when others are offering similar product at a lower price. Likewise, a firm may consistently invest in automation technologies and worker skills to gain a product-processing advantage (known

| FIGURE 1.1 | **Strategy, Competitive Advantage, and Performance** |

as cost-leadership strategy—for example, Timex) that allows the firm to lower operational costs and enjoy higher gross margins than rivals. The important point is that strategy focuses on the advantages needed for superior performance to occur. It provides a firm with a sound basis for allocating financial, informational, and human resources that foster competitive advantage that, when exploited, results in superior company performance. Figure 1.1 illustrates this point.

What Is Competitive Advantage?

Competitive advantage refers to an edge or strength a firm has over its rivals. This may arise from high brand visibility, a dominant market share, a capability to make the product at a lower cost, or higher perceived value. Thus, a firm's competitive advantage may be due to a favorable market position, a unique internal capability, or a combination of the two. A firm's competitive advantage, then, is a strength built and nurtured over time that few or no rivals in the industry possess. *The benefit competitive advantage bestows is the potential for earning superior profits.*

Competitive advantage must be sustained in order for a firm to continue to enjoy superior profits. Only when a firm continuously invests in resources that generate the advantage does the firm maintain its leadership position. Intel, for example, invests approximately 15 percent of its sales revenue each year on research and development to remain the technological leader in microprocessors.* Kodak, among its other missteps, failed to consistently enhance the photographic film technology, the source of its competitive advantage, and allowed its advantage to evaporate.

While competitive advantage is a fundamental requirement for earning superior profits in most industries today, some industries are inherently more favorable for generating higher profits than others.[19] For example, toiletries, pharmaceuticals, and tobacco are industries that offer attractive opportunities for superior profits. In these industries, high entry barriers and the absence of substitutes allow firms to enjoy a higher rate of return on their invested capital.† By contrast, in industries such as steel, airlines, and basic building materials, the commodity nature of the product, declining demand, and excess industry capacity lead to price wars among firms, resulting in extremely low or near-zero rates of return. Therefore, a firm's profitability depends on both industry conditions and the firm's own competitive advantage. In industries with narrow profitability, a firm needs a strong market position and exceptional internal capabilities to earn an adequate rate of return.

---

*Intel Corporation, *Annual Report*, 2003.
†Invested capital = stockholders' equity plus borrowed funds

What Is a Successful Firm and How Do We Measure a Firm's Success?

Several measures of business success exist: size of the firm, market share, technological leadership, innovation frequency, survival (that is, longevity), and profitability. *Profitability is a financial measure of success; all of the other examples are strategic measures of success.* At a given point in time, depending on the competitive landscape, a firm's strategic goals may include any or a combination of these strategic measures of success. For example, a firm may aim for market-share leadership in an industry where the product's design is stable and, as a result, volume production is critical in competition. Another may seek innovation frequency in an industry where products go out of circulation rapidly. But market share or innovation frequency are not ends in themselves. The purpose of seeking them is only to use them as a basis for attaining a firm's ultimate goal: profits. In other words, strategic goals represent the competitive advantage the firm seeks for earning superior profits. *Hence, profitability is the fundamental measure of business success; firms aim for strategic goals as stepping-stones to profitability.*[20]

Gross profits and net profits are general indicators of a firm's profitability. Gross profits* indicate the efficiency of the firm's operations, and net profits indicate a firm's overall efficiency and effectiveness. To make meaningful comparisons, profits are computed as a ratio of sales, stockholders' equity, or total invested capital. One can evaluate a firm's profit performance by making historical comparisons of these ratios—that is, by examining the firm's current profit percentages relative to prior-year profit percentages. These calculations would indicate the profit growth rate of the firm over a certain period, but such evaluations are meaningless unless they are made within a competitive context. In other words, it is not a firm's profitability *per se* but the relationship of its profitability to that of its competitors that indicates the firm's success. Therefore, *a firm is deemed to be successful when it enjoys above-average profitability in its industry.* We define above-average profitability as *returns earned by a firm on its invested capital that are greater than the average earned by all firms in the industry.*[†] Thus, in an industry where the average rate of return on invested capital is 10 percent, firms with higher than 10 percent return are deemed to be successful.

While profitability is a necessary condition for business success, viewing a firm as successful based on its current profitability alone could be misleading, because today's profitability is no guarantee that the firm would be profitable in the future. Therefore, it is essential to measure success based not only on the firm's current profitability, but also on its ability to earn superior profits in the future. Researchers say that this is done by examining the firm's potential to earn future profits as evidenced by the competitive advantages gained through the pursuit of strategic goals, side by side with an assessment of current profitability.[21] In the resulting situation, *a successful firm is one that not only earns above average returns today, but also has the strength and overall health to be highly profitable in the future as well, as evidenced by the competitive advantages it possesses.*[22]

---

*Gross profit is the difference between sales revenue and cost of goods sold. To facilitate comparisons, gross profit is often expressed as a ratio of sales, known as gross profit ratio (or gross margin ratio). Gross profit ratio = (sales − cost of goods sold)/sales.

†Some define it as returns that are in excess of what an investor expects to earn from other investments with a similar amount of risk. See M. A. Hitt, R. D. Ireland, and R. E. Hoskisson, *Strategic Management* (Cincinnati, Ohio: South-Western Publishing, 2003), p. 7.

The Strategic Management Process

Strategic management is a process through which managers select and implement strategies to create sustainable competitive advantages and achieve superior profitability. The detailed steps in this process include the following:

- defining the firm's business
- setting a vision and long-term company goals
- environmental and internal analyses to identify opportunities
- strategy selection and implementation
- evaluation of company performance to determine whether strategies have produced the desired effect

This description may sound as if strategic management is a sequential process in which each stage is elaborately planned without input from other stages, followed by a rigid implementation of the selected plans. In actuality, it is not a lockstep exercise. It is instead a process that involves frequent experimentation and adjustment based on results. It is a highly **interactive process**. *An interactive process is one in which information is continuously exchanged across individual stages to refine decisions and actions so as to enhance the quality of final outcome.*

Some scholars describe strategic management activities in logical order implying that strategies should be deliberately planned and rigidly implemented in a linear fashion.[23] According to these scholars, a deliberate approach allows for quality and thoroughness in strategy selection and efficiency in strategy implementation. Moreover, they say that it helps a firm to clearly define where it wants to go and methodically plan how to get there. Others dispute this rigid and sequential representation of strategic management, saying it ignores the reality that sound strategies can also *emerge serendipitously* without formal planning.[24] For these latter scholars, strategic management is a process in which strategies should be allowed to evolve, and not be rigidly planned. We will describe these alternative models of strategy making in the next section. But, to organize our discussion of strategic management concepts here and in the rest of this text, we need an illustrative model. In Figure 1.2, we provide such a model. The model portrays strategic management activities as resulting from a combination of planning and adaptation—that is, strategic management is a process that is both linear and interactive. This implies that strategies are not only carefully selected through planning, but they are also refined or altered as new information becomes available through successive stages of strategy implementation and evaluation of results. Thus, strategic management as defined and discussed in this textbook is a dynamic process in which strategy formulation and implementation activities are reciprocally connected. The following section briefly describes the components and processes involved in our model.

Mission

The starting point necessary for strategic management to occur is a clearly articulated company mission. *A **mission statement** is a comprehensive articulation of what the firm is and wants to be in the distant future.* It describes what the firm currently does and what it aspires to become in the future—that is, the firm's **vision**, the ideals

FIGURE 1.2	The Strategic Management Process

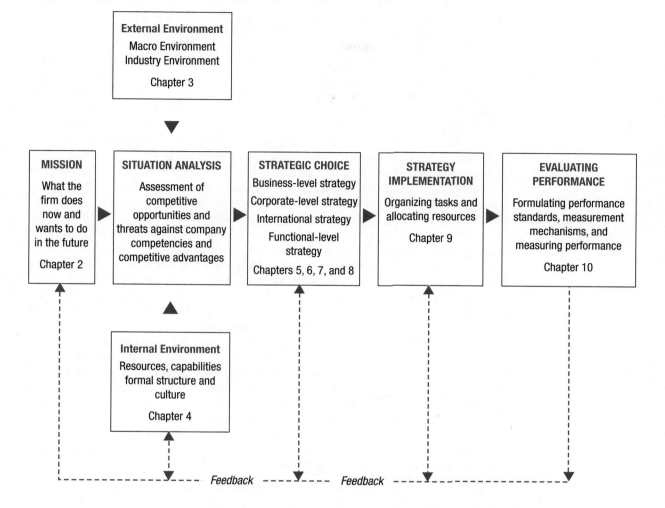

the firm is committed to, and the long-term goals it aims to achieve in pursuit of its vision. When clearly presented, the mission statement indicates the firm's current products and customers it serves. It also indicates activities or businesses the firm hopes to pursue in the future. While a mission statement serves multiple purposes, three in particular stand out:

1. It serves as a guidepost for long-term survival and success by creating a link between the firm's present and the desired future state.

2. It gives managers the focus for developing the competencies and competitive advantages necessary to lead the firm to its desired future.

3. It differentiates the firm from competition; it is by nurturing unique dreams and aspirations among organizational members that a firm sets the stage for sustained superior performance to occur. [25]

Situation Analysis

To attain superior performance on current operations and move closer to the firm's stated vision, managers must identify opportunities. At the same time, they should watch for threats that could hurt current business or constrain progress toward the future. **Opportunities** include a rise in demand for current products, emergence of a new market segment, or the potential to develop a new product as a result of the firm's R&D efforts. **Threats** may include declining demand, new competitor entry, introduction of new technologies by rivals, and increasing power of suppliers and customers over a firm. For Kodak, digital photography was a major opportunity, which the company missed, while Fuji's entry into the film business was a major threat.

Situation analysis provides managers with information on opportunities and threats emerging in the industry and their firm's competencies to exploit them or deal with them. Situation analysis involves a continuous examination of company strengths and weaknesses against industry opportunities and threats. Situation analysis is thus an exercise that evaluates what a firm can do and what possibilities exist. The external environment, comprising the *macro-level forces* and the more specific *industry forces,* frequently changes, which can create a favorable or unfavorable market climate for a firm. Macro-level changes alter demand but leave very little scope for a firm to control demand to suit its needs. The best that a firm can do is to forecast change and be ready to adapt when change occurs. Industry-level changes alter competitive conditions but allow a firm the ability to control them or defend itself against them.[26] Managers assess these environmental changes against company **resources** and **capabilities** to determine whether strengths *match* the demands of the environment—that is, whether they are adequate for exploiting opportunities or defending against threats. *A popular view in strategic management is that superior performance occurs when a firm's competencies and competitive advantages are a match to environmental challenges.* A firm achieves this match either by continuously enhancing its strengths (adaptation), by controlling or altering the environment to suit its strengths (proactive environmental management), or by moving to new environments where its current strengths are appropriate (diversification). These are strategic choices, which emerge from situation analysis.

Strategic Choice

Strategic choice represents the examination and selection of possible strategic alternatives, given a firm's strengths and weaknesses in the face of opportunities and threats. Managers select alternatives based on the potential a selected alternative offers for sustained competitive advantages. However, before a firm selects a strategic alternative, it must first decide whether it wants to be a single-business firm or a diversified, multibusiness firm. This choice is followed by a series of other choices in which a firm decides how it proposes to gain the necessary advantage in its chosen business or businesses: through market positioning, development of unique internal capabilities, or a combination of the two. Several strategic choices are available to a firm. Each provides different types of advantages and opportunities for attaining superior performance.

Business-level Strategy: Business-level or business-unit strategy focuses on gaining advantage within a single business and offers four alternatives: *cost leadership,* *differentiation, focus* (that is, *niche*), or a combination of these. A *cost leader* aims for a cost advantage in the industry through operational efficiencies; a *differentiator* focuses on product or service advantage through unique features; the *focus strategist* tailors its product to the special needs of a small group to gain a niche advantage; and the *combination strategist* aims for cost and differentiation advantages simultaneously. A firm chooses an alternative based on its competencies and the potential for success that the industry offers for that strategy.

Corporate-level Strategy: Corporate-level strategy focuses on gaining advantage by performing a series of value-chain activities, known as *vertical integration*, and/or by managing a portfolio of businesses, known as *diversification*. In *vertical integration*, a firm performs successive activities in product processing (from component production to final assembly and distribution), eliminating supplier and distributor control in product operations. In *diversification*, a firm exploits a common operational or managerial competency across several businesses, thus gaining advantages associated with *economies of scope.** A firm's choice depends on its competencies and the opportunities available for exploiting them in different businesses.

International Strategy: International strategy offers opportunities to a firm to gain advantage through international diversification. By making and selling the product differently in each country (*multidomestic strategy*) or making a uniform product efficiently by locating process operations in favorable international regions (*global strategy*), a firm gains product- or process-related learning that is not available to domestic firms.

Functional-level Strategy: Functional-level strategy involves the choices a firm makes to achieve strengths internally within its functional areas: manufacturing, marketing, research and development, human resource management, and finance. Such strengths help a firm to gain competitive advantages based on unique internal capabilities and to successfully implement its strategies.

Strategy Implementation

To put strategic decisions into action, a firm needs appropriate competencies—skills and knowledge that add value for a firm's customers. For example, cost strategy requires the ability to process products efficiently. Product differentiation requires the ability to add unique features to the product. A firm obtains these competencies from the tangible and intangible resources (human, machinery, informational) it procures and employs. Competencies emerge from these resources not by themselves but from how they are put to use. In an organizational situation, this involves integration of resources—managers integrate multiple resources so that these resources coordinate or harmoniously adjust to function as one unit. Different ways of coordinating resources foster different competencies within a firm. The focus in strategy implementation is thus on *organizational design* and appropriate policies and procedures that managers use to bring about resource coordination.

---

*Economies of scope are efficiencies arising from the use of a single asset (machinery, skills) in several product/service or process operations.

One must continuously monitor organizational performance to determine whether strategies and implementation tools are creating the competitive advantages a firm needs to attain long-term goals. **Strategic control** is the mechanism a firm employs for this purpose. Strategic control comprises decisions and actions in which a firm sets performance standards, selects measurement tools, measures performance, and compares performance to standards. Based on its performance measurement findings, a firm alters its long-term goals, strategies, or organizational mechanisms as the case requires. It is worth emphasizing that strategic management is an ongoing process of strategy formulation, implementation, and verification of results. It is an interactive process in which a firm decides, acts, and frequently modifies future plans through a continuous cycle of learning and adjustment.

Alternative Models of Strategy Formulation

Strategic management is an eclectic subject. Ideas in strategic management, especially those on strategy formulation, have been borrowed from several disciplines: economics, political science, and military science. As a result, alternative models of strategy formulation exist. This has created a certain degree of conflict within the field regarding which strategy formulation process is most suitable for a firm. These conflicting schools of thought have, however, strengthened the strategic management field with innovative models that have emerged from a synthesis of disparate ideas. We will discuss these models, when relevant, later in the text. For now, it is essential that we familiarize ourselves with some of the alternative models of strategy formulation in order to gain a balanced understanding of the subject.*

Recall from our earlier discussions that one popular belief in strategic management is that strategies should be formulated based on an "organization-environment fit." That is, strategies must be selected by examining the match between the competitive advantage they will create and the challenges posed by the firm's industry environment. According to this principle, managers should first thoroughly research industry *opportunities* and *threats* and compare their findings to company *strengths* and *weaknesses* (commonly referred to as SWOT analysis). Based on this comparison, they should select a strategy that is most appropriate for meeting industry needs and commit technological and organizational resources to implement it. Assuming this approach, we might declare that the successful firm is one that continuously adjusts its resources and capabilities to effectively meet the current needs of the market or customers.

Some scholars criticize this approach as too reactive, suggesting that the potential for performance in this approach is restricted to existing company strengths and environmental opportunities only.[27] According to these scholars, superior performance will occur when managers envision and proactively create new opportunities by iden-

---

*For an exhaustive list and discussion of alternative models of strategy formulation, read H. Mintzberg and J. Lampel, "Reflecting on the Strategy Process," *Sloan Management Review* 40, no. 3 (1999): 21–30.

tifying new markets or new customer needs, rather than reacting to current market or customer needs. A firm can do this by setting *ambitious goals* that are far bolder than their current resources would permit (referred to as *stretch goals*),[28] followed by aggressive acquisition and leveraging of resources that would enable them to realize such ambitions. For example, Canon set a lofty "beat Xerox" goal in the 1980s to unseat Xerox from its leadership position in the copier business. Canon followed this aim by investing in resources that created the strategic opportunities it needed to successfully dislodge Xerox. Along similar lines, Komatsu, the Japanese maker of earthmoving machinery, invested heavily in design and manufacturing activities to create opportunities that allowed it to narrow the gap between itself and the industry leader Caterpillar.[29]

Proactive strategy-formulation models (commonly referred to as *resource-based strategy formulation*) assert that strategies should emerge from a firm's resources and capabilities. That is, resources and capabilities should be employed to create opportunities for a firm rather than implement environmentally determined opportunities.[30] Opportunities or advantages are created when managers set a bold vision for their firm and employ resources innovatively to develop new products, create new market segments, or alter the "rules of current competition" to their advantage.* This proactive approach is especially critical for firms that compete in industries where technologies frequently change and erode existing advantages.[31] Consider how Kodak might have benefited from more proactive strategy formulation.

Deliberate Versus Emergent Approaches

As mentioned earlier, the idea that strategies are deliberately planned and implemented is also a popular theme in strategic management. According to this approach, a firm carefully analyzes several alternatives, selects an alternative, and aggressively pursues the selected alternative. In this approach, strategies are deemed to result from careful planning and should, therefore, be rigidly implemented without modification or radical alteration. But, according to Professor Henry Mintzberg of McGill University, this planned approach ignores the fact that strategy can emerge unintentionally, too[32] —that is, a strategy a firm pursues may not be what it initially planned to pursue but one that serendipitously emerged during the course of implementing the original strategy (see Figure 1.3). According to Mintzberg, a firm that rigidly adopts a planned strategy approach may overlook or miss emerging opportunities that could be more profitable. Therefore, he suggests that managers remain more flexible in strategy formulation by recognizing that lucrative opportunities that would require the firm to replace the current strategy could emerge separately.[33] Some research studies have found that firms that employ an improvisational approach in strategy formulation (creatively adjusting strategy through experimentation)

---

*Both Canon and Komatsu succeeded by altering the rules of competition in their respective industries. In the copier industry, Xerox had set the standard of leasing high-speed copiers to businesses and servicing them. To maintain industry leadership, it reacted to customer complaints by improving service quality rather than product quality. Canon dramatically altered this practice—from competition based on after-sales service to competition based on selling quality copiers that required minimal service. By investing heavily in design activities, it made compact, high-quality copiers that businesses were eager to own rather than lease. Likewise, in the construction industry, Caterpillar had built and nurtured competition based on after-sales service. Komatsu effectively shifted the model to one based on product quality and succeeded.

| FIGURE 1.3 | **Deliberate and Emergent Strategies** |

Source: H. Mintzberg and A. McHugh, "Strategy Formation in an Adhocracy," *Administrative Science Quarterly* 30, no. 2 (1985): 160–197.

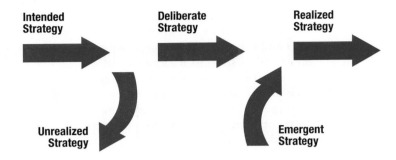

are more successful than those that employ a "rigid planning and implementation" approach.[34]

Is There a Right Approach?

Should firms choose strategies reactively or proactively? That is, should they select strategies based on an assessment of current market needs and company competencies or should they boldly set ambitious goals and strategies and then create the market environment suitable for realizing them? Should they methodically plan, select strategies, and rigidly implement those strategies or should they remain flexible in the face of evolving conditions and allow strategies to emerge through a process of experimentation or trial and error? Some authors suggest that the answer to these questions lies somewhere in between these extreme views.[35] According to these authors, a firm should be proactive sometimes and reactive at other times, keeping in mind the need to maintain at all times a strategic fit between a firm's competencies and its market environment. More importantly, by periodically switching from reactive to proactive and vice versa, a firm may identify new and at times revolutionary opportunities. In regard to planning versus emergent approaches, these same authors say that a planned approach alone is no guarantee for the identification of sound strategies. At the same time, it is equally silly to pretend that good strategies will always emerge through trial and error. Successful firms employ a combination approach, based on the demands of the situation. Our model illustrated in Figure 1.2 follows this combination view.

Strategic Managers, Levels of Strategic Management, and Strategic Leadership

Strategic Managers

Strategy is the responsibility of top managers because only they have the comprehensive understanding of a firm and its external environment that is fundamental for strategy formulation and implementation. Typically, it is the *general manager*, often referred to as the president or the CEO, who acts as the chief strategist. In this capacity, general managers decide, articulate, and monitor the overall strategic direction of a firm. Through formal statements, policies, and informal leadership, they convey a firm's vision, businesses in which it will participate, long-term goals and strategic choices, and how resources will be procured and allocated to develop the competitive advantages the firm needs for its strategy implementation.

While the general manager is certainly the chief architect of the firm's strategy, strategic decision making is not an individual exercise but a collective one. To be effective, strategic decision making requires the analysis and incorporation of several pieces of specialized information:

- hard data, such as technological information concerning a firm's production capacity and financial resources
- forecasts, such as market information concerning demand
- judgments, such as opinions about competitors' intention regarding future moves

Understandably, the general manager cannot be expected to have all the information needed for effective decision making and must therefore rely on the help and support provided by several specialists. The *functional managers* in R&D, production, marketing, and finance help the general manager by providing and interpreting hard data and forecasts, whereas *staff specialists* in planning and business development help with judgmental data. However, data alone will not suffice. To arrive at effective strategic decisions, the general manager needs objective advice and words of wisdom concerning how the firm's decisions will affect its stakeholders and whether they will react to the decisions positively. It is the *board of directors* who, backed by their industry knowledge, connections, and varied general experience, provide the balanced information and counseling the general manager needs in strategy formulation and implementation. In most firms, strategies are developed by a planning committee that includes members of the board, top managers, functional experts, and staff specialists. The general manager typically assumes the lead role in this committee.

Levels of Strategy

Single-business firms, facing a single competitive environment (for example, McDonald's in fast food and Coca Cola in soft drinks), need only a single strategy to guide their business activities. As such, they need only one general manager and a team of functional managers to perform strategic management tasks. Multibusiness concerns that oversee distinctly different business units that operate in dissimilar markets require different strategies for each business unit as well as a comprehensive strategy that will guide the management of a business portfolio. As a result, general managers and functional managers are needed at different levels to perform the strategic management tasks. For example, Eastman Kodak competes in three different market segments: photography, health imaging, and commercial imaging. General Electric competes in several unrelated businesses: aircraft engines, broadcasting, consumer appliances, financial services, lighting products, medical systems, and plastics. For such firms, strategic management is necessary at the corporate, business, and functional levels as shown in Figure 1.4. Let us examine management responsibilities at each level:

Corporate-level management consists of the board of directors, the chief executive officer, and senior executives responsible for staff functions such as planning,

| FIGURE 1.4 | **Levels of Strategic Management** |

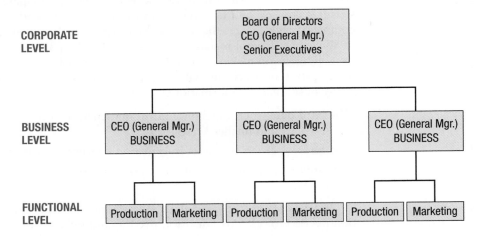

finance, human resources, legal, and general administration. The corporate CEO is the chief strategist responsible for the success of the total enterprise. In that capacity, he or she determines the firm's overall strategic direction: the businesses in which the firm will compete, the businesses of which it will divest itself, the long-term objectives the firm will pursue, and the distinctive competencies it will develop and share among its businesses.

Business-level management consists of the general manager of that business unit, functional managers (R&D, production, marketing), and staff specialists (planning, business development). The business unit CEO is the chief strategist for that particular business and is responsible for its success. In that capacity, he or she determines the business unit's long-term goals, how it will compete in its industry, and how resources will be procured and allocated to attain business goals. Multi-business firms generally allow sufficient freedom to the business-level CEO in strategy formulation and implementation in exchange for business unit performance. Nonetheless, business unit strategy generally falls within the overall strategy formulated by the corporation.

Functional-level management consists of a functional head to which subordinate managers report. Functional heads (vice president of marketing, product design, manufacturing, or R&D) are responsible for formulating functional strategies pertaining to their function. For example, the head of marketing would decide what strategy should be employed to achieve the firm's marketing goal of, say, increased brand awareness. The head of manufacturing would decide what strategy is appropriate to achieve the firm's manufacturing goal of increased productivity. Functional strategies thus focus on the operational competencies necessary to support a firm's business-level and corporate-level strategies.

Strategic Leadership

Thus far, we have argued that a firm is successful when it manages its activities strategically—by articulating a mission, assessing the situation, and selecting and implementing strategies to realize that mission. A clear mission, a sound situational assessment, appropriate strategies, and matching strategy implementation tools are thus fundamental requirements for the success of a firm. But management scholars insist that these alone will not suffice; an additional and equally vital requirement is *strategic leadership*.[36] Strategic leadership allows a firm to successfully employ the strategic management process.[37] The leadership capabilities that managers demonstrate, especially in selecting a vision and convincingly guiding a firm toward it, significantly influence company performance. Strategic leadership is thus viewed as a competitive advantage in strategic management discussions.[38]

    Strategic leadership *broadly refers to the ability of managers to conceive an inspiring vision, formulate clear goals, articulate them, and successfully guide a firm toward the envisioned future.* Managers are characterized as strategic leaders when they possess certain attributes: anticipatory skills, flexible thinking, speed in decision making, persuasiveness, and an ability to motivate others toward the firm's vision.[39] Effective leaders anticipate environmental changes and prepare for them by investing ahead of time in resources that will effectively deal with those changes rather than reacting to them haphazardly. They are quick to exploit opportunities as they emerge but do not wait indefinitely for them to occur. Instead, strategic leaders create opportunities, when necessary, by proactively altering the situation. Most importantly, they zealously develop an organization that is spirited and that voluntarily assumes responsibilities toward the firm's vision and long-term goals. To summarize, strategic leadership involves: *visionary thinking, planned preparedness, a combination of adaptive and proactive skills, people development, and a sense of commitment to achieve the desired end.* Not surprisingly, research evidence strongly suggests that, in addition to a clear mission and other strategic management variables discussed in this chapter, what separates successful firms from the rest is strategic leadership.[40]

Summary

Evidence suggests that successful firms not only manage their internal resources competently but also monitor and proactively manage their industry environment. In short, they manage their business (or multiple business units) strategically. Strategic management involves a series of long-term decisions and actions in which managers articulate a mission for the firm and select and implement strategies. The purpose of these strategies is to build the firm's strength through market positioning and/or accumulation of internal resources that will give the firm the competitive advantage it needs to realize its mission. The key to a firm's success is thus competitive advantage, and strategy is the source of competitive advantage. When a firm exploits this advantage, it earns superior (that is, above-average) returns in the industry. Competitive advantage must be sustained to make progress toward the mission.

    Strategic management is a process in which managers decide on the firm's mission and its components, conduct environmental and internal analyses, select strategies, implement them, evaluate performance, and take corrective actions if necessary. It is an interactive process in which information is frequently exchanged across individual stages so as to enhance the quality of the decision outcome. The clarity of the mission and the appropriateness of the strategic choices made to realize the mission significantly affect a firm's long-term survival and success.

    Strategic management decisions are made at the top and, typically, it is the CEO who has the major responsibility for determining the strategic direction of the firm.

In single-business firms, strategic management occurs at the business and functional levels whereas in multibusiness firms, it occurs at the corporate, business, and functional levels. To the extent that managers show excellent leadership skills when pursuing strategic management, the likelihood of a firm emerging as the industry leader is high.

Chapter 1 Discussion Questions and Projects

Discussion Questions

1. Discuss the importance of strategic management for a firm's competitive performance.
2. Discuss the alternative models of strategy formulation. Which one appeals to you and why?

Projects

1. Microsoft is a dominant firm in the operating systems segment of the software industry. Read about Microsoft on the Internet and in the business press and prepare a brief report on this firm's product and market strategies. Do you think that Microsoft is proactively managing its industry environment?
2. Jack Welch, former CEO of General Electric, is often cited as a good example of an effective strategic leader. Read about Jack Welch's years at General Electric and write a two-page report describing what he did that can be characterized as effective strategic leadership.

Mission, Stakeholders, Governance, and Social Responsibility

CHAPTER OBJECTIVES

After reading this chapter, you should be able to:

- Explain the importance of a mission statement for a firm's long-term success

- Discuss the effect of different mission components on a firm's competitiveness

- Construct a mission statement for a firm or examine an existing statement for effectiveness

- Identify critical stakeholders for a firm and discuss how they can have an impact on mission implementation

- Describe corporate governance, outline the board of directors' role in corporate governance, and explain the importance of good governance in mission implementation

- Describe corporate social responsibility and discuss the need to incorporate social and ethical concerns into a company's mission

Opening Case

Southwest Airlines started in 1971 as a regional carrier flying between Houston, Dallas, and San Antonio in Texas. It had just three aircraft, which were 90 percent financed by Boeing, and virtually no money to meet day-to-day expenses. What little money Southwest had when it started business had financed the court battles it waged against competitors that challenged its right to operate in Texas. The firm could not afford to advertise and relied solely on word-of-mouth publicity. It borrowed tools from rivals for aircraft repairs and maintenance. Often, managers had to pitch in with personal credit cards to pay for fuel.

Industry conditions were no better, either. At the time of the firm's inception, competition was intense, fuel prices were rising, and established firms sought relentlessly to drive Southwest Airlines out of business through predatory pricing. As if these external forces were not enough, the U.S. government deregulated the airline industry in 1978, intensifying competition further. Price wars became a common industry practice, and Southwest's prospects for survival were bleak.

From these humble beginnings and trying conditions some thirty years ago, however, Southwest Airlines emerged as the most profitable firm in the airline industry. In an industry where losses are common, Southwest has been profitable every year for the last thirty years, rewarding shareholders more than any other firm in the Standard & Poor's S&P 500 index. In 2004, its profits exceeded those of all the other U.S. airlines combined. Its performance in other areas was equally stellar. In 2004, Southwest boarded more domestic passengers than any other U.S. airline. It has been consistently ranked number one in customer satisfaction, safety, on-time performance, and employee morale and has frequently been cited by *Fortune* as one of the most admired firms in the United States. Southwest's workforce has been judged the most productive in the industry, and surveys frequently name the firm as one of the most sought-after employers in the nation. Surely, Southwest is a business success story, pure and simple.

What is the secret of Southwest's success? How has it been successful year after year in an industry where profits are rare, productivity is mediocre, and customer satisfaction levels are low? Researchers and industry analysts say that it has to do, among other things, with Southwest's passion for, and commitment to, its mission. Southwest defines its mission as providing superior service to customers; company managers demonstrate their devotion to this mission by enthusiastically talking about customer service during corporate functions and community activities. Moreover, they ensure companywide acceptance of the firm's mission through policies, employee selection and training procedures, rewards—and by providing inspirational leadership. As a result, Southwest's employees have not only internalized the firm's mission but also take special pride in it because it allows them to feel unique about themselves and what they do. Because of the company's policy of keeping customers fully informed about company activities, Southwest's customers also are fully aware of the firm's mission and, as a result, they feel valued. All of these factors have generated a highly motivated, productive workforce and a band of loyal customers, resulting in higher revenues and superior profitability in the airline industry.[1]

The moral of Southwest's story is that a firm is more likely to succeed when its *mission* is realistic and inspiring, when company personnel and critical outsiders believe in it, and when managers make conscious efforts to live up to the firm's stated mission.[2] This chapter defines what a mission is and explains its importance to company performance. We will begin by defining a business mission and describing how an inspiring and clearly stated mission influences company performance. We will examine the components of a mission statement, its influence on company performance, and how a firm can formulate an effective mission statement. Then, we will look at a firm's key constituencies—called *stakeholders*—and discuss how they affect progress toward the stated mission; we will also talk about the need to maintain a good relationship with them. This chapter then describes a *company's board*, the role the board plays in mission formulation and management supervision, and the need for strong boards to ensure that managers are faithful to the stated mission. Finally, we will conclude this chapter with a discussion of a corporation's *social responsibility* and the importance of including social goals in a firm's business mission.

The Mission Statement and Its Importance

Successful people are said to have a mission in life. A mission is an inner voice that tells people who they are and what they are destined to become. It provides them with a solemn purpose to strive for and strenuously work toward. It creates a distant vision and inspires them to move in that direction by shaping their beliefs and behavior. And, by incessantly reminding people about their destiny, a mission ensures that they stay committed to it. It is this sense of purpose, direction, inspiration, and commitment that leads people, even lures them, to their ultimate goal, making them successful in life. Mohandas Gandhi, Abraham Lincoln, Martin Luther King, Jr., and Mother Theresa are examples of successful people whose success is often attributed to clear knowledge of their life's mission and unflinching commitment to it.

Like successful individuals, successful businesses, too, are said to be mission driven. There is no universally accepted definition of a business mission, but most agree that it refers to a firm's long-term purpose and its solemn resolve to achieve it.[3] Since a mission has relevance to organizational insiders and outsiders, a firm communicates its mission through formal statements. Such mission statements describe in philosophical terms who the firm is, what it intends to become in the future, and how it plans to realize those intentions. In specific terms, a **mission statement** describes the firm's current business, customers and markets served, company values and attitudes, intended future business makeup, markets to be served, goals to be attained, and the resources and behaviors that will be employed to realize that future. Current business activities are spelled out in detail while future plans are intentionally left vague so as to remain flexible and open to change.[4] *A mission statement is thus a description of the firm's current task or business and market position (what the firm presently is), its vision for the future (what it intends to become), and how it plans to get to its future position (values and targets that will guide its actions toward the vision).* In a nutshell, a mission statement puts forward a firm's *corporate purpose* and the *business philosophy* it will employ to realize it. Figure 2.1 provides a visual representation of a firm's mission components and their relationship to each other.

| FIGURE 2.1 | **Mission Components and Their Relationship** |

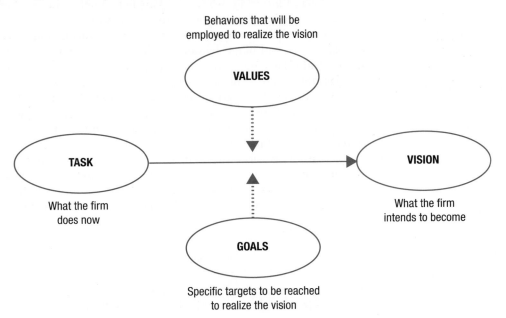

Importance of a Mission Statement

Evidence indicates that one striking difference between successful and unsuccessful firms is the existence of a stated mission.[5] After analyzing long-surviving firms, some researchers conclude that mission-directed behavior can positively contribute to organizational longevity.[6] Others, after studying firms with and without a stated mission, observe that managers of firms with a declared mission are better focused when making strategic decisions.[7] Still others have found that firms with a stated and widely publicized mission have a committed workforce, allowing them to effectively pursue their missions.[8]

A mission statement *per se* will have very little impact on company performance. Evidence suggests that it is the mission contents and how they are articulated that influence performance.[9] What differentiates an effective mission statement from an ineffective one is clarity, an inspiring theme, and the degree to which its contents satisfy company insiders and outsiders.[10] Mission clarity gives company personnel precise knowledge of the firm's tasks, its goals, and its expectations of them. For managers, mission clarity provides the focus in strategic decision making, especially in future planning such as resource allocation and development of competencies. For company outsiders—suppliers, customers, and the community—a clear mission unambiguously explains the firm's business and character, allowing them to make informed choices for building a lasting relationship with the firm. In the absence of such a mission and a document proclaiming its contents, a firm lacks a serious purpose, a sense of direction, pride and commitment, and a positive public image and legitimacy.[11] Without these advantages, its potential for higher performance cannot be great.

Apart from clarity and inspiring tone, a mission must be acceptable to company insiders and outsiders. Employees must internalize company goals and values so that they can conscientiously work toward them. Outsiders must agree with the firm's purpose and philosophy before they will extend cooperation. A firm's vision and values will not satisfy these groups if they perceive them to be irrelevant to the firm's future. Studies have found that unrealistic goals and empty rhetoric in mission statements evoke cynicism among employees and outsiders, undermining managerial credibility.[12] On the other hand, salient statements and those that are congruent with the personal values of insiders and outsiders have tremendous appeal.[13] In firms whose mission was jointly developed by insiders and outsiders, and whose policies strongly support mission contents, employee commitment and outsider cooperation in mission implementation has been found to be high.[14.]

Mission Statement Components

A mission statement has several components: descriptions of what the firm does now, what it intends to be doing in the future, and how it proposes to get to its future. By examining each component closely, we can understand how they individually influence company performance and how a firm's mission can be conceived, constructed, and analyzed for effectiveness. In Figure 2.2 we will use a hypothetical company to illustrate these components. But, before we go any further, a word of caution is in

FIGURE 2.2   ABC, Inc. Task, Vision, Values, and Goals

TASK	*(What ABC Does Now)*	ABC, Inc. designs and makes superior-quality dress shoes and leather accessories for fashion-conscious young women and markets them through prestigious department stores. We continuously seek innovations that add value and comfort to the lifestyle of our customers.
VISION	*(The Future Toward Which ABC Is Moving)*	We wish to be known in the industry as the most innovative and customer-responsive organization. Our dream is to become the indisputable leader in the women's fashion footwear and leather accessories market segment.
VALUES	*(Ideals to Which ABC Is Committed)*	We value our customers and their needs. We are strongly committed to customer satisfaction. We believe that our employees are our greatest assets. We invest in their development to effectively implement our mission. We value our relationship with suppliers. We are strongly committed to fairness and integrity in our supplier relationship.
GOALS	*(The End Results ABC Wishes to Reach)*	Our primary goal is to become the market-share leader in the fashion footwear and leather accessories business through product innovations, continuous product enhancements, and total customer satisfaction.

| FIGURE 2.3 | Southwest Airlines Vision, Mission, Goals, and Values |

SOUTHWEST AIRLINES MISSION STATEMENT

Southwest Airlines is dedicated to the highest quality of Customer Service delivered with a sense of warmth, friendliness, individual pride, and Company Spirit.

We are committed to provide our Employees a stable work environment with equal opportunity for learning and personal growth. Creativity and innovation are encouraged for improving the effectiveness of Southwest Airlines. Above all, Employees will be provided the same concern, respect, and caring attitude within the Organization that they are expected to share externally with every Southwest Customer.

Source: Courtesy Southwest Airlines Co.

order. The hypothetical mission statement provided in Figure 2.2 has been broken down into components to facilitate easy explanation and comprehension, but we do not intend to suggest that this format is ideal. In fact, no two firms state their mission in exactly the same form and fashion.[15] Some highlight their vision and long-term goals, while others give importance to stating their ideals and business philosophy. Some state their mission broadly, while others treat mission and vision distinctly. Some state what strategies they will employ to realize their mission, while others do not.[16] Such differences, however, are matters of style and semantics rather than substance, as a quick comparison of the Southwest Airline's mission statement, reproduced in Figure 2.3, to the hypothetical example illustrates.

In general, a firm's mission statement comprises a description of its:

1. *Task*—what the firm currently does
2. *Vision*—what kind of business enterprise the firm dreams of becoming in the future
3. *Values and Beliefs*—the ideals that the firm is committed to, that will lead it to its vision
4. *Goals and Objectives*—the targets and milestones the firm aims to reach in pursuit of its vision

Task

The **task** of a firm is what it currently does in terms of products offered and markets or customers served. A company's task might include making energy conservation products for homes and offices, minivans for families, sports cars for racing enthusiasts, or sprint shoes for active runners. Ben and Jerry's says its task is to make and sell the finest quality all-natural ice cream and related products in a rich variety of innovative flavors. Levi Strauss states its task more simply: creating and selling jeans and casual clothing. When well defined, a task indicates what the firm does now, why it does it, and for whom.

Some firms describe their task more philosophically and call it their *purpose,* or the reason why they exist. Merck, a leading pharmaceutical firm, says that it is in the business of preserving and improving human life. Nokia states its purpose briefly as "connecting people." Likewise, Xerox says that it is "in the document business."

It is easy for a firm to describe its task when it makes a single product and sells that product in a single market. But how do diversified firms that make multiple products for multiple markets describe their task? They use a philosophical description that focuses on the fundamental needs their products satisfy. Procter & Gamble, a diversified firm that makes toiletries, detergents, and personal-care products, describes its task as "providing branded products and services of superior quality that improve the lives of the world's consumers."*

An unambiguously defined task gives managers clear focus on the *firm's competition,* suppliers, customers, and substitute products and thus the industry to which the firm belongs. Precise information concerning the firm's industry (or segment) is essential to accurately observe market trends, technological changes, and competitor moves that are prerequisites for strategy formulation. For employees, task clarity gives better focus on activities that must be completed so that the firm can be successful in its *current* business.

Vision

A task directs managers' attention to the choices that must be made for success on current operations, but it does not encourage thinking about the firm's future. It is necessary for managers to look beyond the present and think strategically to build an enterprise that will grow and successfully meet the challenges of a changing environment. A firm's mission statement, therefore, generally includes a description of the type of business the firm intends to become—its vision, its dream. *A* **vision** *is a description of the future toward which the firm is moving.* It is not a forecast; rather, it is a mental image of what the firm yearns to become. A vision describes a desired end in inspirational terms and induces purposive action. Although a firm may never arrive at its desired destination, that does not stop it from trying. Arriving at the destination is not the important part; it is trying to get to the destination through continuous improvement that matters.[17]

A vision is generally stated as an ambitious long-term target, such as "to be the most admired firm in the industry," "to be the best in our business," or "to be the technological leader." Boeing's vision is to become the leader of the aerospace industry. McDonald's wants to emerge as the leader of the global food-service industry. Sony aspires to be known as the most creative firm in the audio, video, and digital electronics fields. While these are abstract aims, they still provide managers with a focus by calling for excellence in a specified business, technological field, or competency. *Vision is thus the foundation for strategy*—decisions and actions managers must take to achieve superior performance on current operations and strengthen the firm for future operations. While all firms in an industry perform similar tasks, vision is

---

*www.pg.com

unique to each firm and differentiates it from the competition. Some scholars, therefore, refer to vision as the strategic intent of a firm.[18]

A vision forms the inspirational foundation for managers to make the right strategic choices that will move the firm from its current position to the desired future position. The exact choices managers make will depend on the firm's culture, current technology, and market position, as well as on the competitive environment it faces. But when clearly conceived and defined, a vision sets the stage for strategic decision making: what new technologies and competencies must be developed, what new resources assembled and allocated, to take the firm to its desired future position. In short, a vision describes the firm's ideal future and induces managers and employees to reach it. The more inspiring and acceptable it is to them, the better is the quality of their decisions and efforts to realize it.

Researchers have found that firms with a clear vision stay focused on the firm's future and engage in activities that lead them to the desired future.[19] An ill-defined vision or lack of a vision may take the firm in an unintended direction, as Quaker Oats belatedly realized (see Strategy in Practice 2.1). Quaker Oats' managers made acquisitions that did not fit well with the firm's current operations or market image. Absence of a clearly stated vision led managers to move the firm in several wrong directions and further rationalize actions that turned out to be detrimental to the company. But when management attempted to correct the situation by divesting these acquisitions, it was too late.

Values

Values *are the core beliefs of a firm, the ideals to which it is committed.* Through policies and practices, a firm defines its values and indicates how its members will conduct themselves. Values are thus the foundation of a firm's culture; they do not easily change. Ralph Larsen, the former CEO of Johnson & Johnson, is reported to have said: "The core values of our firm might have given us a competitive advantage, but that is not why we have them. We have them because they define for us what we stand for, and we would hold them even if they became a competitive disadvantage in certain situations."[20] Values are thus durable and deep rooted; they are not the firm's response to any specific market requirement but are fundamental to the firm across all market situations.

An organization's value system can explain why a firm frequently pioneers new technologies, is a successful copycat, a cost leader, or an aggressive market-share leader. Strong values shape the strategic thinking and behavior of managers by conditioning their perception. Exactly what opportunities managers will recognize and vigorously pursue or summarily reject depends on the company's entrenched values. By cultivating appropriate values and reinforcing them, a firm ensures that its strategies for realizing its vision and overall mission are faithfully executed. For example, Johnson & Johnson declares in its value statements that its primary responsibility is toward mothers and fathers. The idea is to make sure that company personnel act in ways that build the trust the firm needs to function as a leading baby-care-products company.

Goals/Objectives

A **goal** *(or objective) is a specific target that the firm intends to reach in the long term.* By setting such targets in key areas and systematically working toward them, a firm

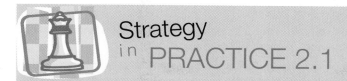

Strategy in PRACTICE 2.1

HOW ABSENCE OF A CLEAR VISION COST QUAKER OATS ITS INDEPENDENCE

Quaker Oats was born in 1901 when several oat milling companies in the midwestern United States combined their operations to make and sell oats to consumers. The newly formed company prided itself on the superior quality of its product and chose the Quaker man to symbolize its purity. The company grew rapidly by gaining the trust of American consumers and before long Quaker Oatmeal became the number one brand in the hot cereal market. Other products introduced subsequently such as Granola bars and Fruit & Oatmeal bars soon catapulted the company to greater fame. The company thrived in the breakfast cereal industry by popularizing the Quaker brand name but had not articulated a clear vision that would have given the firm a direction for its future. As a result, when demand for breakfast cereals started declining during the 1970s and 1980s due to dramatic shifts in American lifestyles, the firm looked at various nonfood businesses for diversification. It aimlessly moved in and out of grocery, restaurant, toy, clothing, and optical businesses, losing money on each deal and weakening its financial position in the process.

The company had mistakenly believed that its strong brand name would allow it to reap success in any product it touched. In 1983, it bought Gatorade, which turned out to be a success—it saved the firm from financial disaster but also moved it from a traditional food company to a sports beverage marketer. Buoyed by its newfound success, the company went for a repeat show in 1994 when it bought Snapple for $1.7 billion, only to fail miserably this time. Snapple was a "cult" drink sold through convenience stores and gas stations and had nothing in common with Quaker's traditional distribution outlet—the supermarket. Unable to generate the volume needed to be profitable, Quaker sold Snapple in 1997 for $300 million. Soon, the huge debt left behind by irrational acquisitions and a demoralized organization searching for new directions were weighing heavily on Quaker Oats. In December 2000, the company succumbed to takeover pressures and was acquired by PepsiCo.

Source: Quaker Oats, *Annual Report* and press releases (various years).

strives to realize its vision. Goals thus provide the basis for measuring the firm's performance and the progress it is making toward its vision. To achieve its vision—to emerge as the leading firm in the global food-service industry—McDonald's set a goal of opening some 2,500 new stores annually, two-thirds of them outside the United States.* By working toward this goal, and periodically measuring its performance against it, McDonald's sought to realize its vision. Similarly, 3M's predominant goal is to realize one-third of its sales revenue from products that are less than four years old. This goal is pursuant to 3M's vision of being recognized as the most innovative company in the world.

Goals say in concrete terms what the firm's vision says in abstract terms. They thus describe in quantitative or qualitative terms what is important to the firm. Goals give the organization's members a sense of purpose; when clearly described, realistic, and challenging, they motivate employees.

---

*In 2003, the company modified this goal. It now wants to grow by adding customers to existing restaurants through food and service quality rather than just adding new restaurants only. See company annual report.

Firms generally pursue two types of goals:

■ **Financial goals** focus on achieving a certain level of financial performance (e.g., higher return on equity, growth in revenues).

■ **Strategic goals** focus on achieving a strategic or competitive advantage within the industry (e.g., technological leadership, superior customer service, frequent innovations).

Most firms highlight strategic goals in the mission statement but avoid mentioning financial goals. Why? Because profits are a necessity for all firms, profit-oriented goals do not help a firm differentiate its aims from rivals, nor do they inspire employees and managers to strive for excellence.

Table 2.1 summarizes how the different components of a mission statement influence performance.

Analyzing a Mission Statement for Effectiveness

How do we analyze the effectiveness of a mission statement? Mission statements can be analyzed from two broad perspectives:

1. How effectively has the firm defined its business and its intended future?

2. How realistic and genuine are its stated values?

TABLE 2.1 **Mission Components and Their Impact on Performance**

COMPONENT	MEANING	ATTRIBUTES AND PERFORMANCE IMPACT
Task	What a firm does now	• Common to all the firms in the industry • Indicates who the firm's competition, customers, and suppliers are • Allows employees to better focus on activities to be completed when clearly defined
Vision	What a firm wants to become in the future	• Unique to the firm; differentiates it from the competition • Inspires and unites when compelling and consensually developed • Provides the foundation for making strategic decisions
Values	The ideals the firm is committed to	• Create the cultural environment necessary for developing and implementing strategies • Make strategy implementation easy when company personnel internalize values
Goals	The long-term targets the firm aims to reach in its activities	• Act as milestones in the firm's journey toward its vision and provide a basis for performance measurement • Motivate employees when they are clearly described, realistic, and challenging

Business Definition

Defining a business is effective when it focuses attention on the customers the firm serves and the needs a firm satisfies rather than the products it makes.[21] A customer- and need-oriented definition allows a firm to closely monitor changing customer needs and adapt its competencies to effectively satisfy customers. By contrast, a product-oriented definition blinds a firm to market opportunities and threats and creates a deep chasm between the firm's competencies and evolving customer requirements, as Eastman Kodak painfully learned. Kodak had initially described itself as being in the *film* photography business (a product-based focus) instead of in photo imaging (a need-based focus). As a result, it failed to note the developments occurring in imaging technology, missing new opportunities and allowing digital camera manufacturers to carve inroads into its business.

Realistic and Genuine Values

A firm's values will inspire organizational insiders and outsiders when those values are realistic, genuine, and consistent with the firm's actions.[22] Mission statements must reflect the values and ideals embedded in the firm's culture. Empty and high-sounding statements that are more symbolic than real and that have no bearing on the firm's business serve only to create cynicism in employees, alienate customers, and undermine managerial credibility.[23] An effective mission statement relies on an observed conformity between what the firm claims it stands for and what it actually does. Managers achieve this conformity by formulating and implementing policies that truly reflect what has been stated in the firm's mission.[24]

Does a Firm's Mission Change?

Two crucial components of a firm's mission are its *vision*—the mental image of what the firm ardently wants to become, its everlasting dream—and the *values* that are entrenched in its belief system. Dreams and values are born out of strong convictions. Changing conditions that result in adversity or misfortunes are not supposed to force the firm to alter or abandon its vision and values. Instead, both vision and values should rally the firm during trying conditions by inspiring managers and employees around the firm's cause. As such, a firm's vision and values are an enduring attribute.

Nevertheless, the firm's current tasks and goals are pathways to its vision and, as such, they should change as external conditions change.[25] By continuously adapting its current operations, a firm remains stronger and makes effective progress toward its vision. Changes in customer preferences or in the technologies used in production and distribution of goods can alter the competitive environment. And such changes require appropriate adjustment by the firm. For example, the Internet has significantly altered how people shop for certain products. Many people today find it convenient to shop for books, toys, appliances, cosmetics, and personal-care items through the Internet. As a result, retailers of these products have added an online shopping alternative to their traditional brick-and-mortar stores. Companies that fail to make this sort of adaptation may well lack the readiness to satisfy changing market needs, resulting in weaker current performance and an inability to perform effectively in the long term.

Stakeholders

To effectively pursue its mission, a firm requires resources and support from the environment. The business environment consists of a web of diverse but intricately connected groups, each pursing its own mission. In this environment, the behavior of one group affects, positively or negatively, the opportunities of other groups and invites reactions from them. As a result, a firm's mission-focused actions affect the interests of other groups in the business environment—suppliers, investors, and special interest groups. Depending on how these groups are affected, they may offer cooperation and support for the firm's activities, withdraw support they are already providing, or pressure the firm to stop pursuing a certain activity. Understandably, a firm will seek to minimize conflict and maximize harmony with key groups by effectively managing its relationships with them. Besides legitimizing its current activities, this approach creates a supportive climate for the firm to realize its long-term goals. However, the complexities and costs of developing and maintaining good relationships with key environmental groups make this a challenging exercise. A firm that manages these relationships effectively and efficiently can, therefore, expect to have competitive advantages.[26]

Identifying and Understanding Stakeholder Relationships

Individuals or groups in the firm's environment that affect, or are affected by, the firm's actions in pursuit of its mission are called **stakeholders** *because they have a stake in or an enforceable claim on the firm's performance.*[27] A firm must identify these individuals/groups and assess the power each group has over the firm before it can decide how to effectively manage its relationships with them. To keep things simple, we can classify stakeholders as *primary* and *secondary.*[28] **Primary stakeholders** are those who provide valuable inputs to the firm's business activities and without whose support the firm cannot survive. In return, these stakeholders expect the firm to satisfy their interests; they thus have a direct exchange relationship with the firm. Primary stakeholders may be employees, managers, stockholders, creditors, customers, suppliers, local communities, and governments. Employees provide skills and work commitment in exchange for fair wages and treatment. Managers provide talent in exchange for power and prestige. Stockholders provide capital in exchange for an attractive return on their investment. Customers provide loyal clientele in return for quality products. Suppliers provide quality components on a timely basis in exchange for an enduring business relationship.

The key to success in a primary stakeholder relationship is reciprocity on the part of the firm. If reciprocity or trust is lacking, or perceived as being deficient, the relationship can suffer. Stakeholders may threaten to withdraw support unless the firm changes its behavior. During the 1990s, many institutional investors (pension funds that own large blocks of stocks) were dissatisfied with the financial performance of General Motors, IBM, and Eastman Kodak and suggested to the respective boards of directors that their CEOs be replaced. When the firms did not act in a timely manner, the pension funds threatened to unload their shares in these companies, which could have had a disastrous effect on the share price. The threat produced the desired effect and institutional investor confidence in the firms was soon restored. Customers, too, may react negatively when they perceive a firm to be lacking in reciprocity. During 2000, when Firestone's most popular tires were linked to several auto accidents and deaths, the company was slow to issue product recalls and future product safety assurances. Customer confidence declined sharply, resulting in massive losses in sales, market share, and company reputation—all of which should prove extremely hard for Firestone to regain.[29] Continued distrust, moreover, can lead to a total loss of stakeholder support that seriously jeopardizes a firm's financial strength and ability to survive. Reportedly, Kmart often delayed payments to suppliers during 2000 and 2001 to finance the lavish lifestyle of its corporate executives. Frequently, it broke promises, leading to supplier mistrust of Kmart's top management and eventual withdrawal of support by suppliers. As a result, Kmart's ability to keep its shelves fully stocked during holiday seasons waned, leading to continuous erosion in its customer base and consequent filing for bankruptcy protection in 2002.[30] While the company came out of bankruptcy in 2003, its ability to regain the suppliers and customers it lost should prove to be an uphill battle.

Table 2.2 summarizes what the primary stakeholders offer the firm, what they expect in return, and how they react when they perceive a lack of reciprocity on the part of the firm. In contrast to primary stakeholders, **secondary stakeholders** do not have any direct economic transaction with the firm. Such stakeholder groups include the media and a wide range of special-interest groups. They do not provide inputs to the firm's task and, therefore, do not materially affect its day-to-day business. However, secondary stakeholders are affected by the firm's activities and can, in turn, seriously threaten a firm's long-term survival. They have the capacity to mobilize public opinion—or even boycotts—against a firm (or an industry) when they perceive that its activities are causing harm to them or to society at large. For example, environmental groups induced Exxon's customers to cut up their Exxon credit

TABLE 2.2 **Primary Stakeholder's Relationship with the Firm**

STAKEHOLDER TYPE	PROVIDE THE FIRM WITH	EXPECT FROM THE FIRM	WHEN DISSATISFIED WITH THE FIRM
1. Employees	Skills, work commitment	Fair wages and treatment	Lack motivation, lower productivity
2. Managers	Talent	Power, prestige	Leave the firm
3. Stockholders	Capital	Attractive returns	Sell shares, refrain from future investments, sue management
4. Unions	Productive workforce	Fair wages, job security	Refuse to cooperate
5. Customers	Loyal clientele	Quality product at attractive prices	Switch to competitors' products/services
6. Suppliers	Quality components	Enduring business relationship	Seek business elsewhere
7. Communities	Local infrastructure	Job creation, philanthropy	Refuse to cooperate
8. Governments	Enact laws to facilitate business formation, growth, fair competition	Abide by the laws, participate in economic and social growth plans	Enact regulations

cards and return them to the company after Exxon spilled 11 million gallons of oil in Alaskan waterways in 1989 and did not, in their opinion, responsibly undertake its cleanup.[31] Evidently, secondary stakeholders are just as potent as primary stakeholders and cannot be ignored by a firm as it plans for stakeholder relationship management.

Stakeholder Management

Businesses need stakeholder cooperation and support for their survival and growth. Stakeholder management aimed at achieving maximum stakeholder cooperation and support is, therefore, a strategic imperative. Successful stakeholder management involves identifying stakeholders—those with the potential for cooperation and those with potential to be threats—and developing and implementing strategies to enhance cooperation and deal with threats.

Three steps lie at the heart of stakeholder management:

1. Identify key stakeholders.
2. Classify them according to their potential for cooperation and potential to threaten the firm.
3. Develop and implement strategies to minimize threats and maximize cooperation.

Building on the classification of stakeholders as primary and secondary, we can sort them into four subcategories with attendant strategies [32]

1. *Low threat–high cooperation*: Staff employees and managers belong to this category. They are the least threatening and most cooperative. In stakeholder management, firms generally overlook these two groups and their potential for cooperation. By actively involving these groups in relevant issues, however, a firm can enhance their overall potential for cooperation.

2. *Low threat–low cooperation*: Consumer activist groups and professional organizations to which employees belong make up this group. Because of their low threat potential, a firm can feel safe—it needs to monitor their activities only periodically. However, a firm can also pursue cooperation with them to minimize or eliminate future threats. The beer manufacturers have effectively pursued this strategy by joining forces with Mothers Against Drunk Driving through commitment of financial and managerial resources in order to minimize threats from this group. In contrast, cigarette manufacturers long ignored secondary stakeholder complaints about nicotine's health effects, thus seriously undermining the legitimacy of their product and the future of their business.

3. *High threat–low cooperation*: Competing organizations, unions, the government, and the media belong to this group. A firm employs defensive strategies against the threats posed by these groups, but it may also explore ways in which it can elicit cooperation so as to minimize or eliminate future threats.

4. *High threat–high cooperation*: Employees with skills that are in short supply and customers belong to this group. The best way to manage them is to collaborate with them on relevant projects. The more the firm collaborates, the harder it will be for potentially threatening stakeholders to oppose the firm.

Despite the clear-cut appearance of the preceding categories, stakeholder management is riddled with complexities and inherent conflicts. The fundamental challenge to a firm is this: how to satisfy primary stakeholders without angering secondary stakeholders. Even within primary stakeholder groups, a firm can experience conflicts; for example, should customer demand for product quality and service take precedence over stockholder demand for higher returns? Conflicts get compounded when a firm faces large numbers of secondary stakeholders unfriendly to its business, as illustrated in Figure 2.4. Philip Morris International, a division of Altria Group, has to deal with several secondary stakeholders with whom it has a conflictive relationship. Under these circumstances, the best a firm can do is to increase transactions with those stakeholders who have a high potential for cooperation while seeking ways to lessen conflicts with those who can be threatening, possibly through collaboration.

FIGURE 2.4   **Philip Morris International Primary and Secondary Shareholders**

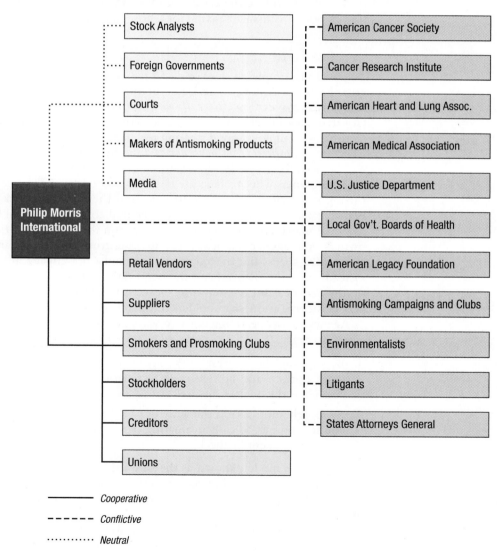

Corporate Governance

A clear, inspiring mission and stakeholder support are necessary but not sufficient to achieve success. Firms also need managers to reliably pursue the firm's stated mission. Any disparity between stated intentions and eventual action creates mistrust in the minds of stakeholders, causing them to withdraw support. Who ensures that managers are in fact pursuing the firm's mission and are not engaged in self-serving activities (for example, pursuing acquisitions that fatten managers' pockets but add no value to the firm's net worth)? *The board of directors oversees and governs management to ensure that it faithfully pursues the firm's mission.*

How does a board achieve effective oversight and governance? How do we define ineffective or poor governance and how does it differ from good governance? *The tools the board uses to govern management, the objective manner by which it governs, and its own competency to govern will indicate the quality of governance.* In this section, we will explore these issues to understand what is corporate governance and how "good governance" is vital for a firm's survival and long-term success.

What Is Corporate Governance?

To govern is, simply, to steer or direct the activities of the governed. The aim in governance is to achieve a desired outcome from the behavior of the governed. **Corporate governance** *literally means directing the activities of the corporation.*[33] Governance is effective when the governor (the board) is competent, objective, and truthful and employs sound steering mechanisms. Thus, *corporate governance also focuses on the qualities of the governor and the mechanisms employed in governance.*

The need for corporate governance has evolved historically. In today's large firms, founder-owners who manage the business are no longer the rule. Corporations grew through the sale of stock to outsiders, and the resultant stock dispersion over the years created innumerable owners and shifted corporate control from owners to professional managers. In essence, managers run today's corporations as agents of the owners. Managers control vast resources entrusted to their care. For this arrangement to be successful, the agent-manager must not engage in self-dealing but must instead act in the owners' and the corporation's best interest. Self-serving behavior on the part of managers seriously weakens the corporation—and can even cost it its very existence, as the shareholders of Enron and WorldCom painfully learned.

Agency theory recommends two ways to prevent the self-seeking behavior of the agent-manager:[34]

1. By aligning the interest of the agent with that of the owner—that is, through stock options and bonuses tied to performance—agents can be made to think and act as the owners themselves.

2. By closely monitoring the activities of the agent—that is, through auditing accounts and periodically evaluating performance—potentially self-serving managers can be kept in check.

An alternative model, known as the stewardship theory, suggests that managers are intrinsically responsible and cooperative. Through empowerment, they can be made to act in the best interest of the corporation and its owners.[35] Some combination of these two models provides the basis for most corporate governance mechanisms. Many believe that, to be effective, boards must combine control with collaboration; a board must function as a supervisor and a leader.[36]

Board of Directors

The board is authorized by the owners to govern the corporation through supervision, rewards, and empowerment. The board performs the following roles:

1. *Strategic Role*: examine and approve the firm's mission and overall strategic direction; help in procuring resources needed for strategy implementation; and monitor the efficient use of such resources

2. *Supervisory Role*: plan, monitor, and evaluate CEO and top management performance; hire and fire the CEO; scrutinize financial statements for accuracy and truthfulness; examine and decide on compensation packages for top management; ensure ethical behavior and compliance with the laws

3. *Leadership Role*: provide counsel and guidance to senior management, especially the CEO; periodically assess its own effectiveness

But corporate governance involves more than the board's roles and responsibilities in supervising management. Corporate governance also focuses on the merits of the board itself. *In a nutshell, corporate governance refers to all the systems, structures, and processes employed to ensure that managerial activities focus on the goals of the corporation and its owners. The board structure (composition, competency of the board members), monitoring mechanisms (rules of management supervision, reward structure), and monitoring process (steps in CEO evaluation) are all components of corporate governance.*

Board Structure

A board usually has between ten and twelve members, who are elected by the stockholders. By law, they are obligated to act in the stockholders' interest as their fiduciary. Board members are classified as inside and outside directors. Insiders comprise the CEO and other top managers. Their presence on the board is vital because they have crucial information about the company's business. Directors who are friends or relatives of the CEO, retired executives, or individuals with business ties to the firm are also deemed to be insiders. Outsiders are major shareholders, responsible members of the community, business leaders, or academics. Most boards today have outside directors in the majority (approximately eight out of ten). By having outsiders as the majority, the firm ensures that its board (a) functions independently without pressure from the CEO and (b) brings objectivity to the process of evaluating management.

The board operates through committees. By keeping insiders off crucial committees, the board can ensure objectivity in its supervision of management. The *audit committee*, comprising only outsiders, reviews the firm's financial reports and evaluates the adequacy of internal control systems. The *compensation committee*, consisting mostly of outsiders, evaluates senior-management performance and determines compensation. The *nominating committee*, comprising mostly outsiders, is responsible for nominating candidates for the board and for senior management positions. The *executive committee*, comprising internal and external directors, is responsible for formulating corporate policies.

Board Effectiveness

A board can be effective when it is independent (outsiders are in the majority), is competent, and demonstrates seriousness of purpose by faithfully executing its legal and moral responsibilities.[37] Nevertheless, inside directors have historically sought to influence board decisions in their favor despite their minority status. Managerial control over company resources and information enables them to do so. Reliance on managers for information undoubtedly weakens the board's supervisory power. And in boards where the CEO is also the chairman of the board, or outsiders do not put in quality time because they sit on several boards, insider influence can be stronger.

Several other factors strengthen insider influence over the board and compromise board objectivity and effectiveness. For example, outside directors with long tenure on the board may develop friendly ties with managers. Accounting illiteracy among outside directors can weaken the board's ability to effectively scrutinize financial statements. Lack of knowledge about the firm's mission and strategic goals or a clear understanding of industry competition can limit the ability of outside directors to lead the firm.[38] In boards where such conditions exist, board effectiveness cannot be high. Such boards have been found to blindly rubber-stamp management's proposals and statements without scrutiny, approving inaccurate financial results of company performance for release to investors. They also have been found to approve large salaries, stock options, or bonuses to top managers in return for attractive perks or consulting fees for themselves. As a result, there have been numerous stockholder suits against board members, and in many instances courts have found board members personally liable for dereliction of their fiduciary obligations to stockholders.

Good governance, like good government, epitomizes integrity, transparent actions, and accountability of results. Opaque activities, unethical behavior, and self-dealing are indicative of *poor governance.* Accounting frauds, executive crimes, and managerial self-dealing reported at Enron, Tyco International, WorldCom, and several other firms once viewed as America's most admired companies have raised serious doubts about the quality of governance mechanisms used by companies, especially board structure, board-member qualifications, and competence.[39] To regain stakeholder trust, some firms are presently overhauling their entire governance structure, and several boards are becoming more assertive in the management of corporations.[40] In the last decade alone, boards have fired or forced the resignation of CEOs for incompetence or corrupt behavior at American Express, Archer-Daniel-Midlands, AT&T, Eastman Kodak, Lucent Technologies, General Motors, Tyco International, and WorldCom, to name a few. Board members are voluntarily curtailing the number of boards on which they serve, thereby enhancing their quality of management supervision. Since 2002, several firms have instituted board-related reforms (either voluntarily or because they have been legally required to do so), such as separating the CEO from the board chairman's function, limiting board-member tenure, and mandating the inclusion of directors with finance and accounting backgrounds.*

Firms with a poor record of governance should find it difficult to obtain the level of stakeholder support necessary for company survival and growth. To regain trust and rebuild a tarnished corporate image, the mission statements of several firms declare their resolve to be truthful and transparent in conduct. You can see from Strategy in Practice 2.2 the commitment that Colgate-Palmolive Company makes to the pursuit of good governance. Colgate's board has been cited frequently by *Business Week* for best governance practices based on a survey of institutional investors. You may also want to refer to *Business Week*'s periodic survey of best and worst boards to learn more about board effectiveness and company performance.

---

*The Sarbanes-Oxley Act passed by the U.S. Congress in 2002 mandates five financially literate members on each board, appointed for a five-year term. Two of them must be certified public accountants.

See also Table 2.3 to understand what criteria distinguish best boards from worst boards.

Social Responsibility

Obviously, managers have an economic responsibility to manage organizational resources efficiently so as to generate a fair return to owners. But do they have any responsibility toward stakeholders who are nonowners? In addition to their economic responsibilities, what responsibilities may managers have for other groups in society? In other words, should firms pursue social goals side by side with economic goals? Today's society strongly believes that a firm's responsibility does not stop with the pursuit of economic goals. Instead, it is expected to fulfill certain social, legal, and ethical obligations as well.[41] **Corporate social responsibility** *is defined to broadly include, besides philanthropic activities, a firm's endeavors to be economically efficient, fair, and just in dealings with customers, suppliers, employees, and competition; and to obey the law and be involved in socioeconomic projects, side-by-side with the government.*[42]

Institutional and individual investors are reported to increasingly prefer stocks of firms that demonstrate a genuine concern for ethics and social responsibility.[43] Similarly, consumers are known to favor products of companies that are honest and have a good track record in fair business dealings. Along the same lines, today's skilled job applicants seem to prefer employers that support a social cause; employee morale in such firms is reported to be relatively higher.[44] Incorporation of ethics and social responsibility beliefs in the mission statement and managerial commitment to actively pursue them has therefore become crucial for business success. Corporate social

TABLE 2.3	Best and Worst Boards	
BEST BOARDS		**WORST BOARDS**
1. Boards have no more than two inside directors.		There are more than two inside directors.
2. Directors are unrelated to the CEO.		CEO has close ties with several directors.
3. Directors own significant company stock.		Directors own minimal company stock.
4. Boards meet frequently.		Boards meet occasionally.
5. Boards evaluate CEO performance annually.		Boards do not evaluate CEO performance.
6. Boards evaluate their own performance regularly.		Boards do not evaluate their own performance.
7. Boards place limits on other board membership.		Directors are on several other boards.
8. Entire board is elected annually.		Members serve for several years.
9. Member knowledge of industry high.		Member knowledge of industry low.
10. The board demonstrates leadership skills.		There is an overall lack of leadership skills.

Source: "The Best and Worst Boards," *Business Week* (www.businessweek.com), October 7, 2002; "The Best and Worst Boards of 2002," *Chief Executive* (www.chiefexecutive.net), October 2002.

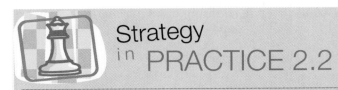

Strategy in PRACTICE 2.2

COLGATE-PALMOLIVE COMPANY: CORPORATE GOVERNANCE COMMITMENT

Board and Committee Independence: Since 1989, Colgate-Palmolive has strived for total board independence. The board comprises entirely of outside directors, with the exception of the CEO. Crucial committees such as the Audit Committee and the Nominating Committee have only outside directors as members. None of the outside directors receives consulting, legal, or other non-director fees from the Company.

Board Experience and Diversity: Colgate is committed to maintaining an experienced, ethical, and diverse board. It values experience in business, education and public service fields, and international experience. Among the eight current independent members, four are women or minorities. The board emphasizes moral conduct in its dealings.

Director Compensation in Stock: 89 percent of a director's compensation is paid in Colgate stock. Board members also receive stock options each year. Board members own significant amounts of Company stock.

Strategic Role of Board: The Board plays a major role in the formulation of Colgate's business strategy. It reviews the Company's Strategic Plan and receives detailed briefings throughout the year on critical aspects of its implementation. These include subsidiary performance reviews, product reviews, and reports on R&D initiatives.

CEO Evaluation Process. The CEO evaluation is a formal annual process. The CEO is evaluated against the goals set each year, including both objective measures (such as earnings per share) and subjective criteria reflective of the Company's core values.

Board Size and Directorship Limits: Designed to maximize board effectiveness, Colgate's By-Laws fix the number of directors between seven and 12. Currently, the Board has nine directors. To devote sufficient time to properly discharge their duties, no director presently serves on more than three other corporate boards.

Meeting Attendance. Each director attended 100% of the meetings of the Board and the Committees on which they served in 2003.

Executive Sessions of Outside Directors: The outside directors of the Board meet without the CEO present as necessary during the course of each year.

Shareholder Rights Plan—Periodic Evaluation Policy: Recently, the Board designated a committee, made up of outside directors, to evaluate the Company's Rights Plan every three years to determine whether it continues to be in the interests of the Company and its stockholders.

Sources: Adapted from www.colgate.com/app/Colgate/US/Corp/ Governance/Boardofdirectors/GovernanceCommitment; "The Best and Worst Boards" *Business Week* (cover story), October 7, 2002.

responsibility appears in a firm's mission as value statements focusing on non-economic goals such as resource conservation, reducing pollution, enhancing consumer/employee/community safety, solving urban housing and drug problems, training the disadvantaged, or promoting the arts and philanthropy, to name a few.[45]

Professor Archie Carroll suggests that a firm has the following four responsibilities:

1. *Economic*: Produce goods and services, of value to society, efficiently so as to repay creditors and stockholders

2. *Legal*: Obey all laws

3. *Ethical*: Conduct itself in ways that are generally deemed by society to be right

4. *Discretionary*: Assume voluntary obligations, such as making philanthropic contributions[46]

According to Carroll, a firm must first meet its economic goals to fulfill its responsibility toward owners. To continue pursuing its economic endeavors, it must act legally. Ethical conduct and discretionary activities comprise the firm's social responsibility. Ethical responsibilities enhance the firm's public image by placing it in society's good graces. Discretionary responsibilities positively add to the firm's public image.

An opposing viewpoint is offered by Professor Milton Friedman,[47] who argues that the business of business is economic efficiency only and social goals should not be part of its mission. According to Friedman, pursuit of social goals increases business costs, thereby minimizing profits, making such pursuits unfair to stockholders. But some researchers have found that by voluntarily pursuing certain social programs (for example, investing in new technologies to reduce industrial pollution) firms have in fact been able to reduce costs related to regulatory compliance.[48] Some scholars suggest that highly ethical firms develop trustworthy relationships with stakeholders, which increases their ability to achieve economic goals efficiently.[49] Professor Michael Porter suggests that social responsibility is not a burden to a firm but a source of competitive advantage when judiciously undertaken. According to Porter, in the long run, economic and social goals of a firm are not conflicting but integrally connected.[50]

Summary

A well-articulated and inspiring mission statement is the starting point for a firm's path to success. It provides managers and employees with a clear destination and a route to follow. When a mission statement carries a steadfast purpose that is widely accepted by company personnel, it provides a shared vision, exhorting employees to deliver higher levels of performance. When outsiders believe in the firm's mission, it gives legitimacy to the firm's business, allowing it to survive and grow.

To successfully realize its mission, a firm needs stakeholder support. Primary stakeholders provide the resources the firm needs for realizing its mission in exchange for satisfaction of their own goals. Secondary stakeholders who have no exchange relationship with the firm can harm the firm if they are adversely affected by its activities. To receive and maintain strong stakeholder support, a firm must manage its stakeholder relationship in a way that maximizes cooperation with those who have a high potential for good and minimizes conflict with those who have a high potential for harm.

A clear and inspiring mission is necessary but not sufficient for success. A firm should also ensure that managers truly pursue its aims. Stakeholders will withdraw support if they find significant disparity between the firm's stated mission and eventual actions. Responsibility for ensuring that managers are faithful to the firm's mission and do not engage in self-serving activities rests with the board of directors. An effective board is thus a *sine qua non* for a firm's success. A board is effective when its members meet frequently, have industry experience, possess accounting competence, are independent of CEO influence, and objectively assess managerial performance.

Today's society strongly believes that a firm's responsibility does not stop with the pursuit and realization of economic goals. Instead, a business has social, legal, and ethical responsibilities as well. To be successful, a firm should be mindful of society's expectations by incorporating such goals in its mission and actively pursuing them.

Chapter 2 Discussion Questions and Projects

Discussion Questions

1. Is an inspiring and clearly articulated mission statement important for the long-term survival of a firm? Discuss.

2. Define corporate governance, describe the governance mechanisms used by firms, and discuss the relevance of good governance to organizational performance.

Projects

1. Intel is a leader in the semiconductor industry and Advanced Micro Devices is a distant follower. Obtain a copy of both companies' mission statements, either from their websites or annual reports. Compare and contrast them on their vision, goals and strategies, business philosophy, and importance attached to corporate governance and social responsibility. Which of the two has a greater chance of long-term survival? Provide reasons for your answer.

2. Using the Internet and the business press, read about the role of the board in corporate governance. Write a three-page paper that summarizes the changes presently taking place in board composition and responsibilities and show how likely those changes are to make boards more effective in corporate governance.

Continuing Case

Southwest Airlines—Reevaluating the Business Mission and Stakeholder Relationships in Changing Times

Company Origin

In 1966, Herb Kelleher, an enterprising lawyer, and Rollin King, a Texas entrepreneur, identified a unique opportunity in the airlines business. They believed that people who drive or take a bus to make intercity short-distance trips would rather fly if attractive fares and convenient schedules were offered. Talks with businesspeople in Texas had convinced them that a lucrative market existed for a low-fare carrier offering direct flights between San Antonio, Dallas, and Houston. In 1971, with limited cash and three small planes borrowed from Boeing, the two men started Southwest Airlines as a niche player in the airline industry. The company defined its business as a short-distance carrier providing point-to-point flights (that is, direct flights) between midsize cities. Within this niche, it posi-

tioned itself as a low fare airline—presenting itself as an attractive alternative to traveling by car or bus. Lamar Muse, an industry veteran, was hired as the company's CEO while Kelleher assumed the role of the chairman of the board.

Business Mission

People close to Kelleher described him as a maverick with a penchant for fun, frolic, and humor and an ability to make friends quickly. Guided by his strong personality and visionary thinking, Southwest chose customer service as the cornerstone of its business mission. Kelleher believed that, while low fares and convenient schedules were important, customer service was the critical discriminating factor for success in the airlines business. By providing customers with an enjoyable and fun flying experience, he argued,

Southwest would become the airline of choice in the fare-conscious market in which it competed. Southwest thus stated its mission as "providing the highest quality of service to customers, delivered with a sense of warmth, friendliness, individual pride, and company spirit." Company reports frequently interpreted the essence of this mission to employees and outsiders along these lines: "We are in the people business, we just happen to be an airline; we offer a cause to strive for, not a career; our cause is to treat customers right and with a fun-loving attitude."

Pursuing the Mission

A mission is a verbal statement that describes a firm's intentions. To put it into action, policies that will induce the organization's members to work toward the mission are necessary. Southwest's policies predominantly sought employees who would voluntarily work toward its mission by a process in which the firm would attract and retain several "mini Herbs." Kelleher wanted to create an organization after his own image, filled with individuals who had the same spirit, passion, and enthusiasm to serve people as he did. In so doing, he reasoned that the firm would have the kind of employees who could internalize the company mission as their own and faithfully pursue it, as defined and unsupervised. Consequently, Southwest's recruitment guidelines focused not on the candidates' skills, but on attitudes that closely matched Kelleher's. "If you don't have a fun-loving, sociable attitude," said Kelleher, "we don't want you. We can change or enhance the skill level through training, not the attitude." To retain the selected employees and to motivate them, Southwest's policies emphasized the creation of an informal work environment in which employees would feel happy to stay and wholeheartedly pursue the firm's mission. Employee empowerment and teamwork were the favored approach in people management while individual performance evaluations, close supervision, and layoffs were shunned. Profit sharing and stock options were provided to ensure employee productivity through a feeling of ownership in the company. More importantly, Kelleher's leadership style itself acted as a crucial motivating factor. Kelleher viewed employees as the firm's most valuable stakeholder, even ahead of customers and stockholders. In Kelleher's thinking, a satisfied employee will satisfy the customer; productivity and profits, key to stockholders' satisfaction, will automatically follow. Kelleher even placed employees ahead of managers in importance.

Company Performance

Southwest's clear mission and consistent policies did not take long to show their positive effect on company performance. Almost from its inception, Southwest's performance has been nothing short of stellar. It has set an impressive record in the airline industry for customer satisfaction levels, passengers carried, employee productivity, and lowest cost per passenger mile. It has been consistently ranked high for flight safety and on-time arrival. It has posted profits uninterruptedly for the last thirty years in an industry where monumental losses are more common. It has steadily grown to be the fifth-largest airline in the United States, with 2004 sales of $6.5 billion.

The Future

While Southwest's achievements are impressive, events that are occurring in the U.S. airline industry and within the firm itself seem to portend that the future may not be smooth sailing for the firm. Industry analysts, who contend that the firm may have to reevaluate its mission and stakeholder relationships, cite the following as reasons:

1. Saturation of the U.S. short-haul, low-fare market due to entry by competitors such as JetBlue, Air Tran, and Frontier raises concerns for Southwest's growth. The company has responded to this threat by pursuing opportunities in the long-haul market (for example, U.S. cross-country flights). In the not-so-distant future, entry into the international segment can be expected. The majority of customers in these long-haul segments are business travelers with complex itineraries whose preferences are more for a seamless connection of routes and flights than a pleasant in-flight experience. In light of this, some industry analysts suggest that Southwest reevaluate its current mission, which focuses primarily on providing friendly customer service.

2. Southwest's relationship with employees, its most valuable stakeholders, and its unions has started showing signs of strain. No longer a small company suitable to Kelleher's paternalistic management style, Southwest is a giant firm with an employee strength of 33,000. It is also the most unionized in the industry, with 85 percent of its employees represented by six different unions. In 2001, for the first time in company history, pilots and flight attendants threatened to strike, claiming they were being underpaid even though the firm was the most profitable in the industry. In July 2004, the company settled issues after marathon two-year negotiations that ended in significant pay increases to employees. Industry analysts fear that it may not be long before Southwest faces the same problems that legacy carriers have long experienced—employer-employee distrust, mounting payroll costs, and below-average productivity—unless the firm reevaluates its stakeholder relationships and identifies ways to strengthen them. Increasing both the level of communication and shared governance mechanisms are mentioned in this context.

Discussion Questions

1. Do you think that Southwest's actions are consistent with its mission? Explain ways in which the firm's actions are consistent or inconsistent with its mission.
2. In light of Southwest's entry into the long-haul market and the likelihood that it might enter international markets, how might the firm's mission be modified?
3. Why is it critical for Southwest to maintain a close relationship with its employees and the unions? Suggest some ways by which the firm can strengthen its stakeholder relationships.

Source: A. A. Thompson and J. E. Gamble, "Southwest Airlines, Inc.," in A. A. Thompson and A. J. Strickland, *Strategic Management: Concepts and Cases* (New York: McGraw Hill-Irwin, 2003), C-590–629; S. B. Donnelly, "One Airline's Magic," *Time*, October 28, 2002, 45–47; D. Reed, "Southwest's challenges grow," *USA Today*, October 17, 2002; M. Trottman, "Inside Southwest Airlines' storied culture feels strains," *Wall Street Journal,* July 11, 2003; D. Koening, "Southwest's profits sag: CEO quits," *San Diego Union-Tribune*, July 6, 2004; "Southwest Reaches Deal with Attendants," *Forbes*, June 25, 2004; A. Serwer and K. Bonamici, "The Hottest Thing in the Sky," *Fortune*, March 8, 2004; "Drop the Pilot," *Economist*, July 16, 2004; W. Zellner, "Southwest's New Direction," *Business Week*, February 8, 1999, 58-59; Company annual report.

PART Two

Situation Analysis

The External Environment: Assessing Competitive Opportunities and Threats

CHAPTER OBJECTIVES

After reading this chapter, you should be able to:

- Discuss the importance of environmental scanning and identification of opportunities and threats for a firm's survival and long-term success

- Discuss how managerial mindset affects perception and interpretation of opportunities and threats

- Describe the components of the macro environment, how they change, and how these changes create opportunities or threats for a firm

- Define an industry and describe how industry forces change, creating competitive opportunities or threats for a firm

- Analyze changes occurring in a specific industry using Porter's Five Forces model to determine how attractive it is for profits

Opening Case

During the 1950s and 1960s, the Big Three U.S. automakers—General Motors, Ford, and Chrysler (now a division of DaimlerChrysler)—together controlled about 95 percent of the U.S. market for automobiles. Mass production of interchangeable parts and assembly-line techniques enabled them to produce diverse models of standard quality economically in large volume. Aggressive pricing, distribution, and acquisition of smaller firms helped them rapidly secure a large market share. With demand stable and no radical change in automotive technology in view, the U.S. firms retained their market dominance throughout these decades simply by making styling changes and advertising aggressively. Improvements in the product's quality or performance (e.g., long-term reliability of the car and fuel efficiency) were unnecessary for competitive purposes and were therefore ignored. The U.S. automakers' prolonged dominance was largely due to the market's penchant for large, powerful, and stylish cars and the ability of these firms to build and deliver such cars economically. The Big Three had adapted to the needs of their environment and they were highly successful.

The U.S. environment of the 1970s was, however, dramatically changing economically, socially, and culturally, altering the type of car that people demanded. Economically, skyrocketing fuel prices and the rising cost of living were steadily forcing the U.S. consumer to demand a fuel-efficient car. Sociologically, the average American family was shrinking in size and, with more and more women working full time, one big family car was not economical anymore; instead, many families wanted two compact cars. Culturally, concern for quality was rising, and Americans valued product reliability and safety more than size or style in a car. In brief, the 1970s environment increasingly demanded cars that were unlike those demanded in previous decades. It had to be a compact that was fuel efficient, of high quality, safe, and competitively priced.

These buyer preferences changed not overnight, but over a period of time. Nevertheless, they caught the U.S. automakers by surprise because the automakers had not anticipated them. The automakers remained oblivious to changes in their environment, blinded by past success and their resulting inability to entertain alternative views of the marketplace. Environmental scanning might have forewarned them, allowing them time to adapt, but they did very little of that because prolonged market dominance had lulled them into complacency. To meet the changed consumer preferences, however, the U.S. automakers had to make radical changes to product design and manufacturing tools, both of which were expensive. The automakers resisted. As a result, the internal resources and capabilities of the Big Three could no longer effectively meet the U.S. demand for high-quality, fuel-efficient compacts. This inability led to a massive entry into the U.S. market of foreign auto firms that had been building high-quality and fuel-efficient small cars for quite some time based on forecasts that indicated to them the rapidly emerging need for such cars. The result was a dramatic end to the Big Three's dominance over the U.S. market. In 1980 alone, they collectively lost over $4 billion. By the end of that year, their share in the domestic market had eroded to 75 percent. By early 2005, their share stood at about 56 percent. Industry analysts predict that this share is likely to fall further to about 50 percent by 2007.[1]

The automotive industry experience tells us that environments change and affect business performance. Advance perception and understanding of environmental change will help a firm plan more effectively for the resources it needs to deal with such changes. This chapter describes how environments change, what key trends managers observe to forecast change, and how their own beliefs influence the perception and interpretation of change. We will discuss two types of environments and the changes occurring within them:

1. The **macro environment** undergoes generic changes due to socioeconomic trends and affects all businesses alike.

2. The **industry environment** undergoes specific changes in response to competitive dynamics and affects firms differently in each industry.

After reading this chapter, you should have a clear understanding of the role the external environment plays in a firm's current and long-term performance and the frameworks available for predicting and assessing change.

Environmental Change

Environments change—sometimes frequently, sometimes dramatically—bringing growth opportunities to some firms while threatening the short-term profitability and long-term survival of others. Managers prefer stable and simple environments that let them pursue company goals as planned. But most environments are neither stable nor simple; instead, they are ever changing and complex. Environmental change alters the volume of demand for current products, creates demand for new products, and alters the technology used to make products. It introduces new competitors into the arena, as the U.S. automakers witnessed; intensifies competition among existing firms; or even lessens competition among existing firms. As a result, environmental change creates sometimes favorable and sometimes hostile business conditions. To be successful in its endeavors, a firm must frequently adapt to environmental change by modifying its internal systems and competencies. Alternatively, it must proactively shape the environment so as to match environmental conditions to its own systems and competencies. Failure to do so can create a mismatch between what a firm can do (its capabilities) and what the environment demands, threatening the firm's ability to move toward its desired future.

Environmental Awareness

Before managers can decide how to respond to environmental change, they must observe relevant environmental events on a regular basis and forecast change. In short, they must become environmentally aware. **Environmental awareness** *involves continuously scanning and interpreting environmental trends to generate informed forecasts.* Forecasting provides the lead information managers need to choose an appropriate response to environmental change. To determine whether emerging conditions are favorable or unfavorable for their business, managers observe changes in demographics, consumer spending levels, competitor moves, and availability of supplies. *Favorable conditions are* **opportunities** *that, when effectively exploited, will lead a firm to its desired end. Unfavorable conditions are* **threats** *that, when not effectively dealt with, can harm a firm's current business and profitability and its future plans.*

A general complaint about the managers of the U.S. automotive industry of the sixties and seventies is that they were not environmentally aware or vigilant; instead, they were oblivious to changing consumer preferences and potential competitor moves, and it cost their firms dearly.[2] Today's managers routinely observe environmental trends and incorporate them into their strategic decision making. But what they observe and how they interpret what they have observed influences the strategic choices they make and, consequently, the firm's performance.[3] Cognitive psychology tells us that individuals selectively observe events based on what is *familiar* to them (that is, what they learned and stored as knowledge) because their capacity to observe information is limited.[4]

Managers, like all individuals, employ filtering mechanisms as they make environmental observations. Because the environment is complex, they cannot exhaustively scan the environment; instead they are selective in what they take note of.[5] What they select to watch depends on what is familiar to them—their cognition, their mindset. Mindset results from the personal beliefs of managers and their understanding of the firm's vision and values.[6] It guides them in their observation: what is relevant and should be perceived and what is irrelevant and therefore discarded. Depending on what they observe and how they interpret it, they may recognize an opportunity or threat early on and gain competitive advantages because of it. Or they may misperceive or fail to perceive a potentially lucrative opportunity or lurking threat, incurring lost sales or revenues.

The Risks of Misperception

Business history is filled with instances of misperceptions and missed opportunities and lost fortunes. Hewlett-Packard, famous for scientific calculators during the 1960s, missed the opportunity to be the first to market personal computers when it turned down a proposal by its own employee (Stephen Wozniak, who eventually founded Apple Computer), saying that it did not want to be in that kind of a market.[7] Digital Equipment Corporation misperceived an emerging opportunity in 1977 (a few months before Apple pioneered the first PC) when its CEO Ken Olsen observed that there was no reason for individuals to have computers in their homes.[8] Western Union missed a golden opportunity when it turned down Alexander Graham Bell's offer to license the telephone technology, saying that the telephone would never replace the telegraph.[9] Obviously, the mindset of managers in these organizations failed them because it did not direct their attention to the attractive opportunities that were emerging in their business environment.

As these examples illustrate, environmental analysis is more than a mere description of opportunities and threats—it includes discussions of how company personnel recognize them as they unfold. Successful firms have managers who are highly aware of pertinent trends emerging in their business environment. Through their leadership, other members of those firms continuously learn and develop an ability to recognize opportunities or threats in a timely manner. As you read through this chapter, bear in mind that more important than a general understanding of what an opportunity or threat is is the ability to recognize it and act on it when one emerges. We will return to this topic in Chapter 4 when we discuss the competencies of a firm. For now, let us focus on organizational environments.

For our discussion, let us divide the business environment into the *macro (or generic) environment* and the *industry environment,* as shown in Figure 3.1. The sections that follow describe the components of each and how they change to create favorable or unfavorable business conditions.

The Macro Environment

The **macro environment,** also known as the generic environment, comprises economic, social, cultural, technological, and political-legal sectors. Because of the international nature of today's business, the global sector is an important additional element in this environment. The changes occurring in this environment are common to all organizations and impact all firms alike. These impacts are not immediate and may not be felt by a firm for a long time. Also, not all the sectors of this

| FIGURE 3.1 | The Firm and the Forces in Its Environment |

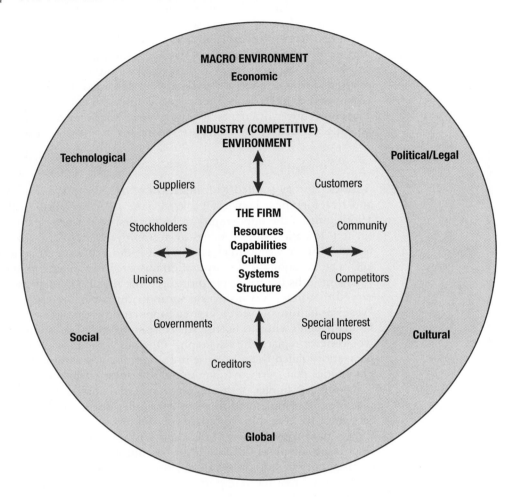

environment are equally relevant to all the firms. Some sectors and the changes occurring within them affect some industries more than others.

The Economic Environment

The economic sector reflects the living standards and general well-being of a society. Businesses are particularly interested in the rate of economic growth, which increases consumer income and, therefore, spending levels. Higher consumer spending reduces competitive pressures, increasing opportunities for businesses to realize higher sales and profits. By contrast, economic decline leads to reduced consumer income and spending, resulting in declining demand, price wars, and reduced sales and profits. Managers study growth rates in *gross domestic product (GDP)* and *employment levels* to assess long-term economic growth. Near term, they watch for movements in *interest rates, inflation, currency exchange rates,* and *stock market indices.*

Let us quickly examine how some of these changes affect businesses:

- Higher *interest rates* reduce consumer incentives to borrow, limiting the demand for durable goods such as houses and cars. Lower interest rates have the opposite effect on consumer borrowing and spending. Periods of rising interest rates are, therefore, a threat to businesses, and periods of falling rates are an opportunity. However, these changes affect luxury and big-ticket manufacturers more than makers of necessities.

- *Inflation* represents erosion in the value of a currency. Inflationary conditions adversely affect a firm's capital costs and restrict its expansion plans. High rates of inflation make investment planning difficult because a firm cannot accurately predict the value of future returns on new investments; as a result, they will not make such investments. Reduction in new business investments slows down economic activity, creating an unfavorable condition for business growth and profitability.

- *Currency exchange rates* (the rate at which one currency exchanges for another) affect the price of goods in international markets. Wide currency fluctuations affect the competitiveness of firms in export markets. When the dollar rate falls in relation to other foreign currencies, U.S. goods become cheaper in international markets, thus becoming more attractive to foreigners. A declining dollar is thus an opportunity for U.S. exporters, whereas a strong dollar produces the opposite effect.

- *Stock market* performance affects the discretionary income of consumers. Significant rises in stock indices create wealth (or the perception of wealth) for stockholders, increasing the demand for luxury goods such as expensive cars and boats. Decreases in stock valuations produce the opposite effect.

The Social Environment

Social change comprises demographic and lifestyle trends. These trends indicate to managers the opportunities or threats emerging as a result of changes occurring in the composition of population, consumer needs, and consumer preferences. For example, the U.S. population is becoming increasingly diverse in ethnicity and buying habits, limiting opportunities to mass marketers of consumer products but increasing opportunities for those that can economically customize or offer variety.[10] The senior-citizen age group of the U.S. population is presently growing faster than any other, producing unprecedented opportunities for firms offering "adult community or active adult" housing. Opportunities have also increased for health care firms, optical product manufacturers and distributors, and retirement counseling specialists that market their products to this age group. On the other hand, decline in the young-adult population is shrinking the market size for brewers, pop music producers, and manufacturers of hip clothing. Similarly, the changing lifestyle of Americans (fast-paced, late-night socializing and eating out more often) has increased opportunities for trendy restaurants and nightclubs, but has produced the opposite effect for supermarkets and manufacturers of prepared food like breakfast cereals (See Strategy in Practice 3.1).

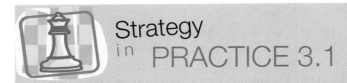

Strategy in PRACTICE 3.1

HOW LIFESTYLE CHANGES ARE AFFECTING THE BREAKFAST CEREAL INDUSTRY

Demand for cereals is presently in a steady state of decline. U.S. sales of ready-to-eat cereals that totaled $8.5 billion in 1996 have been dropping by 3 percent on average each year. Changes in American and Western European lifestyles are hurting the cereal industry.

Cereals used to be an important food item on the American breakfast table. But now, Americans and Western Europeans are consuming less and less cereal. In fact, even the breakfast patterns have changed for many. The traditional and leisurely breakfast at home is becoming a rarity. Most people are on the run in the morning, rushing to get to work, and find no time for a comfortable "sit and eat" breakfast.

For these people, it is breakfast on the go or "deskfast"—eating cookies and croissants at work. Cereal companies such as Kellogg and others are responding to these changes with convenient hand-held breakfast foods such as cereal bars, cereal and milk bars, and oatmeal bars. Industry experts forecast significant growth in demand for such on-the-go food in the coming years but flat or declining sales for breakfast cereals.

Sources: www.preparedfoods.com, February 2002 and September 2003; "Honey I Shrank the Box," www.forbes.com, November 10, 2003; "Cereal Products," *Encyclopedia of Global Industries,* 3rd ed. (Gale Group, 2003) (www.galenet.galegroup.com).

The Cultural Environment

Cultural change refers to changes in the customs, values, and beliefs of a society. They point managers to products that a society may value, emerging patterns in consumption and lifestyle, and overall trends in people's attitudes toward work and business practices. In recent years, concern for health and fitness has emerged as a predominant value for people all over the world. As a result, providers of health spas and manufacturers of natural food, exercise equipment, and weight-reduction products discovered abundant opportunities. Some of these opportunities have been so immense that they have transformed the makers of these products from mom-and-pop operations into big businesses. Vitamin and health-food firms are experiencing unprecedented demand for their products that has turned them into multibillion-dollar businesses.[11] In contrast, producers of fatty foods, starchy snacks (e.g., Krispy Kreme), and cigarettes are experiencing a strong negative reaction to their products and face product-liability lawsuits that threaten their long-term survival.

Public perception and attitudes toward big business also affect corporate performance. Reports of financial wrongdoing, employee mistreatment, layoffs, and unethical managerial conduct tarnish big business's image, adversely affecting long-term corporate performance. Today, several surveys indicate a downward trend in the public's trust of corporations, due to the accounting frauds reported at Enron and WorldCom and widespread media accounts that businesses have become indifferent to product quality, customer service, and environmental health.[12] In light of these developments, a positive reputation is today considered an important intangible asset that corporations actively seek to acquire and hold.[13] Since reputations take time to establish, companies that already have a good reputation (e.g., Johnson & Johnson) enjoy immense opportunities in the form of sustained customer loyalty for current products and solid support for new products.[14]

The Technological Environment

Technology refers to engineering or technical know-how. A common definition is that it is the process used in converting scientific knowledge into commercial goods.[15] When broadly defined, it refers to the know-how used in activities pertaining to developing, processing, and delivering goods; servicing customers; and running an organization. Technological change occurring at societal and industry levels affects businesses. At the societal level, the present trend is toward the increased use of computer technologies to automate factories and offices. This has provided opportunities for all firms to simultaneously achieve higher quality and lower costs, attributes that were once deemed to be trade-offs. It has also permitted firms to speed up new product development, innovate more frequently, offer greater variety, and respond to market demands more rapidly.

At the industry level, technological change is intensifying competition by *altering the rules of competition, blurring industry boundaries,* and *lowering entry barriers.* For example, the Internet has altered the rules of competition in most industries, especially in consumer retail. Most consumer electronics and books retailers now compete through the Internet in addition to location-based competition. New technologies that integrate voice, video, and data have blurred the boundaries between the computer and communications industries, thus intensifying competition between them. Radical technologies emerging in the consumer electronics, healthcare, automotive components, and aerospace industries have intensified competition by lowering the entry barriers in these industries.

Today's technological change is not confined to specific industries. It may impact firms, positively or negatively, within and across several industries. Because of its pervasive influence, managers pay serious attention to technological developments when assessing environmental change.

The Political-Legal Environment

Political-legal change occurs when the government alters its perspective toward business, which leads to increased or decreased government oversight of businesses. Pro-business sentiment in government creates, obviously, a favorable climate for companies since they can operate without fear of antitrust or other types of accusations. Anti-business sentiment threatens operations as it increases the potential for conflict with the government.

Lately, the general trend in the United States and elsewhere has been toward less governmental intervention in business, which has led to deregulation of many industries. Deregulation eliminates legal barriers to entry in an industry, allowing new companies to enter the market. Deregulation in the U.S. airline, banking, and telecommunications industries during the seventies, eighties, and nineties provided immense opportunities for many small firms to enter these industries and quickly emerge as giant companies. But it also brought threats to existing firms in the form of new competition and reduced profitability.

The Global Environment

Global change involves changes occurring in markets, economies, and political systems of the major regions of the world. Because today's markets and economies are interconnected, political changes, economic downturns, supply shortages, or price increases that occur in one region may fairly rapidly bring opportunities or threats to firms operating elsewhere. For example, the shift in India's political ideology during the 1990s, from a socialistic to a market-oriented economy, provided unprecedented growth opportunities for U.S. firms to enter India's markets with their high-tech projects. However, this is making India self-sufficient in certain electronic fields and, as a result, is reducing opportunities for several other U.S. firms that have been exporting such products to India.

Even epidemics and natural calamities occurring in one region impact far-off businesses. The outbreak of the SARS (severe acute respiratory syndrome) epidemic in China during 2003 created a windfall for the makers of surgical masks, who could not meet the exploding demand when many people, not just medical professionals, started wearing masks in public every day. But the epidemic brought significant losses to international airlines serving China, due to massive cancellations by tourists and business travelers. It even wrecked the livelihood of small businesses in Australia that export fish to China. Restaurants in China, the biggest buyers of Australian reef fish, halted their purchases when SARS prompted diners to stay home in large numbers.[16]

Dealing with Macro Environmental Change

How do firms react when environmental factors alter business conditions? Under favorable conditions, a firm may wish to rapidly expand its production and sales or service operations to exploit an emerging opportunity, whereas unfavorable conditions may pressure it to rapidly contract to minimize losses. For established firms, however, neither of these alternatives can be undertaken expeditiously. That leaves them with two options: either control the external factors to prevent change, or anticipate change and remain flexible so as to quickly adapt the firm's operations to suit external conditions. Control of macro environmental trends is an enormous task for a firm. It may be able to influence only some sectors—for example, swaying political thinking and business legislation through lobbying.[17] For the most part, however, the best a firm can do is forecast change and be prepared to adapt when change occurs. The history of the U.S. automotive industry tells us what happens when firms assign low importance to environmental forecasting and accumulate internal assets that are resistant to change. Firms that have excellent forecasting and adaptation skills survive and succeed. Firms that refuse to change suffer serious economic losses, as Levi Strauss learned recently (see Strategy in Practice 3.2).

How Do Firms Forecast Macro Environmental Change?

Of course, no one has a crystal ball to forecast precisely what will happen in the future. But companies can make estimates based on changes that occur in specific sectors over a period of time. Some estimates are derived from simple trend extrapolation. For example, one can predict the rate of U.S. economic growth for next year based on its average growth rate over the past ten years. Other forecasts are more sophisticated, using multiple regression models to predict economic growth based on the impact of several variables, such as, for example, interest rate, inflation, and money supply. Yet others are qualitative models in which predictions take the form of scenarios developed by experts. Let's now examine four types of forecasting that firms do in individual generic environmental sectors.[18]

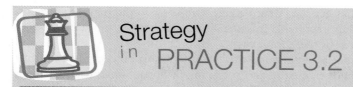

Strategy in PRACTICE 3.2

RESISTING CHANGE, LEVI STRAUSS & CO. LANDS ITSELF IN TROUBLE

Levi Strauss & Co. is a 150-year-old marketer of jeans and an American icon. Its brand enjoys high global visibility, similar to Coca-Cola's and McDonald's. Its jeans have been the most sought-after wardrobe items of teens worldwide for decades. *Time* magazine's millennium issue named Levi's brand 501 as the best fashion of the century. But today, the company is in trouble. Its sales have plummeted from a peak of $7.1 billion in 1996 to $4 billion in 2003, a 43 percent drop. Market research firms say that Levi's market share has been cut in half in a period of six years.

To avert a serious financial crisis, the company started laying off workers, a first in its long history of paternalistic management, and shutting down plants in the United States and Canada. Today, Levi Strauss does not make the jeans it sells. Instead, it outsources manufacturing to subcontractors in low-wage Asian and South American countries. Levi concentrates on design and marketing only. Industry experts say that it will take years before Levi regains its lost sales and market share.

What caused Levi's prolonged and sharp slide in sales? Analysts unanimously agree that it has to do with the firm's rigid thinking and lack of adaptability. Levi continuously ignored or remained oblivious to a changing marketplace. It refused to believe, time and again, focus group and market research findings that indicated how today's teens (the largest customer for jeans) viewed its brand: it was not hip and it was for mature audiences only. A misguided notion within the firm that each generation will adapt to its traditional design and styling, rather than the other way around, kept the company away from innovation and change. It was this self-assuring mindset and resulting unwillingness to change that landed Levi in trouble.

Source: Nina Munk, "How Levi Trashed a Great American Brand," *Fortune,* April 12, 1999; Wendy Zellner, "Lessons from a Faded Levi Strauss," *Business Week,* December 15, 2003; John Boudreau, "Levi Strauss Looks for the Fight in Changing Market," *Mercury News,* December 13, 2003; Lionel Seah, "Fading Jeans," www.straitstimes.asia1.com, July 4, 2003.

Economic forecasts predict economic growth using trends in money supply, interest rates, employment data, growth in personal income, consumer sentiment, new orders for durable goods, business investments in plant and equipment, and manufacturing inventories. Analysis of these data provides a general indication of whether the economy is expanding—if so, the rate of expansion; if not, when it will fall into recession. While very large firms do their own data gathering and analysis, most others obtain forecasts from research firms such as Data Resources and Wharton Econometric Forecasting.

Social forecasts predict demographic and lifestyle changes using trends in population growth, life expectancies, education and training, family formation, and travel and leisure activities. Managers generally obtain the information needed for analysis and forecasting from the U.S. Census. But when specific forecasts have to be made, such as how many people are likely to visit Disney World in Orlando next summer, managers conduct mail and telephone surveys to gather data, analyze it, and make predictions.

Technological forecasts predict what types of technologies are likely to emerge in the future using trends in private and public sector R&D investments, growth rate in categories of scientific personnel, patents awarded, and rate of technological obsolescence (i.e., how quickly an existing technology is replaced). The *Statistical Abstract of the United States* provides key data that managers need to do the required analysis. Some organizations consult experts from several scientific and technical fields who develop futuristic scenarios for these forecasts.

Political forecasts predict government legislation likely to emerge using public opinion trends on matters of economic and social importance. Some forecasts focus on specific regions of the world and predict the likelihood of political stability in those regions. Firms that have multinational operations are interested in such forecasts. Most firms rely on political consultants such as Arthur D. Little for political forecasts.

Table 3.1 summarizes the effect of key trends in the macro environment on businesses and the sources from which data about these trends can be obtained.

The Industry Environment

In addition to the macro environment, a firm's **industry environment** imposes conditions that may be favorable or threatening to the firm's survival and sustained profitability. Industry conditions are assessed and described by the degree of competition occurring within the industry.[19] Competition may be intense or mild depending on such factors as growth in demand for the industry's products, technological change, and the number of sellers within the industry. Intensely competitive industries offer very little potential for profit; industries where competition is relatively mild are favorable.

No two industry's environments are alike because the factors contributing to competition differ from industry to industry. Thus, the degree of competition and profit potential in the PC industry differs entirely from that of sporting goods manufacturing or consumer retailing. This point requires special emphasis because, as we will see later, a firm's choice of strategy to reach its strategic and financial goals is based on the competitive environment prevailing in its industry. For now, it is essential to highlight the following about the industry environment:

1. Industry environments are created by the competitive conditions unique to each industry. Therefore, industries widely differ in regard to opportunities and threats.[20]
2. To a large extent, a firm can alter the industry conditions in its favor.[21]

In the following sections, we will describe what an industry is and how managers analyze the industry environment. A clear description of a firm's industry is an essential prerequisite to identifying the firm's competitors and understanding their motives.

What Is an Industry?

An **industry** *is a group of firms offering products or services that are similar or are close substitutes for each other.*[22] Consumers perceive these products as satisfying the same basic need and are willing to substitute one for the other. In other words, companies in an industry compete directly with each other to satisfy the same consumer need. Based on this definition, Dell and Gateway belong to the same industry because their PCs and servers compete to satisfy the same need (information storage and processing) and consumers perceive their products as close substitutes. Similarly, makers of gas and electric ovens, despite differences in their technology, belong to the same industry (home appliances). Likewise, Avon and Revlon belong to the same

TABLE 3.1   Macro Environment: Key Trends, Impact, and Data Sources

KEY TRENDS	HOW THEY IMPACT INDUSTRIES	DATA SOURCES
Economic		
Interest rates Inflation Stock indices GDP trends Unemployment Money supply	Economic change increases or decreases demand (i.e., volume) for current products by altering consumer income and spending levels. Economic decline affects luxury products more than essentials.	Economic reports by the U.S. Dept. of Commerce (www.bea.gov); The Conference Board (www.conference-board.org); Federal Reserve Bank (www.federalreserve.gov)
Social		
Population distribution Birthrates Family formation Education level Leisure and work trends	Changes in population distribution increase or decrease demand for current products within population segments. Lifestyle change creates demand for unique products and services.	U.S. Census Bureau, (www.census.gov); Yankelovich Population Surveys (www.yankelovich.com)
Cultural		
Attitudinal trends Changes in the belief system	Cultural change alters demand for current products and creates opportunities for new product and service offerings	Yankelovich Values and Attitudes surveys (www.yankelovich.com)
Technological		
Public and private investments in R&D Society's scientific pool Patents awarded Rate of technological obsolescence	Technological change impacts competition by resegmenting industries, altering the rules of competition, lowering entry barriers, and creating new products or processes.	Statistical Abstract of the United States (www.census.gov/statistical-abstract); industry experts' opinions
Political-Legal		
Trends in government-business relationship Tax reform trends Corporate legislation trends	Political change creates a favorable or unfavorable business climate. It affects growth and profits by increasing or decreasing competition.	Political survey reports by independent consultants; for example, Yankelovich, Arthur D. Little Company (www.adl.com)
Global		
Political, economic, social, and technological trends in major global regions	Global change creates new demand for current products. It increases entry threats by lowering barriers. It increases risk for foreign operations.	Country Industry Forecast by Frost & Sullivan (www.frost.com); political forecasts by Arthur D. Little.

industry (cosmetics) even though Avon largely sells directly to customers while Revlon sells through stores. The focus in defining an industry is on the consumer's perception of products as easily substitutable in their need satisfaction, resulting in direct competition between the firms offering these products, and not on the products' technical characteristics or the channels used for marketing and distributing them. It is important to understand this point clearly. Otherwise, a firm may pit itself against other firms that it perceives as competitors but that are not, in fact, its rivals.

Sometimes, the boundaries of an industry may not be clear, making it difficult to tell who a firm's competitors are. Technological change can blur industry boundaries, as has happened in the case of computer, telecommunications, and office automation businesses. Firms in these businesses that once offered products within their respective industries now offer them across all three of these industries. This is an important distinction when defining a firm's industry, because technologies emerging in closely related industries may widen the circle of a firm's competition, making yesterday's substitutes into today's close substitutes.

Industry Segments

Firms strive to differentiate their products from competitors' offerings in order to cater to differences in consumer tastes and preferences. The goal in differentiation is to closely match the firm's offerings to the unique needs of the consumer so as to restrict competition. Differentiation may occur on the product's features, customer service, product breadth, or distribution channels. Differentiation creates **segments** within an industry and products are perceived as close substitutes (that is, direct competitors) within these segments only. For example, while BMW and Hyundai both make autos, the design quality and added features of the former make consumers perceive it as a different category of car and they are willing to pay a higher price for it. Therefore, BMW and Hyundai are not viewed as close substitutes* and they belong to different competitive segments in the automotive industry. BMW follows a *product-differentiation strategy* and competes with Mercedes, Lexus, and the like, whereas Hyundai follows a *cost-leadership strategy* and competes with Chrysler or Honda's low-priced cars.

Strategic Groups: Recognizing segmentation within an industry and identifying the strategic group[23] a firm belongs to is critical for businesses. **Strategic groups** *are clusters of firms within an industry that pursue common or similar strategies.*[24] Firms within each strategic group are similar in their competencies, product offerings and price, and distribution channels. An industry may have only one strategic group (a homogenous industry) or it may have several groups (a differentiated industry). In the automotive industry, we can identify four distinct clusters, as shown in Figure 3.2. Firms in these clusters compete within their respective clusters only.

The strategic group concept helps managers in many ways. By clearly delineating a firm's industry segment and rivals, it gives managers focus in environmental and competitor analysis. Opportunities and threats differ from segment to segment, and a clear description of the segment to which a firm belongs helps managers achieve precision in environmental analysis. It also helps managers effectively analyze other segments in the industry as to their relative attractiveness. Such analyses are a prerequisite to deciding whether a firm should enter another segment or should develop strategies to bar potential entrants from other segments. Toyota moved from the

---

*But Hyundai's premium models may become an attractive substitute if BMW continually increases its price.

FIGURE 3.2   **Strategic Groups in the Automotive Industry**

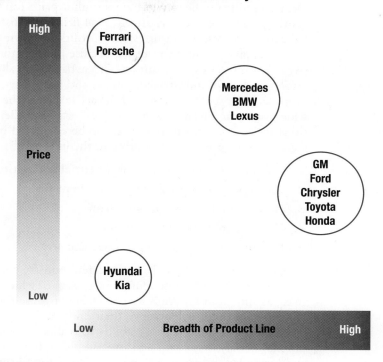

Mercedes and Chrysler (part of DaimlerChrysler) are separated for purposes of illustration.

Source: Adapted from G. G. Dess and G. T. Lumpkin, *Strategic Management: Creating Competitive Advantages* (New York: McGraw Hill, © 2002), p. 63. Reprinted by permission of The McGraw-Hill Companies.

standard car segment to the premium car segment* when it introduced Lexus and became a direct competitor of BMW and Mercedes.

Before proceeding, we need to make a distinction between a "close substitute" and a "not close substitute." To avoid confusion, we will henceforth refer to businesses making close substitutes as the firm's *rivals* or *incumbent firms.* Firms making similar products that can satisfy the same basic consumer need—but compete in a different segment of the same industry or in an entirely different industry—will be referred to as *substitutes.*

Industry Analysis: The Five Forces Model

A firm's financial performance is most closely tied to the developments occurring within its industry. Changes in demand, costs of supplies, and moves of rival firms affect its sales and profits rather rapidly. A firm's goal is to secure an advantageous position in the industry that is conducive to profits. Some industries are inherently more attractive for earning above-average returns than others because they experience a continuous surge in demand and an absence of meaningful competition. Such

---

*Technically, Toyota did not move from one strategic group to another. Movements between strategic groups can be difficult. Toyota overcame this obstacle by creating a new division and a separate line of cars under the Lexus brand name.

industries soon invite entry by new firms, however, leading to increased competition. Or, powerful suppliers negotiate a higher price for their components, reducing a firm's gross margin. Alternatively, rival firms or substitutes thwart the firm's ability to increase prices. To ensure steady profits, a firm must prevent competitive entry, control suppliers and distributors, or raise prices without fear of losing customers to rivals or substitutes. Deciding exactly what a firm should do requires an informed understanding of industry conditions and how they are changing. A model for this purpose proposed by Professor Michael Porter of the Harvard Business School is in wide use in the business world today. Porter's model suggests that industry conditions and a firm's profit potential can be estimated by analyzing the following five forces and the pressures they bring to the industry:[25]

1. The threat of entry by new or **potential competitors**
2. The degree of rivalry among **incumbent firms**
3. The bargaining power of **suppliers**
4. The bargaining power of **buyers**
5. The threat of **substitute products** and services

According to the **Five Forces model,** industry conditions emerge from the pressures exerted by the contending forces, each of which is striving to achieve its objectives, as shown in Figure 3.3. The stronger these forces are, the more successfully contending forces will achieve their ends by altering industry conditions in their favor and threatening a firm's ability to realize sustained profits on its invested capital. Conversely, weak competitors, suppliers, buyers, and substitute manufacturers and low entry threats signal an opportunity for a firm to raise prices and realize significant profits.

Unlike the macro environment, the industry environment can be altered by a firm. A firm is not a prisoner of industry forces. It can defend itself against industry pressures by choosing a *secure market position* or *proactively altering industry conditions in its favor.* Porter contends that a firm will be successful when:

1. The industry has a high profit potential but new competitors cannot easily get in due to high **entry barriers.**
2. The industry has a low profit potential but the firm has an **advantageous market position** that allows it to effectively neutralize the threats posed by the five forces.

The goal of industry analysis, therefore, is to obtain the advance information the firm needs to bar potential entrants or to build a defensible competitive position against contending forces. Let us now examine in more detail Porter's five forces, the pressures they exert, and the conditions under which they will be successful or unsuccessful. (In subsequent chapters, we will describe the strategies available to a firm to defend itself against the five forces or to proactively alter industry conditions in its favor.) As you read through the following discussion, remember we are analyzing the forces operating in the firm's industry, not the firm itself.

Threats of Entry

The term **threats of entry** *refers to the likelihood that new firms can easily enter the industry and carve inroads into the profits of incumbent firms.* For example, telephone companies are emerging as a potential threat to cable firms because new information technologies offer the potential to carry video images through telephone lines and thus take away business from cable companies.

New entrants intensify competition by increasing industry capacity or by altering existing product design and production technologies. A high risk of entry reduces the ability of incumbent firms to raise prices, which threatens their profitability. Entry threats are prevented when an industry has high *entry barriers* or when incumbent firms are known to *retaliate* strongly.*

Entry barriers make it costly for new firms to enter a market and are thus advantages that incumbents have over potential entrants. The following factors, when present in the industry in the right form and strength, endow cost or differentiation advantages to incumbents and act as entry barriers.

FIGURE 3.3   Competitive Pressures in an Industry

Source: Adapted from Michael E. Porter, *Competitive Strategy* (New York: The Free Press, 1980), 3–33.

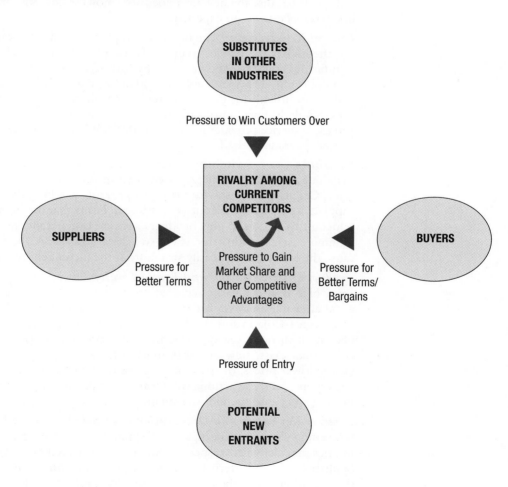

---

* Incumbent firms with substantial cash resources, excess productive capacity, or great leverage with distribution channels can be expected to stage a strong retaliation.

Economies of Scale: **Economies of scale** *are cost advantages that accrue as a result of an increase in the volume of output.* As production volume increases, fixed cost is spread over a larger number of units, bringing per-unit cost down. In industries where incumbent firms enjoy scale economies, entry is difficult because the new firm must either enter on a large scale (risky since it will increase industry supply and depress prices) or accept cost disadvantages associated with low-volume output. Besides production, an incumbent firm may enjoy scale economies in other functional activities as well, such as purchasing, advertising, distribution, and R&D.

Experience-Curve Effects: In some industries, per-unit cost declines successively because firms gain cumulative experience in making the product. This phenomenon has been observed in the aerospace, automotive, and consumer electronics businesses. In mature industries, established firms have significant experience that helps them to achieve overall efficiency. Entry into these industries is difficult because the new firm does not enjoy the cost advantages an incumbent has developed through experience.

Capital Requirements: The higher the capital needed to do business in an industry, the higher the barrier to entry. During the 1970s, IBM and Xerox created significant capital barriers to entry by leasing their products rather than selling them outright. This increased the working capital requirements for new entrants, making it difficult for them to enter the copier and computer mainframe industries. Similarly, entry into aerospace, automotive, semiconductor manufacturing, and cable service provider industries is difficult because of the large amount of investment capital needed.

Switching Costs: **Switching costs** are those that the buyer must assume when switching from the product/service of an incumbent firm to that of the new entrant. Cellular phone service providers prevent switching through contracts that stipulate a penalty if the contract is broken. Firms that use high-tech products are reluctant to switch to new products because it generally involves employee retraining costs. In industries where switching costs are high, entry is difficult because the buyer will not easily switch from the incumbent to the new entrant.

Product Differentiation and Brand Loyalty: Existing firms in an industry may enjoy high **brand loyalty,** achieved through high product quality, uniqueness, or good after-sales service. Incumbent firms may also have well-recognized brands (e.g., Coca-Cola in soft drinks and Marlboro in cigarettes) whose visibility has been built through years of advertising and promotion. In industries where such conditions exist, new entrants must offer a higher-quality product/service, charge lower prices, or spend large sums on advertising to win over brand-loyal customers. All these actions will mean lower profit margins for the new entrant, making entry into the industry unattractive.

Access to Key Supply and Distribution Channels: In some industries, incumbents who enjoy close relationships with suppliers and distributors due to long-standing ties may derive cost, speed-to-market, and related benefits or what Professor Spulber of Northwestern University describes as *transaction advantages.*[26] In industries where incumbents enjoy these advantages, entry is difficult because such advantages will not be readily available to new entrants.

Government Regulations: Industries such as cable TV, radio broadcasting, liquor retailing, electric and gas utilities, and nuclear power distribution are regulated by governments. Safety concerns and the need to ensure that the public receives uniform quality service force governments to selectively permit firms to operate in these industries through licensing. Also, to recoup the high capital investments needed to operate in these industries, governments generally grant businesses monopoly status that further restricts entry by new firms.

Despite these various strategies used by incumbent firms to thwart entry, most barriers are permeable and thus do not offer permanent protection. For example, economies of scale and experience curve advantages disappear if the market expands or the production technology changes. Transaction advantage ceases if the product technology changes or alternative distribution channels emerge. Differentiation-related advantages disappear if the tastes of consumers change.[27]

Rivalry Among Incumbent Firms

Rivalry *refers to the intensity of competition among incumbent firms.* If rivalry is weak, incumbents increase prices and earn above-average profits. If it is strong, price wars occur, minimizing the ability of incumbents to realize higher returns. The extent of competitive intensity in an industry depends on the *structure of the industry, demand conditions in the industry,* and the *ability of firms to exit the industry* if they wish to.

1. *Industry Structure:* The number of firms in an industry and their size indicates the structure of the industry. An industry with many small- to medium-size firms, each with a low market share (e.g., muffler shops, real estate brokerage firms), is a **fragmented industry.** Due to its low market share, no firm has a dominating influence over the industry. By contrast, a **consolidated industry** (e.g., commercial aircraft, overnight mail, or express mail) has a small number of large companies that dominate the industry. Such an industry is an **oligopoly.** Lacking market power, firms in a fragmented industry are in no position to prevent new entry. Due to their small size, these companies lack the resources needed to differentiate their products and build brand loyalty. Consequently, the market, rather than the sellers, sets the price, and price wars break out. A fragmented industry, therefore, experiences high levels of competition and is a threat to a firm. Unable to raise prices, the firm must strive to minimize cost to realize profits. Alternatively, it must differentiate its product or gain significant market share to assert control over price.

   Consolidated industries also experience price wars, since the competitive pricing behavior of one firm directly affects the market share of others. However, such price wars are relatively less common in a consolidated industry. Since every firm has almost equal strength, a collusive behavior often prevails, with one firm (generally the dominant firm) setting the price and others following the leader to avoid competitive battles. While explicit collusion is illegal, companies cooperate in subtle ways that tend to minimize competition. Tacit collusion generally occurs when firms closely monitor what others say or do in regard to price and act in concert. A consolidated industry thus experiences relatively less competitive intensity and is, therefore, less threatening to a firm's profitability.

2. *Demand Conditions:* An industry's growth rate and demand conditions affect the nature of competition within that industry. Growth in demand, as a result of new customers entering the market or existing customers making additional purchases, minimizes the degree of competition by increasing opportunity for every firm. By

contrast, stagnant or declining demand intensifies the degree of competition since each firm must now fight to retain its market share and profits.

3. **Exit Barriers:** In some industries, firms stay in business and continue to operate even when demand is declining or profits are low. Certain economic and strategic factors, such as high investments in plant, contractual obligations (e.g., employee pensions), or dedicated technology (e.g., equipment that has no alternative use), prevent firms in these industries from exiting. On occasion, government subsidies or special grants such as the one provided to the airlines following the September 11 tragedy prevent exit by encouraging weaker firms to stay. Under such conditions, excess industry capacity results, leading to price wars. The need to maintain sales pushes firms to offer discounts, rebates, and price concessions that intensify rivalry. Conversely, when exit from an industry is easy or occurs freely, competition among rivals is less intense and a favorable climate for profit exists.

Bargaining Power of Suppliers

Suppliers may have high or low power over the firm, depending on their ability to negotiate price and delivery terms. When the bargaining power of suppliers relative to the firm is high, they can successfully negotiate a higher price for their supplies or force the firm to accept reduced quality and frequent delivery delays. Supplier strength adversely affects a firm's profitability and, therefore, is a threat. Weak suppliers provide opportunities to a firm by allowing it to negotiate favorable price and delivery terms. Suppliers are powerful when:

- There are only a few suppliers or a single supplier has a dominant market share.
- The product sold by suppliers is unique and has no substitutes.
- Suppliers have a proprietary technology.
- The buyer firm must incur a high cost to switch to another supplier.
- The buyer firm is unable to make the necessary supplies in-house.

In the personal computer industry, Microsoft and Intel supply key components (operating system and microprocessor, respectively) to PC assemblers such as Dell, Gateway, and Hewlett-Packard. Both have enormous power over PC assemblers for the following reasons:

1. There are only a few suppliers of operating systems or microprocessors, and both Microsoft and Intel dominate their market segment.
2. Microsoft and Intel use patented technology, and PC assemblers cannot make these components without violating those patents.
3. PC assemblers do not have the technological or capital resources needed to make the operating systems or the microprocessors themselves.[28]

Bargaining Power of Buyers

Like suppliers, powerful buyers threaten a firm's profits because those buyers can force down price, demand higher-quality products, or exact other concessions. When buyers are weak, a firm can raise its price or negotiate more favorable contracts and earn greater profits. Buyers may be end users of the product or retail/wholesale firms that distribute the products. Buyers are most powerful when:

- There are many sellers.
- The product sold is identical (that is, not differentiated).
- Buyers purchase in large quantities.
- Switching from one seller to another is inexpensive for the buyers.
- Buyers can make the needed product themselves.

In the personal computer industry, the buyers of the finished product are the end users (individuals and institutions) or the retailers. These buyers have immense power over the PC assemblers because there are many brands to choose from, the product offered is identical, switching is virtually cost free, and both institutional buyers and retailers buy in very large quantities.

Substitute Threats

Substitute products are those that consumers perceive as alternatives to a firm's products. The greater the number of substitutes and the more that consumers perceive them as effective alternatives that satisfy their needs, the harder it is for a firm to raise its price to generate higher profits. For example, if consumers perceive tea as a substitute to coffee, the ability of coffee producers to raise price without losing sales to tea manufacturers is limited. Absence of meaningful substitutes, however, enables a firm to raise the price for its products and generate additional profits.

Availability and Price of Complementary Products

A complementary product is one that is necessary for using another product. For example, because gasoline is necessary for using a car, cars and gasoline are complementary products. Both the supply and price of a product's complement will affect that product's sale and profitability. Thus, gasoline shortages and a rise in gasoline prices will adversely affect the sales and profitability of auto manufacturers.

Table 3.2 summarizes the pressures exerted by the five forces and the conditions under which they will be successful or unsuccessful. Table 3.3 provides an information checklist and format for conducting industry analysis. Although the items listed there are not exhaustive, it is a good starting point, a model that you can use and refine to suit your needs.

Five Forces Model: Summary and Critique

Industry conditions affect competition and a firm's ability to realize superior profits. Therefore, managers need information on the nature of competition and how it is changing in order to determine the firm's strategic courses of action. Managers use the Five Forces model to analyze and understand industry competition. The model describes the pressures that potential competitors, rival firms, suppliers, buyers, and substitutes exert to gain unique advantage for themselves and the industry conditions under which these forces will succeed. Armed with this tool and the information it generates, managers can gauge the level of industry competition and the resulting profit potential before they decide what actions to pursue.

When entry threats are low, substitutes cannot win customers over, suppliers and buyers have little negotiating power, and rivalry is mild, managers may conclude that competition is not intense and the profit potential of the industry is high. Under

TABLE 3.2	Industry Forces, Types of Pressure, and Conditions Under Which They Will Be Effective

INDUSTRY FORCE	TYPE OF PRESSURE AND ITS EFFECTS	IMPACT DEPENDS ON
Potential competition	*Entry Pressure:* Brings new capacity or alters industry technology	Scale economies Capital needed Brand loyalty Switching costs Other cost advantages Government regulations Access to distribution channels Expected retaliation by incumbents
Current competition	*Competitive Advantage Pressure:* Initiates price wars, introduces new products, enhances customer service	Industry concentration Industry growth Exit barriers Switching costs Brand loyalty
Suppliers	*Pressure for Better Terms:* Increases price or reduces supply quality	Number of buyers Quantity purchased by buyers Ability of buyer to backward integrate Switching costs to buyer Availability of substitutes
Buyers	*Pressure for Better Terms/ Bargains:* Forces down price, demands higher quality, exacts other concessions	Number of sellers Quantity bought Ability of seller to forward integrate Switching costs Availability of substitutes
Substitutes	*Pressure to Win Customers Over:* Restricts ability to raise price	Number of substitutes Closeness to industry's products Switching costs

such conditions, their decisions will focus on excluding new competitors by erecting entry barriers and solidifying their current market position. Under the opposite scenario, their decisions will focus on altering the industry structure and competitive conditions in a way that establishes their firm in an advantageous market position. In essence, according to the Five Forces model, *market position* yields competitive advantages and superior profits. The goal in industry analysis, therefore, is to assess the strength of competitive forces so as to select an appropriate market position (e.g., a cost leader, a differentiator) that will generate competitive advantages and sustained profitability for the firm.

The Five Forces model has been a popular topic in business management education ever since it was proposed in 1980.[29] Although praised for its intuitive appeal, it has been criticized as relevant to static markets only, where changes are slow and sustaining a chosen market position makes sense. Because today's markets are highly dynamic, some scholars suggest that a continuous development of new advantages is necessary for company survival and the Five Forces model is an inappropriate analytical tool for today's environment.[30] In addition, stronger criticisms have been leveled

TABLE 3.3	Information Checklist and Format for Industry Analysis
Industry size	Dollar sales volume (also volume in units, if available)
Industry growth	Rate of growth in percentage terms (increase in industry sales averaged for a five-year period). Where is the industry in the life cycle (emerging, rapid growth, maturity, decline)?
Market segments	Is the end product highly differentiated (e.g., toothpaste—low price, medicinal, whitening, good tasting)? If so, entry from outside the industry is difficult.
Growth of segment	Are segments within the industry growing faster than others? If so, threats of entry from other segments are high.
Vertical integration	What is the degree of backward or forward integration? Are there a series of intermediaries processing material input or distributing/ retailing the end product? If so, the profitability of firms making the end product is likely to be low.
Technological change	Is the industry technology changing rapidly? Are there segments where it is changing more rapidly? If so, barriers to entry are low.
Ease of entry	Analyze cost, differentiation, and transaction advantages enjoyed by incumbent firms. Based on this analysis, rate entry threats as high, medium, or low.
Rivalry	Assess the degree of rivalry in each segment. How does competition occur? Are there price wars and/or frequent innovation? Analyze demand, industry structure, and exit barriers and rate rivalry as intense, medium, or weak.
Supplier segment (key inputs only)	Is the segment consolidated or fragmented? Is suppliers' technology patented? What is the availability of substitute inputs? Can suppliers forward integrate? Rate supplier power as high, medium, or low.
Buyer segment (individuals and institutions)	Is the segment consolidated or fragmented? Can buyers easily switch? What is the quantity bought? Can buyers backward integrate? Rate buyer power as high, medium, or low.
Substitutes	Are there few or many substitutes? Are they well-recognized brands? How competitive are they in price and product features compared to the industry's products? Rate substitute threats as high, medium, or low.
Industry favorableness	Summarize the industry conditions based on the above information. List the five forces under high, medium, and low categories. How would you characterize the attractiveness of the industry as a whole? Are there segments that are more favorable than others? Can firms from one segment easily move to other segments?

against the Five Forces model by researchers writing under the rubric of the "resource-based view" (RBV) of the firm.[31] For these scholars, it is not market position but the firm's *internal resources and capabilities* that are a source of competitive advantage. In other words, by setting a bold vision and by acquiring and exploiting unique internal resources and capabilities in pursuit of that vision, firms create competitive advantages.[32] We will examine this alternative approach to competitive advantage in the next chapter. For now, we leave this chapter with the understanding that both industry forces and a firm's market position in the industry affect company performance. A strong market position in an industry where other forces are relatively weak gives a firm competitive advantage.

Summary

Environmental conditions change and create a favorable or unfavorable climate for the firm's current profits and future plans. Understanding environmental change is a necessary first step toward company profits and progress. A firm cannot fully control macro environmental changes, but it can remain ready to adapt based on forecasts. Good forecasting and adaptation skills enable a firm to survive and succeed. At the industry level, on the other hand, a firm can influence or alter competitive forces to its advantage. The Five Forces model provides the firm with a tool for analyzing the industry and assessing the strength of competitive forces. The Five Forces model recommends that the firm select a market position that defends it against competitive forces or alters the industry conditions in its favor. Thus, a firm that has a strong market position in an industry where other forces are relatively weak enjoys competitive advantages. Some scholars criticize this thinking by suggesting that it is through developing and exploiting unique internal competencies, not through market position, that a firm gains enduring competitive advantages.

Chapter 3 Discussion Questions and Projects

Discussion Questions

1. Environmental analysis is more than a mere description of opportunities and threats. Discuss.
2. Discuss the importance of industry analysis in strategic management.

Projects

1. Using Table 3.1 as a tool, briefly analyze the changes occurring in the macro environment (economic, social, cultural, political, technological, global sectors). Based on your analysis, discuss a product that enjoys a favorable climate and one that confronts an unfavorable climate.
2. In the Internet service provider industry, firms use three distinct technologies to service customers: the telephone dial-up system, cable, and wireless. Using Internet sources, read about this industry. Write a brief report describing the types of competitive pressures firms face in this industry and how they deal with them (e.g., price wars, technological innovation, service quality).

Continuing Case

The Competitive Environment of the U.S. Airlines Industry

In 2004, U.S. airlines carried 685 million passengers, a record for the industry. The number of passengers has been increasing every year since 1991, except for 2001 and 2002 when traffic declined due to the September 11 tragedy. However, despite a net increase in traffic over the past decade, the financial strength of the industry at the end of 2004 was not encouraging. A depressed economy, intense price competition, and mounting fuel and labor costs had left most airlines in a financial crisis, the worst in their history.

Industry History

The U.S. airline industry began in the 1920s primarily for carrying mail, but by the 1930s passengers were its prime customers. At first, safety concerns made people reluctant to fly, but demand picked up as aviation and navigational technologies improved. A rise in demand for air travel and resulting competition led Congress in 1938 to establish the Civil Aeronautics Board (CAB) to regulate the industry. The CAB made decisions on interstate routes, what airlines would operate in those routes, and what fares they could charge. The rationale behind these decisions was that air travel is a utility and hence must be regulated by the government, not by market forces. Consequently, route selection was based more on a need to connect far-flung areas than to meet market needs. To ensure that the airlines stayed in business, the CAB limited competition within routes and, further, set fares based on a "cost plus reasonable profit" formula. The result was an inefficient system in which the airlines could act as monopolies, resisting service improvements and passing increased costs on to customers. New entries that could have been beneficial to the public on both these counts never occurred.

Deregulation

By the early 1970s, public dissatisfaction with the airline industry was running high. A non-market-oriented route system and ever-rising fares drew public clamor for reforms. At the same time, an emerging political trend favored less governmental oversight of business and greater reliance on market forces to do the job. The culmination of these events was the passing of the Airline Deregulation Act of 1978, which abolished the CAB together with the route and fare restrictions. The airline industry was now open for unrestricted competition. Along with a massive entry by new firms came price wars. A shakeout period followed in which those that could not withstand cost competition died. Survivors strengthened their position through acquisition, through alliance with a major competitor, or by seeking bankruptcy protection to gain temporary breathing room. As of 2004, acquisitions, alliances, and chapter 11 bankruptcies were still common in the airline industry.

While routes and fares are no longer regulated, safety is. In addition, airlines must obtain boarding-gate and landing permits that are limited in number. Landing permits are designed to avoid congestion in busy airports serving such cities as New York, Chicago, and Washington, D.C.

The Industry After Deregulation

After deregulation, established airlines focused on efficient routing as a way to achieve competitive advantage. Many developed "hubs" in key cities that would allow them to compete nationally from a position of regional dominance. The hub-and-spoke system, as it is known, involves flying passengers from several locations into a hub airport and redirecting them to their final destination. Several advantages accrue: it erects a barrier to entry into the region because most gates and landing slots are already leased, it allows high capacity utilization on flights leaving the hub, and it permits airlines to provide integrated service to passengers flying to far-off locations. However, there are major disadvantages too: it can be expensive as a result of cumbersome scheduling and idling of planes in hubs, and it can increase the travel time for passengers.

These disadvantages led to entry by new airlines that employ a point-to-point system in which passengers are flown directly between cities in a commuter-type fashion. While point-to-point carriers cannot provide an integrated service, they save passengers time and money by avoiding congested airports and flying into secondary airports. Thus, the airline industry after deregulation has evolved into two broad segments: the majors, offering high connectivity through a hub-and-spoke system, and the new entrants, offering speedy and economical travel between cities via a point-to-point system. One other factor differentiates these two segments: the majors offer value-added services such as meals and entertainment and charge a premium price; the niche airlines offer no frills, which enables them to offer discount fares. However, these two segments are not quite distinct. Several markets or city pairs exist where both majors and niche airlines operate, and that puts them in a direct competition with one another.

tablished firms to raise fares. First, airline seats are sunk costs, and empty seats are revenue lost forever. As a result, the pressure to cut fares frequently to fill seats is high. Second, air travel is increasingly perceived as a commodity, and fare increases cannot be easily justified. Third, the new entrants operating as no-frills discount carriers are so successful that they have been able to keep the pricing power of majors in check. Because of these conditions, price wars are a common occurrence in the airline industry, especially on routes that are served by both the majors and the discount carriers.

In the absence of pricing power, cost control is the only other alternative available to all airlines to reach their profit goals. A sizable portion of airline expenses is consumed by wages, fuel, and debt/lease payments. Except for fuel, these are all fixed costs, suggesting that a firm with a lower fixed-cost structure will have a significant edge over rivals. The industry is highly unionized, and expensive labor contracts are common. Established airlines have

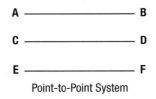

Point-to-Point System

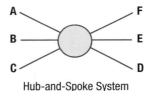

Hub-and-Spoke System

Current Competitive Environment

Presently, airlines have emerged as the dominant mode for long- and medium-distance travel in the United States, while cars, buses, and trains are the preferred choice for distances of 200 miles or less. Trends indicate a steady growth in demand for air travel, paralleling the nation's economic growth, but much of it is occurring in the discount segment. Entry is minimal due to the high capital costs and limited airport availability, and carriers that entered after deregulation have been discount carriers. Overcapacity among hub-and-spoke majors limits their ability to raise fares. Overcapacity is attributed to chapter 11 bankruptcy protection and the generous grants provided by the U.S. government following the September 11 tragedy that have allowed losing firms to avoid exiting the industry. Other factors besides overcapacity also limit the ability of es-

stricter labor contracts as a result of their long-standing union environment, and management's ability to control costs in this area is limited. In addition, the airlines' huge real estate investment in hubs is an added drag on profitability. In regard to fuel, while airlines have no direct control over its price, they have sought to lower the expense by reducing idle time at the hubs by improving on-time flight arrivals, shedding uneconomical routes, and rapidly loading passengers at the gates.

Aircraft are expensive items for the airlines, but they have a long life. As such, attractive financing is necessary to induce airlines to replenish their fleet. Although there are only two commercial aircraft manufacturers, Boeing and Airbus, intense rivalry between the two provides the airlines with an attractive climate in which to negotiate and obtain favorable purchasing terms.

The Future

Industry analysts predict that the airline industry is likely to face the following difficulties in coming years:

1. Historically, business travelers have preferred flexible flights, destinations, and in-flight entertainment, whereas leisure travelers have focused solely on economical fares. Present trends strongly indicate that both these groups expect airlines to offer a combination of these features.

2. Airports are limited in number. Despite the growth in air travel ever since deregulation, only one major airport has been built—Denver. While the demand for the service provided by point-to-point carriers is rapidly rising, their ability to expand is limited unless they can successfully negotiate code-sharing agreements with carriers who have landing slots to spare.

Discussion Questions

1. Following the Five Forces model and using the information provided in this case, analyze the U.S. airlines industry. Prepare a brief report highlighting opportunities and threats.

2. Assume that your firm is an established major using the hub-and-spoke system. Using the information provided in this case, describe the threats facing your firm.

Source: E. Ben-Yosef, *The Evolution of the U.S. Airlines Industry* (Norwell, Mass.: Springer Publishing 2005); R. M. Grant, "The U.S. Airline Industry in 2004," in R. M. Grant, *Contemporary Strategy Analysis* (Oxford: Blackwell, 2004); P. R. Costas, D. S. Harned, and J. T. Lundquist, "Rethinking the Airlines Industry," special issue, *The McKinsey Quarterly* (2002); E. D. Greenslet, "Airlines 1001—A Primer for Dummies," *Airline Monitor,* November 1998.

The Internal Environment: Assessing a Firm's Competencies and Competitive Advantages

C H A P T E R   O B J E C T I V E S

After reading this chapter, you should be able to:

■ Define competitive advantage and explain its importance for a firm's long-term success

■ Define resources, capabilities, and distinctive competencies and explain how they create competitive advantage

■ Discuss ways by which a firm can sustain its competitive advantage

■ Discuss entrepreneurial and operational competencies and describe how to assess a firm's strengths in these areas

■ Analyze a firm's internal environment and assess its competencies against industry opportunities and threats

Opening Case

In the late 1960s, a small UK manufacturer of music and electronics goods by the name of Electrical Musical Industries (EMI) invented a medical device for scanning human bodies. The product, known as the computerized axial tomographic (CAT) scanner, was acclaimed as a major medical technology breakthrough. It generated finely detailed, three-dimensional views of the human body, which were in stark contrast to the output of the conventional x-ray machine, which produced smudgy, flat images of lesser clarity. The invention was viewed as so significant that it earned the Nobel Prize for the EMI scientist who invented it.

Several reputable firms approached EMI either to license the new technology or to make and market the product collaboratively, but EMI turned their offers down. It wanted to pursue the opportunity alone because it believed that the CAT scanner carried an immense profit potential. However, commercial production and marketing of the product proved to be a challenge. The scanner was a complex synthesis of medical imaging and computer technologies in which EMI had only limited expertise. Most of the electronic components needed for assembling the scanner could not be made in-house, forcing EMI to rely on outside vendors for critical components and after-sales service. Despite these drawbacks, EMI decided to enter the scanner business (or, rather, to plunge into it) because of the positive industry demand forecasts. Analysts estimated the initial global demand for scanners at 200 units, rising to 2,400 within ten years. At an average unit price of $400,000, this translated to a market size of $1 billion. Radiologists believed that the scanner would become standard equipment in hospitals soon after introduction.

EMI began marketing the scanner in Western Europe in 1972 but soon realized the need to rapidly commercialize it in other regions of the world to prevent competitive entry. In 1973, the firm entered the U.S. and Japanese markets, where the scanner was an instant success, with demand far exceeding forecasts. In three years, EMI had sold and delivered 450 units globally for total revenue of $200 million, and it had firm orders for delivery of another 300 units. Customers paid a significant portion of the purchase price up front as down payment and were willing to wait six months to a year for product delivery. By all counts and estimates, EMI had by now secured a leadership position in medical diagnostic products and its fame as a pioneer was getting to be well established. By 1976, its market share in the CAT scanner business was around 65 percent, indicating its dominance in the medical imaging industry.

EMI's success, however, did not last long. Order backlogs put pressure on component suppliers, which eventually resulted in missed delivery deadlines and mounting customer complaints. EMI also was unable to provide satisfactory technical support and after-sales service on such a technologically complex product as the CAT scanner, further enraging customers. More importantly, EMI grossly lacked the resources to continuously improve the scanner technology and maintain its leadership position. Its inability to service current customers, effectively meet new demand, and undertake product enhancements to sustain technological superiority soon brought newcomers to the scene. Initial entrants were small medical electronics firms with limited resources. Large and diversified firms such as Technicare and General Electric soon followed. These latter firms had excellent R&D resources to develop a competitively enhanced scanner and, unlike EMI, also possessed in-house capabilities to manufacture, market, and service CAT scanners. EMI's competitive edge—built around its patent, pioneering fame, and **first-mover–advantages***—was not enough to stop these new entrants, who—with excellent design, manufacturing, and marketing capabilities—began grabbing its customers in large numbers. By 1978, EMI lost the leadership position to General Electric. As a result, it sold the scanner business, which was no longer profitable, to Thorn Electrical Industries and Thorn later sold it to General Electric. By 1979, less than eight years after it pioneered a radical technology and developed a lucrative market for it, EMI was no longer in that business. Others who arrived late were enjoying the fruits of its labor.[1]

---

*Advantages a high technology firm derives by being first to develop and market a radically new product. Among others, a crucial advantage it provides a firm is the opportunity to establish itself in the market and prevent new entry.

T he EMI experience tells us a different story about the sources of **competitive advantage** than does the Five Forces model presented in Chapter 3. Recall that the Five Forces model points to *market positioning* as the key to realizing competitive advantage. It recommends that a firm analyze the structure of its industry, choose a sustainable market position (for example, a cost leader, a broad differentiator, a focuser), and strengthen that position by erecting entry barriers. In other words, a strong market position creates competitive advantages leading to a firm's success, and, to the extent it is defensible, a firm enjoys continued success. By contrast, the EMI experience points to a firm's internal **resources** and **capabilities** as key to company success. It suggests that company resources and capabilities create competitive advantages, which lead to a firm's success. To the extent that these resources and capabilities are unique and difficult to imitate, a firm will enjoy continued success. We devote this chapter to examining this latter proposition and developing a response to the question: What causes competitive advantage and company success—strong market position, unique internal resources and capabilities, or both?

In this chapter, we will look inside a firm to identify characteristics that are a source of its strengths. Strengths include both *tangible assets* and *intangible ones*—such as leadership skills, personnel capabilities, and organizational values—that endow a firm with competitive advantage, enabling it to reduce costs, add significant value to products and services, or identify and exploit new opportunities rapidly and thus earn higher profits. We will describe how these strengths emerge from a firm's *resources,* its *capabilities* to effectively exploit those resources, and the **distinctive competency** the firm derives in the process. We will explain how distinctive competency forms the bedrock for generating and sustaining one's own *competitive advantage* or disrupting that of rivals. Our discussion is organized into four distinct, yet closely related, areas:

1. *Competitive advantage*—the edge a firm has over rivals that allows it to earn superior profits and the alternative sources from which a firm derives its advantage

2. *Resources and capabilities*—the stock of inputs held by a firm, its abilities to process them, and the ability of exceptional resources and capabilities to make a firm distinctively competent, endowing it with competitive advantage

3. *Sustaining competitive advantage*—the conditions under which a firm retains its distinctive competencies and thus its competitive advantage over the long haul

4. *Identifying a firm's competencies*—the means of evaluating a firm's competencies to determine whether they are adequate to lead the firm to competitive success

Competitive Advantage

What is the key to a firm's success in its industry? Why do some firms earn significantly higher profits than their rivals—and consistently do so? As discussed in Chapter 1, strategy research invariably identifies competitive advantage as the predominant reason for a firm's superior profits.[2] **Competitive advantage** *refers to an edge or superiority a firm enjoys over its rivals, emerging either from a powerful market position or from a unique internal competency.* It is a strength the firm possesses that is relevant for successful competition in its industry (or market segment) and that no or very few rivals have.[3] In other words, it is a required strength that is rarely found among firms in an industry, hence conferring an edge to those who have it over others who do not. *The benefit competitive advantage bestows on the firm is the potential or ability for higher performance.* When a firm effectively exploits that potential, it earns above-average profits in its industry or market segment. Note that this does not necessarily mean superior profits, only significantly higher profits than the industry average or the average for the firm's market segment.[4] In other words, all firms earning above-average profits in an industry or market segment, as the case may be, enjoy some sort of competitive advantage. An important caveat, however, is that profitability must be higher consistently, year after year, if a firm is deemed to possess a competitive advantage.

How do we know whether a firm enjoys a competitive advantage? One way is by comparing its profitability with that of its peers. Higher profits result when a firm makes its output at a lower cost or sells it at a higher price due to its strong market position or because customers perceive more value in the firm's output. In Table 4.1 the gross profit margin (operating income as a percentage of sales) of McDonald's is compared with that of its rivals*—Wendy's, Darden Restaurants (Red Lobster, Olive Garden), and Jack in the Box. McDonald's profitability is far higher, indicating that it possesses significant competitive advantages. Its advantage is in operational efficiency—ability to control operational costs—as evidenced by its higher gross margin ratio.** Similar comparisons using return on invested capital (ROIC)[†] would indicate McDonald's overall efficiency and effectiveness in its industry.

TABLE 4.1 Profitability of Firms in the Fast Food Industry

	McDonald's			Wendy's			Darden			Jack in the Box		
	2002	2003	2004	2002	2003	2004	2002	2003	2004	2002	2003	2004
Net sales	15,405	17,140	19,064	2,730	3,149	3,635	4,369	4,655	5,003	1,966	2,058	2,322
Cost of goods sold	2,866	3,167	7,378	1,379	1,630	1,916	3,385	3,634	3,903	1,514	1,620	1,129
Other expenses	9,711	10,825	7,961	962	1,104	1,282	587	631	682	288	296	348
Operating income	2,828	3,148	3,695	389	415	437	397	390	418	164	142	145
Profitability (%)	18.4	18.4	19.3	14.2	13.2	12.0	9.0	8.4	8.3	8.3	6.9	6.2

Figures in $ millions. Data are from the websites of the respective firms.

---

*Burger King, the second-ranking firm in the industry, is presently privately held by a group of investors. Financial data for this firm are unavailable.

**gross margin $= \dfrac{(\text{sales} - \text{cost of goods sold})}{\text{sales}}$

[†]invested capital = stockholders' equity + borrowed funds

$\quad$ ROIC $= \dfrac{\text{profit before taxes}}{\text{invested capital}}$

Routes to Competitive Advantage

How can a firm gain competitive advantage? In broad terms, there are two possible routes: *by building a strong* **market position** or *by acquiring and deploying unique internal* **resources** and **capabilities.**[5] While these two strengths may appear distinct, as we will explain later, most firms generally employ a combination of positional and resource-based strengths, each reinforcing the other.[6]

Market Position

Porter explains a firm's competitive success by pointing to favorable industry conditions.[7] A firm is successful because the industry in which it competes has a structure that is inherently conducive to profits (for example, pharmaceuticals, soft drinks).[8] Steady product demand and high entry barriers allow all firms in these industries to realize higher profits. However, a more convincing explanation, according to Porter, is that the successful firm enjoys a strong market position in the industry that allows it to control industry forces and grab a larger share of industry profits. Or, the firm has positioned itself in a secure segment of the industry (a niche) that insulates it from the rest of the industry and allows it to reap monopoly profits. *Thus, in Porter's view, market position endows a firm with a competitive advantage that leads to significant profits.* Specific ways by which a firm can gain a strong market position and derive position-related advantages include the following:[9]

1. *First Mover to the Market:* EMI was the first to move into the CAT scan business. Being the first with a breakthrough product gave the company a monopoly position (at least in the short-term), helping it to garner industry sales.

2. *Geographic Location:* A niche provides a secure market position. Wal-Mart began business in the early 1960s by strongly positioning itself in the small towns of the midwestern United States, preventing entry by others and thereby enjoying monopoly profits.

3. *Market Share:* A large market share gives a firm a strong market position due to volume strengths, allowing it to successfully bargain with suppliers and obtain raw material/components at a lower cost.

4. *Channel Partnerships:* Close ties or partnerships with distributors give a firm ready and unlimited access to distribution channels not easily available to rivals.

5. *Brand Name:* A widely recognized brand name positions the firm's product as the leading and reputable brand in the market, allowing the firm to command premium shelf space and premium price. Additionally, it gives the firm an ability to successfully exploit the popularity of its brand in new products.

6. *Government Protection:* Government protection, for example exclusive defense contracts, gives a firm monopoly status and results in higher profits.

According to some scholars, most market environments evolve and, as a result, positional advantages cannot be permanent.[10] When markets dramatically change as a result of a radical shift in industry technology or government regulations, positional advantages erode or become irrelevant, and cannot contribute to performance.[11]

EMI lost in the CAT scan business because new entrants continuously changed the scanner technology in a way that disrupted and dislodged EMI's market dominance, which was built solely on its positional advantage as a pioneer. Kodak is presently suffering a steady decline in sales because the emergence of digital photography has eroded its positional advantage (brand strength) built around film photography. In a nutshell, some deem positional advantages to be effective only when industry conditions are static, not when they are rapidly changing.[12] The question then arises: What should a firm do to build more enduring advantages?

Resource-Based View

An alternative approach explains competitive advantage as the result of a firm's internal strengths, claiming that that advantage is more enduring. Proponents of this approach, called the **resource-based view,** suggest that performance differences in firms—and why some firms achieve superior performance even under unfavorable or rapidly changing industry conditions—can be better explained on the basis of their internal strengths.[13] For example, ownership of scarce resources or an ability to respond to market changes rapidly may enable a firm to create unique and, therefore, sustainable superiority in competition. Thus, according to the resource-based view, it is the firm's internal strength that is the true source of competitive advantage. Figure 4.1 illustrates this model and its components, which we'll examine later.

Where do internal strengths come from? Internal strengths emerge from the firm's stock of *resources* and its *capabilities* to effectively employ them. The resource-based view assumes that the strengths of firms in an industry will differ because of differences in the resources they own and the capabilities they possess. The distinct choices that strategic managers make in their respective organizations create, over time, disparities in the resources and capabilities of firms, giving some an ability to perform at higher levels. When a firm's resources are valuable and its ability to employ them in competition is superior, its potential for above-average performance is greater. When resources are rare and capabilities are exceptional and competitively relevant, a firm is able to sustain its edge over rivals for a long time.[14]

Differences in strengths inhibit low performers from quickly imitating high performers' strengths, allowing the latter to retain their competitive advantage. Prudent managers of successful firms continuously invest in resources responsible for superior performance, thus constantly enhancing their uniqueness and preventing imitation. More importantly, by investing in **core competencies** that are not tied to a single product but that instead have broad application, successful firms perform effectively under varying market conditions and ensure the longevity of their competitive advantage.[15]

Resources and Capabilities

Businesses have productive assets, commonly referred to as **resources.** *Resources are the stockpile of assets held by a firm to be used as inputs in its business activities.*[16] Some of these resources are *tangible* (that is, visible or quantifiable); they include plants,

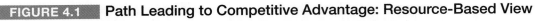

FIGURE 4.1 Path Leading to Competitive Advantage: Resource-Based View

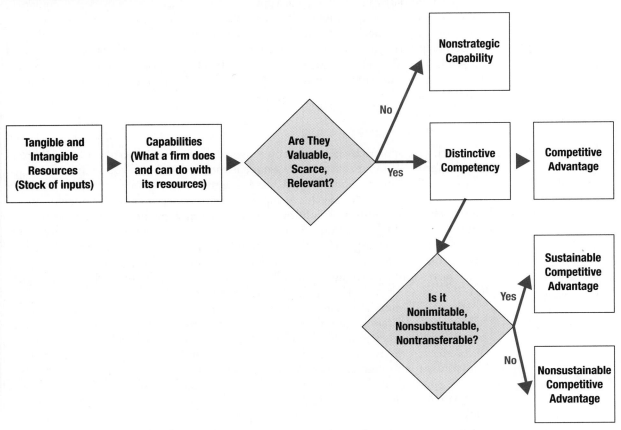

facilities, equipment, and liquid funds. Others are *intangible* (that is, not visible or easily quantifiable); they include employee skills, leadership and managerial capabilities, patents, brand names, and strategic partnerships. Table 4.2 provides a detailed list of tangible and intangible resources.

Resources on their own cannot be productive; they must be combined and collectively processed to achieve organizational tasks. The ability of a firm to combine resources, collectively process them, and complete organizational tasks is its capability. **Capability** is not an input like resources; *it is the firm's skills or knowledge in transforming inputs into outputs.*[17] Capability is the firm's proficiency in certain activity areas, indicating the level of learning the firm has attained in those areas. It is this proficiency that makes a firm claim, "*we have the know-how*" or "*we know how*" to perform a certain task. For example, 3M's capability is developing radically new products frequently, Sony's is making high-quality consumer electronic products in compact sizes, and Toyota's is manufacturing cars efficiently.

Capability emerges from the firm's stock of knowledge, employee skills, and organizational routines, which are developed over time through complex interactions among the firm's resources.[18] Years of experience in combining inputs and collectively processing them give birth to a firm's capability. *Capability is thus specific to a firm and is intangible.*[19] How capable a firm is in performing an activity depends on how effectively it integrates diverse resources toward completion of that activity. Some activities require integrating specialized resources within a function, while others require integration of resources across functions. Yet others require integrating several fields of technological expertise. For example, Toyota's manufacturing efficiency requires integration of specialized resources within the production function: procurement of material, component manufacturing, assembly, and quality control. Likewise, 3M's ability to frequently innovate requires integration of resources across several functions: R&D, manufacturing, and marketing. Sony's ability to miniaturize designs requires integration of several fields of technological expertise: knowledge in materials, mechanical, and transistor circuitry technologies. A firm's capability is thus measured by its ability to integrate several tangible and intangible resources (materials, tools, information) in completing organizational tasks.

Strategic Leadership: A Vital Resource

Resources and capabilities of a firm do not simply emerge; they are consciously acquired and developed. This process takes a long time. Needless to say, the quality and competitive relevance of a firm's resources and capabilities at any given time is

---

TABLE 4.2   **Tangible and Intangible Resources**

TANGIBLE RESOURCES	
Financial resources	Cash
	Short and long-term investments
Physical resources	Plant, equipment
	Land, buildings
	Distribution facilities
	Mines (deposits), materials in stock
Human resources	Years of education and experience
	Employee strength
	Technical personnel as a percentage of total personnel
Organizational resources	Formal structure, procedures, planning and control mechanisms, coordination mechanisms
INTANGIBLE RESOURCES	
Technological resources	Patents
Intellectual resources	Technical knowledge, skills, and stored information
Organizational culture	Positive work climate, employee loyalty
Reputation	Brand name, goodwill, company image
Network resources	Strategic alliances, linkages, and partnerships

the result of the choices that the strategic managers made in the past. The ability of strategic managers to make the right choices in the acquisition and deployment of resources and capabilities that will meet the current and future needs of the firm is thus a crucial requirement for competitive success. Researchers refer to this ability as **strategic leadership,** or the leadership skill of strategic managers.[20]

In their decision making, successful strategic leaders are simultaneously concerned with the firm's present and its future. They are concerned not only about the firm's current performance but also about what needs to be done today to build the firm's long-term health and potential for future performance. Toward this end, they not only formulate strategies for the efficient utilization of current resources and capabilities but also for developing new resources and capabilities in anticipation of the firm's future.[21] To put it precisely, successful strategic leaders do three things:

1. They articulate a vision for the firm after examining the firm's current strengths and potential opportunities.

2. They formulate strategies that would effectively utilize current strengths and build new strengths to realize the expected future.

3. They guide the firm to its future through facilitative techniques.

Visionary thinking, anticipatory skills, persuasiveness, and an ability to adapt or to proactively create the environment necessary to achieve the desired future characterize successful leaders. Bill Gates (the chairman of Microsoft), Jack Welch (former CEO of General Electric), and Herb Kelleher (former chairman of Southwest Airlines), to name a few, are reported to possess these traits and are often cited as effective strategic leaders. The remarkable success their organizations achieved is attributed largely to the visionary thinking of these men and their uncanny ability to realize that vision.[22] Strategic leadership is thus an important intangible asset and a source of competitive advantage for a firm.

How Do Resources and Capabilities Create Competitive Advantage?

Resources as *productive inputs* and capabilities as *skills* are essential for completion of business tasks. When resources and capabilities of firms in an industry are similar to each other, no firm has a differential advantage in its ability to perform. Profitability of each firm under such conditions is just equal to the industry average. Comparable resources and capabilities among industry players do not confer a relatively superior potential for performance on any of these players.[23] But the very nature of competition means that firms strive to distinguish themselves from one another; thus their resources and capabilities do not remain similar. Differences in individuals' cognitive capabilities, organizational culture and experience, and quality of leadership endow some firms with exceptional resources and capabilities, allowing them to create a competitive difference in the industry. One caveat, however: such exceptional resources and capabilities must be in areas that are pertinent for competition and competitive success. When they are, the firm has a **distinctive competency** (or *distinctive capability*).[24] Distinctive competency provides a firm with a potential to perform competitively critical tasks at higher levels—that is, it bestows competitive advantage. Figure 4.2 summarizes how resources and capabilities lead to competitive advantage and performance that is above the industry average.

Distinctive Competency

A distinctive competency is the ability of a firm to perform competitively critical tasks relatively well. A firm with a distinctive competency can complete competitively critical tasks that rivals cannot perform or cannot perform as well. For example, in the automobile manufacturing business, production costs represent a major share of the total costs. Profitability, therefore, hinges on the ability of a firm to keep production costs under control. Through its *lean production methods* (just-in-time procurement, rapid design-manufacturing changeover), Toyota has learned to build cars far less expensively than others in the industry.[25] Toyota thus has a distinctive competency in the economical production of cars. Firms may have distinctive competency in product design production, speedy product innovation, efficient distribution, customer service, or a combination of these.

Earlier, we said that exceptional resources and capabilities make a firm distinctively competent. Resources and capabilities are exceptional when they are *valuable, scarce*, and *relevant* to competition.[26]

> *Valuable:* Sophisticated tools, patents, a well-trained workforce, and organizational learning are examples of valuable strategic resources and capabilities that enable a firm to be distinctively competent and achieve better performance in its industry. Proctor & Gamble has well-known brands in its personal-care and laundry business and has proven experience in brand marketing. This experience has provided Proctor & Gamble with a distinctive competency in *brand management* that is critical for success in the consumer products industry. Sony has gained expert knowledge in designing consumer electronic products in miniature sizes due to a prolonged R&D investment in transistor circuitry. This technical knowledge has given Sony a distinctive competency in *miniaturization* (designing high-quality, portable consumer electronics products in compact sizes) that is viewed as critical for success in the consumer electronics business. Southwest Airlines has a well-trained workforce and a team of talented managers who motivate this workforce through a "fun work culture," making it the envy of others in the industry. This valuable people resource, combined with an exceptional talent for exploiting it, has given Southwest Airlines a distinctive competency in *operational efficiency* (minimal waste and maximal employee productivity), fundamental for success in the airline industry.

> *Scarce:* Obviously, resources and capabilities possessed and widely used by every firm in the industry are a prerequisite for competing in that industry. Standard resources and capabilities do not endow a firm with distinctive competencies. But when they are rare in the industry and a firm has them and others do not, the firm can undertake tasks or do things in ways that others in the industry cannot. Wal-Mart's capabilities in the development and use of point-of-purchase data-collection systems are rare in the retailing industry, and they give Wal-Mart a significant advantage over others in inventory control.[27] As a result, Wal-Mart's gross margin is much higher than the industry average.

> *Relevant:* A firm must have strengths in activities that are relevant for competition in order to derive competitive advantage. Resources and capabilities, however exceptional they may be, will not generate a competitive advantage if they are in activities that are unrelated to competition. Mercedes-Benz's leadership position in the premium automobiles segment is due to significant strengths in design engineering that are relevant for successfully competing in that segment.

Before we leave this section, we wish to emphasize a point that might already have become clear to you, and that is: *it is the firm's capabilities that eventually give birth to distinctive competencies.* Just think back to EMI's failure to maintain its lead in CAT scanners. Resources alone, no matter how unique they are, are of no avail unless the firm has requisite capabilities to exploit them effectively. Thus, unique resources and ordinary capabilities are a weak combination; they are less desired than ordinary resources and exceptional capabilities. Ideally, unique resources and exceptional capabilities generate distinctive competencies that endure for the long term.

Figure 4.2 illustrates how resources and capabilities generate competitive advantage and above-average industry performance.

Sustaining Competitive Advantage

Because competitive advantage allows a firm to earn significantly above-average profits in its industry, it attracts the attention of average performers who want to duplicate it or find alternative ways of gaining a similar advantage for themselves. The market leader may feel pressured when other firms attempt to identify the resources and capabilities underlying its competitive advantage and imitate them, either by developing a substitute or purchasing them through acquisition. When the sources underlying a firm's competitive advantage *resist imitation, substitutability,* or *mobility,* the firm can sustain its advantage for a long time.[28]

FIGURE 4.2   **Resources, Capabilities, and Competitive Advantage**

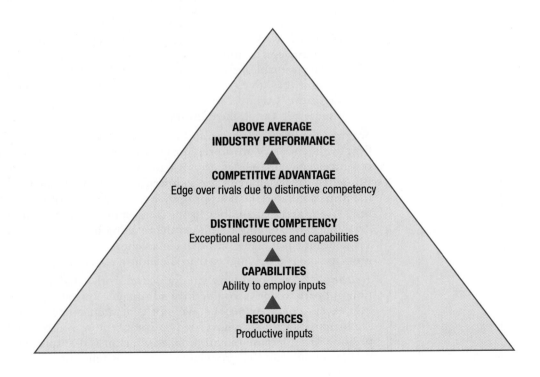

**ABOVE AVERAGE
INDUSTRY PERFORMANCE**

▲

COMPETITIVE ADVANTAGE
Edge over rivals due to distinctive competency

▲

DISTINCTIVE COMPETENCY
Exceptional resources and capabilities

▲

CAPABILITIES
Ability to employ inputs

▲

RESOURCES
Productive inputs

Imitation: In general, competitive advantages based on tangible resources are quickly copied because they are easily visible. Advantages stemming from technologies or capabilities are more durable because they are not easily discernible. However, even they are vulnerable to imitation if they are not intricate. EMI lost its advantage in CAT scanners because its technology was weak, allowing GE to leapfrog EMI by inventing and marketing a more advanced scanner.[29] One way firms can prevent imitation is by continuously investing in the resources and capabilities that generated the competency in the first place. Such investments enhance the complexities of the technology and skill base, making it difficult and often expensive for competitors to duplicate them. In short, competitive advantages resist imitation when they stem from complex technologies and intricate capabilities.

Substitution: A firm's advantage can be neutralized by competition through substitution. For example, Caterpillar's competitive advantage is in its worldwide service-and-parts supply network that allows it to service and deliver parts for any of its heavy construction equipment anywhere in the world, within two days. Komatsu, its Japanese rival, has virtually neutralized Caterpillar's service advantage by building better equipment through its design and manufacturing strengths. Thus, Komatsu's design and manufacturing resources have enabled the firm to achieve competitive parity, not by imitation, but by developing a strategic alternative—reliable equipment that requires minimal maintenance and repairs.[30]

Transferability: An easy way by which a rival can come to have a firm's competitive advantage is through acquisition: acquiring a firm that has the requisite resources and capabilities. When resources and capabilities can be easily acquired and absorbed by a rival, the competitive advantage of a firm cannot be sustained. Tangible resources can be easily absorbed. However, capabilities are not easily transferable from one firm to another because they become specific to a firm, emerging from its culture, learning, and cumulative experience. Thus, to the extent that a firm's competitive advantage is due to its unique capabilities, the sustainability of that advantage is more promising.

Identifying and Assessing a Firm's Competencies

Our concern in this chapter is not just to understand a firm's resources and capabilities, per se, but in relation to competition. How do we understand, identify, and assess a firm's relative competencies, those that can be identified as **core competencies** and those that are identified as **distinctive competencies?*** In a nutshell, it is difficult. Competencies cannot be understood by looking at a firm as a whole. However, by examining a firm's competencies (task input) and performance (task output) in discrete activities, we can inferentially assess its overall competency.

---

*Several authors use core and distinctive competencies interchangeably. In this text, we treat them as separate terms following A. A. Thompson and A. J. Strickland, *Strategic Management* (New York: McGraw Hill, 2003), 122–123. A *core competency* is defined as something a firm does well compared to other internal activities. It is an activity in which the firm has deep knowledge. For example, 3M's core competence is in bonding and adhesive technology. Using this competence, 3M successfully makes and markets several sticky products: "Post-it" notes, coated abrasives, pressure-sensitive tapes, and Scotch tapes. Distinctive competence, on the other hand, refers to something the firm does well relative to competition. Read C. K. Prahalad and G. Hamel, "The Core Competence of the Corporation," *Harvard Business Review* (May–June 1990): 79–91, to learn more about core competencies.

In broad terms, a firm's competencies may be broken down into (a) an ability to identify product and market opportunities and (b) an ability to exploit them. Opportunity identification requires *entrepreneurial* (visionary) *skills,* whereas opportunity exploitation requires *operational skills* (ability to develop and market products of superior quality, at a relatively low cost, or in a timely manner). To be successful, a firm must possess a combination of entrepreneurial and operational competencies.

Entrepreneurial Competence

Some industries offer attractive opportunities because of the absence of entry threats, intense rivalry, or substitute products. Others provide new opportunities due to frequent changes in consumer tastes. In still others, continuous R&D efforts by firms generate new scientific information, resulting in lucrative new-product opportunities, as was the case with EMI's CAT scanner. In these instances, a firm that recognizes and seizes these opportunities first (referred to as the **first mover,** or **pioneer,** if the firm introduces a new technology) stands to gain substantially. In other words, a firm whose managers have the *vision* to see an emerging market or a technological opportunity before the competition does and have the *will* to exploit that opportunity will enjoy significant strategic advantages. Scholars call this the entrepreneurial competence of a firm.[31] Established firms pursuing entrepreneurship are called corporate entrepreneurs or intrapreneurs because entrepreneurship occurs within the firm.[32]

History is filled with examples of dominant firms that failed to recognize, or totally ignored, potential opportunities in their industries, leaving the field open for entry by aspiring entrepreneurs.[33] Apple Computer, Dell Computer, and Federal Express entered established industries and emerged successful, not only because of their founders' entrepreneurial vision, but also because incumbent firms lacked such a vision. EMI had the entrepreneurial vision to pioneer a new technology, but its managers did not have the foresight to invest in internal competencies that would have sustained the leadership position, thus losing the business to followers. Among established firms, Sony and 3M are examples of firms with excellent entrepreneurial skills. Aided by the visionary, creative, and enterprising skills of their managers, they have pioneered several new products and successfully defended them in the marketplace.[34]

Advantages of Entrepreneurship

For an established firm, entrepreneurial competence offers several strategic and financial benefits:[35]

1. *Prevents Entry:* By recognizing and seizing new opportunities in its industry early on, a firm can prevent entry by potential competitors. Sony's avowed aim of being proactive in the consumer electronics business (audio, video, communication, and information-processing products)[36] and its repeated success in attaining this aim has acted as a deterrent to new competition entering its business segments.

2. *Lead Advantage:* Pioneering enables a firm to gain a lead advantage. Customers associate the product with the entrepreneur's brand, endowing it with high brand recognition and market leadership. FedEx, for example, has a lead advantage over its rivals because it was the first to market overnight mail service.

3. *Cost Advantage:* The early mover's higher volume of output and cumulative experience confers on it a lower unit-cost position compared to followers.

4. *Significant Profits:* Absence of competition during the initial stages enables the entrepreneurial firm to garner substantial profits.

Sources of Entrepreneurial Competence

A firm's entrepreneurial competence becomes evident when it frequently pioneers new products, introduces new administrative or manufacturing processes, or proactively creates new markets for its products. R&D spending generates the technological information, while environmental scanning generates the market information the firm needs for developing new products or new markets. But new information is of no avail unless a firm recognizes and learns from it. As we discussed in Chapter 3, cognitive psychology tells us that people observe and recognize environmental events only when they can interpret them based on past learning and experience.[37] Biases, beliefs, and work routines in organizations shape member thinking, determining what opportunities they will perceive and analyze and what they will discard. As a result, organizations that cling to outmoded assumptions and favor the continuation of the past seriously constrain the ability of their members to perceive new opportunities. Such opportunities are either not noted or are ignored because of their unfamiliarity. For example, Sears failed to perceive significant changes occurring in its industry, created by specialty retailers, because of its commitment to the traditional ways of doing business and consequent rigidities in its thinking.[38] On the other hand, firms that adopt a learning and adaptive culture and that promote a knowledge-sharing environment frequently identify new opportunities because of their wider knowledge and information base. Some researchers call this the **absorptive capacity** of the firm[39]—that is, *the ability of the firm to absorb new information as a result of previously stored information*. A learning and adaptive culture is thus an intangible asset for a firm, helping it to recognize new opportunities in a timely manner.

But, timely recognition of an opportunity is only one part of successful entrepreneurship. Willingness to take the necessary risk in exploiting the perceived opportunity is an additional requirement. Some firms are averse to risk taking because of their conservative managerial culture; they would not be willing to make the first move on a new opportunity. These firms would rather wait for someone else to take the lead, acting as followers and content with the average returns that result. Extremely conservative companies would even let a lucrative opportunity pass by, thus denying themselves the chance to earn significant profits. Risk taking is an important additional component of entrepreneurial competence. It reflects a firm's courage and determination to pursue opportunities by committing large resources to uncertain projects. Flat organizational structures, employee empowerment, rewarding achievement, and absence of penalties for failures are characteristics of firms that promote entrepreneurial risk-taking.

By recognizing opportunities early and pursuing them vigorously, a firm may enjoy significant profits for a period of time. Over time, attractive industries draw the attention of other opportunity seekers, thus inducing new entry. Soon, entrepreneurial firms find the once-hospitable environment becoming less friendly. To sustain an early-mover advantage, a firm must also be uniquely competent in several operational activities of its business. We now turn our attention to understanding these competencies, their source, and how they bestow sustainable competitive advantages.

Operational Competence: Value Chain Model

Michael Porter proposed a model, called the **value chain,** to identify and assess a firm's operational competencies.[40] Any product must go through stages of activities during which value is added to the product at every stage before it is sold to the consumer. This sequence, involving the transformation of an input into an output, is called the value chain. Research, product design, procurement, component manufacturing, assembly, marketing, sales, distribution, and after-sales service are activities in this sequence that add value to the product incrementally (see Figure 4.3). By analyzing these strategically relevant activities, managers can identify activities in which the firm is relatively more capable. *A firm is more capable in any or a combination of activities when it performs them better (that is, it adds comparatively more value to the product or service in those activities), performs them at a relatively lower cost, or performs them in a relatively shorter time.*

For easy comprehension and analysis, Porter divides value chain activities into two broad groups: *primary* and *support.* Primary activities (also called *line* activities) are directly related to the creation, making, and marketing of the product—for example, engineering, production, marketing, sales, and after-sales service. Support activities (also called *staff* activities) provide the expert help necessary for the primary activities to take place. Figure 4.4 shows these classifications and how they are linked. The following sections describe them and show how each of them provides opportunities to create value and increase the profit margin for a firm.

Primary Activities

Procurement and inbound logistics entail purchasing of raw materials and components from vendors, storing them, and transmitting them to production. Skilled management of these activities ensures a steady and timely flow of inputs to the firm's operations, eliminating the need for large inventories. These activities provide opportunities to lower inventory ordering and storage costs, thereby minimizing overall operational costs. Efficient management of these activities is especially critical for firms in the discount retail and mass-merchandising business where inventory turnover is high.

Product design (or product engineering) deals with the product's features, functionality, and physical appearance. Superior skill in product engineering enables a firm to design products that are durable, high in performance capabilities, easy to use, and attractive to consumers. Mercedes-Benz automobiles and Rolex watches

FIGURE 4.3 **Value Chain**

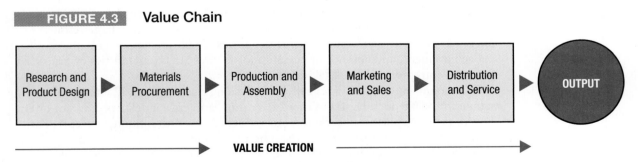

Source: From *Strategic Management: Concepts and Cases,* 13th Edition by J. Thompson and J. Strickland, p. 130. Copyright © 2003. Reprinted by permission of The McGraw-Hill Companies.

FIGURE 4.4 **Primary and Support Activities**

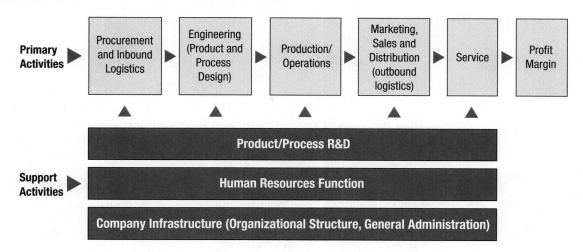

are examples of design quality. Efficient and effective management of this function is critical to firms pursuing a product-differentiation strategy.

Process design (or manufacturing engineering) is concerned with planning the layout and construction of the manufacturing process. Several firms presently use the computer to integrate stages of manufacturing (component production, product assembly, storage) in order to design a manufacturing process that is efficient (minimizes production cost), accurate (minimizes defects), and responsive to design changes (that is, it can shift the manufacturing process to undertake new designs rapidly and without increasing costs).

The term *production/operations* pertains to the processing of materials and components into finished goods. For a manufacturing firm, processing involves the transformation of materials into a physical unit before it is delivered to the consumer. For a service firm, processing occurs at the time the product or service is delivered to the customer (e.g., when a hospital treats a patient). On average, approximately 60 percent of the total costs of a firm are production-related costs. The production function thus offers a significant opportunity for a firm to reduce total costs, thereby adding value to the customer in the form of lower prices. Besides cost containment, the production function can also create value by shortening the processing time to facilitate fast delivery of products.

The *marketing* function is concerned with market segmentation, product positioning, and delivering the message to the consumer. Marketing adds value by creating a favorable image of the company and its products in the minds of the consumer. Inappropriate positioning and inappropriate message content can result in poor sales. Marketing also adds value by bringing to the firm information about changing consumer needs and preferences that can be used to design user-friendly and salable products.

Service provides after-sales service such as product installation, parts delivery, maintenance and repairs, and technical assistance. By attending to these activities in a timely and courteous manner, the service function creates a positive impression about the company and its products in the minds of buyers, thereby adding value.

This function is especially critical for firms that sell products that are technologically complex or bulky and difficult to transport (e.g., copiers, earth-moving equipment).

Support Activities

The most common support activities are research and development, human resources, and company infrastructure.

Research and development (R&D) combines two distinct, yet related, functions. Research focuses on identifying scientific information needed to develop new products and processes or enhance current products and processes. Development focuses on the actual design of products and production processes. Research is, therefore, viewed as a support activity, helping the firm's innovation efforts, whereas development is viewed as a primary activity. The value that research creates is through the superior product design or efficient production system that emerges from its results, making the firm more competitive.

The *human resources* function is responsible for attracting and retaining the right mix of skilled people on the job. It also conducts work analysis and develops training and compensation mechanisms for enhancing employee morale, job satisfaction, and productivity. The human resource function adds value by helping the firm achieve its workforce and productivity goals in a timely, efficient, and effective manner.

Company infrastructure comprises the organizational structure, the administrative mechanisms, and the firm's culture or value system. A firm's infrastructure creates value by facilitating the timely identification of opportunities and threats and by fostering the necessary internal environment to develop distinctive competencies.

Value Chain Analysis

The value chain divides a firm's operations into a chain of activities and indicates how they are linked. Primary activities are sequentially linked, whereas support activities are linked to several primary activities simultaneously. By analyzing these linkages, managers understand the kinds of coordination needed to enhance workflow efficiency, quality, and speed. By analyzing each activity, they understand their firm's overall internal cost structure vis-à-vis that of the competition. They identify activities in which the firm has a cost or differentiation advantage and those in which there is scope for improvement. They learn the unique competencies their firm possesses that others do not, and hence get the job done through outsourcing. Such cross-company comparisons are necessary to ensure that a firm's operations are adding as much value to the product as possible—and as cheaply as possible. In the event they are not, managers have the opportunity to decide whether the value chain sequence must be rearranged or some of the activities outsourced. Alternatively, they may decide to acquire the competency through a vertical merger. Thus, value chain analysis is a vital tool that managers can use to understand their firm's strengths and whether they are in areas relevant for competition—that is, whether they can generate distinctive competencies and competitive advantages.

Function-Based Approach

A functional approach identifies a firm's capabilities within each functional category. Table 4.3 lists common organizational functions and capabilities associated with those functions. The advantage of a functional approach is that it lends itself to easier analysis and comprehension because most firms organize their activities along func-

| TABLE 4.3 | Function-Based Capabilities | | |

FUNCTION	CAPABILITY	FIRMS
R&D	Capability in basic research	Pfizer
	Capability to develop unique new technologies	Sony
Product design	Ability to design products high in functionality	Canon
Manufacturing	Defect-free manufacturing	Honda
	Manufacturing efficiency	Toyota
	Rapid design changeover	Benetton
Marketing	Effective exploitation of a brand name	Ralph Lauren
	Effective promotion of a brand	PepsiCo
	Effective brand management	Proctor & Gamble
	Quality customer service	Nordstrom
	Development of customer trust	Johnson & Johnson
Human resources	Selection, motivation, and retention	Southwest Airlines
Distribution	Speedy delivery	Federal Express

tional lines. One problem with this approach is that it identifies a firm's capabilities within functional units only and ignores cross-functional capabilities. To obtain realistic results, functional analysis needs to be combined with the value chain analysis.

Table 4.4 provides a broad information checklist and format for conducting an internal analysis. Although it is not a comprehensive model, it is a good starting point and it can be refined to suit different requirements. To be meaningful, the analysis suggested in this table should be undertaken from a historical perspective.

Competitive Advantage: Market Position or Resources and Capabilities?

We are now ready to answer the question posed earlier in this chapter: What causes competitive advantage and company success: strong market position, unique internal resources and capabilities, or both?

Some firms are successful because they are well positioned in attractive industries. These firms deliberately choose to compete in such industries only, by searching for and selecting industries that show a high profit potential. Generally, they are the first to enter the industry, and they quickly achieve market dominance by building customer volume. A dominant market position allows them to prevent new competitor entry, generate advantages over rivals, and derive superior profits. Colgate-Palmolive, for example, has a positional advantage due to the high visibility and market share of many of its branded products.

Other firms are successful because they possess certain unique and deep-rooted internal capabilities. These firms consistently outperform the rest of the market even under hostile and unfavorable industry conditions because they systematically invest in skills that are competitively relevant. For these firms, it is not a dominant market position but an ability to perform certain activities relatively well that gives them the competitive edge. In short, they have a capability-based advantage that generates

TABLE 4.4	**Information Checklist and Format for Internal Analysis**
1. Profitability comparisons	Using Table 4.1 as a model, compute and compare the profitability of your firm to its rivals. For industry average profitability, refer to Dun & Bradstreet's *Industry Norms and Key Business Ratios*, and Value Line's *Investment Survey: Ratings & Reports*.
2. Operational efficiency	Compute gross margin of your firm and compare it to that of rivals. Significantly higher gross margin than the industry average indicates relatively higher efficiency in operations.
	Divide sales by fixed assets and compare to rivals. A higher ratio indicates efficient use of fixed assets. In industries where capital investments are huge (e.g., automotive), efficient use of fixed assets is critical for successful performance.
	Divide cost of goods sold by inventory. A relatively low ratio indicates management's ability to control investment in inventory.
3. Productivity	Divide total sales by the number of employees and compare to rivals. A higher ratio indicates employee skills emerging from, among other things, strengths in human resource management practices.
4. R&D strengths	Divide R&D expenditure by total sales or divide number of technical personnel by total personnel and compare to competition. A higher ratio indicates R&D strengths.
	Number of patents issued in a given period, industry awards received for technological excellence, and R&D personnel qualifications and experiential background are also indicators of R&D strengths.
5. Innovativeness	Number of new products introduced in a given period, relative to competition, indicates innovativeness/speed in innovation.
6. Strength of intangible assets	Multiply the value of the firm's physical assets by the average return on assets (ROA) for the industry. Deduct this amount from the operating earnings of the firm. The difference is the value added by intangible assets.
7. Marketing strengths	Divide marketing expenditure by sales and compare to rivals. A higher ratio is a rough indicator of pricing power, distribution reach, and ability to launch new products as line extensions.
8. Human resource strengths	Qualitatively assess HR practices of the firm (employee selection, training and development, rewards, job satisfaction levels) vis-à-vis competition. Articles appearing in the business press are a good source of information. Additionally, examine how strongly the firm has stated its policies for developing human capital.
9. Financial strengths	Cash holdings, absence of debt, and credit ratings by agencies such as Moody's and Fitch would indicate the financial strengths of the firm.
10. Organizational culture	Qualitatively assess the culture of the firm from the company's value statements and press reports of employee attitude surveys, management style, and union activities. Categorize the firm's culture and examine whether it fits with the firm's strategy.

superior profits. For example, Nucor Steel consistently invests in processing capabilities and employee training to sustain its advantage in low-cost steel production.

Still other firms are successful because they possess certain unique internal strengths (for example, ability to be creative) that help them to attack and disrupt the competition's advantage.[41] These firms outperform others not by sustaining an existing advantage but by frequently creating new advantages for themselves that disrupt the status quo. For example, Sony has consistently pursued miniaturization in audio listening devices (from reel-to-reel tape recorders to portable tape recorders and compact discs) that have altered industry standards in its favor. Intel has pursued a similar strategy in computer chips.

The Need for Both

Current views take a balanced approach and suggest that a strong market position and unique internal assets complement each other and that both are, therefore, necessary for competitive success.[42] A strong market position alone cannot be a sufficient source of competitive advantage for long. The firm needs the resources and capabilities necessary to defend that position. Similarly, strengths in internal resources and capabilities are effectively deployed in securing competitive advantages only when a firm has a strong market position.

Let's use a hypothetical example to examine this argument. (Also read Strategy in Practice 4.1.) Imagine a new restaurant that rapidly becomes popular solely because of its prime location. Location advantage and resulting success can only be sustained if the restaurant soon acquires any or a combination of internal strengths in food quality, menu variety, and customer service. The restaurant's positional advantage (prime location) helps in the hiring and retention of talented chefs and service personnel and the timely delivery of fresh supplies. Eventually, location strengths and internal strengths widen the restaurant's popularity further, providing it with an identifiable brand name and opportunities for opening new restaurants. Thus, positional advantage and resource-based advantage reinforce each other, contributing to the firm's long-term success.

SWOT Analysis

In Chapter 3 we described the tools managers use to assess industry opportunities and threats. In this chapter, we described the tools available for assessing a firm's strengths and weaknesses. Before we conclude this chapter, we should familiarize ourselves with a simple technique called **SWOT analysis** that examines a firm's strengths and weaknesses relative to its competitive environment. SWOT stands for Strengths, Weaknesses, Opportunities, and Threats. Managers use the SWOT technique to compare company strengths and weaknesses with industry opportunities and threats. The purpose is to assess the firm's overall strength in relation to the competitive environment and determine the strategic courses of action that will maximize company performance. After evaluating company strengths and weaknesses, and industry opportunities and threats, the SWOT process places the firm in one of the following four categories:[43]

1. Abundant environmental opportunities and significant internal strengths
2. Abundant environmental opportunities but significant internal weaknesses
3. Major environmental threats but significant internal strengths
4. Major environmental threats and significant internal weaknesses

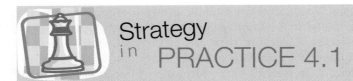

Strategy in PRACTICE 4.1

GOLDEN WEST FINANCIAL BANK'S POSITIONAL AND CAPABILITY-BASED ADVANTAGES

Golden West Financial is a thrift bank. With nearly five hundred savings and lending offices situated across thirty-eight states in the United States, it is a national bank. As of 2003, it had assets valued at $75 billion and was the second largest mortgage lender in the United States. But Golden West is a niche player in the mortgage industry—it offers residential mortgages only, and within that segment it specializes in adjustable rate mortgages for homes in the value range of $200,000–$250,000. Within this narrow focus, Golden West has a dominant market share. This dominance has endowed it with positional advantages, allowing it to generate funds for lending at a relatively cheaper rate than other lenders can and, as a result, enjoy a higher gross margin in the industry.

But Golden West also has an internal advantage emerging from its capabilities. It has one of the lowest cost structures in the industry. Its administrative expenses represent just 0.95 percent of average assets, the lowest ratio among major U.S. financial institutions. That enviable cost structure allows Golden West to underprice competitors, generating strong loan originations while posting net profits that are higher than the industry average.

Source: "Dilemma for Innovators," *Forbes,* November 6, 2003; "Golden West Flexes ARM Strength," *Thrift Investor* 16, no. 10 (2002).

Obviously, category 1 is the most favorable situation. The firm's strategy should be to pursue aggressive growth that will use its internal strengths to exploit the abundant external opportunities. In category 2, the strategy should be to eliminate weaknesses by acquiring the needed competencies either through joint ventures and alliances or vertical mergers so that opportunities can be effectively exploited. In category 3, the strategy should be either to alter industry forces using the firm's strengths (depending on the threats) or diversify into more attractive industries. Category 4 is an extremely unfavorable situation. This is a firm, according to Porter, that has a weak competitive position in an unattractive industry. The firm should consider repositioning by moving into another segment in the industry or gain the required strengths through horizontal mergers.

Summary

A firm is successful when it has internal strengths relevant for effectively competing in its industry. These strengths enable the firm to identify new opportunities before the competition does, successfully exploit them, and defend its position against competitors' moves. Strengths emerge from the firm's resources, its capabilities to effectively use them in competitive activities, and its learning and adaptive culture. When a firm's resources and capabilities are valuable, scarce, and in activities relevant for competition, it has a distinctive competency. Distinctive competencies bestow on a firm a competitive advantage that is essential for earning superior profits. To continuously earn superior profits, a firm must sustain this advantage. Competitive advantage is sustained when the resources and capabilities underlying the advantage resist imitation, substitution, and mobility.

To periodically assess their firm's strengths relative to competition and take corrective action, managers use value chain analysis and SWOT analysis. Value chain analysis breaks down the firm's task into subactivities and examines them to determine whether the firm has strengths in any primary or support activities relative to competition. SWOT analysis compares the firm's strengths and weaknesses to industry opportunities and threats and suggests strategic courses of action to enhance the firm's profitability.

Chapter 4 Discussion Questions and Projects

Discussion Questions

1. Are resource-based advantages more sustainable than positional advantages?

2. Define value chain analysis and describe how it helps managers to assess the strengths and weaknesses of their firm.

3. Describe and discuss the reasons that the capabilities of firms in an industry will differ.

Projects

1. Using the Internet and the business press, read about Federal Express and United Parcel Service in regard to their strengths, weaknesses, competitive advantages, and performance. Write a brief report that will answer the following questions:

   a. Using Tables 4.1 and 4.4 as models, prepare a table and a write-up, comparing Federal Express's strengths to those of United Parcel Service. You may modify the table to suit your needs.

   b. What competitive advantages accrue to Federal Express? Broadly categorize the firm's positional and resource-based advantages.

2. Using the Internet and the business press, answer the following questions about Eastman Kodak:

   a. What are Kodak's distinctive competencies?

   b. What are Kodak's competitive advantages and the sources of these advantages?

   c. What internal weaknesses would you cite as reasons that stopped Kodak from being first-to-market with digital photography?

Continuing Case

Southwest Airlines: Capabilities and Competitive Advantage

When Herb Kelleher, the founder and former CEO of Southwest Airlines, was asked the single most important reason for his firm's continued success, his response was "its people." Asked to elaborate, he said that it was Southwest's customer-oriented culture and the ability of its employees to treat the customer right that was responsible for the firm's astounding success. Other airlines that tried to imitate Southwest's twin approach—low fare and high customer orientation—have so far met with limited success. Southwest thus remains the unmatched star performer in the airline industry, ever since its inception in 1971.

Serving Customers in the Airline Industry

Two different models are available to airlines for serving customers. In one, the emphasis is on connectivity. An airline seeking to maximize connectivity uses a hub-and-spoke system that links several locations and allows passengers to reach far-off places conveniently. The benefit to the airline is the optimal utilization of its capacity. In the second model, the emphasis is on fare and travel time. An airline seeking to minimize fare and travel time uses a point-to-point system that links two locations directly. The benefit to the airline is the rapid turnaround time between locations that reduces cost. To achieve an enduring competitive advantage, airlines add to these two basic models certain service components: meals, in-flight entertainment, frequent-flier benefits, or courteous treatment of passengers. However, notwithstanding the basic model and the service mix a firm chooses, low fare has become a principal factor for success in the airline industry.

The Southwest Model

Southwest uses a point-to-point system, making direct flights between fifty-nine cities in the United States. Most are short-haul flights with an average distance of four hundred miles or less that can otherwise be covered by surface transportation. In pioneering such an airline, its founders believed that people who drive or take a bus to cover short distances would rather fly if it were cheaper, convenient, and pleasant. Southwest has thus positioned itself as an attractive alternative to travel by car or bus, thereby avoiding direct competition with major airlines and creating in the process a defensible niche.

Southwest chooses its cities carefully, based on traffic volume and the route's long-run sustainability. Once a route is chosen, Southwest maintains a high flight frequency on that route by having airplanes spend just twenty minutes on the ground between flights. Southwest offers only economy-class travel and no in-flight meals or movies. What it does offer, however, are deeply discounted fares, pleasant treatment by the crew, and an enjoyable flight experience. Fun, frolic, and peanut fares are what customers can expect from us, claim company officials.

Systems and Processes

To keep costs below those of rivals and to satisfy customers, Southwest performs its operational tasks differently from the industry norm. First, it flies only one type of aircraft—Boeing 737s. This fleet standardization reduces training costs, equipment maintenance, and spare parts inventories. Second, it avoids congested airports and, instead, operates only from secondary airports that are near major metropolitan areas. This reduces cost by minimizing flight wait time and by lowering airport fees. Third, the company does not assign seats to passengers; boarding passes are distributed on a first-come-first-served basis, and passengers choose their own seats. This procedure speeds up boarding at the gate, facilitating on-time performance. While these are, indeed, standard techniques, they still provide Southwest Airlines with an enduring advantage because they are inappropriate for the hub-and-spoke system. For example, differences in the traffic volume in routes served by the hub-and-spoke carriers require that they use different size aircrafts and different airports. In addition, since the hub-and-spoke airlines offer both first- or business-class and economy-class travel, they have to assign seats to passengers.

Besides its operational techniques, Southwest's organizational approaches make a strong contribution to its cost and customer-satisfaction goals.

Airlines require a near-perfect coordination among pilots, flight attendants, baggage handlers, mechanics, caterers, and the gate crew to achieve low-cost, high-quality service. Southwest's ability to achieve the desired level of coordination among its operational units has been the envy of its peers. The firm's coordinative capabilities emerge from (a) the innate skills of its employees to mutually adjust and (b) the work environment the company has created for this purpose. To be precise, Southwest selects people for their aptitude for team spirit, fun, and frugality, thus creating a workforce that has the natural potential to work cooperatively toward the firm's goals. Selected workers are then placed in a structure that is relatively flat—operational employees function without supervision. A flatter structure reduces supervisory costs and, in addition, empowers employees to coordinate their task with other work groups, as they deem fit.

Incidentally, the freedom to coordinate at one's discretion allows employees to learn, as they perform, what is needed to complete their task. The resulting knowledge gets internalized and consequently endures. In the case of Southwest Airlines, employee learning on issues important to the firm's success—cost control and customer care—is relatively high as a result of the worker-selection methods and flatter organizational structure the firm has used from inception.

Stakeholder Relationships

Southwest's strengths do not stop with operational systems and organizational processes but extend to strong stakeholder relationships as well. From the beginning, Southwest's managers have promoted an informal work climate within the firm. Managers act more as coaches, helping employees to learn from their mistakes, than as formal executives evaluating employee performance on the basis of predetermined criteria. It is not uncommon to see the CEO work side by side with the cabin crew, help load the luggage, or engage in a friendly conversation with the operating personnel. Treat the employees well and they will treat the customers well, summarizes the firm's motto. And, besides employees, Southwest managers have developed a strong relationship with the firm's customers as well. Periodically, they take time to write to customers, sharing with them Southwest's plans for the future and soliciting feedback. This strong rela-

tionship has helped the firm successfully convince customers to buy tickets directly from it. Nearly three-fourths of its tickets are sold through its website, against an industry average of one-half, saving the firm millions of dollars in commissions to travel agents.

Emerging Opportunities and Challenges

With competition intensifying in the short-haul market, Southwest has added some long-haul routes. Travelers in the long-haul segment are mostly managers, who are believed to prefer a "business like" service, not the "zany like" acts of Southwest's flight attendants. The firm is also contemplating international expansion, but that could require the use of more than one type of aircraft, a change in training methods, and possibly the adoption of a hub-and-spoke system. Industry analysts believe that the firm's current capabilities are appropriate only for the niche in which it is presently operating and any major attempt by the firm to move out of that niche will require the acquisition of radically different strengths.

Discussion Questions

1. Describe Southwest's tangible and intangible resources.

2. Draw a table showing Southwest's strengths and weaknesses.

3. Does Southwest Airlines have positional advantage, resource-based advantage, or both? Describe the sources of these advantages.

4. Explain why is it difficult for competitors to imitate Southwest's capabilities.

5. What resources and capabilities would Southwest need if it planned to expand significantly into the long-haul and international markets?

Source: J. H. Gittell, "Paradox of Coordination and Control," *California Management Review* 42, no. 3 (Spring 2000): 101–117; U. K. Bunz and J. D. Maes, "Learning Excellence: Southwest Airlines' Approach," *Managing Service Quality* 8, no. 3 (1998): 163–169; A. C. Inkpen and V. DeGroot, *Southwest Airlines 2002,* Thunderbird University Case #A07-02-0009 (2002); A. A. Thompson and J. E. Gamble, "Southwest Airlines, Inc.." in A. A. Thompson and A. J. Strickland, *Strategic Management* (New York: McGraw-Hill Irwin, 2003), C590–629.

Part Three

Strategic Choice

Business-Level Strategy: Building Competitive Advantage in a Single Business

CHAPTER OBJECTIVES

After reading this chapter, you should be able to:

- Define business-level strategy

- Discuss the importance of business-level strategy for a firm's competitive performance and long-term success

- Describe generic business-level strategy choices, the competitive advantage each creates, and the conditions under which each strategy will be effective

- Identify congruent resources and capabilities to effectively pursue the generic business-level strategies

- Describe a cost-differentiation combination strategy, discuss the conditions under which it may be relevant, and identify the resources and capabilities needed for effectively pursuing it

- Describe how the industry life cycle could influence business-level strategy selection and discuss the choices most suitable for different life cycle stages

Opening Case

Wal-Mart is a discount retailer. With over 5,000 stores in operation globally as of 2004, and 1.5 million employees, it is the world's largest retailer. In 2004, its revenues were $285 billion, making it the biggest company in the world in terms of sales for the third year in a row. During the same year, General Motors, which until 2000 had been the world leader for fifteen straight years, was a distant fourth with revenues of just over $193 billion. Analysts predict that there is still much growth left in Wal-Mart and its number one rank in sales is secure for many years to come. In 2003 *Fortune* named Wal-Mart the world's most admired company in the use of corporate assets, thus putting its stamp of approval on the retailer's quality of business management. Never in the sixty-year history of *Fortune's* annual rankings has a firm achieved these twin laurels in the same year: number one in sales and most admired company. Many wonder how a retail business, born in 1962 in rural Arkansas, could achieve so much glory and prominence in such a short period!

What underlies Wal-Mart's astounding success? How did a small-town retailer emerge as the world's number one business in sales, a position that has historically been held by manufacturers of big-ticket items? How could Wal-Mart grow its sales by 15 percent every year when Sears, the industry pioneer, had flat sales of just $40 billion for almost a decade, and when Kmart, which began business around the same time as Wal-Mart did, was seeking bankruptcy protection in 2002? Analysts and researchers point to Wal-Mart's business-level strategy and the supporting decisions it makes in pursuit of its strategy as the reasons for its success. Wal-Mart's strategy in its retail business is to continuously reduce operational costs relative to rivals, allowing it to offer "everyday low prices" to its customers. To pursue this strategy, the firm has acquired and deployed internal resources and capabilities that not only fit remarkably well with its cost goals but also are unique and unmatched in corporate history. In other words, a clearly conceived business-level strategy, accompanied by coherently matching resources and capabilities, has brought about Wal-Mart's success.

The late Sam Walton, founder of Wal-Mart and its CEO and chairman of the board until his death in 1992, always wanted to be in consumer retailing. His philosophy in retailing was that merchandise and other day-to-day items would sell if they were of acceptable quality and offered at a low price. More importantly, he believed that his business would be most successful if it targeted customers in little one-horse towns that other retailers were largely ignoring. What soon emerged were several niche locations in the rural Midwest, not served by the major discounters, where Wal-Mart established itself as the sole discount retailer, deriving monopoly profits. Wal-Mart quickly strengthened this dominant market position by investing in expensive and proprietary technologies that not only controlled costs in inventory and retail operations but prevented entry into the niche by both established retailers (Kmart, Sears) and new firms. Additional investments in supplier management, merchandising, employee relations, logistics, and store management further strengthened Wal-Mart's competitive position as a cost leader in the retail industry as a whole. Over time, abundant opportunities for expansion within and outside its niche combined with its ability to achieve cost reduction that is yet unmatched by others have enabled Wal-Mart not only to achieve dominance in the entire retailing industry but also to become the biggest firm in the world.[1]

Wal-Mart's story exemplifies the importance of a coherently conceived business-level strategy for a firm's competitive performance and long-term success. Business-level strategy provides a central theme around which firms can organize their business decisions and actions against competitive threats. Wal-Mart's strategy for succeeding in its business is **cost leadership.** That is, Wal-Mart aims to continuously lower costs in its retail business, relative to competition, as a means to attain success in that business.

This "cost leadership" theme gives Wal-Mart a basis for making decisions concerning what resources and capabilities it must invest in to gain a cost advantage over rivals. Without a business-level strategy, a firm's competitive decisions and actions can lack focus and thus compromise its ability to be successful.

In this chapter, we examine business-level strategy, also known as business-unit strategy or **competitive strategy**.[2] We start with a brief description of what business-level strategy is, followed by a discussion of certain generic and alternative strategy choices available to a firm in its quest to outperform competition. We then discuss the resources and capabilities needed to pursue these strategies and how they position the firm to deal effectively with the industry pressures described in Chapter 3. Later, we discuss the merits and problems of each generic strategy, knowledge that managers need in order to make an informed strategic choice. Finally, we conclude by highlighting how different stages of the industry life cycle need different strategies at the business level, an additional factor that managers should take into account when selecting a strategy for their business.

What Is Business-Level Strategy?

Recall from Chapter 1 that there is no single, universally accepted definition of the term *strategy*.[3] But most agree on the context in which, and the purpose for which, it is used. Strategy is discussed in the context of achieving a goal when hurdles exist that inhibit goal achievement. In the absence of hurdles, there is no need for a strategy. Hurdles emerge from the actions of others who are competing for the same goal. The aim of strategy is to equip the firm with the strengths it needs to overcome hurdles. Strategy does this by providing advantages—through a strong market position or exceptional internal capabilities—that lead to goal achievement.

Given this general description of strategy, we can understand business-level strategy from the context of the firm's business goals and the hurdles it faces in realizing them. A firm's business comprises the product offered, the customer group or industry segment served, and the skills and technologies employed to make and market the product. Several forces compete with the firm, directly and indirectly, for a share in this business and the potential it offers for profit. To be successful, a firm must have the strengths to effectively deal with these competing forces. Business-level strategy is the means the firm employs to gain this strength, providing the firm with a foundation on which to organize its business decisions and actions. These decisions and actions involve the allocation of resources to achieve a favorable market position or unique internal capabilities that endow the firm with the strengths it needs to overcome competition.

Business-level strategy is thus a comprehensive mechanism the firm employs to gain competitive advantage or superiority in a *particular business*.[4] It specifies the advantage the firm will seek in that business, relative to competition (e.g., advantages in product design, efficient manufacturing, or brand visibility), and how available resources will be deployed to acquire it. The following summarizes the characteristics of business-level strategy:

1. *It is a strategy for a single business.* The focus of business-level strategy is competitive success in a single business. Multibusiness firms, whose businesses are independent of each other and compete in distinct industries, need a business-level strategy for each of their businesses.

2. *Its main focus is dealing with competitive threats.* Business-level strategy is the firm's (or the business unit's) overall and integrative approach to overcoming competitive threats. It is, therefore, also called competitive strategy.

3. *It facilitates the attainment of business goals by building and nurturing competitive advantages.*[5] Business-level strategy leads to higher performance by building competitive advantages—through a favorable market position and/or the acquisition of unique internal competencies (see Figure 5.1).

Business-Level Strategy Choices

Selecting a business-level strategy for a firm essentially involves answering the question: how will the firm compete in its business or industry? The choice a firm makes in this regard is generally influenced by beliefs, values, and past experiences of managers concerning business and competition.[6] For example, Sam Walton's belief that standard-quality products offered at everyday low prices will guarantee success in retailing influenced Wal-Mart's selection of a cost-leadership strategy. But managers' beliefs and business philosophies are only part of the input in strategy selection. A firm also uses information gained through industry analysis and assessment of its own competencies to select an appropriate strategy for its business. Industry analysis lets managers identify the competitive pressures in the industry and determine whether they should pursue their opportunities in the overall industry or within specific market segments. For example, through retail industry analysis Sam Walton discovered the existence of a niche segment within the industry (rural Midwest), and he initially chose to position Wal-Mart as a cost leader within this segment only. Internal analysis, on the other hand, indicates to managers the firm's overall strengths and whether there are unique capabilities that offer relatively more competitive potential. For example, you may recall from Chapter 4 how Komatsu identified internal strengths in design and manufacturing and proactively used those strengths as a basis to compete on product quality rather than after-sales service, the general practice in the construction equipment industry.

FIGURE 5.1 **How Business-Level Strategy Influences Performance**

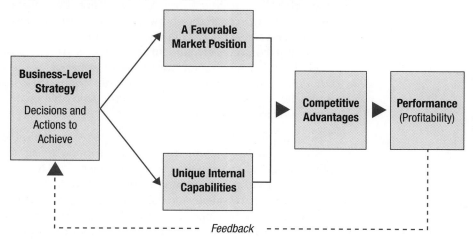

Evaluating industry conditions side by side with internal strengths enables a firm to select an appropriate business-level strategy that meshes industry opportunities with the firm's competencies. When carefully chosen, business-level strategy effectively aligns the firm's competencies to the needs and conditions of the industry or a segment within it. Successful strategies are those that create a good fit among the firm's several competencies, its overall strength, and the needs of the external environment.[7]

Scholars propose business-level strategy choices to help managers select an appropriate way to compete in their business. Some strategies are called *generic* because their proponents believe them to be appropriate for all firms, whether manufacturers or service providers, and suitable for all industry conditions. Other scholars, however, believe that different industry conditions demand different competitive choices and have proposed strategies based on the industry life-cycle stages—industry evolution, growth, maturity, and decline. We'll now examine two distinct sets of generic strategies proposed by Porter and by Miles and Snow, followed by a discussion of strategies proposed by others that are based on the industry life cycle.

Porter's Generic Business-Level Strategies

Michael Porter presents managers with three generic or standard competitive options from which to choose.[8] These options emerge from the *distinct ways* in which value chain activities can be configured, allowing a firm to be *different* from rivals. According to Porter, *the essence of business strategy is competitive advantage, which is achieved by organizing and performing value chain activities differently from competitors.*[9] Porter contends that performing similar activities *better* is not strategy; it is *operational effectiveness*—the ability to execute similar activities more efficiently than rivals do. Operational effectiveness may endow a firm with competitive advantages for a while, but sustainable advantages require a firm to be different from competition, either in how it performs similar activities or in its ability to perform entirely different activities. *To summarize Porter, doing well on what rivals do is not strategy; doing well on what rivals cannot do is.*[10]

Porter's generic strategy options rest on the following competitive themes:

1. *Do what competition does but do it differently.* By engaging in similar activities but performing them differently, a firm aims for a cost advantage. Compare Continental Airlines to Southwest Airlines. Both must plan and execute activities related to flying passengers between destinations economically. By choosing to operate as a full-service airline, Continental must provide long-distance scheduling, flight connections, and in-flight meals. In contrast, by choosing to be a limited-service carrier, Southwest focuses only on short-distance, point-to-point scheduling, eliminating the need for flight connections, baggage transfer, and in-flight meals. As a result, Southwest has been able to do what Continental does but at a relatively lower cost.

2. *Do entirely different activities compared to competition.* Here the firm deliberately sets itself apart from competition in the manufacturing, marketing, or distribution of the product. The aim is to serve customers who have unique product or service preferences and gain a premium pricing advantage. Steinway makes pianos using handcrafted parts while its rivals use mass-produced parts. This has enabled Steinway to build a niche clientele—those that seek handcrafted quality in a piano. Several automobile makers offer unique cars for sports, utility, and luxury segments to differentiate their offerings from standard car manufacturers.

Using these two broad competitive themes, Porter suggests firms choose from the following four specific alternatives.[11] (Note that the third and the fourth alternatives emerge when the firm decides to pursue either of these two options within a narrow industry segment. See Figure 5.2.)

1. **Cost leadership** is a strategy in which a firm aims for the lowest cost position, industry-wide, as a way to beat rivals. By offering the same product but performing activities differently compared to competition, a firm intends to gain a sustainable cost advantage.

2. **Differentiation** is a strategy in which the firm positions its product, or the way it offers it, to be perceived industry-wide as distinct, thereby outperforming competition. By offering a unique product or service, requiring the completion of activities that are different (i.e., are not or cannot be performed by the competition), a firm intends to achieve a product advantage that is sustainable. One way in which a firm differentiates is by focusing on the product's design to improve the design features as opposed to process design that reduces the cost of making the product.

3. **Cost focus** is a strategy in which the firm strives to outperform rivals by concentrating on a narrow product line or a narrow market segment and competing in it based on low cost. By choosing an appropriate niche that avoids industry-wide competition and by tailoring activities to the specific needs of the niche customers, a firm intends to derive a sustainable advantage.

4. **Differentiation focus** is similar to cost focus. In this strategy a firm strives to outperform rivals by concentrating on a narrow product line or a narrow market segment and competes in it based on product or service differentiation.

Porter recommends that a firm select and vigorously pursue any one of these strategic positions in its industry to be successful.* That is, a firm must deliberately choose an identifiably distinctive position in the industry—so as to be perceived as an industry-wide cost leader, an industry-wide differentiator, or a focus strategist—and

---

FIGURE 5.2

Source: Adapted with the permission of The Free Press, a Division of Simon & Shuster Adult Publishing Group, from *Competitive Strategy: Techniques for Analyzing Industires and Competitors* by Michael E. Porter. Copyright 1980, 1998 by the Free Press.

Cost, Differentiation, and Focus Strategies

Competitive Advantage Pursued

	Lower Cost	Differentiation
Broad Cross-Section	Cost Leadership	Differentiation
Narrow Segment	Cost Focus	Differentiation Focus

Market Segment Targeted

---

*As explained in Chapter 1, positional views of strategy take their roots from military science. Military science prescribes different troop positions and maneuvers as strategies to gain an advantage over the enemy. Read R. D. Sawyer, *Sun-tzu: The Art of War* (New York: Barnes & Noble Books, 1994) to learn more about positional views of strategy.

must defend that position by erecting entry barriers. Porter lists six fundamental principles (see Table 5.1) for a firm to follow when selecting and maintaining a distinctive strategic position. He claims that each of these strategic positions is significantly so different from the others, in regard to competitive goals and organizational needs for their implementation, that they should not be combined.[12] Firms that attempt to combine them, and seek to be all in one, will get "stuck in the middle" for want of a clear focus and as a result of conflicting resource allocations. The result is below-average performance, as the sad saga of Sears highlights in Strategy in Practice 5.1.

| TABLE 5.1 | Six Fundamental Principles in Strategic Positioning |

1. *Start with a right goal: superior long-term return on investment.* A strategy must focus on sustained profitability. Profits arise when customers are willing to pay a price for the product or service that exceeds the cost of producing it. When company goals are defined in terms of volume or market share leadership, with profits assumed to follow, poor strategies result.

2. *A firm's strategy must enable it to deliver a set of benefits different from those offered by competitors.* Strategy is neither a quest for the *best way* of competing nor an effort to be all things to every customer. It defines a way of competing that delivers unique value in a particular set of uses or for a particular set of customers.

3. *Strategy needs to be reflected in a distinctive value chain.* To be distinctive, a firm must perform different activities from its rivals or perform similar activities in different ways. A firm must configure the way it conducts manufacturing, marketing, human resource management, and so on differently from rivals and tailored to its unique value proposition. If a firm focuses on adopting best practices, it will end up performing most activities similarly to competitors, making it hard to gain an advantage.

4. *Robust strategies involve trade-offs.* A firm must forgo some product features, services, or activities to be unique at others. Such trade-offs are what make a firm truly distinctive. When improvements in the product or in the value chain do not require trade-offs, they become new best practices that are imitated because competitors can do so with no sacrifice to their existing ways of competing. Trying to be all things to all customers almost guarantees that a firm will lack any advantage.

5. *Strategy defines how all the elements of what a firm does fit together.* A firm's product design, for example, should reinforce its approach to the manufacturing process, and both should leverage the way it conducts after-sales service. Fit not only increases competitive advantage but also makes a strategy harder to imitate. Rivals can copy one activity or product feature fairly easily, but will have difficulty duplicating a whole system of competing. Without fit, discrete improvements in manufacturing, marketing, or distribution are quickly matched.

6. *Strategy involves continuity of direction.* A company must define a distinctive value proposition that it will stand for, even if that means forgoing certain opportunities. Without continuity of direction, it is difficult for companies to develop unique skills and assets or build strong reputations with customers. Frequent corporate reinvention is usually a sign of poor strategic thinking and a route to mediocrity. Continuous improvement is a necessity, but it must always be guided by a strategic direction.

Source: Reprinted by permission of *Harvard Business Review.* From "Strategy and the Internet" by Michael E. Porter, vol. 79, no. 3, p. 71. Copyright © 2001 by the Harvard Business School Publishing Corporation; all rights reserved.

Strategy in PRACTICE 5.1

HOW SEARS GOT STUCK IN THE MIDDLE AND SUFFERED

Sears Roebuck started in 1886 as a mail-order business but soon began operating retail stores in malls to sell clothing, home furnishings, and household appliances. The company positioned itself as a general merchandiser where mainstream Americans could shop with confidence for standard-quality products at low prices. Before long, Sears emerged as a household name and a favorite place for the cost-conscious middle class to shop for the family. Buoyed by its success, the company diversified into other consumer retailing such as insurance, real estate, and financial services products. By the 1980s there were over eight hundred stores in operation in the United States and Canada, and Sears was the acclaimed leader of the retail industry. *Fortune* extolled Sears as the paragon of retailers. Analysts and academicians alike cited it as the true exemplar of cost-leadership strategy.

The America of the 1960s and 1970s was, however, dramatically changing, portending problems for Sears. Changes in lifestyle, shopping habits, and consumers' concern for quality as well as price brought discounters like Wal-Mart and specialty stores like factory outlets onto the retail scene. The ability of these businesses to offer quality products at competitive prices soon made inroads into Sears' market base, causing serious erosion in its sales and gross margin. Sears decided to move away from its acclaimed position as a low-price, high-volume retailer and to reposition itself as a merchandiser of above-average, exclusive-quality soft goods (clothing and furnishings) that would allow it to earn higher gross margins

through premium pricing. To effectively implement this upscale strategy, it stopped carrying low-end merchandise, introduced fashionable clothing, and brought in Cheryl Tiegs, a supermodel, to promote its line of women's apparel. The result was contrary to what Sears expected; it was a disaster. The traditional price-conscious consumer no longer perceived Sears as a place to shop. Nor did the high-end shopper believe that Sears was an acceptable alternative to the traditional premium stores. More erosion in sales followed and losses were monumental. Once again, Sears altered its strategy, this time as a deep discounter, and challenged Wal-Mart. That strategy, too, failed. By late 1990s, the company again repositioned itself in its original position: America's middle-class department store carrying a full line of quality merchandise at low prices. But, by then, it was late in the game—it had lost a sizeable portion of its customers to Wal-Mart and Target. In 2004, eighty years after it opened its first retail store, Sears' sales were just $36 billion. During the same year, Wal-Mart, half its age, had sales of $285 billion. In November 2004, the struggling Sears was acquired by another beleaguered retailer, Kmart, for $11 billion.

Source: R. Lal and S. Sood, "Sears Roebuck and Company," *Graduate School of Business,* Stanford University, Case #M278 (October 1997); P. Sellers, "The Turnaround Is Ending: The Revolution Has Begun," *Fortune,* April 28, 1997; R. Berner and J. Weber, "Eddie's Master Stroke," *Business Week,* November 29, 2004, 35–36; www.sears.com; www.walmartstores.com.

After examining each of Porter's generic strategies in detail, you may want to peruse Table 5.2 to see how they differ from one another in terms of the resources and capabilities needed to pursue them. See also Table 5.3, which compares the advantages and disadvantages of using these strategies.

Cost Leadership

The aim in a **cost-leadership strategy** is to secure an industry-wide advantage over rivals in the overall cost of running the business. Specifically, the firm attempts to control the operational and administrative costs related to designing, manufacturing,

| TABLE 5.2 | **Comparing Porter's Generic Business-Level Strategies** |

	COST LEADERSHIP	DIFFERENTIATION	FOCUS
Target customers	Broad cross section of the industry	Several distinct markets in an industry	A narrow segment within an industry
Strategic focus	Achieving lower overall cost than competition	Achieving product advantage over rivals in several segments	Achieving cost or product advantage in a niche segment
Product line (breadth)	One or two standard designs (acceptable quality, no variety)	Several unique designs to suit distinct needs in several segments	Customized to suit the needs of the chosen niche
R&D	Only process R&D	Heavy product R&D	Product or process R&D depending on strategic focus
Manufacturing	Large volume production; emphasis on lot size	Medium volume production; emphasis on zero defects	Small lot size and custom production
Marketing	No segmentation	High segmentation Heavy advertising	Single segment Heavy advertising
Organization	Skill, work, and tool standardization; centralization of resources	Broad job scope; worker autonomy; decentralization	Depends on strategic focus
Sustaining the strategy	Design standardization for mass appeal Aggressive market-share growth goals	Continuous product innovation Creating brand loyalty through aggressive advertising	Commitment to the needs of the niche Defending niche through pricing or product enhancements and aggressive promotion

and marketing the product. The objective is to achieve a lower cost position relative to others in the industry. The focus of this strategy is thus on internal costs and their control as the predominant means to outperform competition. Some examples of companies pursuing a cost-leadership strategy are Nucor (steel), Hyundai (automobiles), Timex (watches), and Wal-Mart (retailing).

A cost leader earns profits by keeping costs lower than the market-offered price for its product. It earns superior profits in the industry when it maximizes the spread between cost and market price. A second way in which a cost leader earns higher profits is by using its cost advantage to lower prices and win over competition's customers, thereby generating higher revenues through volume. Because low-cost market segments often witness price wars, only a firm that has a significant cost advantage over others will be continuously profitable.

Requirements for Pursuing a Cost-Leadership Strategy

Successful pursuit of a cost-leadership strategy requires that the firm offer no frills, extras, or premium features in the product's design or customer service, as they tend

TABLE 5.3	Advantages and Disadvantages of Porter's Generic Business Strategies	
	ADVANTAGES	**DISADVANTAGES**
Cost Leadership	Volume procurement and distribution strengths give strong negotiating power over suppliers and buyers.	Technological change can nullify past learning and experience curve–related economies.
	Market share and investment strengths in fixed assets prevent entry.	Fixed assets providing cost advantages can be easily imitated by newcomers.
	Low cost structure enables dealing with substitute threats through price reductions.	Frequent investments in costly automation to keep costs under control are needed.
	Cost leaders can use price to compete offensively or withstand price wars initiated by rivals.	High investments in fixed assets make exit difficult.
Differentiation	Product or service uniqueness and brand loyalty prevent new entry.	Protecting the bases of differentiation and brand image is costly.
	Differentiation helps create unique product or service identity and minimizes threats from rivals.	Buyers may forgo some of the unique features and switch to rivals' products if cost savings are high.
	Pressure from suppliers' increased prices can be balanced by ability to increase product price.	Differentiation cannot be sustained if the underlying advantage can be easily imitated.
	Powerful buyers/distributors are not a threat because brand is popular with customers.	Lifestyle changes may make the bases of differentiation less important to buyers.
	Brand loyalty minimizes substitute threats.	
Focus	Small size of the niche provides protection from major industry players.	Small size does not permit economies of scale.
	If the focuser is a first mover, brand recognition prevents entry.	Adverse change in demand can affect a focuser drastically.
	Buyer power is minimal since the focuser satisfies buyers' precise needs.	Focuser's advantage will fast dissipate if an industry-wide competitor can offer the same product/service at a lower price.

to increase the overall cost of the product. The emphasis is on the functionality of the product, not its distinctiveness or sophistication. This does not mean excluding the basic features or compromising the minimum acceptable quality, which would make the product substandard. For customers to buy the product, the firm is still expected to include features essential for the product's normal performance. As a result, the ideal approach for pursuing this strategy is to incorporate the standard features and performance characteristics in the design of the product, while focusing on the manufacturing and distribution aspects of it (delivery, if it is a service business) to derive the necessary cost efficiencies.

A low-cost strategist thus avoids investing in new product research and development because it is unnecessary, expensive, and defeats the purpose of the strategy. For the same reason, it also avoids offering several designs aimed to meet the unique needs of distinct market segments. Instead, it prefers a single or few standardized designs that would satisfy several market segments. To make this standard product at the least cost and to identify new ways of achieving manufacturing efficiency, the firm invests in process research—research that focuses on improving the production/operations process. Successful pursuit of the low-cost strategy requires competencies in materials procurement, manufacturing/operations, distribution, and the management of information technology. Several operations-related factors associated with the pursuit of a low-cost strategy are *economies of scale, factory and office automation,* and *work standardization*—all learning and experience effects.

Economies of Scale

The term **economies of scale** means lower unit cost at higher volume levels. The unit cost (i.e., average cost) of a product falls as more units are produced. Assume a firm has incurred $2 million in fixed costs ($1 million to design and another $1 million to set up machines) to make a new model sports car. Also, assume that no variable costs (labor and material costs) will be incurred in production (though this is a crude assumption). In the resulting situation, the cost of making the first unit is $2 million, but the second unit costs only $1 million and, if a hundred units are produced, the cost per unit is $20,000. Thus, a firm that utilizes its fixed assets to the fullest enjoys a lower cost structure compared to competition. Obviously, the economies-of-scale approach requires a high market share for a low-cost strategist to absorb the high volume of production.

Incidentally, economies of scale are not restricted to the production activity. A firm can derive such economies in other value chain activities—in R&D and advertising, or anywhere that costs can be spread out over a larger sales volume.

Factory and Office Automation

Factory and office automation encompasses the aggressive construction of facilities of an efficient scale and automation of the production line (or operations workflow if it is a service company), both of which are necessary to achieve economies associated with high-volume production. With only a single or few designs to make, assembly-line automation becomes easy for a low-cost strategist. In the early 1900s, Ford Motor Company was able to achieve assembly-line automation by limiting its offerings to the Model T in one color (black). In addition, automation of office procedures (e.g., receiving customer complaints) enables a low-cost strategist to meet volume demands through technology rather than expensive human labor.

Work Standardization

Work standardization, or routinization of tasks allows a low-cost strategist to help workers to thoroughly learn the job, thereby increasing volume levels and minimizing waste. (In Chapter 9, which deals with strategy implementation, we will learn more about the organizational mechanisms used by a low-cost strategist to achieve efficiencies.)

Differentiation

The aim in **differentiation strategy** is to achieve a product quality or service advantage over rivals as perceived by consumers. Specifically, a firm attempts to add significant value to its product, or services related to the product, to differentiate it from the standard and more generic offerings. The objective is for customers to perceive the product or related service as unique, so that it appeals to those with distinct needs. Thus this strategy focuses on the product and its features, or the way it is offered (e.g., through fast service—Jiffy Lube) as the predominant means of gaining an advantage over rivals. Competitive advantage results when customers perceive uniqueness in the firm's offerings and become loyal to the brand because it fits their special needs.

Differentiation can be achieved through the product's features and performance, how it is marketed, the customer service provided, or other attributes widely valued by buyers. For example, Mercedes-Benz focuses on *product design and safety* issues to differentiate its cars. Rolex focuses on *product styling* and prestige factors. BMW focuses on *product engineering* to build *high-performance* cars. Ralph Lauren concentrates on *marketing* to build an *exclusive image* for its brand of clothing. Caterpillar focuses on *customer service* by rapidly responding to customer demands for parts through its vast dealer networks. Domino's Pizza focuses on *fast delivery*, while Federal Express concentrates on *reliable and timely delivery*.

While the cost leader maximizes the spread between cost and price by keeping costs down, a differentiator maximizes this spread by selling its product at a premium price. Customers are willing to pay a higher price for the firm's product or related service because of the superior value they see in its uniqueness. This ability to sell the product at a sum far higher than what was spent to create it enables the differentiator to earn significant profits. Although cost control is not a priority for the differentiator, such firms do keep costs low to maximize revenue. Its market position allows the differentiator to periodically increase prices as an additional way to generate more revenue. Because of their attachment to the brand, customers remain committed to it and do not generally switch unless they perceive a significantly higher value in rivals' brands.

Requirements for Pursuing a Differentiation Strategy

Successful pursuit of a differentiation strategy requires that the firm continuously improve its product or the factor on which differentiation is based. Such improvements maintain the fit between what the firm offers and the customers' changing needs, thereby ensuring their continued loyalty. More importantly, improvements set the firm's offerings and the underlying competencies farther apart from competitors, thus providing a safety buffer against attempts at imitation. The more a firm's product or service is unique—and resists imitation—the more sustainable is the competitive advantage that the firm derives from it.

Unlike cost leaders, a differentiator generally offers its product in several designs that appeal to distinct buyer groups. Since buyer tastes and preferences often differ, a differentiator uses product variety to compete in several niche market segments. Such a firm is known as a **broad differentiator.** A different type of differentiator is the **focused differentiator,** which competes in a single niche market with only one or two designs. Mercedes-Benz, for example, is a broad differentiator, offering several models within the moderate- to high-price range, targeting a distinct range of price and prestige needs of people in the middle- and upper-income earning groups.[13] To maintain its differentiation status, the price of its cars in each model category is slightly higher than the price of its direct competition.

Strengths needed to pursue a differentiation strategy depend on the type of differentiation pursued. Firms focusing on the product's features need significant strengths in R&D and product engineering. Those focusing on product reliability and performance need strengths in defect-free manufacturing. These strengths may derive from a high R&D budget, investments in quality control, and a management culture that fosters product innovation and total quality. Firms seeking to build a unique product image also need to develop strengths in advertising and promotion. Customer service differentiators need strengths in sales, technical assistance, or repair services, depending on their focus.

Focus

A **focus strategy** concentrates on a geographic segment (e.g., marketing the product in the United States only), a buyer group (e.g., marketing products for people of Hispanic background only), or a narrow product line (e.g., marketing only garden furniture). A firm can be more effective and efficient if it concentrates on a single geographic segment, a single customer group, or a few product lines, rather than several.

A focus-strategy firm first chooses a market segment or product line and aims to achieve a cost or a differentiation advantage within that segment. In other words, it offers a standard product or differentiated product/service within a niche. It competes with broad-based differentiators or cost strategists, except that it does so within the niche only. For example, a local stationery store that focuses on a narrow geographic segment may use a cost strategy to compete with Staples, the national cost leader. Absence of large overhead costs that are common to big firms (e.g., warehousing, advertising, and payroll costs) may give the local store an edge over the national rivals. Rolex, the premium watch manufacturer, makes only expensive watches and competes with Cartier, a diversified firm that makes and markets a broad selection of premium watches and other products (precious jewelry, fashion accessories). In essence, a focuser offers the product for a niche segment only and competes with a cost strategist or differentiator that offers its products to a broad section of the industry.

Requirements for Pursuing a Focus Strategy

A successful focuser is one who understands the specialized needs of its niche segment well. Not only must it customize the product to fit its niche market, the firm must also have the ability to adapt rapidly to the changes occurring within that market. Because niche segments are comparatively small in size—meaning opportunities for economy-of-scale benefits do not generally exist—a focuser must be able to control costs to be successful. Because of its low overhead burden, a focuser generally enjoys a cost advantage over its large industry counterparts. Focusers typically minimize product variety to reduce the number of suppliers and distributors—while maintaining a good relationship with them—to further help manage costs.

Advantages and Disadvantages of Porter's Generic Strategies

The merits of Porter's generic strategies stem from the unique advantages they offer in countering the five forces (see Chapter 3) in an industry. These advantages come in the form of the firm's competitive market position, entry barriers to prevent new competition, and the ability they confer to deal effectively with supplier and buyer threats. By choosing a strategy and organizing congruent internal resources and activities, a firm can expect to outperform competition in the long run. However, each advantage a strategy offers is accompanied by a disadvantage, as illustrated in Table 5.3.

The Choice of Strategy

Porter does not suggest that any one generic strategy is better than the others. The generic-strategy model unwittingly leaves managers with a wrong impression—namely, that they can pursue any of the three strategies without regard to industry conditions and still emerge successful if the supporting choices are congruent. In most established industries, however, very few broad differentiators (three or four) are generally successful, and still fewer broad cost leaders (one or two) are. These firms are first movers or close seconds that have positioned themselves well in the industry and, as a result, for most industry rivals the only available competitive option is focus. In short, strategy selection for most firms is not whether they should choose differentiation or cost leadership. Instead, the issue for them is: Which untapped niche segment exists in the industry that can be successfully exploited?[14] The only exception would be firms that have unique resources and skills with which they can challenge the industry majors. In fact, one researcher strongly suggests that broad differentiators and cost strategists who are unsuccessful in their industry reposition themselves as focusers.[15]

Some product and market conditions demand the pursuit of one strategy versus another. For example, the cost-leadership strategy is more appropriate when the product is a commodity and brands do not matter much to buyers. Differentiation strategy is more appropriate when several clearly identifiable market segments exist for the product. A focus strategy is more appropriate when a large niche segment exists but has not been exploited by any firm. In other words, managers may want to consider industry conditions first before they decide which of the generic strategies they should choose and pursue. Table 5.4 describes industry conditions under which each of these strategies will be appropriate.

Cost-Differentiation Combination Strategies

Can a firm compete using a combination of cost and differentiation strategies? Contrary to Porter's claim that it is an inconsistent position whose adoption will result in poor performance, some scholars suggest that a combination approach is not

TABLE 5.4	When Would a Cost-Leadership, Differentiation, or Focus Strategy Be Appropriate?

Cost Leadership

- Price competition in the industry is intense.
- The industry has reached maturity.
- The product is a commodity.
- Brands do not matter to buyers.
- Switching costs are low.
- Buyers have high bargaining power.

Differentiation

- Buyer needs and uses of the product are diverse.
- Buyers would perceive value if the product were differentiated.
- Brands matter to buyers.
- Several ways to differentiate the product exist.
- Rapid changes are occurring in the product's technology.

Focus

- The niche is big enough to be profitable.
- The niche has high growth potential.
- The niche is not crucial to the success of big competitors.
- The niche strategist has strengths to effectively serve the niche and defend it.

only technically feasible but advisable, especially in hypercompetitive industry conditions where technological changes are rapid, product cycles are short, and new competitor entry is frequent.[16] Some firms have successfully employed combination strategies,[17] and, in some instances, combination-strategy firms outperformed those that pursued either cost or differentiation.[18]

A **cost-differentiation combination strategy** involves aiming for an integrated "product-cost-service" advantage. For example, a cost strategy firm may add value at the market-offered price—incorporating new features in to the product, offering variety, enhancing customer service—and still strive for cost leadership. A differentiator may reduce its costs and pass the savings on to customers in the form of lower price—and still strive for enhanced product features or service quality.

The cost-differentiation combination is a critical factor for success in several industries today, especially automobiles, apparel, audio, video, consumer home electronics, and retailing. Changes in consumer values and preference, dynamic industry conditions, and the search by businesses themselves for new competitive advantages are prompting many firms to employ combination strategies.

1. *Changing consumer values:* Historically, consumers sought to minimize cost for themselves by accepting a standard product. Alternatively, they chose to maximize product quality and were willing to pay more. Today's consumer values and demands higher quality in all products and services but is not willing to pay more

for it. Globalization of trade has given consumers several alternatives to choose from, increasing their power to bargain for value-added products and services at competitive prices. Hence, products that offer more value at standard prices find favor with consumers.

2. *Dynamic industry conditions:* Most industries today are dynamic because reliance on a single competitive position is risky. Consider the case of Xerox. In the 1960s, after a careful analysis of the copier market, it chose to position itself in the corporate reproduction market by offering high-speed copiers. The company steadily strengthened its position by building copiers that fully met corporate needs for speed and by leasing the product rather than selling it outright. Soon, its market position was formidable. Both IBM and Kodak, firms that subsequently entered the same market segment with similar high-speed copiers, could not unseat Xerox and, furthermore, failed miserably in the copier business. However, the corporate market for copiers was not standing still. Businesses were looking for a copier they could own, rather than lease—a copier that offered higher quality and lower cost. Sensing an opportunity, Canon came on the scene with a high-quality, competitively priced copier that it sold rather than leased. Xerox soon lost its dominant position to Canon and has yet to recover. Today, competition in the corporate market for copiers is based on a cost-quality-speed combination.[19]

3. *Search for new competitive advantages:* Businesses themselves have been opting to compete across several dimensions with a view to gaining new competitive advantages. For example, cost leader Toyota has consistently raised the bar for competing in the automotive industry. Using its enormous cost advantage, the automotive maker has been adding quality, innovation, and customer service at no extra cost to the consumer, allowing it to steadily increase its global market share.[20] The result is that the traditional "cost-premium product" distinction in the automotive industry is slowly disappearing, and most firms presently compete on a cost-differentiation combination approach just to stay in business.

The cost-differentiation combination has become possible today, especially in manufacturing industries, as a result of the introduction of information technologies in product operations. Traditional automation did not permit design changes when cost efficiencies were the firm's goal. A cost strategist had to limit design changes (that is, standardize the product's features) to make the product in large volume and derive scale-related economies. Thus, a cost strategist could focus on cost minimization only, since a simultaneous concern for product enhancement had the potential to get the firm "stuck in the middle." But today's automation uses the computer in design and manufacturing operations, allowing the firm to offer design variety and undertake product enhancement frequently without jeopardizing cost goals. Computer-aided design (CAD) technologies generate several designs of the product without increasing costs because they have eliminated the need for prototyping. Computer-aided manufacturing (CAM) technologies have made variety manufacturing economical by allowing machines to be programmed and by minimizing the changeover time from one design to another. And, by linking several operational activities—procurement, design, production, storage, distribution—with the help of a computer, a firm can achieve lower cost, product variety, and fast market response simultaneously.[21]

To summarize, combination strategies appear to be relevant today in industries that undergo continuous disruption in market structure due to dramatic changes in technology, buyer preferences, and globalization. In these industries it is futile to search for distinct competitive segments—cost, quality, or customer service. Even if one were identified, it could not be sustained for long. Some industries demand a combination of these attributes. To be successful in these industries, a firm must identify the appropriate combination, position itself accordingly, and be able to defend that position.

Miles and Snow's Generic Business-Level Strategies

An alternative model of generic business-level strategies proposed by Miles and Snow presents three options for managers to choose from—*prospector, defender,* and *analyzer*—plus one to avoid—*reactor*.[22] Table 5.5 summarizes these strategies.

A **prospector** *is an entrepreneurial firm* that constantly explores and exploits new products or market opportunities to achieve high growth. A good example is Sony. It relentlessly invests in R&D and pursues technological innovations to develop and market new products in consumer electronics. To successfully implement the prospector strategy, a firm needs capabilities in opportunity identification, product and market development, and willingness to take high risks.

A **defender** *is a survivor* whose main aim is to protect its current business, maintain current market positions, and prevent competitor encroachment by effectively serving existing customers. One such company is Lincoln Electric Company, a manufacturer of arc welders. It does not invest in product innovation or make welders in different designs to attract new customers. Instead, it focuses on manufacturing existing designs more efficiently through computerized automation technologies and competitively prices them to retain its current customers.

An **analyzer** *is a prospector and a defender combined*. A firm pursuing an analyzer strategy seeks to protect its current businesses and to pursue new opportunities as well. Anheuser Busch is an analyzer, defending its primary business, beer, while also experimenting in theme parks. Many pharmaceutical firms may be viewed as analyzers because, while defending their current drugs in the marketplace, they also pursue the development of new drugs or the identification of new applications for their current drugs. To implement this strategy, a firm must promote creativity and flexibility without increasing cost. An analyzer strategy is relatively difficult to implement, but it may yield higher rewards if successfully implemented.

A **reactor** *has no consistent strategic approach*. It has no coherent plans, does not anticipate change, and reacts to environmental events as it deems fit. During the late 1990s, Kmart was clearly a reactor. By blindly responding to every move Wal-Mart made in pricing, product breadth, and location, Kmart made incoherent decisions that brought financial disaster, forcing the firm to seek bankruptcy protection in 2002.

Business-Level Strategies Based on the Industry Life Cycle

Business research indicates that most industries and the products they offer evolve through distinct stages, from emergence to growth and maturity. Some industries and products go into decline and eventually die. Business researchers have noted that

TABLE 5.5	Prospector, Defender, Analyzer, and Reactor Strategies	
STRATEGY	**DESCRIPTION**	**FIRMS USING**
Prospector	Focuses on continuous exploration of new product or market opportunities Demonstrates aggressive growth orientation Characterized by entrepreneurial orientation and risk-taking	3M Sony
Defender	Focuses on defending current products and market position and on preventing competitor encroachment by effectively serving existing customers	Lincoln Electric Bic
Analyzer	Focuses on defending current business Also pursues new opportunities	Pfizer Merck
Reactor	No coherent plans, aimless, does not anticipate change Reacts to environmental change haphazardly	Kmart

each stage is materially different from the others in regard to the rate of growth in demand, industry structure, technological requirements, and, hence, the intensity of competition. As a result, some researchers claim that the strategy and organizational resources needed to successfully compete at these stages will also be different. Let us now examine the stages of the **industry/product life cycle** and the business-level strategies that researchers have found to be appropriate for each stage.[23]

During **emergence,** a firm is in its formative stages. Sellers are few in number, suggesting minimal rivalry. Growth in demand is uncertain because the product has yet to be fully accepted by potential buyers. As a result, a firm's *aim is to survive* until the industry establishes itself. A firm does this by selling small quantities at a high price and, at the same time, controlling costs so as to break even. A firm must also continuously enhance the product's features to widen its appeal to potential buyers. It therefore employs promotional strategies to gain brand recognition. Strengths in product R&D and marketing are understandably vital for carrying out these activities, suggesting that a firm pursues a *pure differentiation strategy* at this stage. MP3 players and iPods are examples of products in the emergent stage.

At the **growth stage,** the industry is somewhat established. Sellers are many in number but demand expands rapidly, keeping competition subdued. Supplier and distribution segments fully emerge and the product's design undergoes incremental refinement. A firm's goal now is on realizing *rapid growth/market share* and *preventing new entry*. It achieves this by improving the product or service features to ensure a sizeable clientele and aggressively advertises to retain customers. To prevent entry, it locks in suppliers and distribution channels. Strengths in product engineering, advertising, and customer service are vital for performing these activities, suggesting that successful firms at this stage are *differentiators*. Digital photography and broadband Internet service are examples of products in the growth stage.

At the **maturity stage,** demand levels off and the industry is consolidated through mergers and acquisitions. Incumbent firms are now well positioned in the industry with stable market share. Due to the absence of new demand, competition intensifies and a firm's goal is to *retain its current market share*. With the product's design now standardized, the only way a firm can retain its market share is by increasing the level of customer service and holding price levels or even reducing them. A firm achieves this by automating production/processing to reduce costs and maintaining a high level of advertising and promotion to retain customers. Successful firms at this stage are *differentiators who enjoy high brand loyalty, cost leaders who have an above-average cost advantage,* or *focusers in narrow industry segments whose needs are highly specialized.* The cost and focus firms probably entered the industry at the beginning of the maturity stage. The personal computer is an example of a product at the maturity stage.

In the **decline stage,** demand for the product decreases, reducing opportunities for incumbent firms. Competition intensifies because industry capacity exceeds demand. *The aim of a firm is to maintain sales volume in a shrinking market but with a reduced asset base to lower costs.* A firm accomplishes this by (a) acquiring exiting firms to maintain sales volume and (b) selectively retrenching assets that add little value to sales in proportion to costs. Successful firms at this stage are *cost strategists whose costs are sufficiently low that the firm survives until it reinvents itself or is totally liquidated.* Computer disk drives and floppy disks are products in the decline stage.

Summary

Of the several obstacles to the firm's success, competition is the predominant one. Porter offers three generic competitive options by which a firm can organize its fight against competition: *cost leadership, differentiation,* and *focus.* Miles and Snow propose more or less comparable strategic choices: *prospector, defender,* and *analyzer.* Differentiators and prospectors are similar, as are cost leaders and defenders, whereas analyzers combine features of both cost leadership and differentiation, where feasible.

In cost leadership, the aim is to outperform rivals through internal cost minimization; in differentiation, it is through offering unique product or service features; and in focus it is through customizing to the needs of a niche. Porter suggests that the focus of each of these strategies is different; therefore, they require different internal mechanisms. Cost leadership requires product standardization (hence no variety in designs), high-volume production, and no market segmentation. Differentiation requires several unique designs, offered to distinct market segments, and supported by aggressive product R&D, advertising, and promotion. Focus strategy requires product/process customization to satisfy the unique preferences of the niche and to continuously improve the product or the process to defend the niche position.

Although cost leadership, differentiation, and focus are generic strategies, their selection depends on product and industry conditions. Cost leadership is appropriate when the product is a commodity and brands do not matter to customers. Differentiation is appropriate when buyer needs and uses of the product are diverse and buyers perceive value when the product is differentiated. Focus strategy should be chosen when a large unexploited niche for a product exists.

Although Porter recommends that a firm compete on a single dimension, dynamic markets and the need to create new competitive advantages are forcing firms in several industries to compete on a cost-differentiation combination. New technologies that involve the use of computers in operations are endowing firms with the flexibility they need to compete on multiple competitive dimensions—product variety, product quality, processing efficiency, timely customer responsiveness—without getting stuck in the middle.

The industry life cycle seems to influence strategy selection. During emergence and growth, differentiation seems appropriate. During the maturity stage, differentiation, cost, and focus strategies may be successful if effectively implemented. During the industry decline stage, cost leadership is considered to be more appropriate.

Chapter 5 Discussion Questions and Projects

Discussion Questions

1. Are there products and markets where only cost leadership or only differentiation strategy can be used? Discuss with an example.

2. Do you agree with the criticism of Porter's generic strategies that they are appropriate for stable industry environments only? Provide reasons for your answer.

3. Discuss the similarities and dissimilarities between Porter's generic strategy choices and Miles and Snow's.

Projects

1. Select two firms from the pharmaceutical industry, a differentiator (e.g., Pfizer) and a cost leader (e.g., Abbott Labs). Read about these firms on the Internet and in library sources. Prepare a brief report describing how their activities indicate the strategies they are said to be pursuing.

2. Select an industry that is at the growth stage and another that is at the decline stage. Select three firms from each of these industries and compare their financial performance over a five-year period. Determine the business strategy each of them is using and see whether it compares with what has been suggested in this chapter.

 ## Continuing Case

Southwest Airlines: Focused Cost Leadership

The Strategy

When Rollin King and Herb Kelleher decided to start Southwest Airlines as an alternative to road transportation, they had clearly defined their firm's business-level strategy: it would be *focused cost leadership*. Southwest would be positioned as a point-to-point, commuter-type air carrier appealing to travelers who take short-distance trips by car or bus. Within this niche, the firm would attract customers by offering fares comparable to bus fares and by providing superior customer service.

Southwest thus began business in the airline industry as a rival to ground transportation rather than to the established firms in the industry. By 1980, less than ten years after it began life as a short-haul carrier within the state of Texas, the company had set up commuter-type service between several U.S. cities and was well on its way to becoming a leader in passenger boarding. Identification of a unique market segment, not served by the established carriers, allowed Southwest to pursue its growth almost unchallenged. Selection of an appropriate strategy to compete within this segment allowed the firm to attract customers from substitute segments and to gain a dominant position in the airline industry fairly rapidly.

Consistent Internal Actions

To run its activities consistent with its planned business-level strategy, Southwest undertook several measures. These measures focused on (1) standardizing the firm's operations to lower cost, and (2) creating an informal work arrangement to achieve customer service quality. In operations, Southwest used only one type of aircraft, offered only standard in-flight services, operated from secondary airports only, and sold tickets directly to customers. In work arrangement, the firm used a relatively flat structure that not only reduced administrative expenses but also empowered employees to mutually adjust, allowing them to focus more on customers than on the hierarchy. Additionally, through employee selection the firm created an organization that voluntarily worked toward cost and customer service goals.

Effect on Performance

Southwest's well-conceived business-level strategy and the coherent decisions the firm made in pursuit of this strategy rewarded the firm handsomely. In an industry where the established firms were failing, Southwest was rapidly growing. By the early 1990s, the firm had become the most successful carrier— profitable every year since its inception. In 2004, Southwest enplaned 71 million passengers, the highest in the industry. It was the industry leader in market share with an 18 percent share of the U.S. market.

New Entry into the Niche and Intensifying Competition

Southwest's stellar performance, however, did not go unnoticed. Established hub-and-spoke airlines, recognizing the opportunities in the niche pioneered by Southwest Airlines, reacted strongly by starting their own low-cost subsidiaries. Several entrepreneurial start-ups (e.g., AirTran, ATA, Frontier, Independence Air, JetBlue) entered the niche, imitating Southwest Airlines. Some employed a cost-differentiation combination strategy (for example, discount fares along with in-flight service, such as meals, liquor, entertainment, and an upper-class cabin) to be more attractive. These developments increased the capacity in the most popular short-haul routes, leading to price wars and resulting in the first casualty among the low-cost carriers—ATA. In October 2004, ATA filed for bankruptcy under chapter 11. Soon thereafter, Independence Air indicated that it could follow suit.

Fine-tuning the Strategy

Escalating competition in the popular short-haul markets had the potential to threaten Southwest's top-line growth. To deal with this threat, Southwest Airlines aggressively sought to develop new underserved short-haul markets and, at the same time, seek opportunities outside its niche. During the late 1990s, Southwest developed new short-haul routes and added medium-distance routes (1,000 miles) to its service. In 2002, it entered the long-haul market, flying point-to-point between the East Coast and the West Coast, thus actively competing for business passengers. In late 2004, the company entered into a code-sharing agreement with ATA that would allow it to access major airports in New York, Boston, and Washington, D.C., and further, to offer services to distant locations such as Hawaii. In addition to market penetration and developing new markets, the firm has started to aggressively promote its brand, offering well-defined service to both business and leisure travelers along with its signature discount fares. Southwest's current CEO, Gary Kelly, indicates that the firm is seriously contemplating some value-added in-flight services so as to retain its competitive edge. All these enhancements have led industry analysts to conclude that Southwest Airlines will continue to shape airline industry competition for a long time to come.

Discussion Questions

1. Describe Southwest Airlines' business-level strategy. Are the operational and organizational mechanisms the firm has employed consistent with this strategy? Explain.

2. Identify the threats developing in the short-haul airline segment and describe how Southwest is fine-tuning its strategy to respond to them.

3. How did Southwest alter airline competition when it entered the industry in 1971? How is it altering competition now?

Source: M. Maynard, "Are Peanuts No Longer Enough?" *New York Times,* March 7, 2004, Business section; "Turbulent Times," The *Economist,* July 8, 2004; "Commercial Aviation," *Report to Congressional Committees by the U.S. Government Accountability Office,* August 2004; M. Maynard, "Southwest adds ATA flights from Chicago," *New York Times,* January 14, 2005, Business section.

Corporate-Level Strategy: Gaining Advantage by Managing a Portfolio of Businesses

Opening Case

The Greyhound Corporation began business in 1914 as a small jitney transport service in Hibbing, Minnesota. It carried leisure travelers to nearby attractions and miners to work at the Mesabi Iron Range. The service was an instant success. The novelty of a bus ride and low fares enabled the company to quickly generate a sizeable passenger volume and achieve profitability.

During the next several years, Greyhound grew rapidly, aided by an unprecedented postwar boom in the U.S. economy and the resultant increase in leisure travel. Initial growth came through **geographic expansion strategies.** The company aggressively expanded its bus service to major U.S. cities by acquiring local bus companies and by establishing a network of regional affiliates. Greyhound kept its fares low to prevent competitors from entering the market and to induce people to choose the bus rather than other means of transport for long-distance travel. By the 1950s, Greyhound Corporation was an international bus line, connecting most cities in the United States and Canada. Its five thousand buses generated annual revenues exceeding $300 million.

Greyhound's revenues hit a plateau by the late 1950s, however, because the bus transportation industry had matured. While Greyhound's routes produced a steady cash flow each year, income stopped growing because no new routes were available to generate additional revenues. Fare hikes that would have increased revenues were ruled out because the company was afraid of losing business to Trailways, a major competitor, and to substitutes such as airlines and railroads. At the same time, Greyhound's operating expenses were mounting as a result of rising bus maintenance and payroll costs, which reduced profitability.

Greyhound thought that it could reduce costs by **vertically expanding** its operations into bus production. It estimated saving millions of dollars each year if it built the buses it needed rather than buying them from its supplier, General Motors. An added attraction in this move was that the company could also build buses for sale to others, generating extra revenues. In 1961, Greyhound bought Motor Coach Industries and became a vertically integrated company—building buses and running a bus line. A second acquisition in the equipment leasing business was added to the firm's portfolio in 1963. Greyhound was now a multibusiness firm with a corporate headquarters that made strategic decisions concerning what future **diversifications** should be made to strengthen the firm's growth and profitability.

By the mid-1960s, Greyhound's *vertical integration* and *diversification strategies* were paying off. Revenues had doubled to nearly $600 million and operating expenses had decreased. To further strengthen its position in the bus transportation business, Greyhound diversified into several charter travel, leisure, and tourism businesses. But soon its diversifications were no longer related to its original business. In 1970 it bought a major food business, Armour & Company, which also owned Dial Corporation, a consumer products company. By the early 1980s, Greyhound had become a **conglomerate** competing in five different businesses: bus transportation, bus manufacturing, financial services, consumer products, and food. Its revenues now totaled over $4 billion.

Greyhound's initial moves within the transportation industry were beneficial to the firm, but the later acquisitions proved detrimental since they took the firm far away from the bus business it knew well. Unable to manage a complex set of unrelated businesses about which it knew very little, Greyhound embarked on a **divestment strategy:** disposing of businesses that demanded more attention but contributed less to overall profits. In 1983 it sold Armour (the food business) while retaining Dial. Greyhound was now known as Greyhound-Dial. But soon, problems arose for the bus business. The airline industry was deregulated in 1978, leading to intense competition and price wars in that industry and making airline travel relatively cheaper. The bus industry itself was deregulated in 1981, increasing competitive rivalry and the cost of running the bus business. Compounding these problems, the bus transit workers' union rejected Greyhound's appeal for a wage freeze the firm said it needed to remain viable in the bus transportation business. No longer

(continued)

competitive, Greyhound sold its bus business in 1986 to a Texas-based investor group. It then changed its name to Dial Corporation and now makes and sells personal-care products, toiletries, and detergents.[1]

G reyhound's history points out the strategic options available to a firm when its current business is no longer attractive. Additionally, it highlights the importance of choosing those options carefully for the firm's long-term success. The options, collectively known as corporate-level strategy, are the subject of this chapter. We describe corporate-level strategy, discuss its meaning, purpose, and effectiveness as a tool for building competitive advantage, and explore the dangers of making the wrong choices. We start with a brief description of how corporate-level strategy evolves for a firm. We then define and discuss four important corporate-level strategy choices: **single-business concentration, vertical integration, diversification,** and **divestment.** We describe the merits and demerits of each and the conditions under which they will be effective. We conclude this chapter by describing a framework that diversified firms use to monitor and manage their corporate portfolio of businesses.

How Corporate-Level Strategy Evolves for a Firm

Like Greyhound, almost all firms begin as single-product companies serving a single market. This product-market concentration allows firms to rapidly achieve the sales volume required for profits. But soon, market maturity sets in and competition intensifies, putting a hold on further company growth and profits. Some businesses continue to operate as single-product, single-market firms even under such hostile industry conditions by employing defensive strategies to protect their current sales and profits. But many others explore new strategic opportunities under such conditions to generate uninterrupted growth or even to maintain current sales and profits.[2] These opportunities range from an extension of the current product line to expanding current operations and further moving the firm into entirely new lines of business. The choices a firm makes in this regard evolve over the life of a firm (see Figure 6.1), requiring the addition of a layer of management to coordinate interunit activities.[3] That layer is identified as the corporate level, and the strategies emerging from that level are called **corporate-level strategies** (see Figure 6.2).

For Greyhound, the corporate level emerged when the firm decided to vertically expand* its area of operations from bus lines to bus manufacturing/assembly and to further diversify into new lines of business—financial services, food, and consumer products. As a single-business firm, Greyhound had been most concerned with how to compete in its bus lines business. As a diversified firm engaged in several businesses, its concerns were not only how to compete in individual businesses but also how to develop and manage a synergistic portfolio of businesses for maximal benefits.[†] Thus the decision to pursue a diversification strategy led to the creation of a

---

*Vertical expansion, more popularly referred to as vertical integration, is a corporate-level strategy in which a firm extends its operations along the value chain. If Nike decides to make the components for its running shoes in-house instead of buying them from outside vendors, or to sell running shoes through company-owned stores instead of outside retailers, it is extending its operations—it is pursuing a vertical integration strategy. We will have more to say about this strategy later.

[†]The term *synergy* means the working together of two or more things to produce an effect that is greater than the sum of their individual effects. If two or more tasks or business units, working together, create more value than when they work independently, synergy is supposed to exist among them. Synergy is most likely to occur with related diversification, a corporate-level strategy.

FIGURE 6.1 How Corporate-Level Strategy Evolves for a Firm

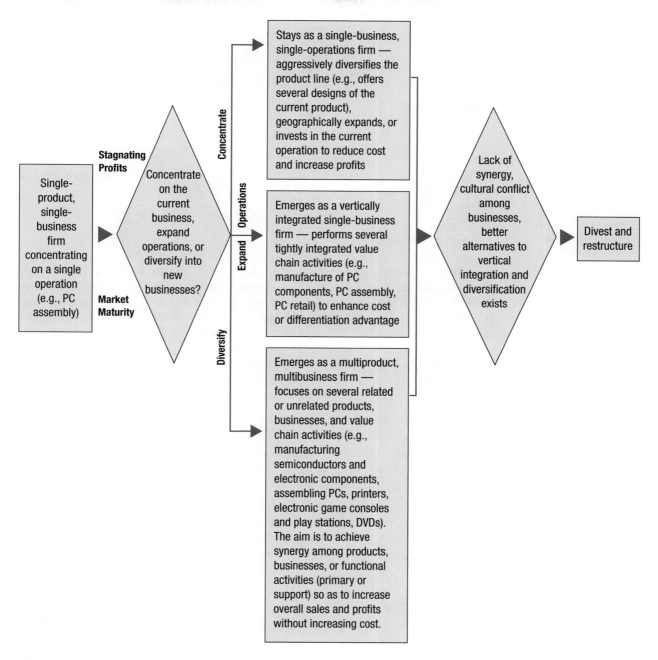

FIGURE 6.2   Greyhound Corporation in 1963

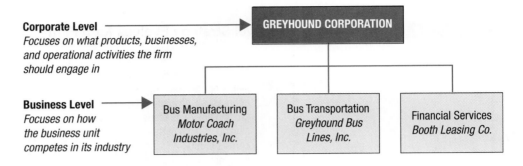

Corporate Level
Focuses on what products, businesses, and operational activities the firm should engage in

GREYHOUND CORPORATION

Business Level
Focuses on how the business unit competes in its industry

Bus Manufacturing
Motor Coach Industries, Inc.

Bus Transportation
Greyhound Bus Lines, Inc.

Financial Services
Booth Leasing Co.

corporate level to administer it. Figure 6.2 illustrates this point by distinguishing the roles that corporate and business levels play in a diversified firm.

Corporate-Level Strategy Choices

Corporate-level strategy represents the firm's decisions and actions to gain advantages over rivals by managing a portfolio of products or businesses. It focuses on the *scope of the business enterprise*—that is, the range of products/businesses in which the firm will compete and the value chain activities it will perform to realize growth or profits. Strategic choices provide the firm with a basis for deciding on the products or businesses in which it will compete and the competencies it must acquire to successfully compete in them. The aim in corporate-level strategic decisions is to assemble a balanced portfolio of products or businesses and matching competitive capabilities that can create a sustainable growth or profit opportunity for the firm.[4] The exact strategy the firm selects will emerge from its response to the following questions:

1. Should our product/market scope *concentrate* on a single business/industry or should it be diversified across several businesses/industries?

2. If a single business, should we pursue *vertical integration* and, if so, in what direction? Should we integrate more toward raw materials and components, more toward retailing and distribution, or toward both?

3. If a *diversified* business, should the businesses share a common technology, share common customers, or be unrelated to each other?

4. Do we have products, businesses, or assets that are unprofitable or do not fit with our overall mission and that should, therefore, be *divested*?

Single-business concentration, vertical integration, diversification, and divestment are thus corporate-level strategy choices. A point worth emphasizing here is that all these choices stress business scope; that is, whatever its decision, the firm should be involved in a range of products, businesses, or operational activities. In a single-business concentration, this range is restricted to one business or industry. In vertical integration, the range is in the value chain activities the firm pursues. In diversification, the firm offers a range of products across several industries. In divestment, the firm adjusts this range through restructuring and retrenchment—that is, disposing of operational assets or businesses that do not fit with the firm's vision and long-term

FIGURE 6.3 How Corporate-Level Strategy Influences Performance

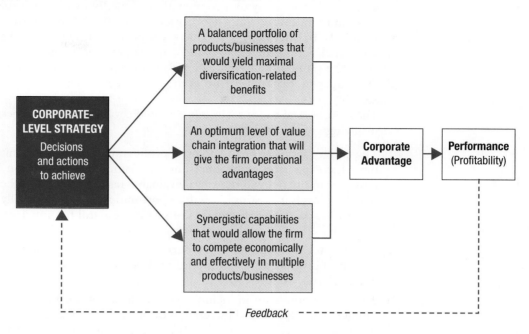

goals. *Thus, corporate-level strategy is the pursuit of diversification within a business, across businesses, or in value chain activities to generate growth or profitability.*

Recall from Chapter 5 that business-level strategy builds a firm's competitive advantage (market position, internal competencies), which, in turn, boosts financial performance. Likewise, corporate-level strategy builds a firm's *corporate advantage,* which, in turn, beneficially influences the firm's financial performance (see Figure 6.3).[5] **Corporate advantage** *is defined as the ability of a corporation to integrate several products and businesses into a cohesive operation that creates more value than the sum of its parts.*[6] This ability emerges from the diversification and divestment/restructuring decisions the firm makes in the selection of products, businesses, and value chain activities in which it will engage. These decisions provide the corporation with a balanced portfolio of closely knit product operations and businesses to manage, making interunit coordination easy to accomplish. They also provide the corporation with an optimal bundle of competencies that each product and business unit can share and thus allow the firm to perform better than single-product firms that have no access to such synergies.

Single-Business Concentration

Some companies opt for a **single-business concentration;** that is, they choose to focus on a single business, pursuing a range of products and markets within that business or industry only. Coca-Cola (beverages), McDonald's (fast food), Starbucks (hot-beverage retailing), and Dell (computers) are examples of such firms. The strategy they pursue for achieving long-term growth or profitability is to explore new product or market opportunities within a single business. The implementation of this strategy includes any or a combination of the following: (a) expanding product lines within a business (Coca-Cola offers over fifty different brands of soft drinks worldwide); (b) offering new products within an existing brand (Cherry Coke was a new product within the Coke brand); and (c) expanding geographically— that is, offering the same product in new markets (Starbucks seeks growth by aggressively developing new markets for its gourmet coffee in the heartland of the United States).

There are several reasons why a firm would choose a single-business concentration for realizing growth or profits.

1. The current industry provides ample profit and growth opportunities through geographic expansion or product-line extensions. Diversification into new businesses or industries will draw away valuable resources, leaving the firm weak and unable to exploit existing growth opportunities. This is especially true for a firm like Starbucks, whose premium coffee business still has much room for growth left both in the U.S. and international markets.

2. Demand for the product in the current market is fairly stable, yielding a steady stream of profits and making product-line extension or business diversification unnecessary.

3. The firm is dominant in its industry and does not need to secure additional advantages through vertical integration or diversification. For example, Intel is dominant in the semiconductor industry and has not felt the need to vertically or horizontally diversify.

4. The firm's knowledge is specialized and limited to the current business. This knowledge is not easily transferable to the management of other businesses. Consider Exxon as an example. It diversified into the office-automation business during the 1970s to offset falling revenues from its petroleum business. But soon it had to divest itself of this business because its specialized skills in oil exploration, drilling, and refining did not fit well with the office-automation business, where R&D, marketing, and after-sales service skills were more critical.[7]

However, focusing on a single business has disadvantages too. It is risky—tantamount to putting all your eggs in one basket. Economic downturns can adversely affect the volume of demand, creating uneven cash flows and disrupting financial plans. Lifestyle changes and industry maturity can reduce the demand for the product, significantly shrinking the firm's revenues. Radical change in the product's technology can make the firm's product obsolete and bankrupt the firm. Besides risk, there is also a second major disadvantage. There is only so much room that a single business can offer for growth: the range of products possible within a single business is limited. For these reasons, some firms explore vertical integration or diversification at some point in time.

Vertical Integration

Vertical integration expands a firm's scope of operations in its business. Vertical integration adds new operations to current operations by sequentially extending the firm's activities along the value chain. For example, a manufacturer of dress shoes that buys the leather for making its shoes from outside suppliers may decide to process the leather in-house. It may implement this decision either by acquiring a tannery or developing the needed skills internally and making the necessary investment in plant and tools. The firm has now extended its shoe manufacturing operation by adding to it the production of supplies for its shoes. Similarly, it may acquire a retailer and sell its shoes directly to the end user. In each of these instances, the firm is said to be using a vertical integration strategy. When this strategy takes the firm further away from the end product and the end user toward raw material and component production, it is called **backward integration.** When it moves the firm closer to the market and the end user, it is called **forward integration.** Figure 6.4 illustrates vertical integration and the directions it can take.

A fully vertically integrated firm sequentially performs, in-house, most of the activities in the value chain: raw material processing, component production, product assembly, marketing, distribution, and after-sales service. The level of integration and the direction in which the firm pursues integration (that is, backward or forward) depends on the competitive conditions in the industry and the extent of control the firm should have over product operations to be successful.

Vertical integration should not be confused with **horizontal integration.** Horizontal integration is the acquisition of direct competition—for example, a shoe manufacturer buys another shoe manufacturer in the same industry segment. The aim in horizontal integration is to achieve a rapid increase in revenues and market share. Exxon increased its revenues from $120 billion to $180 billion when it acquired Mobil in 1999.* Hewlett Packard instantaneously doubled its market share in the personal computer business from 8 percent to 16 percent when it acquired Compaq Computer in 2002.[8] But a more important reason why firms pursue

FIGURE 6.4 **Vertical Integration**

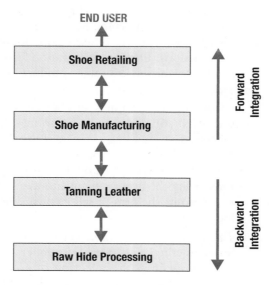

---

* *Hoover's Company Profiles.*

horizontal integration is to reduce competition and gain market dominance that gives them pricing power. In industries that are matured or where the product is a commodity, pricing power is critical for competitive success and horizontal integration is a common occurrence. Telecommunications is one such industry where fixed-line long-distance telephony has reached maturity (it is increasingly being replaced by cellular telephony) and horizontal integration has become extremely common.

Strategic Importance of Vertical Integration

Vertical integration gives the firm control over successive stages of the product's processing, marketing, and retailing. Does this control bestow competitive advantages? How does vertical integration help a firm achieve higher growth or profitability? You may recall from earlier chapters that strategy facilitates higher performance by building strong market positions and/or internal capabilities to overcome threats and exploit opportunities. The following list describes how vertical integration strengthens a firm's market position and internal capabilities, thereby facilitating higher performance.

1. *Deters potential competitor entry:* New entrants intensify competition by limiting a firm's ability to increase price and earn above-average profits. Vertical integration deters entry in two ways: (a) by increasing the cost of entry, since the new firm must similarly integrate to achieve the advantages of integration enjoyed by the incumbent firm, and (b) by limiting or eliminating avenues of supply and distribution to the new firm.[9] The petroleum industry has long pursued vertical integration to prevent new entry. Because oil is a commodity, entry barriers are the only way by which incumbent firms can gain some control over price.

2. *Eliminates threats of powerful suppliers and distributors:* Backward integration frees the firm from powerful suppliers who can curtail shipment or increase prices. It thus ensures ready availability of supplies to meet market demand without an attendant increase in costs. Forward integration eliminates dependence on powerful distributors who can refuse to distribute the product unless they receive higher commissions. Forward integration also provides the firm with direct customer feedback, which is critical for product innovation.

3. *Creates new product and market opportunities:* Vertical integration allows the firm entry into new products and businesses. Greyhound's backward integration into bus production eventually led to its building buses for others and entering the motor coach building business. In the shoe manufacturer we considered earlier, backward integration not only supplies tanned leather to its shoe-making operations but also creates an opportunity to sell leather to other shoe manufacturers, thus giving the firm an entry into the tannery business. Similarly, forward integration permits the firm to sell its own shoes and those made by others, thus allowing entry into the shoe retailing business.

4. *Facilitates cost advantage:* Vertical integration eliminates time and costs incurred in transacting with outside suppliers or distributors.[10] **Transaction costs** are monies spent in the selection of a competitive vendor/distributor, contract negotiations, payment of legal fees, and inventory ordering.[11] By performing several adjacent activities in-house, a firm not only eliminates such costs but is also able to streamline workflow and achieve cost efficiencies through tighter processing.

5. *Facilitates differentiation advantage:* For a firm planning a differentiation advantage through product quality and added value, vertical integration is an appropriate tool. Backward integration by a finished goods manufacturer ensures the quality of input and processing and, thus, the quality of output. Sony is heavily backward integrated into component manufacturing to ensure the quality of its television sets and audio products.[12] Likewise, forward integration by a raw material supplier allows for value to be added to the output, enabling the firm to charge a higher price for its product. By controlling successive stages of a product's processing, a firm can also raise the overall value of its products and services to the customer.[13] Read Strategy in Practice 6.1 to learn how one firm, a raw meat supplier to marketers of processed food, successfully employed vertical integration to achieve differentiation advantage and generate significant growth.

6. *Prevents technology imitation:* For firms with proprietary technology, there is considerable risk of imitation if component manufacturing is outsourced. Backward integration eliminates this risk. An additional problem with outsourcing is that it turns the control of a crucial component over to the supplier, increasing the supplier's bargaining power. For these reasons, Polaroid manufactured its proprietary components in-house for many years.[14]

Problems with Vertical Integration

Vertical integration makes sense when a firm needs to capture any or a combination of the strategic advantages we listed. But vertical integration also has drawbacks, and hence managers must approach it with caution, because once integration has been accomplished, reversing course is often difficult. The following are some of the disadvantages of vertical integration.

1. *Makes a firm less flexible:* Vertical integration requires firms to invest large sums in fixed assets. A highly integrated firm gets wedded to its expensive assets. But rapid technological change or declining demand for the product requires the firm to quickly adapt or exit the industry. Under those circumstances, many integrated firms cling to their costly assets, unable to change or exit. Thus, vertical integration creates inflexibilities for a firm and increases business risk.

2. *Requires new skills to be mastered:* Forward and backward integration both call for businesses to learn and master radically different technical skills. Besides requiring time and money, they divert resources from current operations, which can adversely affect what the firm does best now.

3. *Can entail cost disadvantages:* Vertical integration may not yield the expected cost savings because company-owned suppliers and retailing operations have no incentive to keep costs down since the firm is their guaranteed customer. This commitment restricts the firm's ability to use external sources even if their prices are attractive.

4. *Requires capacity balancing:* The capacities of linked operations must be balanced to obtain a smooth flow of operations. For example, sufficient upstream capacity is needed to adequately feed downstream operations when demand for the end product is high. An imbalance can create bottlenecks along the line or can create excess capacity. Capacity balancing is difficult to achieve and imbalances lead to operational inefficiencies.

Table 6.1 describes when and when not to pursue vertical integration.

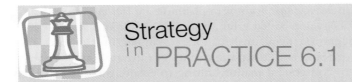

Strategy
in PRACTICE 6.1

HOW ONE FIRM PURSUED VERTICAL INTEGRATION TO POPULARIZE ITS BRAND AND ACHIEVE GROWTH

Grain and slaughtered meat are commodities. The sellers of these products have no control over price. Price is determined by market conditions—quantity of grain and meat demanded and supplied. Since demand and supply conditions fluctuate frequently, the price of these products also fluctuates frequently. As a result, grain and meat suppliers suffer from earnings instability, making financial planning difficult. To achieve a stable and predictable income each quarter, control over product pricing is necessary.

One way grain and meat suppliers have sought control over price is by processing raw grain or meat and offering value-added products. Grain merchants turn wheat into flour and sell processed flour to bakers. Hog and cattle farmers slaughter their animals and sell processed meat, instead of raw meat, to packers. Vertical integration of material input and processing guarantees the quality and consistency of output. Firms use that as a basis to demand higher prices.

Today, grain and meat suppliers are becoming fully integrated, performing every activity from raw material production to food processing, marketing, and delivery. Forward integration has become popular since grain and meat suppliers can sell their products under their own brand name and charge a premium price.

One firm that has pursued full vertical integration in recent times is Smithfield Foods. Started as a slaughterhouse and a raw meat supplier in the state of Virginia in 1936, Smithfield's performance was anything but stellar during its first forty years. Sales in 1975 were a meager $12 million, and the company was in frequent financial distress. To achieve sales growth and income stability, it embarked on an aggressive strategy of vertical integration.

Between 1981 and 2000, Smithfield acquired several firms in meat processing, packing, and marketing. Its acquisitions enabled the company to become fully vertically integrated, especially in the pork business—from raising hogs to processing pork, packing it, and marketing it under its own brand name. Vertical integration allowed the firm to generate high-volume production, reduce costs, and increase profits. But more importantly, it permitted Smithfield to exercise tighter control over operations all along the value chain and to ensure the quality, output consistency, and safety of its products—a combination of strengths that are unique in the meat industry. Armed with these strengths, Smithfield embarked on a marketing strategy, differentiating its products on product quality and safety. The results have been astounding. Today, Smithfield's brands have become extremely popular and command a premium price. The company has significantly increased its sales, market share, and profitability in the pork and beef business. Joseph Luter, Smithfield's CEO, summarized how vertical integration helped his firm: "When hog prices rise, our hog raising group enjoys greater profitability. When they decline, our hog processing companies contribute more to the bottom line. Vertical integration is the reason why we have been reporting record results compared to competition." In 2005, Smithfield's sales were $11.3 billion, many times over its 1975 sales of $12 million.

Source: www.smithfield.com; Smithfield Food Annual Reports for various years; P. C. Squires and L. Waltz, "New Path for Pork Giant," *Virginia Business,* November 2004; "Smithfield Foods report record earnings for fiscal 2005," http://news.moneycentral.msn.com, June 3, 2005.

Alternatives to Vertical Integration

Vertical integration should be avoided if it does not materially strengthen competitive position or provide a distinctive cost or differentiation advantage. Given the high risks associated with it, a firm can consider alternative approaches that yield more or less the same benefits as vertical integration. Following are some of these:

| TABLE 6.1 | When and When Not to Vertically Integrate |

WHEN TO INTEGRATE	WHEN NOT TO INTEGRATE
Suppliers and retailers/distributors are few, the market is inefficient, and transaction costs are high.	There are many suppliers and retailers/distributors, the market is efficient, and transaction costs are low.
The product is a commodity and vertical integration can create perceived difference in the product and allow premium pricing. The firm's product technology is proprietary.	Gross margins are already high and adding value will not enhance pricing power or increase gross margins.
Vertical integration can create market power by raising barriers to entry.	Alternatives to vertical integration can provide the same advantages as vertical integration.
The industry is declining and suppliers and retailers/distributors are exiting the industry.	The industry is not yet established, and demand as well as technological uncertainties exist.

1. *Tapered integration:* In tapered integration, the firm makes only part of the needed supplies in-house, buying the rest from outsiders. Similarly, it sells its output through independent retailers in addition to company-owned outlets. This *partial integration strategy* minimizes risk compared to full integration. For years, AT&T pursued tapered integration by selling the telephones it made through its own retail stores and through Sears and Kmart.

2. *Long-term contract/vertical alliance:* Long-term cooperative contracts with outside suppliers and buyers following a thorough search and selection process enables a firm to build a trusting relationship with them that eliminates the need for vertical integration. Such contracts are generally referred to as **strategic alliances** of the vertical type (that is, between a supplier and a buyer). In these alliances, the contracting parties commit themselves to a sustained and mutually rewarding relationship by finding ways to reduce cost or improve quality in the value creation process.

3. *Issuing threats:* Sometimes, mere threats of integration may do the job. In the automotive industry, General Motors and Ford are known to keep suppliers' urge to raise price in check by constantly threatening to manufacture key components themselves.

Diversification

Whereas vertical integration expands operations within a product or business, **diversification** moves the firm into new products or new lines of business.[15] A diversified firm has a portfolio of products or businesses and competes in more than one industry or market. Most large organizations today are diversified firms.

Why Do Firms Diversify?

A firm contemplates diversification for several reasons:

1. *Limited growth opportunities in the current business:* Market maturity, decline, or intense competition limits growth opportunities in the current business or industry.[16]

Greyhound moved into other lines of business when the bus transportation industry stopped growing. Dell and Hewlett Packard have lately diversified into the consumer electronics business (flat panel television sets) because of stagnation in the computer hardware business.[17] Coca-Cola and Pepsi-Cola have been aggressively pursuing global diversification, especially focusing on developing country markets because demand for carbonated soft drinks in the developed country markets has reached saturation limits.

2. *Income volatility:* Income frequently fluctuates and is unpredictable when current business is cyclical or susceptible to economic change. Smithfield Foods (described in Strategy in Practice 6.1) pursued vertical integration and product/ market diversification to minimize income and profit fluctuations caused by the volatility in its meat packaging business.

3. *Risk:* Radical technological changes are occurring in the current product or industry creating high levels of business risk.

4. *Excess resources:* The firm has excess resources (technological, marketing, or financial) that it can effectively use to move into new products or businesses and increase sales revenues.[18]

5. *Market power:* By competing in several markets, a firm can strengthen its overall competitive position. For example, it can use profits earned in one market to support a price war in another.[19]

6. *Economies of scope:* Diversification allows a firm to exploit existing assets in new operations and derive **economies of scope**, the cost savings arising from the common use of strategic assets.

Diversification into a new business is fraught with risk.[20] One way firms attempt to reduce this risk is by seeking diversification opportunities that can be implemented with current resources, capabilities, and core competencies. Existing raw material resources, production processes, and distribution networks or a certain skill the firm possesses may allow it to offer a second product without jeopardizing current operations. For example, cable service providers now offer Internet service using existing cable lines in a way that does not adversely affect the cable business. Diversifications of this type, which can be implemented with existing strategic assets (tangible or intangible), are called related diversification. **Related diversification** reduces risk by eliminating the need for investments in new fixed assets. Besides minimizing risk, it offers cost savings too, since it permits asset sharing by the firm's different businesses.

But not all diversifications are related to the firm's current business. On occasion, a firm may diversify into new businesses that cannot be implemented with the firm's current strategic assets; they require totally new resources and capabilities. Such diversifications are called **conglomerate diversification.**

Related Diversification

Related diversification implies that the new business the firm is getting into is related to its current core business in some way. It may mean sharing the same technological resources and competencies or customer base and marketing channels. Diversifications based on the same core technology are called **concentric diversifications.** Consider 3M as an example. It initially made and sold bonding products called

FIGURE 6.5 **Concentric and Horizontal Diversifications**

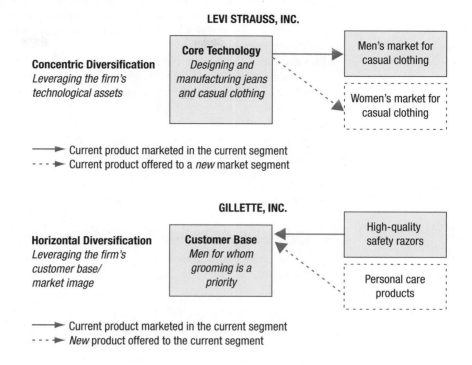

adhesives to industrial clients. Using this same technology, it diversified into the household market with Scotch tape, masking tape, and Post-it notes. Similarly, Levi Strauss initially made jeans for men. Using the same technological resources, it diversified into the women's apparel business by making and marketing dress jeans and casual clothes for women.

In contrast, diversifications that leverage a firm's current customer base or marketing assets are called **horizontal diversifications.** You know that Gillette became popular among men for whom grooming is a priority with its high-quality safety razors. It later exploited this market image to diversify into personal care and skin care products, such as cleansing lotions, facial moisturizers, pre-shave gels, and post-shave soothers, and marketed them to the same quality-conscious, well-groomed men. Figure 6.5 shows concentric and horizontal diversifications.

To summarize, using a "rule of thumb" definition, concentric diversification means offering the current product to a new customer. Horizontal diversification means offering a new product to the current customer. In each case, the firm synergistically employs its existing strategic assets: in concentric diversification, synergy is in the firm's technological assets; in horizontal diversification, it is in the marketing assets.

Unrelated Diversification

When a cash-rich firm plans to diversify into other businesses but does not have unique resources or competencies in its existing business to leverage, unrelated diversification is the only option. The firm acquires and operates a portfolio of businesses that do not have a commonality in their products, markets, or technology. Such diversifications are called **conglomerate diversifications.** Firms such as General Electric, Tyco International, and ITT pursue conglomerate diversification. General Electric, for example, is involved in diverse businesses that make products for both consumers and businesses: consumer appliances, medical diagnostic products, jet engines, electrical transformers, plastics, broadcasting services, and consumer finance services. This form of diversification is pursued predominantly for any or a combination of the following reasons: to generate a higher cash flow, gain market power, reduce the risk of relying on a single business, or avoid government scrutiny that targets firms concentrating in a single industry for possible monopoly behavior. However, because conglomerate diversification lacks technological or market-based synergy, it is expensive to implement. Firms pursuing it attempt to reduce costs by: (1) diversifying into businesses that are stable and offer a steady, positive cash flow, (2) maintaining a lean corporate management structure, and (3) letting acquired businesses operate autonomously.

The Strategic Importance of Diversification

How does diversification generate competitive advantages? The following examples explain how:

1. *Confers market power:* As mentioned earlier, diversification gives a firm certain market advantages not available to a single-business firm. *First,* a diversified firm can use the profits earned in a favorable market to support price wars in a not-so-favorable market (tactics known as **cross-subsidization**) and gain competitive advantage.[21] For example, in the telecommunications service provider industry, the business segment offers more opportunity for pricing and profits than does the residential segment. Using this advantage, and with the help of profits earned in the business segment, diversified telephone service providers have engaged in price wars in the residential long-distance market to gain market share. *Second,* a diversified firm can create a competitive stalemate—that is, keep other similarly diversified firms in check. By threatening to strike them in markets where they are weak, a diversified firm can stop other diversified firms from striking it in markets where it is weak.[22] *Third,* diversification can prevent new entry. A diversified firm can set up a reciprocal buying arrangement with other similarly diversified firms, thus closing markets to potential entrants.[23]

2. *Builds corporate advantage:* Diversified firms have a unique edge over nondiversified firms: corporate advantage.[24] By bringing together several products and businesses and letting them share their skills and competencies, corporations enable each operation to compete more successfully (either by reducing costs or by enhancing differentiation) than if they were independent units. For example, compare Xerox to Canon. Xerox started out in the photocopier business and has stayed in that business. Canon started in the photography business and became known for the quality of its cameras, but it later diversified by adding photocopier and optical equipment (medical imaging, TV lenses) businesses. Using its skills in designing quality cameras, Canon has successfully built and marketed high-quality copiers. For the last several years, Canon has been the market leader in copiers and its success is largely due to its ability to transfer skills from the camera business to the copier business on an ongoing basis.[25]

3. *Offers economies of scope:* The most commonly mentioned strategic advantage in the context of diversification is economies of scope. By employing an existing tangible or intangible asset in several businesses, a firm is able to spread the fixed costs among them and gain cost advantages on each of the products made and sold. For example, the costs to a cable service provider of offering broadband Internet service is far lower than it is for a new firm that must invest large amounts of money to lay the cable network.

4. *Strengthens negotiating power over suppliers and buyers:* A diversified firm operates several businesses. When these businesses need similar components and other supplies and these orders can be aggregated, the resulting order quantity can be enormous. The firm that centralizes the purchasing function at the corporate level can thus enjoy a high degree of negotiating power over suppliers. Likewise, the power of a diversified firm over buyers can be equally immense. Its product diversity and consequent ability to provide total customer solutions or "one-stop" shopping appeals to buyers who seek to minimize procurement costs by limiting the number of suppliers they deal with.

Problems with Diversification

Although diversification offers both competency and market-based advantages, a number of problems are associated with it. Generally speaking, real-world evidence of its beneficial effect on company profits is mixed. Some researchers have found highly diversified firms to be less profitable than those that are focused.[26],* In several instances, diversifications that were initially touted as brilliant, with claims of their huge profit potential, were eventually found to be mistakes and the acquired businesses had to be divested, incurring huge losses.[27] Following are some reasons why a diversification strategy may not deliver the expected result:

1. *Dilutes focus:* In general, a single-business firm has focus and, as a result, can monitor the performance of its operations effectively. For a diversified firm, diversity of operations creates distraction, diluting its ability to effectively monitor each operation. There is no identifiable optimal level of diversification beyond which control becomes problematic. As a result, a firm does not know when to stop diversifying and can end up overdiversified. Overdiversification can lead to inefficiencies in portfolio planning, dilution of corporate control, and a negative impact on overall operational performance. As the opening case indicates, Greyhound could not effectively monitor the performance of its core businesses due to the unmanageable size of its portfolio and, as a result, lost its prize holding, the bus lines.

2. *Encourages empire building:* The goal of diversification is to pursue new opportunities that will increase the firm's revenues and provide more value to shareholders. But some research studies have found that an important reason managers seek diversification is to fatten their own pockets through empire building.[28] By growing the size of the firm, managers enhance their prestige, pay, and bonus; more importantly, by directing diversification in a way that increases the firm's demands

---

*A quick comparison of Coca-Cola's profit performance with that of PepsiCo supports this finding. Coca-Cola is a single-business firm focusing on beverage products only, whereas PepsiCo is a multibusiness firm, diversified into convenience food and beverages. For the five-year period ending 2004, Coca-Cola's net profit margin averaged 18 percent compared to PepsiCo's 12 percent for the same period.

for their particular skills, managers ensure their job security.[29] As a result, the temptation for managers to diversify and grow for the sake of growth (not because it adds any value for the shareholders) and for personal gain is high, resulting in unwanted diversifications and the eventual divestment of acquired businesses, causing the firm significant losses.

3. *Incurs bureaucratic costs:* To be successful, diversification must achieve a higher level of coordination among the business units. Close coordination among distinct operations in various business units is what allows them to share strategic assets effectively to realize economies of scope. The structural mechanisms needed to achieve the required coordination are highly complex. If these mechanisms are not designed carefully, frequent bottlenecks can arise in the flow of work and information among operations. Resolving such bottlenecks requires top management intervention in operational conflicts, wasting managerial resources and increasing administrative cost.

Despite these potential drawbacks, the merits of diversification cannot be denied. It is essential to bear in mind that diversification is an effective strategic tool if it is carefully formulated and implemented. Several studies strongly suggest that moderate levels of diversification are rewarding and that overdiversification is detrimental to a firm.[30] Studies also suggest that diversifications emerging from the firm's R&D investments, core competencies, and strategic vision of top management are preferable, and more beneficial to company profits than unrelated diversification.[31] Needless to say diversifications are more successful when they are directed toward achieving the firm's long-term goals rather than toward achieving managers' personal goals.

How Do Firms Diversify?

In general, a firm can seek diversification in one of two ways: (1) internal venturing or (2) acquisitions.

Internal Venturing

Some firms pursue diversification through internal venturing, also known as corporate entrepreneurship or intrapreneurship. **Internal venturing** means developing and commercializing new products through the firm's innovative capabilities. Significant R&D investments and an ability to use the resultant scientific information to develop and market new products are essential to successful internal venturing. Sony is a good example of a firm that has successfully diversified into such businesses as consumer electronics (television, audio/video equipment), gaming products (play stations), and business solutions (PCs, flat panel monitors) through internal venturing. Major benefits of this form of diversification are (1) control over the new technology, preventing imitation, and (2) first-mover advantages if the new product creates a new market segment. Major drawbacks are (1) the high failure rate in new-product endeavors and (2) its time-consuming nature, which prevents the rapid exploitation of an opportunity.

Acquisitions

Most diversifications occur through acquisitions. Four types of acquisitions are possible:

1. vertical acquisitions
2. geographical acquisitions
3. horizontal acquisitions
4. conglomerate acquisitions

Vertical acquisitions are made either to meet the firm's supply and distribution needs or to exploit new opportunities emerging in other value chain segments of the same industry. Greyhound acquired Motor Coach Industries not only to build buses for itself but also to enter the bus-building business. *Geographic acquisitions* are made to take the firm's current product to a new market or region. Many regional U.S. banks have lately acquired banks in other regions of the country to enter new markets. *Horizontal acquisitions* (in diversification)* are made to enter another segment of the same industry or a closely related industry. Procter & Gamble, maker of shampoos and deodorants that target mostly women, acquired Gillette in 2005 in order to enter the men's market for personal-care products. Likewise, SBC Communications, a regional phone company serving mainly the western United States, acquired AT&T in 2005 so as to enter the long-distance market in a big way. *Conglomerate acquisition* means buying a firm in another industry that is unrelated to the firm's current product or customers served. Greyhound's purchase of Armour, a firm in the food industry, was a conglomerate acquisition.

Diversification through acquisitions has significant benefits. It allows for rapid entry into a new market or acquisition of strategic assets (e.g., new competencies, plants, distribution channels, or new customer accounts) that the firm does not currently possess. It is also a less risky way to expand than internal venturing. And, for a firm with a high price/earnings (P/E) ratio, it provides an opportunity to reduce it by acquiring a firm with a low P/E ratio. Lastly, it allows a firm with excess cash to profitably invest in attractive opportunities.

Nevertheless, there are significant problems with acquisitions. Integration challenges emerge when there are differences between the two companies in corporate values, managerial mindset, or organizational tasks and routines. In the year 2000, America Online acquired Time Warner Company for $165 billion—the most expensive acquisition in corporate history. While many thought that the two businesses complemented each other, the required integration between them never occurred because of their radically opposing cultures—a maverick America Online and a conservative Time Warner. In 2003, after reporting a loss of $99 billion, AOL-Time Warner changed its name to Time Warner, making AOL one of its business units. A second problem in acquisitions is the potential for overpayment,† increasing debt levels and precluding investments in activities that contribute to the firm's long-term success, such as R&D and marketing.[32] Finally, acquisitions consume much of top management's time, often distracting them from other matters that are necessary for the firm's long-term competitive success.[33]

---

*Horizontal acquisitions occurring within the same market segment are referred to as **horizontal integration,** defined earlier in the section on vertical integration.

†Hostile takeovers and bidding wars in acquisitions lead to overpayment, resulting in a huge debt for the acquirer. In 2004, applications software firm Oracle frequently raised its takeover bid for PeopleSoft, another software firm, eventually paying $3 billion more for the acquisition than the initial offer of $7.7 billion.

Divestment

Vertical integration and diversification are expansionary strategies; implementing them results in entry into new operational activities or new lines of business. Not all expansionary moves turn out to be successful, however. Lack of synergy among different products, cultural mismatch among acquired businesses, altered industry conditions, or a huge debt load arising from the acquisitions can result in negative performance, forcing a firm to reconsider its holdings. A firm might also have over-diversified, and the resulting diseconomies of scale may demand a reconsideration of the portfolio. Occasionally, the government's threat of antitrust action due to a perceived or real monopoly may necessitate such a reconsideration. Under those conditions, a diversified firm will plan to exit from some of the vertically integrated operations, a product line, or an entire business.

It can do so by selectively selling assets (for example, selling machinery and closing plants) or by selling an entire business. The idea is to restructure or recompose the firm's business portfolio so as to make it fit for the new situation. The decisions and actions pertaining to this restructuring that result in selective retrenchment and eventual re-composition of the firm's portfolio are called **divestment**.[34]

If diversification is a strategy for expanding by identifying attractive new businesses to move into, divestment is a strategy for restructuring by identifying noncore and unattractive current holdings that must be disposed of. Divestment is a strategy in the sense that it requires careful review and analysis of the firm's portfolio and trimming it to meet changing industry conditions.[35] Managers must determine whether the firm would be better off competitively, and its overall value greater, when certain assets or business units are divested than when they are retained. When done prudently, based on a sound analysis of strategic gains and losses that can arise from restructuring, divestment can be beneficial. Hasty decisions can be detrimental since they could shrink a firm to a level that cannot support its competitiveness. For example, divestment of a product line that shared tangible assets with other operations can create excess resources within the firm, thereby increasing costs. Divestment of an operation by a vertically integrated firm can place it at the mercy of external sources for critical supplies or channels of distribution. In other instances, a firm may lose some of its market power. Successful firms take these risks into account when contemplating a divestment strategy.

Portfolio Analysis

Prudent managers of multibusiness firms periodically analyze and assess the soundness of their business portfolio vis-à-vis the firm's long-term goals. This analysis examines the potential for success for each product line or **strategic business unit** (SBU),* given industry conditions. Its purpose is to determine (1) whether the existing portfolio of businesses should be retained or a change in its composition made, (2) which businesses will be discarded from the portfolio and which will be added, and (3) how available resources should be allocated among the retained busi-

---

*A diversified firm has several products and brands. To effectively allocate resources among them and control performance, firms organize them into manageable groups based on commonality of customers or competitors. These groups are called SBU's. An SBU can be a division within a firm, a product line within a division, or even a single product or a brand.

nesses to achieve maximum overall performance. Managers use frameworks illustrated in Figure 6.6 (BCG or Boston Consulting Group Matrix) and Figure 6.7 (GE or General Electric Business Screen) for performing portfolio analysis.

The **BCG Matrix** requires two types of data for each business unit: relative market share and industry growth rate. **Relative market share** is defined as the ratio of the business unit's market share to the market share held by its largest rival in that industry. If firm A's market share in its laundry detergent business is 20 percent and its largest rival B has a market share of 40 percent, the relative market share of firm A's detergent business is 20/40 or 0.5. **Industry growth rate** is defined as the percentage growth rate of the industry.

The matrix has four cells: stars, cash cows, question marks, and dogs. **Stars** are business units with a high market share in industries that have a high growth rate. They offer the best opportunity for the firm's long-term growth and profitability. As such, they should receive major emphasis in resource allocation to maintain their star status. Market penetration, development of new market segments, and vertical integration are appropriate for stars.

Cash cows have high relative market share in a low-growth industry. They generate large amounts of cash for the firm but need very little financial support because their industry is not growing. The cash generated by them should be used to support other growing businesses in need of cash.

Question marks are businesses with a low market share in high-growth industries. They generate very little cash but can become stars if strongly supported. The decision the firm must make is whether to take the risk and support them or divest them.

Dogs have a low market share in a low-growth industry. They may be self-sufficient or they may be draining money earned by other business units. Dogs should be divested unless they provide intangible support to other business units.

Each circle in Figure 6.6 represents a business unit and the size of the circle indicates the revenue generated by that business unit relative to other units.

FIGURE 6.6　**BCG Matrix**

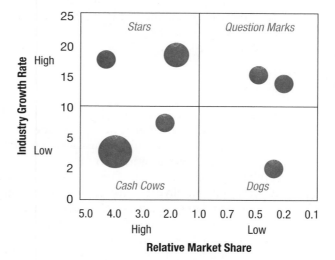

Source: Perspectives, No. 66, "The Product Portfolio." Adapted with permission from the Boston Consulting Group, Inc., 1970. All rights reserved.

FIGURE 6.7   **The GE Business Screen**

		Good	Medium	Poor
INDUSTRY ATTRACTIVENESS	High	Winner	Winner	Question Mark
1. Market Growth 2. Market Size	Medium	Winner	Average Business	Loser
3. Capital Requirements 4. Competitive Intensity	Low	Profit Producer	Loser	Loser

COMPETITIVE POSITION

1. Market Share   2. Technological Know-how   3. Product Quality
4. Service Network   5. Price Competitiveness   6. Operating Costs

Source: From *Strategy Formulation, Analytical Concepts,* 1st edition by Hofer. Copyright © 1978. Reprinted with permission of South-Western, a division of Thomson Learning: www.thomsonrights.com

The **GE Business Screen** (developed for General Electric by McKinsey & Company, a management consulting organization) uses more elaborate data, focusing on industry attractiveness and the firm's competitive position. Industry attractiveness is measured using market growth rate, market size, capital requirements, and competitive intensity. An industry is attractive when it has a high growth rate, is large in size, has minimal capital requirements, and has a low competitive intensity. Under the opposite conditions, the industry is unattractive. A firm's competitive position is good when it has a high market share, superior technological know-how, high product and service quality, competitive prices, and low operating costs. Using the GE Business Screen, a firm decides to aggressively invest in winners and question marks, maintain a status quo in average businesses and profit producers, and sell losers.

The foregoing portfolio models are not without drawbacks. By emphasizing cash flow management, these models ignore opportunities for building linkages across businesses in order to achieve economies of scale and scope.[36] In addition, these models wrongly assume that higher market share would always lead to higher profits.[37] At times, a firm with a low market share may also be highly profitable. Also, these models ignore the fact that a business unit could offer a strategic advantage to a firm even though it was losing money. Caution is, therefore, necessary when using these models to make divestment and restructuring decisions.

Summary

To maintain a steady state of growth and profitability, firms explore new opportunities by expanding their area of current operations or by moving into new products, new markets, and new lines of business. The former is known as vertical integration and the latter, diversification. On occasion, a firm may even plan to exit from an unprofitable business or area of operation, referred to as divestment. Collectively, vertical integration, diversification, and divestment are called corporate strategies. Corporate strategy focuses on the synergistic management of the expanded operations of a single-business firm or the portfolio of a multibusiness firm so as to enhance growth and profitability.

Vertical integration consolidates a firm's position within an industry and prevents new entry but also makes it difficult for the firm to exit the industry if it is threatened.

Diversification offers the advantages of market power and economies of scope but dilutes managerial control and creates coordination problems. Divestment enables a firm to exit an unprofitable business or operational activity but can create excess resources internally or an external dependency on suppliers/distributors. Before a firm adopts these strategies, it must consider viable alternatives, such as strategic alliances.

Chapter 6 Discussion Questions and Projects

Discussion Questions

1. Describe how vertical integration provides cost and differentiation advantages.
2. In the petroleum industry backward and forward integrations are common. Most firms perform exploration, refining, and marketing of gasoline. Based on what you read and understood about vertical integration from this chapter, what do you think are the possible reasons for this industry-wide phenomenon?
3. Based on what you learned from this chapter, explain why Greyhound's diversifications failed.

Projects

1. Using the Internet and business press sources, read about Eastman Kodak Company and write a report that answers the following questions:
   (a) Describe the company's businesses.
   (b) Are the businesses vertically linked?
   (c) Does Kodak pursue concentric, horizontal, or conglomerate diversification? Provide reasons for your answer.
   (d) During the 1990s, Kodak undertook a massive restructuring by divesting pharmaceutical, medical diagnostic, and consumer product businesses from its portfolio even though some of them were profitable. Explain the reasons why.
2. Using the Internet, read about why and how Boeing has pursued a diversification strategy ever since it bought McDonnell Douglas.

 ## Continuing Case

PepsiCo: Diversification, Divestment, and Restructuring

Background

In the early 1960s, Pepsi-Cola Company decided to strengthen its strategic arsenal so as to effectively fight archrival Coca-Cola for industry leadership. Until then, Pepsi-Cola's strategies to realize its lifelong ambition of becoming the number one soft drink company focused on successfully marketing Pepsi, its only product. By differentiating Pepsi through packaging, product image, and claims of better taste, the company sought to reach and surpass Coca-Cola in sales volume and profits. But, despite a prolonged and costly marketing campaign, the company found itself nowhere close to its goal. So, Pepsi-Cola planned to strengthen its position in the core soft drink business through diversification. By adding new products that complemented Pepsi or that could be offered using the company's existing resources in marketing and distribution, the firm thought that it could generate additional cash. This cash could be used to support the costly marketing battles Pepsi waged against Coke.

Product-line Extensions

Pepsi-Cola's initial diversification strategies were confined to beverage products that called on the firm's strengths in the marketing and distribution of soft drinks. Early diversifications were product-line extensions through internal venturing that introduced Diet Pepsi and Pepsi Light, a diet cola with a hint of lemon. But soon the company turned to acquisitive diversification. It bought Teem, Mountain Dew, and Seven-Up, which utilized Pepsi's promotion and distribution skills and exploited opportunities in the rapidly emerging noncola market. These diversifications established Pepsi-Cola in several segments of the soft drink industry, thereby strengthening the firm's capabilities in beverage marketing and distribution. Moreover, they provided the firm with the additional net cash it needed to effectively pursue its rivalry with Coca-Cola.

Some Missteps

Pepsi-Cola's subsequent diversifications were moving the firm into products and markets that were totally unrelated to beverages. During the late 1960s and early 1970s, Pepsi-Cola bought North American Van Lines, Lee Way Motor Freight, and Wilson Sports Company—companines that required for their management a fundamentally different knowledge and experience. The problems that ensued due to incompatibilities in resources and capabilities led the firm to dispose of these businesses during the 1980s. By then, according to industry analysts, the firm had lost some ground in its fight against Coca-Cola. Pepsi-Cola's then-CEO, Donald Kendall, vowed that future diversifications would be confined to businesses that marketed food and beverages.

Adding Snack Food and Restaurant Businesses

In 1965, Pepsi-Cola bought snack food manufacturer Frito-Lay (potato chips, corn chips, pretzels). The company then changed its name to PepsiCo and created a corporate structure that enabled it to coordinate the activities of two businesses—snack food and beverages. Wall Street analysts and the investment community applauded this acquisition because of the commonality between Frito-Lay and Pepsi—both had the same customer base and both could be marketed and distributed through the same channels. A further synergy between the two was that they complemented each other. As Kendall remarked, "Frito-Lay created the thirst that Pepsi was ready to quench." By encouraging supermarkets to move Pepsi closer to Frito-Lay products on store shelves, the company effectively exploited this complementarity, thus significantly increasing the sale of Pepsi. Between 1966 and 1970, Pepsi's market share rose from 16 percent to 20 percent. In addition, the Frito-Lay acquisition helped PepsiCo achieve $1 billion in sales for the first time in 1970 and provided additional net cash to the firm, thus enabling it to continue its fight against Coca-Cola.

Buoyed by the success of the Frito-Lay acquisition, PepsiCo (the parent of Pepsi-Cola) searched for other similar acquisitions that would strengthen the overall sales and profitability of the firm. During the late 1970s and the 1980s, the company acquired Pizza Hut, Taco Bell, and Kentucky Fried Chicken, believing that the restaurant business was synergistically related to the beverage business. For example, these restaurant chains could be marketed along with Pepsi through the same television or print advertisements, providing the firm with a higher return on each ad dollar spent. But a more important reason for the restaurant business acquisition was that it gave PepsiCo control over fountain sales in which Coke had a dominant edge. Fountain sales were rapidly growing during this time due to the popularity of fast foods, especially the "take-out" types. Ownership of large restaurant chains would ensure that only Pepsi brands were sold through their fountains. Incidentally, fountain sales offered a sizeable profit margin and by owning the restaurants, PepsiCo could access these profits, too.

Divestment and Restructuring

With over 29,000 outlets internationally, the restaurant chains increased the sale of Pepsi's beverages significantly. Overall sales of PepsiCo reached $30 billion in 1995, with the beverage, snack food, and restaurant businesses contributing to revenues almost equally. However, the profits generated by the restaurant business were not only below average, they were shrinking every year. In the early 1990s, the operating margins of the beverage and snack food businesses averaged between 12 and 17 percent respectively, whereas during the same period margins for the restaurant business fell from 8 percent to 4 percent. In fact, between 1990 and 1995, PepsiCo's overall net margin averaged a meager 8 percent compared to Coca-Cola's 18 percent. The low margin, according to industry analysts, was due to the fact that the fast food restaurant business was intensely competitive and required periodic large-scale investments in store expansion just to maintain existing sales volume. As a result, PepsiCo found itself diverting huge amounts of cash each year from the snack food and beverage businesses to its restaurant business, leaving very little funds for Pepsi to effectively carry on its rivalry with Coke. In 1997, the company decided to exit the restaurant business and restructure its activities. By the end of that year, it had spun off the restaurant business to shareholders as an independent publicly traded company.

In 1998, PepsiCo once again vowed to stay focused on what it knew well. It declared itself as a marketer of convenience food and beverages only and soon embarked on creating a portfolio of products that could be synergistically managed under these categories. Through new acquisitions, such as Quaker Oats, Gatorade, and Tropicana, and the restructuring that followed, the firm appeared to have succeeded in its efforts. By the early 2000s, PepsiCo

had two broad businesses that not only complemented each other well but shared the same marketing and distribution resources: (1) a convenience food business consisting of Frito-Lay brands and Quaker Oats brands, and (2) a beverage business consisting of Pepsi-Cola brands, Tropicana, Aquafina (water), Gatorade, and SoBe drinks. The company's financial and market performance in 2004 reflected its strengths. During that year, it had sales of $29 billion, an overall operating margin of 12 percent, and two of its brands—Pepsi and Mountain Dew—held the second and third position, respectively, in soft drink sales and market share. Industry analysts contended that the PepsiCo of 2004 was in a much stronger position to challenge Coca-Cola for soft drink industry leadership.

Discussion Questions

1. Describe PepsiCo's diversifications into the convenience food and beverage businesses and explain how they helped the firm effectively pursue its rivalry with Coke.

2. Describe the strategic advantages that PepsiCo derived by diversifying into the restaurant business. Why did this diversification fail?

Source: D. Yoffie, "Cola Wars Continue: Coke and Pepsi in the Twenty-first Century," *Harvard Business School Case* #9-702-402 (2004); C. Moriguchi, "PepsiCo's Restaurants," *Harvard Business School Case* #9-794-078 (2001); "PepsiCo, Inc.," *International Directory of Company Histories*," vol. 38 (St. James Press, 2001); "The Sweet Spot of Convenient Food and Beverages," *Business Week*, April 10, 2000; "Pepsi Gets Back in the Game: The Company Is on the Rebound with a New Vision and an Old Problem: Coke," *Time,* April 26, 1999.

7

International Strategy: Gaining Advantage Through Global Expansion

CHAPTER OBJECTIVES

After reading this chapter, you should be able to:

- Discuss the strategic advantages of expanding internationally

- Describe global and multidomestic industries and how competition occurs in them

- Discuss the conflicting competitive pressures a firm faces when expanding internationally

- Describe global, multidomestic, and transnational strategies and the industry conditions for which each is appropriate

- Discuss the international market entry modes, and the advantages and disadvantages of each

- Plan the international market entry strategy for a given business

Opening Case

Nike is the world leader in athletic footwear and sports apparel. Its branded footwear is sold in over 150 countries around the world. It enjoys a roughly 35 percent share of the world market for athletic footwear; its nearest rivals, Reebok and Adidas, each have 13 percent. Nike has consistently expanded its share of the U.S. and foreign markets since its inception in the mid-1960s, while its rivals have been stagnating. In 2005, Nike's sales of footwear, sports apparel, and accessories totaled $13.73 billion; over $7 billion came from selling branded footwear in the U.S. and international markets. With the U.S. market for athletic footwear now fully matured, Nike is focusing on increasing its global presence and international sales to sustain a healthy growth rate.

Headquartered in Oregon, Nike does not make the footwear it sells globally. It outsources manufacturing to subcontractors in China, Indonesia, and Vietnam, who make the product using designs and product specifications provided by Nike. The finished product is then packed and exported directly from the factory to company-owned stores (Nike Towns) and to over twenty thousand independent retailers in different countries, who place orders in advance with Nike's sales force.

Footwear production is labor intensive, and outsourcing it to manufacturers in low-wage countries yields significant cost advantages. Nike pioneered this outsourcing strategy when it entered the athletic footwear business in the late 1960s, and it has since become industry practice.

Besides low-cost manufacturing, Nike needs strength in product R&D, branded marketing, and global distribution to succeed in the athletic footwear business. Footwear demand is influenced by fads, and the firm must introduce new designs every six months just to stay in business. Because athletic footwear is also expensive, Nike must invest in branding, promotion, and celebrity endorsements. More importantly, since product R&D involves high fixed costs, a large market share that spreads these costs across several units is also essential. And, since the market for athletic footwear is a

niche, Nike can achieve the necessary large market share only by diversifying into several geographic niches worldwide.

To realize the required strengths in product R&D and marketing, Nike invests substantially in these functions, far outspending its rivals. In order to achieve a sizeable market share, Nike aggressively pursues international expansion using a global strategy. *A global strategy assumes the world to be a single market (as opposed to several regional and differentiated markets), permitting the firm to offer the same standard and uniform designs in every international market in which it competes.* Because the needs and preferences of buyers of athletic footwear are uniform the world over, a global strategy is the appropriate avenue for athletic footwear firms that are pursuing international expansion. Firms implement this strategy by centralizing R&D and marketing decisions and undertaking manufacturing activities at a single or a few favorable international locations, instead of at every location where they compete. For Nike, R&D and marketing activities are centralized at corporate headquarters in Oregon, manufacturing activities are performed in select international locations, and sales and distribution occur worldwide through regional representatives.

While every firm in the athletic footwear industry seeks competitive advantages in product innovation, manufacturing efficiency, and brand marketing, what sets Nike apart from others is the aggressiveness it has shown in globalizing its business. With demand for athletic footwear rising relatively faster in the developing countries, Nike has pursued global expansion vigorously in two ways: (1) through international licensing and execution of several wholesale and retail distribution agreements, and (2) by supporting international sports programs and seeking celebrity endorsements from international sports stars to realize the high level of global visibility and brand recognition necessary for gaining worldwide market share. This two-pronged approach of sustained global market penetration and creation of a strong brand awareness, in addition to product innovation and marketing strength, has made Nike the leader in the athletic footwear industry.[1]

International expansion offers firms unique growth and profit opportunities that are not available to domestic firms. But international expansion also carries enormous risks that firms must be careful to avoid if they are to be successful. This chapter focuses on international expansion opportunities and how firms exploit them. We start with a brief overview of how markets have evolved from domestic to global, which expands opportunities for a firm but simultaneously intensifies threats. We define globalization and global industries, explain how competition occurs in a global environment, and outline the strategic advantages and pitfalls of pursuing international expansion. This overview provides us with the foundation necessary to understand the strategies firms employ to gain competitive advantages when expanding internationally. We conclude this chapter with a description of alternative ways of entering international markets, and their relative advantages and disadvantages.

Trends in International Competition

Early-twentieth-century markets were largely local, and businesses competed within the confines of their domestic environment. Competition for the procurement of productive inputs (i.e., raw material, labor, and capital) and the sale of finished goods was a regional or national phenomenon. **International trade** in which firms imported raw material from foreign suppliers or exported and sold finished goods to foreign buyers was relatively uncommon. Equally uncommon was the physical movement abroad of business capital to be invested in foreign plants and other business assets, known as **direct foreign investment** wherein firms engage in offshore production of goods and compete side by side with host-country sellers for a share of the local markets.

Several factors kept businesses localized. *First,* domestic markets and economies were experiencing significant growth, creating very little incentive for firms to seek international opportunities. *Second,* most countries employed high tariffs and import quotas to protect domestic businesses from foreign competition, making international trade and direct foreign investment expensive and unprofitable. *Third,* differences in living standards and resulting disparities in the needs of people across the globe provided few opportunities for products made in one country to be sold in another. *Fourth,* currency regulations, inefficient factor markets, poor infrastructure, and political uncertainties—especially in developing countries—inhibited developed-country firms from physically expanding internationally.

Revolutionary changes occurring worldwide during the last fifty years have dramatically altered the nature of business competition. Changes occurring in the political, social, and technological sectors of all nations have gradually transformed competition into a routinely international phenomenon. Politically, nations have been aggressively enacting free market reforms, driven by economic growth needs that have lowered import restrictions. As a result, cross-border trade and foreign direct investments have become common in competition. Sociologically, trends in the industrialization and urbanization of the developing world have narrowed lifestyle differences among nations, providing huge opportunities for developed-country firms to market their white goods (refrigerators, household appliances) and other branded goods globally. Technologically, new inventions in communication and information technologies (for example, the Internet) have made foreign markets quickly and easily accessible to large and small firms alike. Advances in production and transportation have reduced the cost of moving goods and machinery abroad, inducing domestic firms to profitably pursue cross-border trade and overseas expansion.

Emergence of Global and Regional Trade Institutions

Certain trade institutions have emerged in the last fifty years that also strongly induce international commerce. In 1947, to rapidly revive the war-ravaged economies of the world, advanced nations came together and signed what came to be known as the *General Agreement on Tariffs and Trade* (GATT), giving birth to an organization bearing the same name. The purpose of GATT was to promote trade among member nations by providing each member with an opportunity to obtain from other members a "most favored trading partner" status. In 1995, GATT was replaced by the *World Trade Organization* (WTO), which has the same purpose of encouraging unrestricted international trade except that it has more power to penalize errant members. In 2005, about 150 nations were members of WTO, which indicates just how global trade has become. And, besides global institutions, it is worth noting the emergence of two regional trading blocs as well—*the European Union* (EU) and the *North American Free Trade Agreement* (NAFTA). These organizations, too, aim to reduce and eventually eliminate international trade barriers within their regions. The EU comprises 14 member countries in Europe that trade more or less as a single market using a common currency, the euro. While NAFTA integrates the United States, Canada, and Mexico in order to promote free trade among them, it has no common currency provisions.

The net result of all these changes is the widening of domestic markets and customer bases for most goods and the rise of international competition. Besides finished goods, competition for sourcing of raw material, skilled personnel,[2] capital, and manufacturing plant sites has also become international in character. A worldwide market presence has emerged as a critical competitive factor in several industries—including computer hardware, electronic goods, apparel, and steel—where economies of scale differentiate successful firms from unsuccessful ones.[3] In fact, many believe that competition in several products and industries today is no longer just cross-border or international but global—that is, firms in these industries compete on a worldwide basis.[4]

International Trade and Investment Volume

Some hard data would help us to gauge the extent to which business has become international in character in recent years. In 1970, world exports totaled $1.4 trillion; in 2003, that figure was $9.1 trillion. In 1970, U.S. exports were valued at $57 billion. The corresponding figure for 2004 was $1,146 billion. The share of U.S. imports and exports as a percentage of its gross domestic product has increased from 8 percent in 1970 to 25 percent in 2004, indicating how significant international trade has become to U.S. businesses.* Table 7.1 shows how international trade has grown

TABLE 7.1 **World Trade as a Percentage of Gross World Product**

YEAR	WORLD TRADE ($ TRILLIONS)	GROSS WORLD PRODUCT[a] ($ TRILLIONS)	WORLD TRADE AS PERCENTAGE OF GROSS WORLD PRODUCT
1970	1.4	17	8.2
1980	2.6	25	10.4
1990	3.7	33	11.0
2003	9.1	46	19.7

Source: World Investment Report (various years), United Nations Conference on Trade and Development; *World Trade Report 2004*, World Trade Organization.

[a]Total output of goods and services for final use.

---

*Data from International Trade Administration, U.S. Government (www.ita.gov).

TABLE 7.2	Direct Foreign Investment, Inflows and Outflows, by Region ($ Billions)

YEAR	WORLD INFLOW	DEVELOPED WORLD INFLOW	DEVELOPING WORLD INFLOW	WORLD OUTFLOW	DEVELOPED WORLD OUTFLOW	DEVELOPING WORLD OUTFLOW
1970	12	10	2	14	14	.03
1980	55	46	9	53	51	2
1990	209	164	45	242	216	26
2003	560	367	193	612	570	42

Source: World Investment Report (various years), United Nations Conference on Trade and Development.

in size over the years. Table 7.2 reveals the massive growth in direct foreign investments; a quick comparison of world inflow and outflow of capital for the years 1970 and 2003 will prove the point.

Strategic Advantages of International Expansion

Are there strategic advantages that accrue to firms pursuing international trade and direct foreign investment? There certainly seem to be some noteworthy advantages. One primary advantage we can mention is the *growth opportunity* it offers in the form of new markets for the firm's products. A second advantage is the access it provides to *cheaper or unique resources*. Third, existing assets of the firm can be effectively utilized through *full-capacity production*. Fourth, international expansion allows firms to *preempt or match competitors' similar intentions* or actions. To remain competitive in international business, firms must build strong foreign market positions before competition does or at least be a close second. Other advantages pertain to the *learning opportunity* that internationalization provides because it creates a diverse market experience. Let us examine these advantages in some detail.

Growth Opportunities

Internationalization increases the size of the potential market for the firm's products. It is an attractive option for developed-country firms whose proprietary products, which have attained maturity in their home markets, will enjoy the early stages of the product life cycle in emerging markets.[5] During the 1950s and 1960s, U.S. firms such as IBM and General Electric found growth opportunities for their technologically innovative and branded products in postwar Europe when domestic markets were reaching maturity. Today, these firms and others such as Pepsi-Cola, Levi Strauss, Nike, and Whirlpool are aggressively expanding into developing countries whose markets for consumer products are surging because of the rapid economic growth there.

Cost/Differentiation Advantages

Availability of cheap inputs such as raw material and labor in many developing countries and the resulting cost savings are strategic motivations for developed-country firms to move operations offshore. The opening case at the beginning of the chapter is a good example. When developing countries offer tax incentives and bonuses as inducements for locating on their soil, the cost advantages add up, providing further reasons to move abroad. In addition, critical resources may be available only in certain parts of the world, requiring firms to move closer to them. Many U.S. software firms have moved their product-development operations to Bangalore, India, to take advantage of the many skilled software engineers in that region.

International expansion also offers opportunities for a differentiator by providing a more suitable location for undertaking product research. Canon, the Japanese maker of premium copiers and cameras, chose Silicon Valley instead of a home-country location for its R&D activity because Silicon Valley offered access to a large pool of talented researchers in digital technology.

Volume Production Needs and Capacity Utilization

In commodity industries such as petroleum and basic chemicals, cost advantages are critical in competition. Firms invest heavily in plant capacity to derive scale economies, and high-volume, full-capacity production is essential to keep cost under control. The larger market share that results from internationalization helps a firm to run its plants at full capacity.

Companies such as Nike with high fixed costs (product R&D and design costs) should produce in larger volume to minimize per-unit cost. Since the U.S. athletic footwear market can absorb only so many units of a new design each year, Nike needs several niche markets internationally to sell all its units. Likewise, in many industries such as aerospace and pharmaceuticals where R&D and product-development costs are high, worldwide marketing and sales are essential for firms to recoup their sunk costs.[6]

Preempt or Match Competitor Actions

A firm internationalizes because it wants to either preempt competitors' similar moves or respond to such moves. Failure to do so can leave a firm vulnerable to attack. An unchallenged competitor can grab significant world market share quickly, gain cost advantages due to massive volume, and effectively use these strengths to wage price wars with a firm in its home market. That is what happened to U.S. television manufacturers RCA and Zenith, which stayed domestic and ignored Panasonic's aggressive worldwide buildup during the 1970s and 1980s. Using its global market power, Panasonic cross-subsidized* its U.S. television business, initiating a vigorous price competition. Unable to attack Panasonic in foreign markets that could have relieved their U.S. businesses of pricing pressures, RCA and Zenith were forced into a price war, losing a significant share of the U.S. market to cost-competitive Panasonic.[7]

Opportunities for Worldwide Learning

Internationalization provides opportunities for worldwide learning that are not available to a domestic firm. It exposes field units to diverse environments, allowing them to gain new knowledge and skills and transfer this learning to the parent company, where the knowledge is accumulated within the firm. Moreover, when a firm locates

---

*Go to Chapter 6 and refresh your memory on cross-subsidization, discussed under diversification.

functional activities (e.g., basic research, product design) in the international regions most qualified to perform them and has personnel from diverse cultures work together, it creates opportunities for information sharing and new thinking. This new thinking results from a synthesis of several streams of specialized knowledge and is essential for developing winning products for global markets.[8] The frequency with which consumer products manufacturers like Unilever and Procter & Gamble innovate is due to the knowledge diversity that arises from their global presence.[9]

Disadvantages of International Expansion

Despite all its advantages, internationalization has some disadvantages, too. *First,* it renders strategic decision making more difficult. Diverse economic environments, differing buyer needs and preferences, and international currency fluctuations introduce severe uncertainties in market and financial planning. Cultural barriers and language differences create communication and coordination problems within the organization.[10] *Second,* not all nations receive foreign businesses with open arms, as McDonalds and Starbucks painfully learned when their stores were attacked and vandalized in China and France. *Third,* market failure, political unrest, and prolonged governmental instability in some regions of the world can pose serious threats to profitability and to the safety of a firm's foreign investment. Therefore, firms make international expansion decisions, especially of the direct foreign investment type, after thoroughly analyzing the opportunity/risk trade off.*

Globalization, Global Industries, and Global Competition

Increasing internationalization of trade and foreign direct investment has introduced new terms such as *globalization* and created new types of businesses and competition such as *global industries* and *global competition*. We should explain these terms first before we discuss the strategies that firms employ to successfully exploit international opportunities.

Globalization

Globalization broadly refers to the cross-border integration presently occurring among national markets, resulting in their interdependence for goods, services, and factors of production.[11] More and more, the world is emerging as a single, undifferentiated, and homogeneous market for finished goods.[12] Besides goods, capital, know-how, and skilled personnel freely move across borders, and the traditional trade barriers between nations are rapidly disappearing. This process of a worldwide transformation in which distinct national markets and economies are gradually integrating themselves into a unified, global market is called globalization.

Global Industries and Global Competition

Researchers describe an industry as a **global industry** when it shows signs of worldwide linkages, resulting in a seamless movement of components, finished goods, know-how, and factors of production.[13] Uniformity in consumer needs and government regulations across nations allows some industries to function as a single, homo-

---

*Excellent source material for performing opportunity/risk analysis is the *Global Competitiveness Report* prepared annually by World Economic Forum (www.weforum.org). The report provides a comprehensive assessment of economic strengths and weaknesses of eighty countries and rank orders them.

geneous market for goods and factors of production despite the existence of national borders. Competitive rivalry in these global industries occurs on a worldwide basis, and firms compete for a global market share using economies of scale, brand recognition, and other advantages drawn from a network of worldwide activities (recall how Nike competes with Reebok and Adidas).[14] Because competition is global, firms seek **location advantages** by setting up value chain activities in international regions where they can be performed more efficiently or effectively, and the industry shows signs of cross-national linkages in product processing.[15] Thus, R&D activities are performed in one country, component manufacturing in another, product assembly in a third; the entire chain of activities is coordinated from a central location; and products are marketed worldwide (see Figure 7.1).[16] The more the value chain activities of an industry are sequentially integrated across borders and a standard product is marketed worldwide, the higher is that industry's level of globalization.

Porter contends that it is essential for a firm in a global industry to be as global in its operations as the industry is, because the firm's competitive position in one nation affects (and is affected by) its position in other nations.[17] *A firm's competitive strength in a global industry is thus a function of how globally its own operations are integrated, compared to those of the industry.* In other words, to be successful in a highly global industry, a firm must employ strategies that closely match the characteristics of its industry environment. It should formulate and implement strategies that focus on gaining a global competitive advantage: through global market presence; global branding and promotion of products; global sourcing of skills, materials, and capital; and locating facilities in favorable international regions.[18] Some examples of global industries are commercial aircraft, consumer electronics, industrial chemicals, petroleum, steel, and watches.[19] In these industries, worldwide similarity in consumer needs and government regulations allow firms to produce a standard product in large volume in a few attractive international locations and market it globally.

Multidomestic Industries

Not all industries are global (or globally integrated). Some, such as consumer banking, dairy, processed food, and retailing, have stayed largely domestic.[20] Differences in consumer taste, lifestyle, distribution channels, and government regulations in these industries have prevented them from becoming global. These are called **multidomestic industries** because they are present in each nation in a distinct form. Competition in multidomestic industries occurs locally and is not affected by competition in other regions of the world. Nor can an international firm use its competitive strengths in one nation to positively influence its position in another. Therefore, a firm seeking to internationalize in multidomestic industries must manufacture and market the product in each location according to that region's unique needs; for example, Unilever makes and markets frozen food differently in each major international region to suit the local palate. *The competitive success of a firm in a multidomestic industry will depend on how well the products and marketing practices of its regional units match the demands of the local environment.*

Customization, not economies of scale, matters most in a multidomestic industry. As a result, international firms competing in a multidomestic industry have autonomous, self-contained business units in each region; that is, they do not require material, labor, or informational inputs from other company units for their survival. All the value chain activities, from materials procurement to product design to production and marketing, are performed locally in each region (see Figure 7.1).

FIGURE 7.1 **Multidomestic and Global Industries**

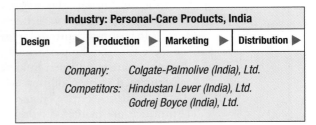

MULTIDOMESTIC INDUSTRY

Industry: Personal-Care Products, USA
Design ▶ Production ▶ Marketing ▶ Distribution ▶
Company: Colgate-Palmolive (USA), Inc.
Competitors: Proctor & Gamble (USA), Inc.
Unilever (USA), Inc.

Industry: Personal-Care Products, India
Design ▶ Production ▶ Marketing ▶ Distribution ▶
Company: Colgate-Palmolive (India), Ltd.
Competitors: Hindustan Lever (India), Ltd.
Godrej Boyce (India), Ltd.

GLOBAL INDUSTRY
Athletic Footwear
Company: Nike, Inc.
(Competitors: Adidas, Reebok)

Source: Adapted from P. Lasserre, *Global Strategic Management* (New York: Palgrave Macmillan, 2003), 11.

Global and multidomestic industries are thus two ends of the globalization continuum. What differentiates them is the way competition occurs within them: in global industries competition for factor inputs, design/manufacturing locations, and finished goods occurs on a worldwide basis; in multidomestic industries, competition is predominantly localized. But no industry will be absolutely global or absolutely multidomestic, and such categorical generalizations are misleading because many firms will fall between these two extremes.[21] It is essential for managers to bear this fact in mind when analyzing the competitive environment of their industry in order to make strategic choices; otherwise, they can make poor choices. More importantly, no two industries can have a similar competitive environment because trends in international business are continuously changing, altering conditions from industry to industry. Changes in lifestyle, technology, and government regulations may allow some industries to become more global while they move others in the opposite direction.[22] Understanding these issues in international business equips managers to intelligently analyze their industry's competitive conditions and decide on the strategies that are appropriate for the context.[23]

Strategies for Competing Internationally

What choices are available to a firm to compete in the international business environment? What competencies should a firm select and pursue to derive the necessary competitive advantages? What strategies would provide the firm with the competitive advantages it seeks? To answer these questions, a broad discussion of the competitive challenges and pressures firms face in the international business environment is necessary. The exact pressures a firm faces in its industry and the competitive advantages it must pursue to overcome these pressures would indicate the strategy that is appropriate for the context.

Researchers suggest that managers face three types of competitive pressures (see Figure 7.2) in the international business arena: pressure to integrate globally, pressure to be locally responsive, and pressure to achieve both global integration and local responsiveness.[24]

> *Pressure to Integrate Globally:* While international business offers enormous opportunities for growth, the risks it carries to the firm are also immense. One risk lies in the investment-return ratio. International expansion requires substantial investments in fixed assets in foreign locations, but there is no guarantee that they will generate adequate returns to be profitable. Prudent managers seek to minimize this risk by controlling the investment cost and increasing its return potential. One way they do so is by efficiently utilizing the existing assets and selling the current product to as large a market as possible. In other words, if the current product could be standardized, made in large volume in a few favorable international locations, and successfully sold worldwide, a firm would have effectively achieved growth at a lower cost. Consequently, managers pursuing international expansion are pressured to pursue global integration of operations that will reduce cost by reducing product variations and by creating the potential to market a standard product globally. In commodity industries such as petroleum and semiconductors, and in industries such as athletic footwear where the needs and tastes of people are uniform across regions, the pressure for global integration is high because high-volume production and large market share are critical competitive advantages.

| FIGURE 7.2 | **Competitive Pressures in the International Business Environment** |

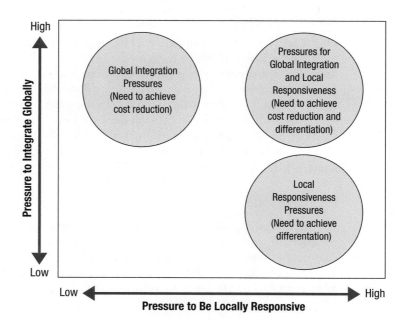

Pressure to Be Locally Responsive: If organizations seek standardization to minimize cost for themselves, customers seek differentiation to maximize value for themselves. Their unique needs and preferences induce consumers around the world to demand customization and the incorporation of unique features in products and services. In addition, regional government regulation of packaging and distribution preclude the adoption of uniform marketing strategies. Fluctuations in currency exchange rates and host-government policies concerning foreign direct investment further prevent companies from adopting standardized practices. All these factors pressure firms to pursue a local responsiveness approach by making a dedicated investment in each region. In other words, a firm designs, makes, and markets the product differently in each region to suit local requirements. Firms that fail to do so under the conditions just described and adopt a global approach instead run the risk of losing local market opportunities.

Pressure to Achieve Both Global Integration and Local Responsiveness: Intensifying competition in some industries forces firms to simultaneously pursue global integration and local responsiveness. A firm expanding internationally, as either a multidomestic or a global firm, must continuously adapt to the diverse environments in which it operates. Pressure builds within the firm to minimize product variations to control costs while at the same time selectively customizing so as to remain competitive. Thus, a firm pursues global integration to reduce cost in some of its activities (for example, manufacturing the product in large scale in a few centralized locations), but it also customizes other activities to be locally responsive (for example, adding certain features to the product at each location or performing marketing and after-sales service activities differently in each location). Computer, automobile, and pharmaceutical industries are now experiencing this dual pressure. Experts suggest that the pressure to integrate globally and be locally responsive at the same time stems from the nature of the international competitive environment, which forces firms to learn and adapt to differing conditions.[25]

Strategic Choices

Our discussion of the competitive challenges in international business provides us with a basis upon which to describe and explain the strategic choices available to a firm. Three distinct strategies are available to firms that compete in the international business environment: *global strategy, multidomestic strategy,* and *transnational strategy.* The strategy a firm will choose depends on the pressures it experiences in its industry. If the firm perceives a strong need for cost advantages, it will pursue a global strategy by integrating operations worldwide. Multi-domestic strategy will be its choice if it finds differentiation needs to be high, and it will opt for a transnational strategy if both cost reduction and differentiation pressures are high.

Global Strategy

A **global strategy** allows the firm to compete internationally by offering a standard product for worldwide consumption. It emerges from the firm's ethnocentric belief that people's needs are the same worldwide and that what was successful "at home" will succeed globally if the product is of standard quality and marketed uniformly in all regions.[26] The company therefore models the product on home-country specifications, makes it in large volume in favorable international locations, and offers it globally. Its international operations, functioning as centers of excellence, are tightly integrated by headquarters with a single purpose: making the product in conformity with planned standards and marketing it globally under a single brand name to derive economies of scale. Cost efficiencies in production and global market share are, therefore, the objectives in a global strategy.[27]

The competitive advantages the firm seeks in a global strategy are: (1) location advantages—situating an optimal number of value chain activities in international regions where they can be efficiently and effectively completed, (2) coordination advantages—linking the geographically dispersed activities in a way that lets the firm effectively serve a worldwide market, and (3) the advantages of a global market presence—marketing and distributing the product in as many countries around the world as possible. Nike pursues a global strategy, competing around the world with local firms as well as with other global firms, such as Reebok and Adidas. So does Pepsi-Cola as it competes with regional beverage brands around the world as well as with Coca-Cola on a global basis.

Strategy in Practice 7.1 narrates the story of Heineken, the Dutch beer brewer, and its pursuit of global domination through the use of a global strategy. A point worth noting from this story is that even though the beer industry shows strong signs of global integration, not all firms in that industry pursue a global strategy. Interbrew, the fourth largest brewer in the world, pursues a multidomestic strategy—brewing local beers and marketing them under the local brand. *The point is that a firm's strategy is not environmentally determined. Managers have choices; strategy results from the conscious choices made by managers.*

Multidomestic Strategy

A **multidomestic strategy** lets the firm compete in each international region by making and marketing the product according to local needs. This strategy emerges from a polycentric business belief—that people's needs differ from region to region and that products will be successful when they are made and marketed in a way that satisfies host countries' unique needs.[28] The company therefore offers a differentiated product for each region and even differentiates its marketing and business practices to closely resemble host-country environments (by, for example, flying the host country's flag and observing local business hours and holidays). Organizationally, a firm pursuing a multidomestic strategy is a loose federation of independently operating international business units that compete within host-country markets only.[29]

The competitive advantage a firm seeks in a multidomestic strategy is product or service uniqueness that closely matches regional preferences. Colgate-Palmolive, a U.S. firm making oral-care, personal-care, and detergent products, has expanded internationally using a multidomestic strategy. Proctor & Gamble (household products) and Gillette (consumer products) are other examples of U.S. firms that pursue a multidomestic strategy.

Transnational Strategy

A **transnational strategy** is a combination type, mixing multinational and global features. A transnational firm competes through product standardization but also adapts through customization where necessary.[30] The underlying business philosophy is

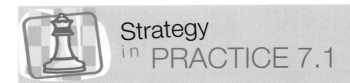

Strategy in PRACTICE 7.1

HEINEKEN'S GLOBAL STRATEGY

Heineken is a 150-year-old Dutch beer brewer. With sales of $13.6 billion in 2004, it is the world's third-largest brewer after Anheuser-Busch and SAB-Miller. But with the Heineken brand selling in over 170 countries, it has a more dominating global presence than its rivals.

Early in its history Heineken believed that beer was not a regional product but one that had universal appeal and could be sold in world markets. It envisioned Heineken emerging as the most international brewer in the world. To realize this vision, the company conceived a global strategy: positioning Heineken as a premium global brand. It embarked on an ambitious export program to implement its strategy by aggressively expanding its domestic brewing capacity and popularizing its brand internationally. By the 1960s, its efforts had paid off and the company emerged as the dominant exporter of beer in the world. However, a steady growth in demand for beer in the emerging markets during this time soon put pressure on its export capacity, forcing the firm to explore other avenues for international expansion. Starting in the 1970s, Heineken pursued licensing and, more importantly, foreign operations using direct investment. The aim in these investments was to acquire foreign brew-

eries that would allow the firm to brew and market the Heineken label in international locations after modernizing the facilities to its specifications. Today, the company has 110 breweries in over 60 countries that cater to the global distribution needs of the Heineken brand.

Heineken's international strategy is guided by a single goal: to create and market "one beer, one brand." While the firm owns eighty regional brands and a second international brand, Amstel, it is the Heineken label that is the focus of its international brewing and marketing activities. This contrasts with the strategy followed by Heineken's closest Dutch rival, Interbrew, which promotes itself as the world's local brewer. The difference between Interbrew and Heineken is this: Interbrew buys local brands and markets them better, whereas Heineken buys local breweries to make and market the Heineken brand.

Source: www.heinekeninternational.com; www.hoovers.com; "Tapping into the World Market," www. brandchannel.com, October 15, 2001; "The Global Beer Industry 2001 Review: Toto, We Are Not in Kansas Anymore," *Modern Brewery Age,* March 25, 2002; "Heineken: One beer, one brand," *Sunday Business Post,* July 2, 2000.

geocentric—the world is a reservoir of resources, skills, and information, and through an intelligent process of selection and synthesis, universal standards and unique requirements can be simultaneously fulfilled.[31] The transnational firm thus centralizes some functions (e.g., R&D, finance), decentralizes others (e.g., human resource management, marketing), and even has some self-contained foreign subsidiaries. They all work closely together to create products that conform to a universal standard and that are therefore cheaper to make while still accommodating local needs.

The competitive advantage a firm seeks in a transnational strategy is the ability to effectively transfer information and experience from one field unit to another and from each field unit to the parent company. Firms in the pharmaceutical, automotive, and computer industries globalize as transnationals. For example, in the computer industry, the commodity nature of the hardware means that companies must reduce costs through high-volume production in central locations. But diversity of software and services creates a need to be locally responsive. Firms therefore perform these activities as an add-on at the local levels.[32]

Table 7.3 summarizes the three alternative strategies from which to choose when a firm plans to expand internationally. What countries to enter and what mode of entry to use are additional choices a firm makes, and we turn our attention to those choices now.

Entry Decisions and Modes of Entering International Markets

Firms contemplating international expansion must decide: (1) which countries to enter and (2) what mode of entry to choose. Country selections are based on an assessment of each country's (a) *market attractiveness* for profits, (b) *economic and political risk* levels for the safety of invested capital, and (c) *cultural orientation* toward business. *Market attractiveness* is assessed by measuring market size, growth, industry structure and competition, availability of productive resources, and government policies and regulations. *Economic and political risks* are determined from an overall assessment of a country's economic climate and growth, transportation and communications infrastructure, political philosophy, and long-term political stability. *Cultural orientation* toward business is evaluated by examining a country's belief

TABLE 7.3	Comparison of Multidomestic, Global, and Transnational Strategies		
	MULTIDOMESTIC	**GLOBAL**	**TRANSNATIONAL**
1. Product/market	Custom products/services offered in each country	Standard products/services offered worldwide	Standardization and customization combined, offered worldwide
2. Strategic objective	Local responsiveness (flexibility)	Efficiency	Efficiency and flexibility
3. Critical issues	Which countries are most promising for revenues and profits?	Where should operations be located to gain maximum cost advantages?	How should local information be integrated with global information for maximum advantage?
4. Competitive advantages	Ability to adapt to local needs	Location advantages; value chain coordination; global brand visibility	Global learning and adaptation abilities
5. Culture	Polycentric	Ethnocentric	Geocentric
6. Control	Determined and administered locally	Determined and administered by headquarters	Determined and administered jointly by headquarters and regions
7. When appropriate	When needs are distinct across world regions	When needs are uniform worldwide	When uniformity must be combined with some local responsiveness
8. Operational characteristics	Value chain activities performed in each region	Value chain activities globally dispersed and integrated	Value chain activities globally dispersed and integrated; some activities locally completed
9. Organizational characteristics	Decentralized federation	Centralized autarchy	Combination of centralization and decentralization
10. Knowledge and skill mobility	Stays within each business unit	Stays at headquarters	Moves freely between business units and headquarters

system and how it affects people's perception of business. Companies develop country profiles that rank the attractiveness of each country in relation to its risks, match them to their own goals, and use those profiles to make country selections and decide on appropriate entry modes.*

International Location Advantages: Michael Porter suggests that firms take into account the distinct attributes of nations when making foreign expansion decisions because these attributes have relevance for competitive advantage. According to Porter, regions of the world differ in their capabilities and infrastructure, conditions that allow different industries to prosper in different nations.[33] For example, Switzerland is famous for watches, Italy for fashionable clothing, Holland for diamonds, the United States for computer hardware, and India for computer software. By situating the whole business or any functional operation (R&D, manufacturing) in international locations where conditions are favorable for that business or operation, a firm can gain competitive advantage.

Following are the attributes according to Porter that shape a country's business environment in a way that favors an industry. Firms of that country excel in a specific industry because these attributes are present in the right quantity and combination, appropriate for that industrial activity. By analyzing these attributes and by comparing the results of that analysis to its own business needs, a firm can make intelligent decisions concerning which countries to enter and where to locate its operations.

Factor Endowments: These are inputs such as skilled labor, material, and infrastructure (roadways, waterways, communication systems) necessary to compete in a given industry. India has become internationally successful in software development because of its huge stock of cheap but highly skilled engineers. Firms whose operations need a large quantity of low-cost knowledge workers may choose India for their location.

Demand Conditions: These refer to buyer taste and preferences in a country for the products of a given industry. A nation's industry gains prominence if the domestic buyers demand quality in the products or services of that industry. The electronics industry in Japan gained international fame because the Japanese are discriminating shoppers for consumer appliances who forced firms in that industry to continuously improve product quality. Japan is thus an attractive location for a firm that makes and markets high-quality consumer appliances both locally and globally because the electronics industry is in a highly developed state there.

Related and Supporting Industries: These include makers of raw material, components, and complementary products for a given industry. Italy is internationally famous for fashionable clothing. Several Italian family businesses have historically been engaged in apparel design and there is a network of highly competitive ancillary businesses tied to the clothing industry. Firms in the fashion goods industry should consider Italy as a potential location for product design.

Firm Strategy, Structure, and Rivalry: These represent the conditions governing how firms are created, organized, and managed and the nature of domestic rivalry in a nation. Germany is renowned for high-quality engineering because top managers of firms generally have an engineering background that induces contin-

---

*Economist Intelligence Unit (www.eiu.com) and LexisNexis (www.lexisnexis.com) periodically publish country reports and profiles containing economic and political risk analysis and forecasts.

uous product and process improvements. Germany is thus an attractive choice for locating the operations of a manufacturer of precision engineered products.

Entry Modes

Once a firm has selected a country or countries, it must decide on a preferred mode of entry. In broad terms, four modes of entry are available to a firm: *exporting, licensing/franchising, joint venture/strategic alliance, and sole venture or wholly owned subsidiary.*[34] These choices differ in their requirements for invested capital and in the degree of control they offer to the firm over its investment. Exporting requires relatively low investment and hence is less risky, but it offers no control over the marketing of the product in foreign countries, thereby limiting profit potential. By contrast, a sole venture is a high investment–high risk alternative, but it offers a higher degree of operational and marketing control to the firm in foreign regions, thus facilitating the full exploitation of international opportunities. Licensing/franchising and joint venture/strategic alliance lie between these two poles.

The exact mode of entry a firm selects depends on industry conditions, the firm's international competitive strategy, its propensity to take risk, and the extent of control the firm desires in its international operations. Some firms employ a gradual approach to entering foreign markets, moving from exporting to licensing and then to joint ventures or sole ownership, so as to minimize risk.[35] Others employ more than one entry mode at a time to optimize benefits; for example, McDonald's uses franchising and sole venture, whereas Heineken uses exporting, licensing, joint venture, and sole venture (see Strategy in Practice 7.1). Yet other firms select an entry mode based on a step-by-step, rational analysis of the situation that seeks to minimize risk and maximize opportunities.[36] While these are important considerations, and exceptions are possible (for example, a firm may not go through the gradual process and instead choose joint venture or sole venture outright), it is important to bear in mind while choosing an entry mode that it is a strategic decision. International market entry requires significant resource commitments, and once a choice has been made and implemented, it is difficult to change without considerable loss of time and money.[37]

Let us look at each entry mode and its advantages and disadvantages. Table 7.4 summarizes these characteristics.

Exporting

Exporting is the simplest and the most common form of international market entry. Most manufacturing firms entering foreign markets for the first time choose this option and later switch to other options, although many stay as exporters only. In exporting, a firm makes the product in one or a few central locations, preferably in the home country, and ships it to another country or several countries for sale. An exporter does not generally require large foreign operations unless it is essential for the firm to pursue offshore manufacturing. However, exporting requires a firm to set up sales and distribution outlets in key foreign locations. An exporter generally meets this need through contracts with host-country firms.

Exporting is an appropriate entry mode when the firm needs control over product design and production operations. Because finished goods (whose value is insured) and not investment capital move across borders, it is a low-risk option. Exporting

TABLE 7.4	Advantages and Disadvantages of Different Entry Modes

ENTRY MODE	ADVANTAGES	DISADVANTAGES
Exporting	Control over design and production operations; least risky Economies of scale Location advantages	Tariff and currency fluctuation problems No control over marketing and distribution in foreign locations Difficult to respond to foreign market changes in a timely manner Logistical problems
Licensing	Control over technology A steady stream of free cash flow An attractive alternative to entering a foreign market that is politically volatile	No control over the quality of licensee's production and marketing operations Possible emergence of licensee as a competitor Income limited to royalty payments
Joint venture/Alliance	Useful information about host-country markets, buyer tastes, and government regulations Knowledge sharing between partners, resulting in enhanced learning and development of new competencies to exploit international opportunities	Risk of losing trade or technology secrets to the partner Compromises a firm's independence Trust problems and tension between partners resulting from cultural and language barriers
Sole venture	Total control over business operations No need to rely on host-country firms that compromise independence	Very expensive; large capital requirements Highly risky—market failure or expropriation of assets by host-country government can result in substantial losses Extremely difficult to move assets out of the country when problems develop

offers economies of scale, and through market expansion a firm can ramp up production and derive volume economies. It is especially attractive to firms whose domestic demand does not permit high-volume production. Another important benefit is the freedom it offers in the selection and location of manufacturing operations: a firm can locate its operations anywhere in the world where they can be efficiently performed and can export the product worldwide from that location. Heineken, the world's most global brewer, produces its flagship brand Heineken in 110 breweries situated in fifty countries and exports it to over 170 countries, which makes the firm the world's number one beer exporter.

Exporting has some major drawbacks, however. Not all products are suitable for export—among them, delicate items, or heavy items (for example, pianos). Manufacturers of heavy items solve this problem by shipping their products in parts and assembling them in host countries. However, import tariffs, currency exchange rate fluctuations (referred to as foreign exchange risk),* and lack of control in mar-

---

*An exporter generally receives payments in foreign currencies that must be converted into its national currency. Fluctuations in the currency conversion or exchange rate can result in losses for the exporter. For example, assume a U.S. firm exports $10,000 worth of computers to a European importer. At the time of sale, the exchange rate between the dollar and the euro is $1 = EUR 1 and the European importer agrees to pay EUR 10,000 when goods arrive. If the euro falls in value when the European importer actually makes the payment, and the new exchange rate is $0.90 = EUR 1, the U.S. exporter has incurred a 10 percent loss. The EUR 10,000 it received is now worth only $9,000.

keting the product in foreign countries are other drawbacks that work against the selection of exporting as an entry mode.

Licensing and Franchising

Licensing is another entry mode in which the entering firm (licensor) authorizes a foreign firm (licensee) to use its patented technology for making and marketing products in the licensee's home country. In exchange, the licensing firm receives an upfront, one-time payment and a regular payment of commissions (known as royalties) on sales. Besides product technology, copyrights and other intellectual properties are also licensable. Every licensing agreement is unique, but terms that are common to most include (1) a territorial clause restricting the market boundaries within which the licensee will make and sell the product, (2) an exclusivity clause indicating whether or not the licensor can enter into a competing licensing agreement with another firm within the specified territory, (3) the duration of the license, and (4) compensation terms.

Licensing is appropriate when the firm: (a) must have control over its technology, (b) has a proven product (or technology) but is short on capital needed to develop foreign operations, and (c) does not want to physically move to foreign locations it considers unsafe. Licensing lets the firm exploit international markets without making any capital investment. In fact, it offers the firm a risk-free opportunity to rapidly recoup the costs initially sunk in the development of the technology. But licensing's strategic disadvantage is that the licensor has no control over the quality of the licensee's operations, which can adversely affect the reputation of the licensor. The firm may encounter other problems as well. Its licensees may become potential competitors in the international scene, and the firm may run the risk of losing its technological know-how to foreign firms.

Franchising is a form of licensing in which the franchiser sells a trademark or a trade secret for a fee and royalty payments. The franchiser retains control over the operations of the franchisee by requiring the latter to strictly follow the rules and business guidelines that the franchiser sets up. Licensing is a strategy generally pursued only by manufacturing firms, and franchising is employed only by service firms. All other conditions are generally the same for licensing and franchising.

Joint Ventures and Strategic Alliances

Exporting, licensing, and franchising do not require investment in foreign facilities, but joint ventures do. In recent times, joint ventures have become a relatively more popular form of entry, fueled by explosive growth opportunities in the developing nations and the guarantees these nations offer to foreign investors in regard to the safety of their capital. **Joint ventures** are partnerships between two or more firms that result in the creation of a third entity.

The partners are called parents of the newly created entity, which functions as a separate corporation. When there are only two partners, a 50-50 stock ownership that provides partners with equal control of the new venture through board member representation is common. In some instances, a 51-49 ownership may emerge when a dominant partner insists on having more control of the venture. Generally, this dominant partner is the firm seeking to enter a new country with its patented technology, and the minority partner is the host-country firm that provides marketing and distribution resources. Several U.S. firms have entered the European, Asian, and Latin American markets by joint venturing with host-country firms along these lines.

On occasion, two firms from different countries may join hands to pursue opportunities globally. A good example of a joint venture of this type is the one between Lever Brothers of the United Kingdom and Margarine Uni of Holland, which gave birth to a new entity called Unilever. Unilever makes and markets frozen food, toiletries, and other consumer products in several countries of the world.

Strategic alliance is another way by which a firm seeks international market entry. A **strategic alliance** is an agreement between firms to *cooperate* in certain ways to achieve strategic benefits. It does not create a new entity. A firm seeking entry into a foreign market executes an agreement with a host-country firm authorizing it to act as its local marketing and sales agent in return for doing the same in its own country. Several European airlines have such marketing agreements with North American airlines; the firms cross-sell each other's routes. However, alliances are not limited to cooperation in the area of marketing alone. Several encourage cooperation in the areas of R&D, new product development, production, and distribution. General Motors helped Isuzu enter the U.S. market by selling its pickup trucks through its U.S. dealerships; in exchange, Isuzu trained General Motors' personnel in small-car production in its plants in Japan.

The major strategic advantage of a joint venture/strategic alliance is that the firm benefits from the host-country partner's knowledge of the market, industry conditions, buyer tastes, and government regulations. A second advantage is that it facilitates knowledge sharing between partners, resulting in enhanced learning and the development of new competencies. Joint venture is thus appropriate when the firm needs complementary technology and information to exploit international opportunities. But a major strategic disadvantage of joint ventures and alliances is the risk the firm takes in sharing its patented information with a foreign partner. International alliances also suffer from cultural and language barriers, mistrust, and partner incompatibility. As a result, they have a lower success rate than other modes of entry.

Sole Venture

A **sole venture,** also known as a *wholly owned subsidiary,* is a foreign business unit in which a firm has 100 percent ownership of the subsidiary's stock. There are two ways by which a firm can establish a subsidiary in a foreign market: by acquiring an existing business in the host country or by launching an entirely new operation from scratch, referred to as *greenfield* investment.[38]

A sole venture makes sense strategically when the firm needs total control of its foreign assets; it allows the firm to safeguard its technology, trade secrets, and business processes. Sole venture is thus a preferred mode of entry for businesses with proprietary technological information such as pharmaceuticals, scientific tools, and diagnostic instruments. It also eliminates the need to rely on a host-country firm for resources or local information that seriously compromises a firm's independence. However, sole venturing has significant problems too. Starting a new operation from scratch in a foreign location (or in several foreign locations) is expensive. Market failure or expropriation of assets by a foreign government can result in a substantial loss of invested capital. Strategically, exit is extremely difficult: when problems develop in a host country due to political unrest, economic downturns, or an adverse change in public sentiment toward foreign businesses, it is a monumental task to close operations and move out.

TABLE 7.5	International Expansion Conditions, Mode of Entry, and Country Choice	
EXPAND INTERNATIONALLY WHEN	**CHOOSE AN ENTRY MODE THAT MATCHES OPPORTUNITIES TO FIRM STRENGTHS AND INVESTMENT RISK TO PROFIT POTENTIAL**	**SELECT FOREIGN MARKETS OR COUNTRY LOCATIONS BASED ON**
Foreign markets offer high growth opportunities.	Export License Joint venture Sole venture	*Market Factors* —Growing/stable demand —Supplier and distributor segments exist or can be quickly developed —Complementary products/segments exist or can be quickly developed —Market structure favorable for profits
Large customer base is needed to gain volume economies or to recoup sunk costs in R&D.	Export License	*Factor Endowments* —Capital market developed —Skilled labor and supervisory talent readily available —Transportation and communication infrastructure adequate
Cheaper, higher quality or unique resources are available in foreign locations.	Joint venture Sole venture	*Political/Economic Climate* —Politically stable —Government regulations favoring foreign direct investment
Competitors are expanding abroad and gaining market power.	Joint venture Sole venture	—Low tariffs and minimal or no quota restrictions —Growing/stable economy —Stable currency —Per capita/disposable income growing
International location experience will offer new learning opportunities.	Joint venture Sole venture	*Socio-Cultural Climate* —Lifestyle —Consumer taste and preferences favorable —Public attitude toward foreign business favorable

Table 7.5 provides a comprehensive framework on which to making decisions: when to expand internationally, what mode of entry will be relevant for the context, and which foreign markets/locations will be appropriate.

Summary

Rapidly falling trade barriers and the emergence of new technologies have opened new opportunities for firms in international markets in recent decades. While international expansion has strategic advantages, it is also punctuated with political and market-related risks. It is essential for firms to analyze these risks and understand industry competition before embarking on international expansion. In deciding what strategy to use to expand internationally, firms have three options. Global strategy focuses on the advantages gained from efficiency and global integration, multidomestic strategy focuses on those gained from local responsiveness, and transnational strategy focuses on achieving both aims. The choice depends on the competitive pressures of the industry and the firm's own preferences.

There are four alternatives available to firms for entering global markets: exporting, licensing/franchising, joint venture/strategic alliance, and sole venture or wholly owned subsidiary. Which option a firm chooses depends on industry conditions, the firm's international competitive strategy, and the extent of control the firm desires in its international business operations.

Chapter 7 Discussion Questions and Projects

Discussion Questions

1. Select a product (one not discussed in this chapter) for which a global strategy is appropriate and another for which a multidomestic strategy is appropriate. Provide your reasons.

2. Discuss why it is critical for firms in the pharmaceutical and petroleum industries to compete on a global scale.

Projects

1. Is the beer industry global or multidomestic? Using the Internet, investigate the international expansion strategies pursued by the top three brewers (Anheuser-Busch, SAB-Miller, and Heineken) and analyze them.

2. Select any two U.S. companies that compete internationally. Using the Internet and sources in the business press, read about their international operations. What is their international competitive strategy? What entry modes have they used in international expansion? Do you think alternative modes could have been more appropriate?

3. Ben and Jerry's is considering marketing its products in international markets. Should the firm use a multidomestic or global strategy? Provide reasons for your answer by discussing the advantages and disadvantages of each strategy for Ben and Jerry's.

Continuing Case

Pepsi-Cola's International Expansion

Background

From zits early years, Pepsi-Cola aimed to transform its flagship brand Pepsi into the leader in soft drink sales. To realize this aim, the firm initially focused on effectively marketing Pepsi in the United States as better tasting than Coca-Cola. Later, it diversified into related products and businesses that, besides increasing Pepsi's sales, provided additional cash to help the firm successfully compete with Coke. Soon thereafter, the firm contemplated international ex-

pansion; marketing Pepsi in other countries could enhance sales and strengthen the firm's competitive position against Coca-Cola. Initial international expansion strategies were limited to exporting packaged bottles to neighboring Canada but in 1934 the company opened a bottling and distribution operation in that country, its first direct foreign investment. In the following year, it set up similar operations in Cuba and in England. However, aggressive steps to introduce Pepsi in several countries and to market it as a global brand did not start until the early 1990s. Domestic growth opportunities and lack of adequate capital to finance foreign operations had kept the firm from pursuing international expansion in a big way. And when the firm finally did commence to expand, it faced an uphill battle, since by then Coke had already established itself as the global leader in soft drinks and was the world's most recognized brand.

Carbonated Soft Drinks Operations: Value Chain

Carbonated soft drinks (CSD) operations comprise concentrate production, bottling and distribution, and marketing. Using proprietary and secret formulas, the concentrate producers blend the raw materials, pack the concentrate in plastic containers or large drums, and ship the concentrate to franchised bottlers. The bottling companies add carbonated water and syrup to the concentrate, bottle or can the soda, and sell the soft drinks to the retailers. Restaurants buy the concentrate for their fountain directly from the concentrate producers. Marketing is the responsibility of the concentrate producers who own the soft drinks brand, although the bottling companies often share the marketing costs with them.

Concentrate production requires very little capital. An investment of $50 million is adequate to meet the U.S. CSD consumption, which was 17 billion gallons (57 gallons per capita) in 2003. Bottling operations are capital intensive, requiring $75 million for a large plant, and eighty such plants are needed to meet the U.S. annual demand of 17 billion gallons. The average pretax margin in bottling is about 9 percent, whereas concentrate sales yield a hefty 30 percent margin. Because of the high capital requirements and low profit margins in bottling, concentrate producers prefer to franchise bottling operations. The franchisee gets exclusive rights to bottle the product and sell it within a geographic area using the franchiser's brand name.

Concentrate firms aim for worldwide franchising since it generates large volume sales and a sizeable royalty income as a result. However, to prevent competitive entry, they also seek forward integration in certain markets. By owning the bottling and distribution resources or taking a controlling interest in the franchisee's business through equity participation, concentrate producers limit the availability of such resources to a potential entrant, thus preventing entry.

International Market Opportunities

Several factors influence CSD consumption in a society. While they include the lifestyle of its people and the percentage of young people in its population, a predominant factor is disposable income. Countries whose population has a significantly higher disposable income consume more CSD than those in which most people live on marginal subsistence levels. For example, the per capita consumption of CSD in the United States in 2003 was 57 gallons compared to 10 gallons in China. In 2003, the world consumed about 50 billion gallons of CSD, and over 70 percent of this consumption occurred in the developed regions of the world (i.e., North America, Western Europe, and Japan), which have relatively higher disposable incomes. But, the developing regions are said to be rapidly catching up. Market research studies project a 5 percent annual growth in world consumption of CSD during the next several years, and much of this growth is expected to occur in the developing countries of Asia, Africa, and Latin America, for two important reasons: (1) demand in the economically developed regions is reaching saturation levels, and (2) the disposable income of people in developing countries is rapidly rising because of the economic development measures undertaken by their governments. As a result, for a soft drinks firm aiming for growth through international expansion, the developing regions appear to offer more promise.

Pepsi-Cola's International Expansion Strategy

To be successful in international expansion, a soft drinks firm needs two key strengths: (1) access to manufacturing and distribution resources in several international locations, and (2) a strong global brand. The following explains why these strengths are critical.

Soft drinks must be bottled and distributed regionally so that supplies (water and syrup) can be economically procured locally, transportation to the end market is cheaper, and manufacturing is able to effectively meet local product-mix and regulatory needs. To ensure uniformity in product taste, plants employ input and process standardization and the use of advanced water purification technologies to further minimize taste variations. Because bottling capacity is limited in each region, a soft drinks firm that has access to bottling resources in several international locations through long-term bottling franchise arrangements has an advantage over others. The firm translates this manufacturing-volume advantage into sales-volume advantage by creating a global brand. A global brand emerges when the firm employs a uniform theme in international advertising and promotion by centralizing marketing decisions and activities.

By moving into many of the attractive foreign markets first, and locking in available production capacity through long-term franchising or outright ownership, Coke secured a manufacturing and distribution advantage. Through consistent marketing efforts that promoted Coke as the real thing, the firm created a global brand. On both these counts, Pepsi remained weak due to its late arrival on the international scene. As a result, Coke has historically maintained a significant lead over Pepsi in international sales. During the1990s, this lead was about 4 to 1—Coke's $12 billion in international sales to Pepsi's $3 billion, on average.

From the mid-1990s, Pepsi-Cola has sought to strengthen its international market presence and performance by using two specific strategies. The aim has been to achieve global visibility and recognition paralleling Coca-Cola's.

1. In the first strategy, the emphasis is on entering emerging markets in which Coca-Cola has a weak presence or that offer a high growth potential, sufficient for both companies to stay and exploit (e.g., China, India, Indonesia). By offering attractive incentives (higher share in equity, profits) to bottlers, entering into long-term joint venture agreements with them, or by acquiring local bottling facilities, the firm has sought to rapidly achieve manufacturing and distribution strengths in these markets. In addition, by aggressively promoting its brand among the young through music and lifestyle themes, the company has striven to establish Pepsi as a global name in soft drinks.

2. In the second strategy, the emphasis is on seeking joint ventures/alliances with leading international food and beverage firms that would give Pepsi entry into developed markets that are currently Coke's strongholds. In 1996, Pepsi-Cola developed jointly with Starbucks a coffee-flavored drink called frappuccino that is presently sold internationally through the latter's retail outlets. In October 2003, Pepsi-Cola entered into a joint venture with Unilever, a large packaged-food and consumer products multinational, to make and sell tea concentrates (Lipton brand) to bottlers.

These strategies have helped Pepsi-Cola not only increase its international sales significantly but also transform Pepsi as a global brand vis-à-vis Coke. In the 1980s, there were about 300 Pepsi plants worldwide and the Pepsi brand was sold in just over 100 countries; in 2004, these numbers stood at 700 plants and 175 countries. And in 2004, Pepsi's international sales were about $9 billion compared to Coca-Cola's $14.6 billion.

Discussion Questions

1. Describe the value chain stages in the soft drinks industry. Is this a global industry or a multidomestic industry? Provide reasons for your answer.

2. Describe the factors critical for success for a soft drinks firm that aims to expand aggressively internationally. Explain why these factors are critical for success.

3. Describe clearly the international expansion strategy employed by Pepsi-Cola from the early 1990s to the present.

Source: P. Sellers and J. E. Davis, "Pepsi Opens a Second Front," *Fortune,* August 8, 1994, 70–76; P. Sellers, "How Coke Is Kicking Pepsi's Can," *Fortune,* October 28, 1996; *"Global Soft Drinks Report 2003,"* Zenith International, 2004; D. Foust, "Gone Flat," *Business Week,* December 20, 2004; L. Jabbonsky, "Room to Run," *Beverage World,* August 1993, 24–29; R. Girard, "Coca-Cola Company: Inside the Real Thing," Polaris Institute, October 2004.

8

Functional-Level Strategy: Building Functional Capabilities for Strategic Performance*

CHAPTER OBJECTIVES

After reading this chapter, you should be able to:

■ Define and discuss the importance of functional-level strategies for a firm's strategic performance

■ Describe each strategy at the functional level and how it is developed

■ Discuss the competencies and competitive advantages associated with each function

■ Develop appropriate functional-level strategies for a low cost firm, a differentiator, a vertically integrated firm, and a diversified firm

■ Discuss the need for a multifunctional orientation in today's businesses

---

*Professor Ed Boyer of Temple University prepared the initial draft for the Marketing Strategy, Human Resources Strategy, and Financial Strategy portions of this chapter.

Opening Case

In July 1995, Amazon.com began business as an Internet-based bookseller. Initially derided by investors as another expensive dot.com gimmick, the company soon emerged as the world's largest online retailer. By 1999, in just four years of existence, Amazon's sales of books and CDs had reached the $1 billion mark. Encouraged by its stellar growth, the company expanded its product line by including DVDs, toys, consumer electronics, cameras, housewares, and related goods to its inventory. Cumulatively, the company is estimated to have served over 40 million satisfied customers since inception and its sales in 2004 totaled $6.9 billion. Industry analysts forecast that Amazon.com is most likely to grow by 20 percent each year for several years to come and could very well emerge one day as the Wal-Mart of the Internet environment.

Amazon.com does business through the Internet only, serving consumers who prefer the convenience of shopping online. It is thus a focuser, serving a narrow segment of the consumer retail market. Within this narrow segment, it emphasizes *selection*, *convenience*, and *service* as key areas that differentiate it from brick-and-mortar stores. In addition, to quickly generate a sizable customer base, the company offers its products at a deep *discount* compared to the regular stores. Amazon.com is thus a focuser competing on a "*cost-differentiation*" combination strategy. To be successful with this strategy, Amazon.com must offer customer service superior to that of the competition, both Internet-based and brick-and-mortar, and its costs must be lower. Achieving a cost advantage in a focused segment, however, is a special challenge to any firm because its narrow focus makes economies of scale hard to come by.

To effectively realize its cost-differentiation combination goals, Amazon.com has sought strength in its *operations functions* (order procurement, distribution) through massive investments in information technology. The company has installed a state-of-the-art computer system that allows it to store over 3 million book titles (compared to 100,000 in a brick-and-mortar store), offering customers both an exhaustive list and speed in product selection. At the same time, the computer system is capable of handling volume and variety without compromising customer convenience. More importantly, it has integrated value chain activities, from sales to billing, to procurement, and shipping, permitting the firm to complete both order execution and account collection speedily and efficiently. In essence, Amazon.com's aggressive investments in computer automation have not only enabled the firm to achieve both cost and differentiation advantages but have also secured it a dominant market position in Internet retailing, creating entry barriers in the process.

But tangible assets alone do not create sustainable advantages. Amazon.com has also accumulated within its operations function intangible strengths that emerge from its effective management of its technological assets. The firm has invested in technological skills and capabilities that allow it to customize generically available software to its unique needs. It has also developed proprietary software that deploys information technology in novel ways, creating a personalized shopping experience for its customers. Overall, it has developed an internal culture that is driven to exploit information technology to serve the needs of the customer. Technological innovation aimed at satisfying the customer is a core value of the company.[1]

The key to Amazon.com's success is that it chose to invest in functional activities that were critical for achieving its business goals. Providing shoppers with a differentiated service at a lower cost required unique strengths in operations. By aggressively automating the operations function and by customizing the technology, Amazon.com gained the needed strengths. In this chapter, we discuss functional-level strategy and its importance to strategic management. Understanding what a functional-level strategy is and what strategic choices are available within each function (i.e., marketing, operations, R&D, human resources, and finance) is essential if managers are to make intelligent strategic management decisions.

We define **functional-level strategy** as a set of decisions and actions managers take to attain superior competency in business functions. A functional-level strategy aims to develop the functional competencies and competitive advantages the firm needs to effectively pursue its business-level and corporate-level goals. Managers thus formulate for each functional unit a strategy consistent with the firm's chosen business and corporate-level strategies. For example, a firm that is pursuing a cost strategy employs the following functional-level strategies: a manufacturing function strategy that focuses on devising high-volume production methods that will reduce unit costs; a marketing function strategy that focuses on creating a mass market for the firm's product(s) that will reduce advertising and promotional costs; and a human resources function strategy that emphasizes the development of work and skill standards that will reduce operational costs by increasing employee productivity. Understandably, a differentiator firm will use functional-level strategies that are entirely unlike these. By the same logic, the functional-level strategies of a multi-business firm will differ from one business unit to another because the competitive goals of these units are likely to vary.

Because functional-level strategies have the potential to contribute to the firm's current and future competitiveness, it is necessary to develop them in concert. In other words, functional-level strategies must complement one another by being internally consistent.

Marketing Strategy

The responsibility of the marketing function is to identify attractive market opportunities for the firm's current or potential products and services and to develop strategies that will fully exploit those opportunities. Toward that end, the marketing function's activities involve (a) selecting suitable market segments based on the product's attributes, and (b) positioning the product in a way that is most appealing to customers in those segments. The goal of the marketing function is to create a marketing-related competitive advantage for the firm.[2]

To develop an effective marketing strategy, managers do three things. First, they segment the market—that is, they divide the market into identifiable customer groups. Second, they select the segment(s) the firm will target or focus on. Third, they decide how they will position the product in the selected segment in a way that will create value for customers. Note what we emphasize here: the focus of marketing strategy is on the *market*, not on the product, and this is where marketing strategy begins.

Segmenting the Market

Market segmentation is the classification of potential customers into distinct subgroups: groups with different needs, characteristics, or behavior. This classification is essential to determine which segments offer the best opportunities for the firm's product(s). Segmentation is effective when it broadly classifies the market based on customer needs and the different ways a firm can satisfy those needs. Companies rarely start out with a well-defined product; instead, they design and supply a product to serve well-defined markets. If Coke had defined its product narrowly as a cola beverage, it would have seen only Pepsi as its competition rather than all beverages that satisfy thirst. As a result, Coke might never have introduced other products like bottled water and orange juice to its line of beverages and could have passed up profitable growth opportunities. Although Amazon.com initially began selling only books over the Internet, it perceived and defined its market in terms of the broader customer convenience and service it could deliver. This focus on customers and their convenience enabled Amazon.com to expand into a range of products.

Targeting the Market

After evaluating the different market segments, managers must decide which segment(s) their firm will serve. A firm cannot effectively serve them all; managers must, therefore, identify those segments that offer the greatest profit-making potential. Several factors influence the selection of the target market.[3] First and foremost, the size of the segment and the rate at which it is growing should justify targeting it. Second, the structure of the segment and competitive conditions within it must be favorable for profits. Third, the firm must possess sufficient superior resources and capabilities to serve the selected segment successfully.

Three different targeting strategies are available to managers to choose from: undifferentiated marketing, differentiated marketing, or concentrated marketing.[4] In **undifferentiated marketing**, managers ignore market segments and, instead, treat the market as a homogeneous unit. Ford's Model T is a good example; Ford hoped the car would appeal to everyone. At one time, Pepsi-Cola perceived the market for cola as undifferentiated and, as a result, promoted only one brand of Pepsi. Undifferentiated marketing is attractive to cost leaders since it offers mass-marketing and economies of scale advantages.

In **differentiated marketing**, managers decide to target several segments by designing and offering the product differently for each. Today, Ford pursues a differentiated marketing strategy by offering a variety of models to appeal to different market segments. Pepsi-Cola offers regular, diet, and decaffeinated Pepsi. Differentiated marketing is attractive to broad differentiators because it allows them to appeal to distinct buyer groups through product modification.

In **concentrated marketing**, managers decide to focus on a single segment (a niche) and aim to capture a high market share within that niche to be profitable. Amazon.com is a good example of a firm pursuing concentrated marketing. It competes in Internet-based retailing only. Focused cost and focused differentiators use concentrated marketing. Figure 8.1 diagrams these three approaches.

Market Positioning

After selecting the segment(s) in which the firm will participate, managers must decide how the firm and its products will be *positioned* in that segment. **Positioning** creates in the minds of target customers a distinctive image of the firm and its products/services, relative to the competition.[5] Thus, a firm may choose to be perceived by customers as offering a standard product, a high-performance product, a utility

FIGURE 8.1 Alternative Targeting Approaches

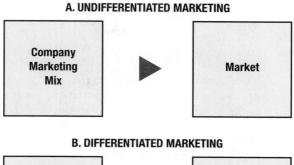

A. UNDIFFERENTIATED MARKETING

B. DIFFERENTIATED MARKETING

C. CONCENTRATED MARKETING

Source: Kotler, Philip; Armstrong, Gary, *Principles of Marketing,* p. 232. Copyright © 1991. Adapted by permission of Pearson Education, Inc., Upper Saddle River, NJ.

product, or a luxury product. Hyundai has positioned its auto as an economy car, Mercedes as a luxury car, BMW as a high-performance car, and Porsche as a sports car. By deliberately choosing a market position and strengthening it through an appropriate *marketing mix (pricing, promotion, and distribution)*, a firm creates strategic advantages. Ineffective positioning (that is, when customers perceive the firm or its products differently from what the firm intended them to) places a firm at a strategic disadvantage.

There are a number of considerations in strategic positioning. Managers must decide whether to differentiate their offerings based on product characteristics or on company image. For example, DiGiorno's Pizza created an advertising campaign that compared its product to delivered pizzas, thereby distinguishing other frozen pizzas as inferior. Alternatively, companies can create a company image. BIC has successfully positioned itself as a marketer of low-priced, disposable consumer products. Sony has developed a reputation for product reliability and performance with the Trinitron picture tube. Dell has distinguished itself with customer responsiveness.

Marketing Strategy Choices

Through segmentation, targeting, and positioning, a firm selects a marketing strategy that is consistent with its strategic goals. Thus, a cost leader chooses an undifferentiated marketing strategy, together with competitive pricing and mass distribution, and positions itself as a firm offering standard products for mass markets. Likewise, a differentiator chooses differentiated marketing strategy along with components appropriate to this strategy (e.g., premium pricing, targeted promotion, and selective distribution channels), and positions itself as a firm offering unique products for segmented markets. A firm is strong in marketing when customers perceive it the way it has positioned itself, and when it satisfies customer needs more effectively in that position than rivals do. A firm is weak in marketing when all the marketing components so far discussed are internally inconsistent.

Product Life Cycle and Marketing Strategies

One important way by which marketing strategies are developed is by examining the product's life cycle (PLC). Most products go through such a cycle, the stages of which are emergence, growth, maturity, and decline. Each stage requires different marketing strategies, due to the unique challenges each presents.

Emergence Stage

The emergence stage is characterized by low sales and absence of profitability. Product acceptance takes time, and sales growth in the beginning is therefore slow. The goal of the firm at this stage is to develop a viable market for the product by creating product awareness and attracting distributors. Toward that end, it must inform consumers of the new product, the firm's brand, and where it is available, and it must induce consumers to try it. The marketing strategy appropriate for this purpose is high-volume advertising and promotion. Advertising creates awareness of the product while promotion provides the necessary inducement to try it.

Growth Stage

At the growth stage, the market expands rapidly, inducing competitors with enhanced product features to enter the market. Promotional expenditures typically increase, but because of the increase in sales, the firm achieves economies in advertising. Prices start to decline because of increasing competition, but economies of scale in production allow firms to earn higher profits. It is essential at this stage to fend off competitors and establish a clear position for the firm and its products in the minds of consumers. In addition, the firm must endeavor to recover its investment and provide investors with a competitive return. This concern, however, may be complicated by the fact that firms may have to make a choice between current profit and future market share. Investing in the product and its wider distribution now, and sacrificing some profits, ensures for the firm a leading position down the road. Thus, marketing strategies at the growth stage focus on product improvements, promotion, and distribution to achieve a dominant and enduring market position for the firm.

Maturity Stage

The maturity stage is burdened by overcapacity leading to increased intensity of competition through advertising campaigns and price wars. The decline in profitability may force some firms to exit the market, resulting in market consolidation. Strategies to expand the market include converting customers who have been reluctant to try the product, extending the product into a new market segment, inducing customers to switch from competitors, and increasing the frequency of product consumption by current customers.

Other strategies to extend the maturity stage are product-modification strategies and marketing-mix strategies. A company can modify the product through quality, features, or style. Marketing mix strategies can change pricing or advertising or make use of extended distribution channels, sales promotions, additional sales force, or added services.

Decline Stage

Sales of most products decline because of a change in the product's technology, a change in consumer taste, or increased competition. For example, digital camera technology has forced photographic film into decline. Likewise, CDs have edged out cassette tapes. As sales and profits decline, some firms may withdraw from unprofitable market segments or exit the industry altogether. Those that stay may reduce the number of their product offerings but intensify the level of competition on the remaining products so as to hold onto their existing market share. The best marketing strategy for a firm at this stage depends on its competitive position in the industry. Firms with a weak competitive position generally exit the industry. But those with a strong brand exit from the unprofitable segments and reposition their product in new and more promising segments. During the 1970s, Miller Brewing Company successfully repositioned its beer from an upper-income segment, where it was perceived as the "champagne of beers" and where demand was declining, to a more populous middle-income segment where demand was rising.

The PLC concept is not without problems, and managers must be cautious when using it. First, it is an overly general concept; it may not apply to particular instances and can thus be misleading. Second, precise identification of the stage a product is in, and predicting exactly when it will move to the next stage, is difficult. Third, if the PLC position determines the marketing strategy that managers select, the selected strategy may also influence the subsequent PLC stages—a product at the maturity stage may revert back to the growth stage, instead of moving to the decline stage, as a result of the strategies that firms in an industry employed.[6]

Marketing Strategy in a Multibusiness Firm

What determines marketing strategy for a multibusiness firm? Generally, marketing decisions in such a firm are decentralized—that is, they are made at the business unit level. Decentralization allows marketing managers to formulate strategies tailored to the distinct needs of products offered by each business unit. But, for firms that have diversified by leveraging a single, strong brand (for example, Sony, GE*), corporate-level "*brand promotion*" in addition to the individual business unit level marketing offers unique benefits. First, a shared brand name provides economies of scope advantages because it spreads the marketing costs across several products/businesses. Second, it offers customers a "single value proposition" in the company's products, helping them in their purchasing decisions. Third, it projects a uniform image of the firm, building trust and confidence in consumers' minds about the company's products. For these reasons, multibusiness firms whose several products carry the same brand name undertake brand-promotion strategies at the corporate level. The goal is to position the brand, rather than products, which allows the firm to integrate its product lines and collectively market them.[7]

Operations Strategy

Operations can be defined as a function or system that transforms inputs into outputs of greater value.[8] Therefore, operations management deals with the input-output transformation process. When Amazon.com invests in new computer hardware to enhance its customer-order-processing capabilities, it is engaged in operations management. When General Motors redesigns its assembly line to enhance the performance and reliability of its cars, it is engaged in operations management. Operations managers make decisions about processing capacity, process layout, technology selection and automation levels, vertical integration levels, and employee control and reward mechanisms. Most of these decisions are complex, affecting a firm's operational capabilities and, eventually, its organizational performance.

A firm's operations create the products and services the firm needs to serve customers competitively. Consequently, operational capabilities affect a firm's ability to be successful in the marketplace. Viewed from this perspective, an effective operation is not necessarily one that promises the maximum efficiency or engineering perfection; it is, rather, one that fits the specific competitive needs of the firm.[9] Operating systems should, therefore, be deliberately designed to support the firm's competitive goals.[10] In other words, a cost leader must have an operating system that is capable of securing a cost advantage for the firm. A differentiator must have an operating system that is capable of output consistency (that is, zero defects) and is able to effectively make different designs. Research evidence indicates that firms whose operations capabilities and business goals match are high performing.[11]

Operations strategy thus involves managerial decisions and actions to ensure that the firm's operations capabilities match the needs of its business and corporate-level strategies. Choices of automation to be used, processing skills to be developed, and related issues are operations strategy decisions. Choosing one type of automation over another or organizing the operations function in one way instead of another creates different operational capabilities.[12] Therefore, to formulate an effective operations strategy, managers must first understand what automation and organizational choices are associated with different operational capabilities.

---

*The GE brand name is common to many products marketed by different GE business divisions—consumer appliances, health care, energy products, and consumer credit and finance.

Operational Capabilities

In broad terms, operations function can be designed for any one of three capabilities: cost (processing efficiency), quality (manufacturing quality—that is, output consistency), and flexibility (producing in different volume, variety, speedy processing).[13] Let us now briefly describe the choices firms make that create these capabilities in their operations. Table 8.1 summarizes this section.

Cost

Cost refers to the ability of the operations function to process units at a lower cost than competitors—that is, achieve a cost advantage in the industry. The manufacturing approach associated with this capability is high-volume production—generally referred to as large batch production as opposed to small batch production. Increasing production volume by keeping the fixed cost constant reduces unit costs.

A prerequisite for this approach is that the firm must minimize its product mix or variety. By offering a few standard designs, the firm is able to make them in large lot sizes to derive economies of scale. The manufacturing technology requirement for this approach is variously known as **fixed automation** or **sequential automation**, in which units are put together in assembly-line fashion. A firm aggressively invests in large-scale operations facilities to achieve the necessary production volume. Output consistency (the achievement of zero defects) is not a priority here, but volume production is, and a certain defect ratio is viewed as acceptable. In regard to the work environment at the operational level, the firm standardizes the task, allowing employees to perform repetitively. Repetitive performance leads to specialized learning, resulting in increased productivity and lower unit cost.

Quality

A product is assessed for quality based on how it is designed and how it is made. **Design quality** refers to the product's features and functionality and is the responsibility of the design engineering function. **Manufacturing quality** (also known as **process quality**) refers to how effectively each unit has been made—that is, whether the finished unit conforms to the specifications of the designed unit. Units that do not conform to the design are considered defective. An operations system's role in quality is thus its ability to make units that consistently match design specifications.

The manufacturing approach associated with quality capability is medium-volume production of a few standard designs. But the emphasis is on a flexible manufacturing system that will permit incremental design enhancements and process improvements to realize zero defects. The manufacturing technology requirement for this goal is **computer-aided manufacturing (CAM)** automation with robots and process-monitoring technologies. CAM allows frequent changes to be made in the product's design. Robots make products with higher precision, consistency, and reliability than people can. Process-monitoring technologies achieve quality by monitoring and controlling the process that produces the product—that is, they prevent defects. The operations work environment for pursuing quality requires multiskilled personnel, cross-functional relationships, and a continuous learning culture.

Flexibility

Flexibility refers to the ability of the operations system to adjust to volume or design changes without affecting cost. **Volume flexibility** is the ability to increase or decrease production volume rapidly when customers frequently change their order or when industry demand fluctuates. Firms competing in cyclical industries such as housing and durable goods make volume flexibility capabilities their priority. **Design flexibility** is the ability to make products in different designs or to frequently change to new designs. Firms that differentiate their product to compete in multiple market segments and those that must frequently innovate seek design flexibility.

The manufacturing approach associated with flexibility is mass customization with an emphasis on "cost, quality, and frequent innovation" combined. Firms achieve flexibility in operations through investment in **flexible automation** that electronically integrates product design and manufacturing tools (generally referred to as computer-integrated manufacturing). Electronic integration of several operations allows information to flow across value chain stages in virtual time, thereby ensuring speed and efficiency in operations. As a result, the firm can make frequent changes in production volume and product design and do so economically.[14] The operations work environment for a flexibility firm emphasizes nonstandardized jobs, broad worker skills, worker autonomy, and continuous learning.

TABLE 8.1	**Technology and Organizational Choices that Create Operational Capabilities**

OPERATIONAL CAPABILITY	TECHNOLOGY AND ORGANIZATIONAL CHOICES
Cost	Fixed automation (dedicated to a single product design) Sequential processing (assembly-line setup) Mass production (large lot sizes) Manufacturing emphasis on increasing productivity Standardized product (no design variety) Work standardization (no task variety in a job) Focused employee skills
Quality	Flexible automation (not dedicated to any one design) Sequential processing Medium-volume production Manufacturing emphasis on adding higher value to the product and zero defects Standard product but incremental enhancement to features Multiskilled operations personnel Continuous learning culture
Flexibility	Computer-aided manufacturing (electronic integration of design and manufacturing tools) Parallel processing Mass customization Manufacturing emphasis on volume and design flexibility Frequent design changes, incremental and radical Multiskilled operations personnel Continuous learning culture

Operations Strategy in a Vertically Integrated, Diversified Firm

Vertical integration and diversification strategies pose unique demands on the firm's operations. Foremost among these demands is the ability to coordinate and harmoniously work with other process operations. Vertical integration requires that a firm's operations sequentially adjust with other value chain stages (e.g., component production, finished goods warehousing). Diversification requires coordination with other product units that share the same manufacturing assets. Firms achieve the required coordination by: (1) electronically linking several machines, known as computer-integrated manufacturing (CIM), which allows real-time information flow among value chain stages, thereby achieving coordination; (2) limiting the number of components used through effective product design, thus minimizing bottlenecks in coordination; and (3) using hierarchical positions (e.g., a chief operating officer) that integrate the activities of several product/process operations. Firms also achieve a smooth flow in the processing of products by locating plants that perform sequential operations close to each other.

Some firms, especially those that pursue a global strategy, employ materials managers at the headquarters level who plan and execute the movement of inputs and semi-processed units across value chain stages into finished units and distribution to the end user. But increasingly, global strategy firms rely more on outsourcing for many of their input requirements than on making them in-house.

Research and Development Strategy

In many industries today, competitive advantage depends on the ability of the firm to develop and leverage new scientific knowledge.[15] The responsibility of the R&D function is to endow the firm with precisely this capability. The R&D function generates new scientific knowledge for meeting the firm's competitive goals—namely, for developing innovative products, efficient processes, or systems to serve customers speedily and effectively.

There are two distinct and yet closely related activities in the **R&D** function: a **research** activity and a **development** activity. Research is a *scientific* activity that identifies new information, whereas development is an *engineering* activity designed to apply new-found knowledge to products or processes.[16] Research activities are further broken down into *basic* and *applied* research. **Basic research**, also referred to as pure research, is exploratory in nature; its purpose is to acquire knowledge for knowledge's sake. It is a quest for radically new scientific information, often characterized as fundamental or frontier knowledge (e.g., recombinant DNA), and thus funding is provided without the expectation of an immediate financial return. In other words, basic research does not directly help current businesses, products, or operations but benefits the firm in the long run with major discoveries, breakthroughs, or by providing a deeper theoretical understanding in a scientific area.

In contrast, **applied research** focuses on the feasibility of transforming into products or processes the theoretical knowledge already obtained through basic research. Through experimentation, applied research simplifies the abstract knowledge emerging from basic research into concrete knowledge (in the form of product specifications and blueprints) needed for developing or enhancing products and processes. Summarily, applied research develops product or process technologies. For example, by using the scientific knowledge of combustion chemistry, researchers developed the internal combustion technology leading to the manufacture of automobiles. Applied research thus has a commercial purpose with benefits for the firm's sales and profits in the near term.

Development is an engineering activity centered on designing products or processes using the data provided by applied research. Through prototyping, testing, and verification, development activities create new products or processes or redesign current ones for better performance. Thus, developmental activities include product innovation, process innovation and product/process redesign. Product innovation allows the firm to create new markets for its products and thus achieve growth. Product redesign makes the existing product easy to manufacture, reducing the defect rates and costs, and thus increases the firm's competitiveness in the current market. Process innovation or redesign improves the efficiency of operations, reducing the overall cost structure and thereby enhancing the firm's competitive capabilities.

What should a firm's R&D focus be? What activities should receive more emphasis? Should the firm stress basic research to generate proprietary knowledge or applied research that will use current knowledge to develop new products and processes? Should developmental activities be directed toward pioneering new products, enhancing current products, or improving the efficiency and speed of operational processes? In other words, what should be the firm's distinctive competency in its R&D function? The answers to these questions will depend on the firm's corporate and business-level strategies. It is the firm's strategic needs at the corporate and business levels that will determine its R&D focus and the competencies it must possess in that function.

A firm's R&D strategy, therefore, involves long-term decisions and actions by managers to ensure that their firm's research and development capabilities are relevant to its business and corporate-level strategy needs. Investment in the R&D function is understandably the primary requirement for achieving this capability. Thus, cost strategists would invest in process R&D since it would give them the strength to efficiently manufacture the current product but avoid product R&D as it is not only expensive but also contrary to their competitive goals. By contrast, product differentiators would invest in product R&D, either to develop new products or redesign current products for better manufacturability and to achieve zero defects. Firms that must develop proprietary products or technologies (e.g., biotechnology, pharmaceutical, semiconductor firms) would invest in basic R&D to gain the necessary fundamental knowledge. However, investments in the R&D function alone will not give a firm the needed capability. By recruiting the appropriate research personnel, creating the organizational climate in which they would stay and perform, and closely linking research and developmental activities for better results, firms gain the necessary strengths in R&D. The close linking of these activities is especially critical for a firm seeking proprietary products because it needs significant strengths in basic research, applied research, and new product development combined.

Research and Development Strategy in a Multibusiness Firm

What constitutes R&D strategy for a multibusiness firm? What type of R&D activities does such a firm perform and at what level? Generally speaking, one would expect the R&D activities of a multibusiness firm to be decentralized at the business unit level for obvious reasons—to get the R&D function focused solely on improving the products/processes of that business unit in order to make that unit more competitive. However, for some diversified firms, R&D activities have to be performed at the corporate level as well in order for the firm as a whole to stay competitive. Firms that have diversified using a common core technology, such as 3M with its bonding technology, have to continuously enhance their core knowledge to sustain the competitive advantage emerging from it. Such firms undertake basic R&D at the corporate level and distribute the results of that research to business units for specific application. In essence, corporate R&D in related diversifiers performs basic research to meet the competitive needs of the firm as a whole; business unit R&D performs developmental research to meet the competitive needs of that particular business unit. Conglomerate diversifiers can be expected to undertake developmental research at the business-unit level but no research at the corporate level.

Human Resources Strategy

The task of the human resources function (HR) is to develop policies and practices to attract, retain, motivate, and utilize competent organizational members. This task is considered to be strategic because organizational members are viewed as a valuable competitive resource.[17] HR strategy, therefore, is a set of decisions and actions managers take to acquire and effectively employ human resource capabilities in pursuit of the firm's business and corporate-level strategy goals. This definition should not be taken to mean that human resources simply implement a firm's predesigned strategies. Many, especially those who subscribe to the resource-based view of strategy, believe that human resources can also create unique competitive advantages for a firm.[18]

Different industry environments and strategies employed by firms demand different HR policies and practices. These policies and practices focus on three broad areas:[19]

1. the flow of employees into and through the organization
2. employee compensation
3. employee relations

When a firm's policies and practices in these areas are congruent with the needs of its business- and corporate-level strategies, the firm is likely to be high performing.

Employee Flow Function

Managing employee flow encompasses a whole arena of interrelated organizational activities such as HR planning, job analysis, employee recruitment, selection, evaluation, career planning and development, and termination.[20] The focus in the employee flow function is to acquire or internally develop appropriate personnel and with the necessary competencies to generate the competitive advantage the firm seeks. There are three primary strategic alternatives for HR policies and practices to accomplish these tasks:

1. The firm can rely solely on the internal labor market.
2. The firm can look to the external labor market for these needs.
3. The firm can use some combination of both.

In the internal approach, hiring takes place through a limited number of entry-level positions. The career path is predetermined and compensation is based on knowledge often gained on the job, which is specific to the firm. Advancement is based on seniority or merit, depending on the type of workforce targeted and the competitive needs of the firm.

A conspicuous strategic advantage of the internal approach is that it allows the firm to retain the intellectual capital it has developed. The time and effort employees invest in gaining firm-specific knowledge discourages them from seeking employment elsewhere because this firm-specific knowledge cannot be easily transferred to a new employer. A second advantage is that the internal approach generates cost efficiencies in hiring. Because the firm hires at only a limited number of entry-level positions, it incurs lower expenditures to staff the hiring function. Other efficiencies derive from lower turnover rates and job security. Lower turnover rates mean fewer hiring and training expenses, and job security often compensates employees for lower wages. These advantages closely match the needs of low cost strategy firms and hence it is their most likely choice in employee acquisition.[21]

There are some potential drawbacks to the internal labor market approach. First, it does not encourage creativity because new ideas do not easily emerge in an internally-focused organization. Second, the internal labor market tends to be rigid and generally myopic and, therefore, is not adequate when speedy responses to customer needs are necessary. Third, if risk taking is important, for example in firms that rely on innovation, quality enhancement, or breakthrough products, the advancement and compensation policies of the internal labor market are a poor match because employees are not rewarded for risk taking. These disadvantages prevent some firms, especially differentiators, from opting for an internal approach in human resource acquisition. For them, external acquisition of personnel is more attractive because it brings new ideas into the firm and offers a wider selection of candidates from which to choose. As a result, a differentiator is able to select individuals whose qualifications and training closely match its unique needs.[22]

Most firms use a combination of the internal and external labor markets depending on the job categories for which personnel are sought. Different worker requirements for different jobs dictate the choice. As suggested earlier, the more firm-specific knowledge and skill are required to compete, the greater the firm's reliance on the internal labor market. For unique skills and for those in which there is an internal deficiency, firms rely on the external labor market.

Compensation Function

The compensation function determines the current pay level for specific job types, monitors market-based pay levels for similar jobs, and establishes the criteria for pay increases. The firm must first decide where it wants to set its pay level in comparison to the market average. This decision will directly affect the firm's profits through the cost of labor. It will also indirectly affect profitability to the extent that the pay level encourages employee attraction, retention, and satisfaction.

A firm's pay structure refers to the relationship between different job types. Consider the following examples: A firm may use at-risk pay* to motivate innovative

---

*At-risk pay is a portion of the pay that employees receive when they reach or exceed a certain goal. It is a lump sum variable pay that is not part of the base pay and is paid contingent upon performance.

behavior. It may substitute pay-for-performance for seniority-based pay when productivity is critical. In other words, the strategy of the firm and the type of people a firm wants to attract and retain affect its pay structure. Suppose that innovation is integral to the firm because it employs a differentiation strategy. To attract and retain creative individuals the firm needs, it has to offer a competitive pay (that is, pay that matches or exceeds what the competition pays) and perhaps include some at-risk pay to encourage risk taking. On the other hand, cost strategy firms that need conforming individuals who faithfully execute planned decisions would pay according to the job category or position within the company, along with a bonus that is directly tied to performance.

Employee Relations Function

The employee relations function is concerned with establishing, enforcing, and reinforcing the psychological contract between the employer and its employees in order to structure the work environment and the corporate culture. The psychological contract is the set of employee beliefs about their relationships with other employees and the impact of these beliefs on their level of commitment to the organization. For example, a company that wants to foster a family-like atmosphere will put in place programs aimed at easing work-family conflicts. Strategically, it is important to develop a work environment that aligns employee interests with those of their employers.[23]

An important area of employee relations relevant to competitive performance deals with work systems. Work systems are the ways in which the firm structures jobs, allocates discretion, and exercises supervision. There are several choices. The firm can adopt direct supervisory control to accomplish the job. Alternatively, it can make jobs standard and routine as a substitute for supervision. Finally, a firm can build more discretion into the employee's job, which also minimizes the need for supervision.

The types of work systems adopted are a function of the firm's strategic needs. Direct supervisory control is employed in skilled occupations such as construction where jobs may differ from period to period. The direct cost of supervision is one drawback of this kind of work system. In addition, highly skilled workers may take exception to direct supervision, leading to employee-employer conflict.

In some instances, work standardization may be sufficient for achieving managerial control. Under standardization, the work process itself provides the control. By eliminating the need for hierarchical control, work standardization reduces cost and hence is appealing to cost strategists. There is also a second reason why it appeals to them: standardization allows workers to become specialized and increases their productivity rate. However, standardization of the job can create monotony for the worker, leading to job dissatisfaction and worker agitation for higher pay. This behavior has been frequently observed in the automotive industry where job standardization on the assembly line is common. The alternative to work standardization is employee self-control—allowing employees to plan and control their activities. This arrangement has been found to be appropriate for differentiators and those firms that must frequently innovate because it gives the workers the autonomy necessary to be creative.[24] The problem in this approach, however, is that the firm incurs risks—employee self-control can result in wasted resources. Given these contradictions, it is prudent to weigh the advantages and disadvantages of standardization versus self-control before making a decision. Managers take a balanced approach that combines autonomy with standardization, mixing more or less of each depending on the strategy pursued.

Human Resources Strategy in a Multibusiness Firm

What is the human resources strategy for a multibusiness firm? Would its HR policies and practices differ from one business unit to another when these units pursue different competitive strategies, or would the policies and practices be uniform? Certainly, it makes sense to say that the HR policies and practices of a diversified firm would not be uniform when its business units seek different competitive advantages. Instead, such policies and practices would be unique to each business unit. Conglomerate diversifiers, competing in different industries using different strategies, can be expected to have decentralized key HR activities such as personnel selection, training, and job design to the business units while performing only administrative tasks such as regulatory compliance at the corporate level. This allows the business units to formulate HR policies and practices that are specific to their competitive needs. Related diversifiers, on the other hand, especially those that have diversified using a common technological resource, are most likely to have centralized key HR activities at the corporate level and pursue a uniform set of policies and practices because the core skills and competencies their business units seek are the same. These policies and practices are most likely to resemble that of a differentiator.

Financial Strategy

The role of the finance function is to raise and manage cash to meet the strategic needs of the firm and to create value for investors. This role encompasses more than simply borrowing money from banks and selling stocks and bonds to investors. In broad terms, the finance function includes activities relating to capital budgeting, raising capital, and managing liquidity. Financial strategy comprises a set of decisions and actions managers take to ensure that the firm has adequate funds available to meet its growth and competitive needs in a timely manner and, further, that the required funds have been economically obtained.

Effective financial strategy creates value for investors. Value creation is captured in the concept of **economic value added (EVA)**,* which suggests that a firm must generate more cash than it raises from investors through stock and bond issues. EVA is expressed as:

$$EVA = (ROIC - WACC) \times invested\ capital$$

In this expression, ROIC stands for the percentage return that the firm has earned on financial capital contributed by investors. WACC is the weighted average cost of capital and represents what investors require as a return on the capital they have invested. Suppose investors have contributed $10 million in capital to the firm. Assume they require a 10 percent return on this investment—that is, WACC equals 10 percent. Finally, suppose ROIC is 12 percent. EVA tells us that the firm has earned $200,000 more than investors required as a return on investment:

---

*The concept of EVA was developed by Joel Stern and Bennett Stewart, co-founders of the consulting firm Stern Stewart & Company. EVA® is a registered trademark of Stern Stewart & Company.

$$EVA = (ROIC - WACC) \times invested\ capital = (0.12 - 0.10)$$
$$\times\ \$10,000,000 = \$200,000$$

The EVA concept embodies the financial activities of capital budgeting, raising capital, and liquidity management in the following way: first, the firm must have a process for valuing investment projects to determine that projects earn at least the cost of capital. This activity is part of the capital budgeting function. Second, the firm must be able to raise capital in such a manner as to minimize the cost of capital. Doing so requires policies regarding debt-equity mix and management of liquidity. Let us look at each of these functions.

Capital Budgeting

The capital budgeting decision relates to investment in fixed assets: plant and equipment. Managers conduct analyses to determine the profitability of this investment, using net present value, or NPV. Assume the firm invests $6 million in plant and equipment to make a new product. Suppose this project is expected to produce a one-year after-tax cash flow of $6.72 million. Cash flow is sales revenue minus operating costs such as labor, materials, and overhead. Also, suppose the required return to investors, as represented by WACC, is 10 percent. The NPV of this project is:

$$NPV = -\ I_o + \frac{CF}{(1 + WACC)} = -\ \$6M + \frac{\$6.72M}{(1.10)} = \$109,091$$

The strategic importance of NPV here is that it tells managers three things: (1) whether the initial investment of $6 million can be recovered; (2) whether the cash flows are adequate to meet the 10 percent return ($600,000) investors seek; and (3) whether additional cash for reinvestment in the firm is available. In present value terms, this latter amount is $109,091.

Raising Capital

In order to take advantage of profitable opportunities, firms need cash. While cash is important for all firms, it is critical for those that experience growth opportunities. A firm can obtain cash externally by borrowing funds or selling stock, or internally by managing cash. Acquiring assets through leasing is also an alternative. Leasing may have some strategic advantages over purchasing assets because operating leases contain cancellation options. Airlines lease a portion of their fleet, since demand is highly variable and they may cancel leases on the airplanes if necessary.

Borrowing: Debt-Equity Mix

Borrowing affects a firm's capital structure—the ratio of debt to equity. The optimal capital structure is defined as that mix of debt to equity that maximizes stock price. In general the mix of debt and equity that will maximize stock price is the one that will minimize the cost of capital. An easy way to see this is to return to the NPV example. If managers could find a mix of debt to equity that would reduce the required return—that is, WACC—to 8 percent from 10 percent, the NPV of the project would increase to $222,222, which is more than *double*! Determining the optimal choice of capital structure requires balancing the advantages and disadvantages of debt financing.

Advantages and Disadvantages of Debt Financing

While there are several advantages to debt financing, one of the major benefits is that the interest cost of debt is cheaper than equity because the interest paid on debt is tax deductible. Even so, there are two major disadvantages to debt financing. The first is that debt financing introduces the potential for financial distress, commonly associated with bankruptcy risk. The second disadvantage is the loss of financial flexibility. Financial flexibility describes the ability of the firm to respond quickly to competitive threats or new opportunities. This ability is diminished if the firm is burdened by heavy principal and interest payments.

The Tax Advantage of Debt

To illustrate the tax advantage of debt, consider the following example. Assume managers have the choice of financing the firm's operations with all equity or with debt plus equity. For simplicity, assume equal proportions of debt and equity. Suppose the firm has $6 million in assets to be financed. Which capital structure will maximize stockholder value?

Suppose managers could sell 600,000 shares at $10 per share in order to raise the $6 million. Also assume a corporate tax rate of 40 percent. Now assume that the firm's earnings before interest and taxes are $600,000. Without debt in the firm's capital structure, there is no debt payment. With a tax rate of 40 percent, net income to stockholders is $360,000 and the EPS is $0.60 with a return on equity of 6 percent. (See Table 8.2, column A. See also, Figure 8.2.)

Now suppose that managers choose to finance with both equity and debt. And, suppose the firm sells 300,000 shares of stock at $10 per share and borrows $3 million at 5 percent interest. Assume the tax rate remains at 40 percent. With an interest rate of 5 percent on $3 million of debt, the interest payment will be $150,000 (see Table 8.2, column B). However, the taxable earnings have gone down from $600,000 to $450,000 and the tax liability has been reduced from $240,000 to $180,000. This represents a tax savings of $60,000. Although the net income has gone down from $360,000 to $270,000, the stockholders have still benefited in the new situation with a significant increase in the EPS and ROE because the number of

TABLE 8.2	The Tax Advantage of Debt Financing		
		A	B
Earnings before interest and taxes		$ 600,000	$ 600,000
Less interest expense		0	150,000
Earnings before taxes		600,000	450,000
Taxes @ 40%		240,000	180,000
Net income		360,000	270,000
Number of shares outstanding		600,000	300,000
Earnings per share (net income/ number of shares)		$ 0.60	$ 0.90
ROE		6%	9%

| FIGURE 8.2 | **Tax Advantages of Debt** |

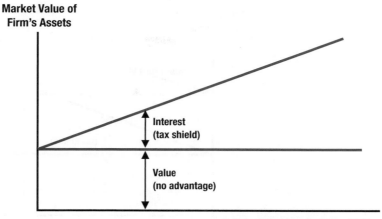

shares outstanding is substantially lower. Obviously, in the absence of any other considerations, stockholders are better off using debt to finance a portion of the assets.

Figure 8.2 shows that with the tax advantage of debt financing, the value of the firm continues to increase as debt financing is used.

Financial Distress

Financial distress refers to the costs associated with excessive debt. It occurs when the firm cannot make the payments on its debt and runs the risk of bankruptcy. Financial distress has both direct and indirect costs. The direct costs of bankruptcy are the legal and consulting fees associated with transferring ownership from stockholders to debt holders. The indirect costs of financial distress are associated with the loss in operating efficiency. For example, managers who are occupied with financial restructuring cannot pay sufficient attention to the competitive and long-term growth needs of the firm. When firms are having financial difficulties, their customers may turn elsewhere, productive employees may leave, and relationships with suppliers may be strained.

Figure 8.3 illustrates that the optimal debt to total assets ratio is found where the value of the firm is maximized. This ratio is indicated by D/A where the trade-offs between the benefits of interest tax shield and the costs of financial distress are in balance.

Financial Flexibility

Loss of financial flexibility is another cost of debt financing. When a firm takes on debt, it has to pay that debt back in the form of principal and interest payments. This debt service requires cash that might otherwise be used to finance new projects. The use of debt financing can also affect the firm's credit rating. The firm will find it more difficult to take on more debt if new projects become available. Second, the interest rate the firm will have to pay on new debt will be higher.

FIGURE 8.3 Debt to Total Assets Ratio

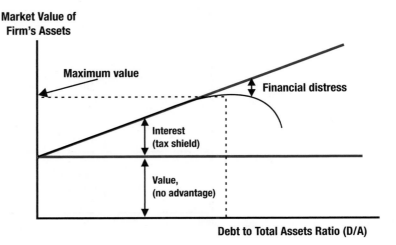

Determining the optimal capital structure requires managers to weigh the advantages and disadvantages of debt financing. Only then will the firm minimize the cost of capital and make projects more profitable and more worthwhile. As firms become more profitable, they can rely less on external financing. And for firms with highly risky assets, the optimal capital structure is often no debt at all. Microsoft is an excellent example. Large portions of Microsoft's assets do not show up on the balance sheet since they are intangible assets associated with the firm's knowledge capital. But Microsoft maintains a considerable amount of cash on hand, given the volatile nature of the technology business.

Liquidity Management

In order to reduce the dependence on debt, the firm may employ strategies aimed at generating cash internally. To do so, companies must develop a working capital strategy, which aims to accomplish three things:

1. The firm must collect accounts receivable in a timely and expeditious manner.

2. It must reduce the time that cash is tied up in inventory.

3. It should stretch the time it takes on accounts payables for as long as it is possible.

There are, of course, trade-offs to all these goals.

Firm Strategy and Financial Strategy

Will the financial strategies of firms differ depending on their competitive and corporate strategies? Using our discussions in this section, we can make some general observations. Rapidly growing high-technology firms (generally product differentiators) would prefer equity and internal financing to debt because the latter limits their financial flexibility. This is because the volatile revenue flows of a high-technology

TABLE 8.3 Matching Functional Strategies to Business-Level and Corporate-Level Strategies

FUNCTIONAL STRATEGY	COST LEADERSHIP	DIFFERENTIATION	VERTICAL INTERGRATION	RELATED DIVERSIFICATION	UNRELATED DIVERSIFICATION
Marketing	Undifferentiated (no segmentation) One price (competitive pricing) Mass promotion Mass distribution	Differentiated (many segments) Different prices for different segments but premium pricing Promotions unique to each segment Distribution channel unique to each segment	Not relevant	Corporate-level brand promotion	Promotional strategies unique to each business unit
Operations	Standard product (no variety) Fixed automation High volume production Narrow job scope for production personnel Repetitive (programmed) task performance	Differentiated products (variety) Flexible automation Medium volume production Broad job scope for production personnel Discretionary task performance	Electronic linkages of value chain stages Hierarchical coordination Locating sequential operations close to each other	Machine programming to achieve economies of scope Structural and behavioral coordination to achieve synergy	Operational decisions decentralized at the business unit level
R&D	Process R&D No product R&D	Product R&D Limited process R&D (focus on zero defects)	Process R&D focusing on the electronic integration of machines to achieve smooth material and information flow	Basic research at the corporate level Developmental research at the business unit level	Developmental research only at the business unit level
Human Resources	Internal recruitment (entry level) Productivity-based training Rewards for high output Process-based control	External recruitment (all levels) Behavior-oriented training Rewards for creativity Output-based control	Multiskilled training and team training for operations personnel	Technology-based diversifiers Adopt policies and pratices similar to that of a differentiator	Policies and practices unique to business units Corporate HR performs administrative functions only
Finance	Debt financing	Equity financing	Not relevant	Equity financing	Debt financing

187

firm, especially during the growth stage would lead to frequent defaults in debt payments and resulting problems with creditors. More importantly, the high-tech differentiator would want to focus more on the market opportunities for growth than on debt repayment issues—hence the avoidance of debt. For the cost leader, however, market conditions are relatively stable and dramatic changes in product/process technology are not likely to occur. As a result, the cost leader would prefer debt to equity so as to enjoy the tax benefits associated with the former while creating a balanced debt-equity portfolio to avoid potential financial distress issues.

In regard to diversification, researchers suggest that related diversifiers are more likely to choose equity financing because creditors generally view expansion based on firm-specific resources as risky and would be unwilling to finance them. But unrelated diversifications do not fall into this category and hence are attractive to lenders. As a result, unrelated diversifiers are more likely to choose debt financing.[25]

Multifunctional Competency

As we mentioned at the outset, an important factor to bear in mind when formulating functional-level strategies is that they should be internally consistent. Unrelated functional-level strategies create internal conflict, which should, therefore, cause firms to experience problems in the effective implementation of their business-level and corporate-level strategies. Table 8.3 lays out how different functional-level strategies and their elements match business-level and corporate-level strategies.

A second factor requiring attention in functional-level strategy formulation is the need to build multifunctional competency within the firm. Today's competitive environment is complex. In several industries—as, for example, the automotive and consumer appliances—the specialized competencies that firms have acquired to compete as a cost leader or differentiator are becoming obsolete. More and more, businesses in these industries are forced to compete using a combination of cost, differentiation, and frequent innovation strategies. As a result, it may not be enough for a firm to be strong in one functional area; instead it must be strong in several. Firms achieve multifunctional strengths by making appropriate investments in those functions, by facilitating cross-functional communication, and by promoting a multiskilled learning environment within the firm.

Summary

Functional-level strategy is a set of decisions and actions that managers take to attain superior competency in business functions. A firm needs these competencies to effectively achieve its competitive goals. The competencies of each function must, therefore, correspond with the needs of business- and corporate-level strategies. In other words, a firm's functional competencies must support the competitive advantages sought by the firm's different businesses. To be congruent with the firm's overall strategy and with each other, functional-level strategies are developed in concert.

Chapter 8 Discussion Questions and Project

Discussion Questions

1. Using the Internet and the business press, read about Gatorade and its marketing strategy. Describe and discuss potential new market segments for this product.
2. How do you think capital structure decisions of a large food chain and a high-technology company would differ? Discuss why you would expect these differences.

Project

1. Assume that Southwest Airlines has decided to enter the international market by offering direct flights to major cities in South America. What market segment should the firm target? How should the firm position itself? Based on your reading about and understanding of Southwest Airlines, develop a marketing plan for the firm's proposed diversification.

Continuing Case

Pepsi-Cola: Marketing and Distribution Strategies

Background

Although Pepsi-Cola began business in 1898, it was not until the 1950s that its vision and business strategy become evident. During that period, "beat Coca-Cola and become the industry leader" emerged as the principal goal and guiding theme for the firm. Ever since that time, the firm's decisions and actions in pursuit of this goal have focused on defining Pepsi as better tasting, hipper, and more in tune with the times. Pepsi-Cola's business strategy can thus be described as one of differentiation. By claiming that Pepsi is unique in taste and image, the firm sought to surpass Coke in industry sales. Realizing this goal required (1) a marketing strategy that would identify appropriate market segments and, through creative advertising and communication, position Pepsi in those segments so that it was perceived as unique and appealing; and (2) a distribution strategy that would make Pepsi widely available to those segments.

Marketing Strategy

By the early 1930s, Coca-Cola was a highly profitable firm and an internationally known consumer brand, while Pepsi-Cola was relatively unknown. The company had twice declared bankruptcy, but through slogans, radio commercials, and cash from enterprising investors Pepsi-Cola managed to stay alive. Later, by offering "more quantity but for the same price as Coke," the company positioned Pepsi as a bargain cola and to some extent resurrected its business. But slogans and price challenges are weak weapons to employ in the fight for industry leadership, especially when the leader is a valued brand and the contender is a distant follower with an inferior bargain-cola image.

The real break for Pepsi-Cola came during the late 1950s when the company conceived a marketing strategy that would reposition Pepsi as unique and different. The impetus for this strategy arose from business surveys of the times that strongly indicated that the teenage market in the U.S. population was rapidly emerging as the biggest demographic segment. By vigorously promoting its product as a drink for the trendy, the whimsical, and the party loving against Coke's appeal to the conservative, Pepsi-Cola hoped to become known as a beverage of the youthful or, at least, of the young at heart. Pepsi-Cola executives reasoned that successful implementation of this strategy would allow Pepsi to grow with the teenage group and eventually emerge as the dominant soft drinks firm.

What followed was an ad campaign with the theme "The Pepsi generation," arguably the longest running in advertising history and one that consistently associated the young and fun-loving with Pepsi. The ads used attractive models and music celebrities to position Pepsi as synonymous with partying and entertainment. Creative commercials showed teenagers and young adults in party scenes and at the beach to create the belief that life would never be boring for the Pepsi drinker. Ads targeted the young American woman, who was the household shopper, with the message that Pepsi was not only wholesome for the family but was a fashionable party beverage as well.

Before long, the strategy had the desired result—Pepsi had emerged as the near-equal of Coke and a respectable contender for the soft drinks industry leadership. In reviewing Pepsi-Cola's marketing strategy, academicians noted that its success was due to two logically related factors: (a) the clear identification of rapidly emerging growth segments to whom a soft drink would be appealing, and (b) an aggressive, well-focused ad campaign that convincingly positioned Pepsi in those segments as the product of choice.

Distribution Strategy

A sound marketing strategy positions the product in the minds of consumers in ways that appeal to them. But for volume sales, a company also needs a distribution strategy that ensures ready availability of the product in retail channels when demand occurs. A traditional outlet for soft drinks in the 1950s was the soda fountain, where—as a first mover—Coca-Cola enjoyed a strong presence. But supermarkets were rapidly emerging as a much larger outlet for soft drinks, and Pepsi-Cola planned to focus on them.

Supermarkets are supplied by independent bottlers who work with retailers to obtain shelf space by offering trade discounts, point-of-purchase displays, and strong service. Obviously, a large, well-trained, and highly motivated bottler sales force that aggressively competes for retail shelf space is a competitive advantage for a soft drinks firm. Pepsi-Cola initially contemplated forward integration that would have given it total control over bottling and distribution operations, but it soon discarded the idea in favor of a vertical cooperation strategy. Alfred Steele, the company's CEO, reasoned that by treating bottlers as business partners, rather than as customers for the concentrate sold by the firm, Pepsi-Cola would be able to build a strong presence at the supermarket.

Accordingly, the firm devised and implemented a sustained distributor-support program that emphasized sales training for bottlers, retail display help, and a share in profits. This program helped Pepsi-Cola gain a significant edge in supermarket sales and thus narrow its market-share differences with Coke. However, Coke employed similar strategies, and the cola wars that ensued soon put many small bottlers out of business, thus threatening Pepsi's distribution. To strengthen its distribution network, Pepsi-Cola began buying out several weak bottlers and consolidating them under a Pepsi Bottling Group. In 1999, the company spun off this group to the public but retained a 35 percent controlling interest in the venture. In 2004, the Pepsi Bottling Group accounted for nearly one-half of Pepsi's supermarket sales in the United States.

Effects on Performance

Nearly four decades ago, Pepsi and Coke were poles apart in their U.S. market share—6 percent and 35 percent, respectively. In 2004, Pepsi was on the heels of Coke, claiming 30 percent of the U.S. market to the latter's 40 percent. Critics attribute Pepsi's superb performance to its marketing and distribution strategies, especially the synergy between the two. By cleverly associating Pepsi with youth, its marketing strategy firmly positioned Pepsi as the beverage of choice for parties, entertainment, and social occasions. By relentlessly pushing Pepsi through the supermarket distribution strategy, Pepsi-Cola successfully targeted and captured the high-volume "home market."

Discussion Questions

1. Describe the elements of Pepsi-Cola's marketing strategy. Explain how these elements helped the firm to differentiate Pepsi from Coke.
2. Describe Pepsi-Cola's distribution strategy. Is this strategy consistent with the firm's marketing strategy? How do the two strategies complement each other?

Source: R. S. Tedlow, *New and Improved: The Story of Mass Marketing in America,* (Boston, Mass.: Harvard Business School Press, 1996), 22–112; D. Yoffie, "Cola Wars Continue: Coke and Pepsi in the Twenty-first Century," *Harvard Business School Case* #9-702-402 (2004); "PepsiCo, Inc.," *International Directory of Company Histories*" (Farmington Hills, Mich.: St. James Press, 2001).

Part Four

Strategy Implementation

CHAPTER 9   Implementing Strategy: Organizing Tasks
and Allocating Resources

Implementing Strategy: Organizing Tasks and Allocating Resources

CHAPTER OBJECTIVES

After reading this chapter, you should be able to:

- Discuss the importance of organizational design and organizational advantage in strategy implementation

- Describe the components of organizational design and discuss how they impact a firm's performance

- Describe the different ways of grouping tasks and the competencies associated with each

- Identify and describe organizational structures appropriate for different business-level, corporate-level, and international strategies

- Design an organization for a particular strategy

Opening Case

Southwest Airlines operates within a narrow segment of the airline industry, offering point-to-point flights that carry a significant amount of business traffic. Within this narrow segment, it competes with other niche players like JetBlue and industry giants like American Airlines by offering competitive fares and superior customer service. Southwest is thus a focus strategist that aims for a cost–customer service advantage within a niche. To achieve this advantage, Southwest Airlines must have the capability to perform organizational tasks more efficiently than most others in the industry; its customer service must be superior to that of its competitors.

Organizational capabilities emerge from the way an organization structures its activities and creates linkages among task groups. Southwest's organizational structure and processes are designed with *operational efficiency*, *administrative cost control*, and *customer service* in mind. To achieve operational efficiency, Southwest has standardized its tasks and skills. Standardization reduces cost by minimizing variations in the work process, which curtails waste and generates more output for every unit of input. To keep administrative costs under control, it uses a flatter organizational structure with only four layers of management. Flatter structures have no middle management to coordinate functions (that is, to link the activities of different departments). Instead, operations personnel mutually adjust, reducing the need for supervisory coordination, which lowers the firm's overhead costs.

To achieve a customer service advantage, Southwest Airlines designs jobs from a "job output and job skill" perspective as opposed to a "job process" perspective. Jobs designed from an output and skill perspective describe the job outcome (in this case customer satisfaction), describe the skills needed for job completion, and give the employee the freedom to decide how to complete the job. Because the needs of passengers differ, an output- and skill-based design is more appropriate; process-based designs prescribe how the job should be completed and are a poor fit for the situation. Southwest's operational jobs describe customer satisfaction as the output and "people attitude" as the required skill for employees. The company encourages pilots and flight crew to use discretion and get the job done, in contrast to many airlines that strictly limit the discretion of operations personnel.

Southwest's flatter structure helps the company serve customers effectively in other ways as well. In flat organizations, employees focus on the customers and their needs, rather than on the chain of command. However, a flat structure alone may not hold the key to customer satisfaction, as most other major airlines also have flat structures. Researchers suggest that it is Southwest's customer-oriented work culture, in conjunction with the flat structure, that is the cause for the firm's superior performance in customer satisfaction. Other major airlines that have tried to imitate Southwest's work culture have not quite succeeded thus far.[1]

The Southwest Airlines case highlights the relevance of organizational design—organizing tasks and allocating resources—to strategy implementation. Organizational design breeds and fosters the competencies the firm needs to implement its strategy. A mismatch between the strategic needs and the capabilities of an organization never augurs well for the success of a firm. In this chapter, we define organizational design and discuss its role in strategy implementation. We start by describing how organizational design gives the firm **organizational advantage**—an ability to integrate disparate organizational resources and process products efficiently, speedily, or with unique features and attributes. We then describe organizational design components, and the way different designs generate different competencies within the firm. After discussing integration mechanisms, we conclude this chapter with a brief description of organizational designs appropriate for different strategies.

Organizational Design and Organizational Advantage

Recall from previous chapters that strategy is a decision the firm makes to achieve performance superior to that of its rivals. To put this decision into action, a firm must possess the requisite competencies. For example, cost strategy requires the ability to process products efficiently, product differentiation requires the ability to add unique features to the product, and vertical integration requires the ability to manage distinct value chain activities efficiently. A firm obtains these competencies from the tangible and intangible resources—machine, material, skill, and informational assets—it acquires and employs. However, a firm's competencies emerge from these resources, not per se, but from the way it puts them collectively to use, integrating several resources so that they coordinate or harmoniously adjust to function as one unit.

Importance of Resource Coordination

Think of an organization as an orchestra. An orchestra is made up of different musical instruments that yield different tones and whose players have unequal competencies. The quality of the orchestra's music depends not on the skills of any one player, say the first violinist, not even on all the violinists, but on the orchestra's ability to coordinate all its players and instruments to perform as one unit. Like an orchestra, an organization too has human resources with distinct skills and tool resources that use dissimilar technologies. The quality of the firm's performance depends on how effectively these disparate resources have been organized to perform in a coordinated manner. The importance of resource coordination can be understood from the fact that even the best scientists and engineers will be of no avail to a high-technology firm if it cannot make them work together to create new knowledge and develop new products. Southwest's stellar performance is not due to the fact that it possesses a unique resource that is rare in the airlines industry; it is due to its ability to seamlessly integrate the work of flight personnel and ground personnel whose cooperation is critical for effectively meeting the firm's goal—customer satisfaction. To sum up, a firm's competencies emerge not so much from the quality of individual resources but from the ability of the firm to organize them and make them act in unison. The focus in strategy implementation is thus on the organizational design the firm uses to bring together various resources and to coordinate work and information flow among them.[2]

Organizational Advantage

Organizational design is a framework the firm uses to get the organizational task accomplished. By dividing work and grouping the divided parts (or through differentiation and integration, as Lawrence and Lorsch put it)[3] an organization assigns tasks to people, achieves unity of effort, and gets the task completed. Division of task—grouping the divided tasks based on commonality of worker skills, output, or other criteria—and integrating several groups through formal and informal mechanisms such as hierarchies, teams, rules, norms, and culture thus form the steps in developing an organizational design. The effectiveness of a design depends on the extent to which the level of differentiation and integration it uses is in balance. Extreme differentiation of task makes integration of the divided parts difficult, but low differentiation denies the benefits associated with differentiation. Not all firms are successful in effectively dividing tasks and integrating workflow among human and tool resources; some have gaps in their knowledge or functionality that make the job of coordination difficult and challenging.[4] If a firm can successfully achieve a greater degree of coordination among its resources, its abilities in product processing can be significant and it may have an advantage over rivals in strategy implementation. We call this the **organizational advantage** of a firm. Organizational advantage is a firm's ability to coordinate the differentiated tasks and resources more efficiently and effectively than the competition. Ability to process products more efficiently or more quickly, or to offer unique and highly differentiated products, are examples of organizational advantage When a firm achieves this advantage more through informal coordination mechanisms (for example, a conducive work culture similar to Southwest Airlines' in which groups voluntarily coordinate their activities), its abilities are superior and it is difficult for competitors to replicate them. Informal coordination mechanisms thus bestow enduring advantages on a firm.[5]

Matching Design to Strategy

Different ways of dividing, grouping, and integrating tasks exist. As we will soon see, the manner in which these activities are carried out fosters different organizational competencies over time. Consequently, it is imperative that managers select the right design for implementing their firm's strategy, because any mismatch between strategy and structure can lead to ineffective performance. And, since strategy as intention precedes organization that connotes action, the dominant thinking in strategic management is that strategy determines the organizational design that the firm must adopt. A pathbreaking historical study by Alfred Chandler,[6] and several other studies following his,[7] strongly confirms this thinking. Chandler found that as firms such as DuPont and General Motors diversified into new geographic regions and new markets, they needed new organizational forms, or new ways of grouping tasks—from simple skill- or function-based groupings to geography-based and multi-product/market-based groupings—to implement their diversification strategies. Firms that failed to adjust their structure to the new strategy experienced below-average performance.

However, some evidence also suggests that in established firms existing structure can determine the adoption of new diversification strategies.[8] Organizational structures, especially when they are bureaucratic, become rigid over time, constraining the number of strategic choices a firm can pursue. In other words, under some conditions and contexts, current organizational structure and design may influence the selection of new strategies. While these conflicting research findings may be puzzling, the general belief seems to be that strategy determines structure. However, conflicts aside, what is important for us to bear in mind is that strategy and structure must be in alignment for successful performance to occur.

Designing an Organization

To design an organization that meets the needs of strategy, we must first identify the components of organizational design. Organizational designs are made up of *tasks, authority structures,* and *integration (or coordination) mechanisms.* The starting point for a design, therefore, is the firm's task and the strategic goals it has set for that task. For example, Southwest's task of *providing air travel* and its strategic goals of *economical fares* and *superior customer service* have both formed the basis for its organizational design. Since the organizational task is a complex mixture of activities that requires inputs from several sources, the concerns in organizational design are: How should the task be divided, authority delegated, and the output of each divided unit integrated without jeopardizing the firm's strategic goals? In other words, what design would give the firm the ability to best achieve its strategic goals? Division of task, delegation of authority, integration devices, and their effect on the firm's ability to achieve its strategic goals thus form the basis for designing an organization. Figure 9.1 sums up this statement and suggests that a firm adjust its design characteristics when they do not meet the needs of strategy.

Division of Task

Division of task, or **horizontal differentiation**, refers to fragmentation of work. Extreme fragmentation (known as narrow or focused division of task) creates many specialized jobs within a firm. To cite Adam Smith's study of a pin-making factory, one worker draws out the wire, another straightens it, a third cuts it, a fourth points it, a fifth grinds it at the top, a sixth and a seventh make the head, and so on and so forth. If the pin maker is a large firm that has a high volume of production, it will employ several people in each of these activities, resulting in several specialized sections and departments. In contrast, another firm may divide the same task more broadly, with one worker being responsible for drawing, straightening, and cutting the wire, another for pointing it, grinding at the top, and making the head, and so on. Horizontal differentiation can thus result in a structure in which workers perform each task repetitively or several related tasks interactively.

Each of these approaches has different implications for the organization. Narrow division of task allows each divided activity to be standardized, tightly controlled, and linked to other activities in assembly-line fashion. The result is high-volume, uniform output due to the specialized learning of each worker. Other benefits are

---

FIGURE 9.1 **Designing an Organization**

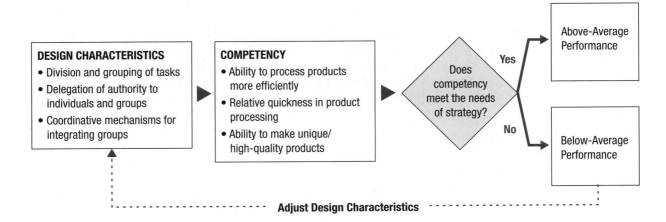

waste reduction because the firm is able to exercise tight control over stages of the divided task and efficiency because the worker has learned to be economical in processing as a natural outgrowth of task repetitiveness. Undoubtedly, these advantages are attractive to low cost firms and to those competing in mass markets (e.g., steel, commodity automotive parts). But the problem here is that it leaves the firm's employees with a narrow task orientation—they do not understand what goes on in other stages of the task sequence. As a result, it is very difficult to make changes to improve the work process or the product's design. Thus, narrow division of task builds a firm's competency in volume production and cost economies but leaves it deficient in skills relating to process or product improvement.

In contrast, a broad division of task enhances worker understanding of the whole task (because the worker performs several related tasks in sequence, as exemplified by the second example of pin making), thereby increasing output quality. It also creates flexibility in the workers' routines, allowing new ideas to be quickly recognized and exploited.[9] These advantages appeal to firms that compete on product quality, innovativeness, and rapid market response. But the firm must be willing to relax control over resources—it must take some risks. A broad division of task entails delegating to workers authority over planning and the use of resources in task execution, and that could be costly. In other words, broad division of task makes a firm competent in innovativeness and fast market response but leaves it weak in resource control.

Historically, organizations favored narrow division of task, with roots going back to the automotive industry of the early 1900s.[10] Until three decades ago, mass production and mass marketing were the popular ways to compete in several industries (e.g., automotive, appliances, and home entertainment) that required firms to produce in large volume to be successful. Firms achieved these capabilities by dividing the task narrowly to permit assembly-line automation and manufacture of a standard product in large volume. But today's markets are not mass markets; instead, they are segmented and rapidly changing. To be successful in this environment, a firm must offer the product in several designs, frequently improve its features, and respond to market changes speedily. Such combination strategies require flexible automation in production and services. Flexible automation, in turn, needs flexible work structures and workers with multiple skills to capture the benefits associated with such technologies.[11] Hence, the present trend in division of task is toward a broad division that allows each employee to perform a family of related tasks.

Delegation of Authority

Delegation of authority distributes the power to make decisions to the divided work units. To accomplish the divided task in ways that achieve the firm's goals (e.g., to assemble ten widgets a day), authority for use of resources and information must be ceded to the worker. When tasks are divided narrowly into specialized jobs, each worker's authority also tends to be narrow. To complete their task, workers must rely on a supervisor to coordinate their activities with those of others. Narrow division of task thus requires supervisory layers to coordinate worker activities, making the structure tall. The opposite occurs when the task is broadly divided since the worker who performs several tasks coordinates activities among them. Thus, horizontal differentiation influences the number of hierarchical levels in a structure, commonly referred to as **vertical differentiation**. The more narrowly divided the task, the taller the structure. A flatter structure emerges when the task is broadly divided.

Traditional approaches to organizational design concentrated authority at the top levels of the firm, an approach known as **centralization**.[12] Tall structures (seven or eight levels, from the CEO to clerical positions) that gave managers total control over resources were viewed as fundamental, because the environment in which firms competed required them. Most industries involved high volume and stable markets, in which the primary condition for success was the ability to consistently supply large quantities of a standard product. Uniformity of output and economical production that would lower costs were additional criteria for success. To meet these requirements, a firm needed an organization in which top managers would make product decisions (such as quantity and delivery schedule) based on the best information available to them, and lower-level personnel would strictly implement these decisions using planned criteria. A tall structure helped the firm to achieve these goals by allowing managers to exercise tight control over worker activities and output. By controlling information and denying the worker the power to alter the task or schedule, managers ensured efficiency, consistency of output, and high volume.

Today's environment, by and large, favors flatter structures. (A structure with four or five hierarchical levels is generally considered to be flat.) Flatter structures offer a significant advantage sought by many firms today: they speed up vertical communication. Markets and technologies are continuously changing; strategic managers need real-time information about changes in customer preferences or about new or emerging technologies that could alter the firm's operational capabilities. Much of this information resides with the firm's sales and operations personnel, who are able to quickly transfer it to the top when the structure is relatively flat.

But flatter structures also offer a second, equally significant, advantage: they push operational decision making to lower levels, where operational problems occur. In other words, in flatter structures, authority is decentralized and operations personnel have autonomy in decision making. There are two reasons why decentralization is advantageous to firms in today's environment. The environment is highly complex, and it is appropriate to delegate authority to operations personnel who have the information needed to deal with day-to-day contingencies (recall that is what Southwest Airlines does). Second, today's environment is cost conscious, and decentralization minimizes cost by reducing the need for supervisory coordination. In a decentralized structure, employees coordinate their activities through mutual adjustment.

Grouping of Tasks

To achieve unity of effort, organizations must group divided tasks under common heads into sections and departments. Moreover, managers rely on grouping to control work, since monitoring the performance of a small number of groups is easier than monitoring the performance of many individuals. On what basis should this grouping be done? Should it be based on business skills and education (engineering, manufacturing, finance), output (cutlery, chinaware), customers served (individual customers, business customers, nonprofit organizations), or any other basis? Different criteria exist for grouping tasks and activities, and they foster different competencies within the firm. It is essential that managers select the right criteria to group organizational tasks, bearing in mind the needs of the firm's strategy.

In broad terms, a firm may group its activities on one of three bases: (1) knowledge or skills needed for task completion—known as a **functional structure**;

(2) products made or markets served by the firm—known as a **product or market structure**; and (3) a combination of functional and product structures—known as a **matrix structure**.

Functional Structure

A functional structure groups tasks according to skill or knowledge categories. A small production firm uses craft-based grouping (cutting, welding, bookkeeping), a large manufacturer uses a body of business skills or functions (manufacturing, marketing, finance), and a professional organization such as a hospital uses disciplines or branches of knowledge (surgery, radiology, oncology). Personnel are assigned to groups based on their education, training, and work experience. Group members share the same body of knowledge or expertise, perform the same tasks, use the same professional jargon, and report to a supervisor who has a similar educational background.

Functional structure results in an organization of skill-based groups that use their collective knowledge to make and market a single product or several related products in high volume. Generally, single-product firms that must produce in high volume or serve a large body of similar clients use a functional structure. But multiproduct firms also opt for a functional structure when those products can be made and marketed in high volume using the same set of skills. Figure 9.2 illustrates how different kinds of firms use this structure.

Advantages and Disadvantages of a Functional Structure

First and foremost, a functional structure promotes skill specialization. Grouping people of similar skills and educational backgrounds creates an opportunity for them to learn from one another and hone their skills. The result is enhanced expertise, improved skill level, and a higher understanding of what they do. Higher knowledge on a specialized task (e.g., purchasing, R&D, product design) allows people to perform that task efficiently, speedily, and with precision. Second, a functional structure requires relatively fewer hierarchical levels since specialists can function with little supervision. It thus reduces supervisory costs. Third, it motivates people by offering opportunities for professional development, thereby creating a productive workforce. But functional grouping also has disadvantages. The emphasis on skills detracts attention from the output. To elaborate, specialists prefer to communicate only with people of their specialization because they lack an educated understanding of other specialties. Cross-functional communication (e.g., among R&D, manufacturing, and marketing) needed for developing new products or quickly responding to market changes does not freely occur at all levels of the firm. As a result, cross-functional issues are pushed to the top, overloading general managers with operational issues that distract them from strategic decision making. Firms resolve this problem by creating cross-functional teams, but this strategy increases costs. A second problem is inflexibility. Specialists resist change because change threatens their current expertise. Functional structure firms that must retool their competencies because of a change in strategy or market conditions will find it difficult to do so. A third problem is the difficulty of assessing the profit contributed by each product. Consequently, a firm may be manufacturing and marketing unprofitable products without realizing it.

FIGURE 9.2 Functional Structure

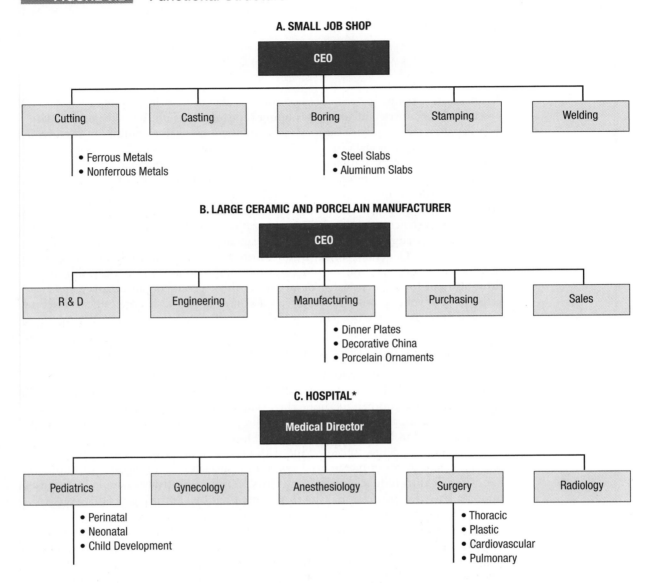

A. SMALL JOB SHOP

CEO

- Cutting
- Casting
- Boring
- Stamping
- Welding

Cutting:
- Ferrous Metals
- Nonferrous Metals

Boring:
- Steel Slabs
- Aluminum Slabs

B. LARGE CERAMIC AND PORCELAIN MANUFACTURER

CEO

- R & D
- Engineering
- Manufacturing
- Purchasing
- Sales

Manufacturing:
- Dinner Plates
- Decorative China
- Porcelain Ornaments

C. HOSPITAL*

Medical Director

- Pediatrics
- Gynecology
- Anesthesiology
- Surgery
- Radiology

Pediatrics:
- Perinatal
- Neonatal
- Child Development

Surgery:
- Thoracic
- Plastic
- Cardiovascular
- Pulmonary

To summarize, a functional structure fosters skill specialization, allowing workers to become experts in their respective fields. By encouraging each group of specialists to apply their knowledge to the organizational task, a firm gains competence in product processing, reaping benefits like processing efficiency, processing speed, and output consistency. However, because a functional structure inhibits cross-functional communication and is inflexible, it is difficult to implement new ideas.

*Adapted from H. Mintzberg, *The Structuring of Organizations* (Englewood Cliffs, N.J.: Prentice Hall, 1979), 109.

Product and Market Structures

A product structure groups tasks according to products made. When a firm diversifies and makes several differentiated products, manufacturing and marketing decisions become highly complex. A functional structure that groups activities under a common set of skills cannot effectively handle this complexity. Consequently, separate resources in design, manufacturing, and marketing must be assigned to each product. A firm thus chooses a product-based grouping in which functional specialists are dedicated to each differentiated product. General Motors was among the earliest firms to use a product structure to successfully make and market its Buick, Cadillac, Chevrolet, Oldsmobile, and Pontiac cars as distinct brands.[13] A consumer products manufacturer similar to the one shown in Figure 9.3, Part A is likely to use a product structure to effectively allocate exclusive R&D and marketing resources to its personal-care, toiletries, and other products in order to make them competitive.

When a firm has diverse customers and when each customer group is large and has distinct needs, a market-based grouping is needed. Imagine a firm with significant technological expertise in the area of electronic controls. It uses this knowledge to make control systems for residential, industrial, and defense clients. Because the requirements of these clients are different and unique, the firm organizes its operational activities under each market segment it serves: home and building market, industrial market, and aerospace and aviation market (see Figure 9.3, Part B). A modified version of this structure groups by geographical areas in which the firm competes (see Figure 9.3, Part C). An insurance company may use such a structure so as to effectively respond to the regional differences in insurance needs.

Strategic Business Unit (SBU) Structure

When firms are highly diversified, a simple product structure is unable to coordinate product groups because the span of control is too large. Under such conditions, firms use an elegant form of product structure known as **strategic business unit (SBU) structure**. (see Figure 9.4). An SBU structure groups several related products into a few manageable divisions to facilitate effective managerial control. When firms become too large as a result of diversification, they combine several SBUs into groups, thus adding another level of management. For example, General Electric has combined several SBUs into ten manageable groups (see *www.ge.com/company/businesses*). The resulting structure is generally referred to as a multidivisional structure.

Each division in an SBU structure operates autonomously as if it were an independent business. Each has its own profit goals and budget, developed jointly by division and corporate managers. Each division has its own functional specialists assisting it, either to effectively differentiate its products or to serve distinct market segments. In exchange for their independence, groups assume responsibility for fully realizing their profit goals, and they report to the CEO at corporate headquarters.

Advantages and Disadvantages of Product and Market Structures

Product and market grouping directs the attention of functional specialists assigned to each group to the exclusive needs of that product or market segment. Because product success or customer satisfaction (as opposed to skill enhancement) is now

FIGURE 9.3 **Product and Market Structures**

A. PRODUCT-BASED GROUPING: CONSUMER PRODUCTS COMPANY

B. MARKET-BASED GROUPING: MAKER OF ELECTRONIC CONTROLS

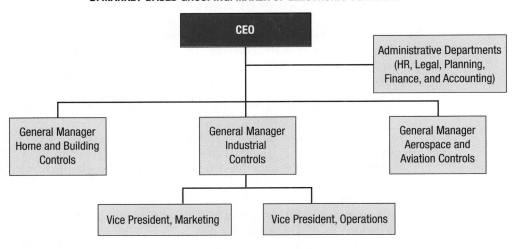

C. GEOGRAPHY-BASED GROUPING: A FIRM IN THE INSURANCE INDUSTRY

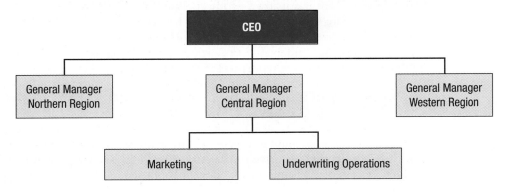

| FIGURE 9.4 | Strategic Business Unit Structure |

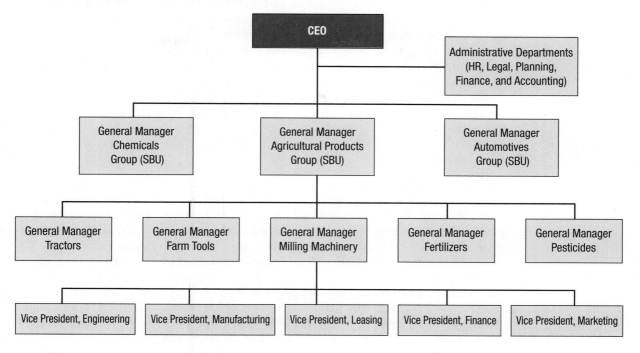

the common goal of specialists in each group, cross-functional communication and cooperation within each group are heightened. This interaction helps the firm respond rapidly to changes in the external environment that affect the product's technology or customer needs.

A second advantage is that the profitability of each product or market served can be clearly assessed. A firm can thus effectively commit more resources to successful products while deciding to exit from (that is, divest) those that are unprofitable. This exit decision can be easily implemented because each product has independent assets assigned to it. A third advantage is that a product or market structure frees corporate managers from product operations issues that are now the responsibility of division managers. The corporate managers can thus focus on the strategic and long-term issues of the firm such as growth and diversification.

The product or market structure entails significant disadvantages as well. First, it is very expensive because of the duplication of resources. Each division must be assigned exclusive operational resources that may not be fully utilized but that increase the overhead costs for the firm. Second, it does not promote functional skill enhancement. The emphasis in this structure is more on achieving cooperation among functional units than on encouraging functional skill enhancement. In fact, product and market structures can even cause the functional skills of an organization's members to quickly get outdated. A third problem is that divisions may fight over allocation of scarce resources, resulting in interdivisional animosity that is detrimental to the total firm. A fourth problem is that the poor quality of one division's products and services may adversely affect the brand reputation of another division and that of the overall firm.

To sum up, a product or market structure enables a firm to achieve product- or market-based advantages. By grouping functional resources around products made or markets served and fostering cooperation among them, it can effectively differentiate products or successfully meet the needs of customers in different market segments. A firm can exploit emerging opportunities rapidly or exit from currently unprofitable operations easily. However, it is an expensive structure because each product group must be assigned separate functional resources. Also, it can cause the skills of functional personnel to get quickly outdated.

Matrix Structure

A matrix structure combines the features of functional and product structures. It attempts to capture the strengths and minimize the problems of these two structures. In a nutshell, it groups functional personnel and product personnel on a project basis. Functional personnel (e.g., engineers) participate not only in activities that enhance their skills but also in projects where their knowledge is required.

Each small circle in Figure 9.5 represents a project to which functional experts are assigned until the project is completed. A functional expert (a design engineer, for example) may be assigned to work on more than one project at a time. The goal is to efficiently utilize available functional resources across several projects. For example, the consumer products firm shown in Figure 9.3, Part A may launch two projects: (1) developing and marketing a new line of cosmetics, and (2) improving the

FIGURE 9.5   **Matrix Structure**

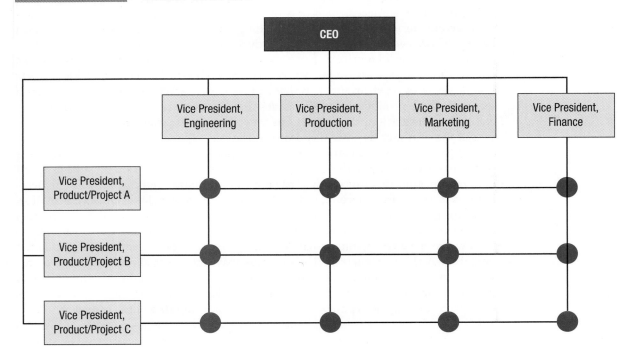

features of its current dental care products to make them more competitive. For each of these projects, it may assign necessary product design, manufacturing, marketing, and finance personnel to the appropriate product managers. Some of these employees may work half-time for each of these products. When the projects have been completed, the functional experts are redeployed to other emerging projects or even ongoing projects that need more personnel. Thus, a matrix structure rotates functional resources across product groups based on where they are most needed. Aerospace firms (e.g., Boeing), engineering consultants, and construction firms that operate on a project-by-project basis generally use a matrix structure. Others use it when resources are scarce (e.g., Dow Chemicals), when exchange of ideas across product groups is needed, and when projects must be completed within specified deadlines (e.g., defense contractors such as Lockheed Martin).

Advantages and Disadvantages of the Matrix Structure

An important advantage of the matrix structure is that it facilitates the efficient and effective use of critical functional resources. Functional personnel who have high expertise but are in short supply can divide their time among multiple projects that must be undertaken simultaneously. This resource sharing, while contributing to efficiency, also enables the firm to respond quickly to changes in the competitive environment. Thus, to a great extent, the matrix structure offers both the efficiency of a functional structure and the flexibility of a product structure. As a result, it is attractive to firms that must compete on a cost-differentiation combination strategy.

A second advantage is that project teams require minimal supervision. The structure builds a sense of professionalism among team members, who learn from each other and monitor each other's actions. Consequently, top managers are freed up to concentrate on the strategic issues facing the firm.

The matrix structure also has significant disadvantages. It creates a dual reporting relationship for its personnel, generating confusion and uncertainty regarding accountability. The functional experts assigned to projects must report to both their functional heads and the project/product managers. This creates tremendous vertical and horizontal coordination problems, requiring extra resources to manage its complexity. Nor is the matrix easy to implement, as the Dow Chemical Company found out when it adopted the structure in the late 1960s to pursue global expansion.[14] It took the firm and its employees more than a decade to understand and adjust to the complexities of the structure. Some scholars suggest that a matrix is not a structure per se, but a frame of mind. As such, its implementation requires a different type of thinking within the firm: a thinking that understands and is comfortable with conflicts and complexities.[15]

To sum up, a matrix structure offers a certain amount of both efficiency and flexibility. It is appropriate for firms that must design and implement specific innovation projects within deadlines but not for firms operating in a structured and unchanging environment.

Table 9.1 summarizes the advantages and disadvantages of different structures discussed thus far. We will now conclude this section with some general comments. Firms are not likely to use a pure functional, product, or matrix structure. Today's business environments are complex and dynamic, and, therefore, a combination structure is more likely. Firms that compete in industries that rapidly change favor a loose, "network type" of structure in which tasks are completed through contracts and alliances with several external parties.[16] Those that compete in *global markets,* as we will soon see, are reported to employ extremely complex structures that combine product, functional, and geography dimensions.[17] More importantly, no two firms may use a typically comparable structure even though they are pursuing the same strategy. Therefore, according to researchers, the best way to assess the effectiveness of a firm's structure is to examine the processes it employs to get specific tasks accomplished and compare them to those used by the competition.[18] For example, one can compare American Airlines to Southwest on employee selection and training processes and conclude which would be more appropriate for customer satisfaction goals.

Integration

Division and grouping of tasks is necessary to achieve focus. It allows each subunit to concentrate on the needs of the divided task so it can be executed according to plans. But, to effectively complete the organizational task, the divided units must act in concert. This is achieved through integration. If customers frequently complain about delivery delays, sales and manufacturing units are probably not coordinating their activities. If the design unit is aiming for a new product design while manufacturing is planning for high-volume production of the current design, there is a mismatch between the goals of product design and manufacturing. These issues emerge naturally from division of task, but they also indicate that the flow of work and information among the divided task groups is not in place or is not effective. The idea in organizational design is to ensure through the selection and implementation of coordination mechanisms that the divided groups work as if they were one unit.

The choice of coordination mechanisms depends on the information needed by each group to complete the assigned task.[19] Some tasks are routine, and each group may have all the information it needs to process the task. Other tasks may necessitate frequent consultation among groups before a group can complete its task. In the first case, integration is easy: all that needs to be done is to select a mechanism that will sequentially link the completed task of each group to the next in an assembly-line fashion. However, in the second case, complex coordination mechanisms such as cross-functional teams are needed to ensure that groups are able to exchange information at the time the task is processed. Today's organizations lean more toward the second type than the first. Even so, these are not the only criteria for selecting integration mechanisms. The ability of the firm's personnel to coordinate their activities with minimal or no supervision and the availability of resources to implement coordination are other determining factors. Most importantly, the strategy of the firm is the overriding factor in the selection of coordination mechanisms.

Integration Mechanisms

In broad terms, integration mechanisms range from planned to informal devices. Hierarchies and rules are examples of planned devices, whereas the organization's culture is an example of informal devices. The more the organizational task is divided, and the more each group must interact with others to complete its task, the more complicated are the firm's integration needs.[20] Complex organizations thus employ several integration mechanisms to achieve the desired coordination.[21] Intel, 3M, and GE are examples of complex organizations because they have many special-

| TABLE 9.1 | Functional, Product/Market/SBU, and Matrix Structures: Advantages and Disdvantages |

STRUCTURE TYPE	ADVANTAGES	DISADVANTAGES
1. Functional	Fosters skill specialization in competitively critical functional areas. A firm can gain competency in processing efficiency, processing speed, or output consistency. Enables large-volume production of products that require similar skills. Can be effectively implemented with few hierarchical levels because specialists need little supervision. Motivates personnel by offering opportunities for professional development, creating a productive workforce.	Functional skill development takes priority over product improvements. Does not facilitate cross-functional communication necessary for innovating. Pushes cross-functional issues to the top, overloading senior management. Inflexible, resists change. New skill development does not easily occur.
2. Product/ market/SBU	Directs the attention of functional experts to the exclusive needs of each product or market segment. Facilitates rapid response to product and market changes. Entry into new products/ markets or exit from current ones is easy to implement without jeopardizing current operations. Relieves top management of responsibility for operational issues.	Costly due to duplication of personnel, tool operations, and other assets. Does not promote functional skill enhancement. Can create dysfunctional competition among divisions. Poor quality product/service in one division may adversely affect the reputation of other divisions or the firm as a whole.
3. Matrix	Fosters innovations and fast market response through functional collaboration. Maximizes efficient use of resources. Offers efficiency-flexibility combination.	Coordination among vertical and horizontal units is difficult and expensive. Highly complex. Not suitable for all firms.

ist groups performing intricate tasks. To achieve unity of effort among them, these organizations employ several integration mechanisms, ranging from informal meetings to formal rules and procedures. But, as we mentioned earlier, most successful firms rely more heavily on informal mechanisms through which organizational members voluntarily cooperate with other groups to coordinate their activities.

Hierarchical Integration

Perhaps the easiest way to integrate two or more work groups is to add a layer of supervision. Direct supervision brings the activities of sections or departments together through a common manager. Information or work that must move from one group to another goes through a supervisor who coordinates the groups' activities and makes the necessary decisions. Hierarchical integration helps managers to exercise control over operations at lower levels, but it also overloads their position. Besides, it brings along with it the problems of centralization that we described earlier. Moreover, hierarchical (or vertical) coordination alone will not be sufficient for large organizations, and thus other mechanisms of a lateral type are necessary.

Lateral Integration

There are several mechanisms for laterally integrating work; the most important are *liaison roles* and *teams*. These mechanisms carry no formal authority but have informal power. Lateral integration achieves coordination among groups through lateral adjustments as opposed to supervisory intervention and thus implies decentralization of authority. Its advantages and disadvantages are similar to those of decentralization.

When the volume of workflow and communication between two groups increases, a firm may create a *liaison* position to act as a coordinator between the two. For example, Galbraith provides the example of a design engineer who is physically located in the manufacturing plant to coordinate activities between design and manufacturing units.[22] Similarly, a marketing person may regularly attend product design meetings to share market information with design personnel and at the same time review the marketing potential of new designs.

A *team* is used as an integrating mechanism when the activities of several work groups or departments require coordination. One member from each functional group is assigned to a team that meets periodically to discuss issues common to the groups. Each member then returns to his or her functional group to apprise it of the discussions. Each team member thus becomes an integrating link for the groups. Southwest Airlines relies more on teams than on any other coordinating mechanism to achieve work-group integration.

Rules and Procedures

Planned mechanisms such as rules and procedures can integrate the activities of task groups. For example, a firm's standard operating procedure may require the manufacturing department to involve the design department in all decisions concerning production setup. Rules make coordination routine, and routines lead to efficiencies. But rules can make a firm bureaucratic and inflexible. Besides, rules require advance planning for all possible contingencies, and that is difficult.

Culture

Culture is a set of beliefs and values shared by a group of people. It acts as a standard for judging what is acceptable behavior. Organizational culture represents member beliefs about the goals of the firm and the type of work behavior expected of them. By promoting a certain culture within the firm and ensuring that employees internalize it, organizations condition member behavior. For employees at 3M, innovation has become a way of life because the policies and reward systems of the company favor creativity. At Nucor, a low cost steel producer, employee concern for productivity is high because the company recognizes it and rewards it. Organizations with a strong culture require very few formal mechanisms to obtain employee cooperation because employees have already internalized the goal of the firm as their own.[23] The benefit of using organizational culture as a coordinating mechanism is its effectiveness. It is also a low cost way to achieve coordination compared to other formal mechanisms that are expensive. Nevertheless, a significant amount of time and resources must be spent on employee selection, training, and motivation to build the type of culture the firm needs.

Matching Design to Strategy

Different ways of dividing, grouping, and integrating organizational activities foster different competencies within the firm. A firm must choose a design based on the competencies it needs to implement its strategy. In this section, let us examine the organizational structure appropriate for each strategy.

Cost Leadership and Structure

A cost leader needs a structure that can process products or serve mass markets more economically than rivals. Efficiency and high-volume output are its key requirements. A functional structure is an appropriate design for these requirements. By dividing the task, developing uniform procedures for completing each task, and grouping units based on skills or functions, a functional structure creates standardization and specialization, allowing for an efficient and productive organization to emerge. Two other factors that promote efficiency in a functional structure strengthen its appeal for cost strategists: (1) it centralizes skill resources, allowing for their economical use in single or multiple operations, and (2) it fosters a professional culture that induces employees to voluntarily coordinate, eliminating the need for the more expensive supervisory coordination.

Nevertheless, a functional structure does not by itself guarantee a firm competitive superiority in efficiency since most cost leaders would use this structure. It is through measured levels of task differentiation and by choosing the right integration mechanisms that a firm builds a competitively capable functional organization. Extreme differentiation makes integration difficult and costly, whereas the opposite does not permit specialization to occur. More importantly, achieving integration of the specialists groups is crucial for a functional organization because coordination among these groups does not naturally occur. As an example, consider a hypothetical firm, a commodity steel manufacturer that competes on cost leadership and uses a functional structure. Its high fixed cost (steel mills require a large investment in fixed assets) and its inability to influence price (because the product is a commodity) bring added pressure on the firm to control cost. As a result, it would avoid extreme levels of differentiation that require expensive integration mechanisms such as rules or direct supervision. Instead, it would keep differentiation closer to the natural workflow—for example, mining, melting, casting, cooling, cutting, sales, distribution—that induces automatically occurring coordination between adjacent groups all along the task sequence. Where differentiation based on such a natural workflow is not possible, cost strategy firms rely on cultural mechanisms to achieve coordination.

Differentiation Strategy and Structure

A *broad differentiator* competes in several niche segments. Abilities to offer different designs, continuously enhance each design, and quickly respond to market opportunities are its key requirements. To realize these, a differentiator must (1) have strengths in product R&D and marketing, (2) be skilled in making the design and marketing groups work together, and (3) be able to effectively manage a portfolio of independent product/market divisions. In short, a differentiator needs an organization that can offer not efficiency, but flexibility in the use of resources.

A differentiator is most likely to choose a product/market structure to meet its needs. This structure allocates critical resources (R&D, marketing) exclusively to each product/market division, giving the firm the flexibility it seeks to customize the product for each segment. An additional factor that makes this structure attractive to the differentiator is that functional units within each division voluntarily coordinate because the success of the product, not skill enhancement, becomes their common goal.

Similar to a functional structure, a product/market structure does not by itself guarantee competitive superiority to a differentiator because most differentiators are likely to use it. The issue of concern here is decentralization: extreme decentralization is expensive and wasteful of resources whereas the opposite constrains the flexibility that divisions need. By selectively decentralizing most relevant resources to divisions while centralizing others at the corporate level, a firm builds a competitively capable product/market organization. For example, Eastman Kodak, which pursues a product line differentiation (digital and film imaging products, commercial imaging products, health imaging products), has delegated product development activities (applied engineering, product design) to the divisions but has centralized basic R&D, marketing, and sales at the corporate level.[24] To ensure the flow of R&D information from the corporate to division levels or between divisions, Kodak uses cross-divisional team integration mechanisms.

A *narrow differentiator* that competes within a focused segment (for example, Rolex Watch Company, which targets upscale customers only) may choose a functional structure because of the absence of volume economies due to the small size of the market and the pressure to control cost as a result. Depending on the nature of differentiation—for example, superior product or superior customer service—the company designs its activities around the needed competency, such as R&D or marketing, as the case may be.

Diversification Strategy and Structure

Diversification creates coordination and control issues for managers. A well-diversified firm that performs several value chain activities and competes in multiple industries (e.g., GE) finds that achieving coordination and control is challenging and costly to achieve because of the firm's complexity. Understandably, managers would prefer an arrangement that would allow them to pursue multiple business opportunities economically and without loss of control. The design that fulfills these criteria is an SBU or a multidivisional structure. These structures minimize complexity issues by dividing the firm's task into distinct business units, each with its own administrative and functional personnel. They solve the control problem by allowing top managers to delegate the responsibility for running the business units to division managers. Division managers accept this responsibility in exchange for their autonomy in divisional matters and the promise of rewards when division performance exceeds expectations. Hierarchical positions, liaison roles, and cross-divisional teams serve as integrating mechanisms.

Most firms pursuing diversification strategies use a multidivisional structure. To achieve a competitive superiority in strategy implementation, a diversified firm must therefore explore additional organizational mechanisms that would give it an edge over rivals. By employing informal coordination mechanisms, such as promoting a certain organizational culture in which interunit coordination voluntarily occurs, a diversified firm gains the necessary advantage.

International Strategy and Structure

What organizational structure would be appropriate for firms that compete internationally? Recall from Chapter 7 the three international strategies that we discussed: multidomestic, global, and transnational. Multidomestic strategy requires the product and marketing to be differentiated to suit the local market and regulatory needs, global strategy requires a uniform product and marketing efforts worldwide, and transnational strategy requires combining uniformity with differentiation. Using these critical requirements, we can examine what structure may be appropriate for each.

A *multidomestic strategy* firm would most likely use a global geographic area structure as illustrated in Figure 9.6. In this structure, a firm duplicates value chain activities in every country in which it operates and decentralizes strategic and operational decisions to regional business units to allow them to effectively compete locally. Since each business unit is almost self-contained, no formal cross-divisional integration mechanisms are employed and coordination among units is informal. In regard to the headquarters–business unit relationship, each unit receives resources or other forms of support from the headquarters and in turn contributes profits back to it. The principal advantage of this structure is that it allows a firm the flexibility to tailor products to local market needs. But two disadvantage must be noted: (1) it does not offer economies of scale associated with global production and marketing, and (2) it makes it difficult for regional business units to share crucial information they may have with other units.

Global strategy firms are likely to use a global product division structure as shown in Figure 9.7. In this structure, a firm locates its critical value chain activities at global locations where they can be performed most economically. Thus, R&D may be performed in one country, component manufacturing in another, and product assembly in the third. Strategic decision making is centralized at the headquarters level where the firm makes crucial decisions concerning location of functional units, market development and entry, and distribution channels. Since the value chain activities are performed in different countries, tight integration mechanisms are necessary. By using cross-functional teams and liaison roles and by locating value chain operations geographically close to each other, a firm achieves the necessary coordination of activities. The major advantage of this structure is the economies of scale benefits it offers. Its weakness is the inability to respond to local needs effectively.

Transnational strategy firms generally prefer a global matrix structure that combines the beneficial features of the geographic area structure and the products division structure. (See Figure 9.8, Part C. Also read Strategy in Practice 9.1.) In Figure 9.8 (C), the product groups with functional resources such as R&D, manufacturing, and marketing are on the vertical axis. On the horizontal axis are the business divisions in the international locations in which the firm operates. In this structure, product managers have control over functional resources and distribute them to overseas divisions based on the firm's overall competitive priorities, but regional managers have the freedom to decide how their business units operate within their respective regions. Due to its team-orientation and the professional culture it builds within the firm, the matrix structure brings about coordination among activities through mutual adjustment. The major advantage of this structure is that it allows for a systematic transfer of skills across business divisions, creating a globally competent firm. However, a crucial problem is the complexities the structure poses for employees in work coordination, resulting in inefficiencies.

FIGURE 9.6 **Global Geographic Area Structure—The Unilever Company, 2005**

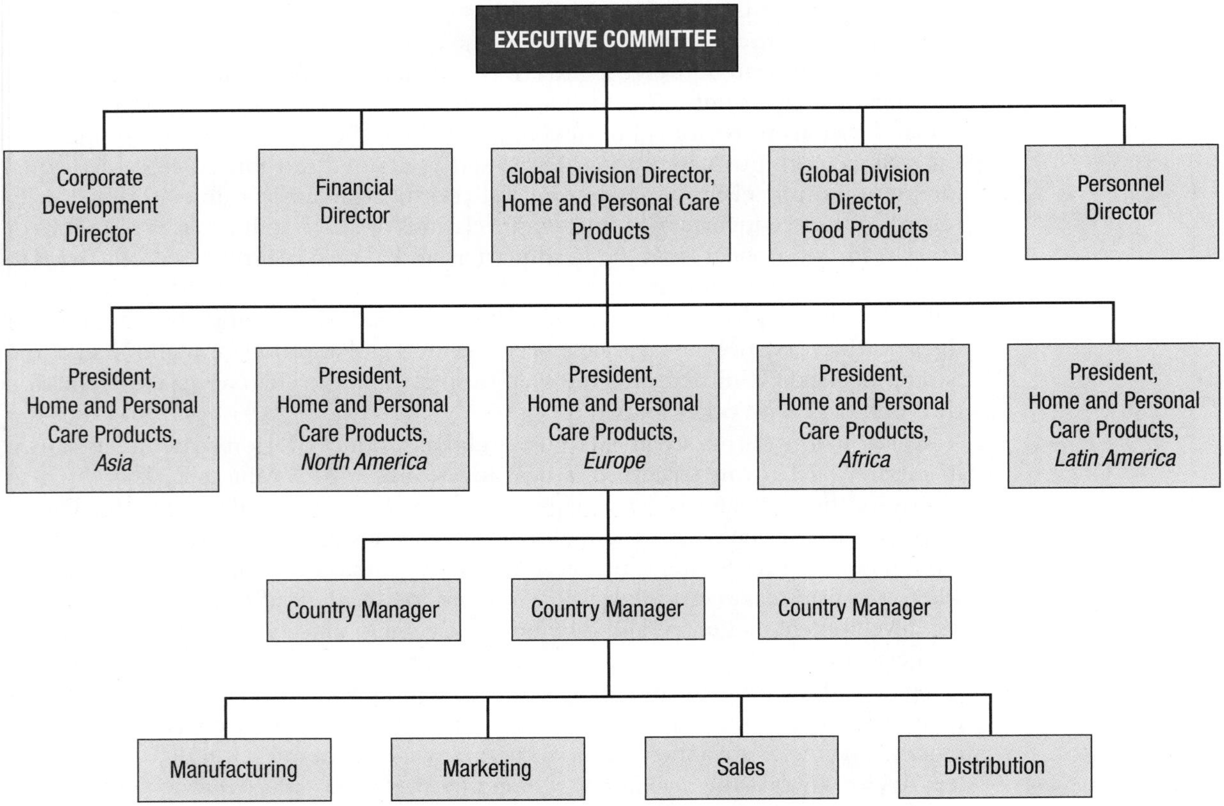

Source: Adapted from www.unilever.com/ourcompany/aboutunilever/companystructure.

FIGURE 9.7 Global Product Division Structure—An Athletic Footwear and Apparel Manufacturer

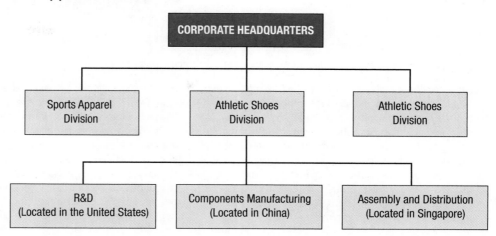

FIGURE 9.8 Global Matrix Structure

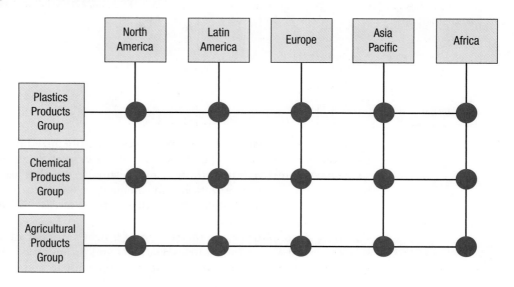

Strategy
in PRACTICE 9.1

THE DOW CHEMICAL COMPANY'S GLOBAL MATRIX STRUCTURE

The Dow Chemical Company is a one-hundred-year-old U.S manufacturer of plastics, chemicals, and agricultural products. Some of its products are chemical intermediates (hydrocarbons, polymers, monomers) that serve the needs of industrial clients, while others are finished goods (plastic wrap, cleaning agents, automobile coolants) for household consumption. Overall, Dow manufactures 3,500 different products in 180 manufacturing plants spread across 37 countries. As of 2003, the company employed 46,000 workers worldwide, served customers in 183 countries, and had $33 billion in sales. Dow is truly a global firm.

The chemical industry is highly regulated by most nations for plant safety, product safety, and pollution effects. Regulations differ from country to country, requiring a chemical firm to be mindful of local laws when designing foreign operations. At the same time, because the output of a chemical firm is uniform, a global integration of procurement, manufacturing, and R&D operations is needed to benefit from economies of scale. In short, an integrative approach that combines local responsiveness (differentiation) and global standardization (efficiency) is essential to achieve competitiveness. Dow pursues such a combination strategy.

To effectively implement this strategy, the company employs a three-dimensional global matrix structure that is organized by business, function, and geography (that is, by country). Along the business dimension, Dow's 3,500 products are grouped into fifteen global businesses that plan and set goals for their units. Along the functional dimension, skills needed for realizing these goals are centralized in functional units such as R&D and manufacturing, letting managers in these units optimally distribute available resources to global business operations based on their respective needs and priorities. Along the geography dimension, country managers are given the authority to act as regional experts, providing market information to business units and regulatory information to functional units.

This structure has helped Dow achieve the twin objectives it needs to remain competitive in a global business environment: flexibility (ability to quickly respond to local needs) and efficiency (ability to be economical in operations). By allowing business, functional, and country managers to collectively formulate strategic and operational decisions, the structure ensures the rapid exploitation of global market opportunities. Through functional centralization, it provides for the efficient use of the firm's resources.

Source: www.dow.com; "Dow draws its matrix again—and again, and again," *Economist* (US), August 5, 1989, p. 55; T. Stevens, "Winning the World Over," *Industry Week*, November 15, 1999.

Summary

Strategy implementation requires resources to be organized in such a way that they function as a single unit. The complexity of a firm's resources may make it difficult to achieve effective integration. As a result, firms that can achieve effective integration have an organizational advantage over competitors. Organizational advantage refers to a firm's ability to coordinate its resources more efficiently and effectively than the competition.

Organizational design is the source of a firm's organizational advantage. Organizational design requires firms to divide and group tasks, integrate the divided tasks, and delegate the necessary authority to individuals and groups to get the tasks accomplished. Different ways of designing an organization exist, and they create different types of competencies within firms. It is imperative that a firm match its design to its strategy to be successful.

Tasks are grouped on the basis of skills or business functions, products made or markets served, or a combination of functions and products or markets. Functional grouping promotes skill specialization, allowing for processing efficiency and volume production of a standard product or of several standard products that require the same skills. This grouping creates inflexibility and impedes product or process change. Product/market grouping makes it easier to dedicate functional resources to each product or market group, enabling the firm to respond swiftly to technological or market changes. However, it is inefficient because separate resources must be assigned to each product/market division. Moreover, it does not promote skill specialization. In fact, skills may soon become outdated in a firm that uses this type of grouping. The matrix structure groups functional experts and product personnel on a project basis. It economically distributes available functional resources to product groups based on needs. Thus it minimizes the functional structure's lack of flexibility and the product structure's inefficiency. Organizations using this structure, however, find it difficult to coordinate functional and product activities effectively. As a result, the matrix structure is difficult to implement.

In selecting an appropriate organizational structure, a firm must first evaluate the competencies needed to implement its strategy. It must then understand the competencies that each of the structures—functional, product/market, and matrix—fosters within the firm. Finally, it must choose a structure that will meet the needs of its strategy. Successful firms frequently assess the match between their strategy and structure and fine-tune their structure to create an ideal fit between the two.

Chapter 9   Discussion Question and Projects

Discussion Question

1. Compare the strengths and weaknesses of functional, product/market, and matrix structures and the competencies each fosters within a firm. In your comparison, answer the question: what structural type will be most appropriate for implementing each of the business- and corporate-level strategy choices presented in this text? Provide reasons for your answer.

Projects

1. Based on your understanding of how your college functions, diagram its organizational structure. Now, obtain a copy of your college's organization chart from its human resources department and compare it with your diagram. What similarities and differences do you find?

2. Using a textbook or other published source, identify a diversified company that presently uses a product structure. Restructure this firm along functional lines.

Continuing Case

Reorganizing Pepsi-Cola, USA: From a Functional Structure to a Matrix Structure

Background

Pepsi-Cola emerged as a multibusiness firm when it made a series of acquisitions in the snack food and restaurant industries during the 1960s and 1970s. The company then changed its name to PepsiCo and added a corporate-level management structure to coordinate the activities of three businesses: beverage, snack food, and restaurant. Pepsi-Cola was now one of the business units of PepsiCo. The corporate structure as of 1986 is shown in Figure 1, with PepsiCo as the parent company and Pepsi-Cola as one of its business units.

While PepsiCo focused on formulating strategies to increase the overall performance of the corporation, the concern at Pepsi-Cola was how to gain competitive superiority in the beverage business. Pepsi-Cola's marketing and distribution strategies addressed this issue by building a distinctive image for Pepsi in attractive market segments and by firmly positioning the Pepsi brand in the supermarket channel. As a result, the Pepsi brand emerged as a strong contender for the soft drinks industry leadership. However, the soft drinks industry was not standing still. Changes were occurring in the industry environment, especially in the supermarket segment where Pepsi was strong, necessitating corresponding changes in Pepsi-Cola's organizational processes.

The Pepsi-Cola Organization in the Mid-1980s

The U.S. Pepsi-Cola division of the mid-1980s had three operating subdivisions: *Pepsi USA, Pepsi Bottling Group (PBG),* and the *Fountain Beverage Division (FBD).* These subdivisions were functionally organized, as illustrated in Figure 2. *The Pepsi USA subdivision,* the oldest of the three, was responsible for concentrate sales and for marketing the Pepsi brand nationally. It developed the overall marketing strategy for Pepsi, designed national campaigns, and worked with both company-owned and independent bottlers to implement these campaigns at the local level. The widely acclaimed Pepsi Generation campaign that radically repositioned Pepsi as a unique beverage was designed by Pepsi USA. Since marketing strengths are crucial for the success of a soft drinks firm, the Pepsi USA division occupied a central place in the Pepsi-Cola organization. The *Pepsi Bottling Group (PBG)* managed the company-owned bottling operations. It bought the concentrate from Pepsi USA, bottled the soft drinks, and sold and distributed the product within its franchised territories. While Pepsi USA marketed the Pepsi brand nationally, PBG focused on marketing Pepsi within its regions through local advertising and by providing in-store display support to local retailers. *The Fountain Beverage Division (FBD)* was responsible for the marketing, sale, and distribution

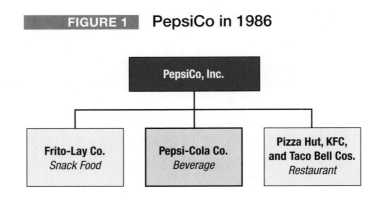

FIGURE 1 **PepsiCo in 1986**

of the Pepsi brand through the fountain. FBD sold the concentrate to two types of customers: (1) restaurant chains and convenience stores that added carbonated water to the concentrate and sold the beverage on-site, and (2) bottlers who bought the concentrate and sold it to local restaurants. FBD and the restaurant chains jointly decided on the marketing and promotion of the Pepsi brand through the fountain.

Division Interaction

Historically, the Pepsi-Cola culture promoted individualism and self-interest. The functional differentiation the firm employed in its operations—*concentrate sales and marketing, bottling and distribution, fountain sales*—and the reward systems the firm used to achieve higher performance in each of them encouraged interunit competition. As a result, the three operational subdivisions acted independently, formulating and implementing plans that essentially focused on their own individual goals. This arrangement led to higher subdivisional performance and, in turn, higher company performance. However, it was losing its effectiveness because it created interunit conflict and limited Pepsi-Cola's ability to satisfactorily serve the retail customer—the supermarket. Precisely stated, the interunit coopera-

tion needed to respond speedily to customer requests for promotion and delivery did not automatically occur at Pepsi-Cola, even though the changes occurring in the supermarket segment demanded that the firm, in fact, have such a capability.

The U.S. Food Retailing Scene: Consolidation in the Supermarket Segment

The traditional food retailers were small grocery stores. Their small volume purchases gave them very little power to successfully negotiate attractive discounts or delivery terms with giant suppliers such as Pepsi-Cola. However, between the 1970s and 1980s, the supermarkets were rapidly replacing grocery stores. The mergers and acquisitions that took place in the supermarket segment during this time had created large retail chains owned by fewer firms. The centralized procurement system employed by these firms resulted in volume purchases that gave them the power to negotiate better terms with the food and beverage suppliers. These terms required speedy delivery to stores located across several states, uniformity in advertising campaign and in-store display support, and rapid decision making in promotions jointly undertaken by Pepsi-Cola and the retailers. Certainly, the Pepsi-Cola organization that encouraged interunit rivalry was a poor fit for

FIGURE 2 Pepsi-Cola in 1986

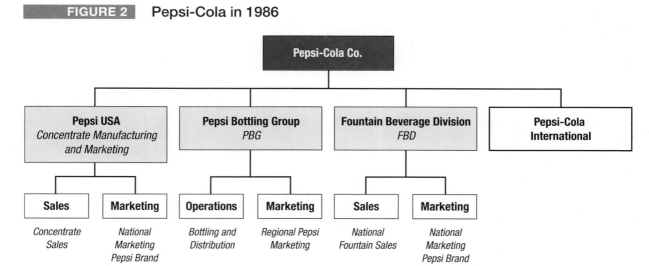

Source: Adapted from "Pepsi-Cola U.S. Beverages (A), Harvard Business School Case #9-390-034, July 8, 1992.

FIGURE 3   Pepsi-Cola in 1988

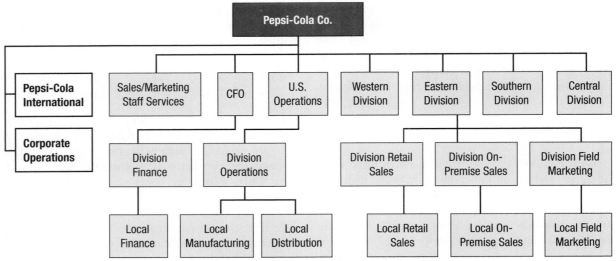

Source: Adapted from "Pepsi-Cola U.S. Beverages (B)," Harvard Business School Case #9-390-035, April 29, 1991.

this market situation. Therefore, Pepsi-Cola had to quickly reorganize.

The Reorganization: Geographic Matrix

Following the recommendations of a task force the company had set up for the purpose, Pepsi-Cola reorganized early in 1988. The goal of this reorganization was to make Pepsi-Cola more of a customer-focused firm than a task-focused firm. The new organization sought to achieve this goal by decentralizing the marketing and sale of Pepsi products under four regional divisions. Operations (bottling and distribution) remained centralized, but the division heads exercised authority over them jointly with headquarters. Each regional division had several local units, and each unit had functional managers who coordinated their activities based on the needs of local customers (supermarkets and restaurants). Bonuses tied to individual efforts and overall sales performance of the local unit motivated the required coordination. The resulting structure, a geographic matrix, is shown in Figure 3. Managers of Pepsi-Cola believed that the new structure would provide com-petitive benefits in two ways: (1) It would help the firm respond to customer needs more rapidly, and (2) it would reduce costs by eliminating the duplication of activities the previous structure had fostered.

Discussion Questions

1. Describe Pepsi-Cola's structure prior to the 1988 reorganization. What advantages did the firm derive from this structure? What part did Pepsi-Cola's culture play in fostering this structure?

2. Describe the reasons that Pepsi-Cola reorganized. Describe the new structure and the advantages the firm expected to derive from this structure. Explain how the new structure was expected to provide these advantages.

Source: "Pepsi-Cola U.S. Beverages (A)," Harvard Business School Case #9-390-034, July 8, 1992; "Pepsi-Cola U.S. Beverages (B)," Harvard Business School Case #9-390-035, April 29, 1991; D. A. Garvin, "Leveraging Processes for Strategic Advantage," *Harvard Business Review* 73, no. 5 (September–October 1995): 77–90; R. S. Tedlow, *New and Improved: The Story of Mass Marketing"* (Boston, Mass.: Harvard Business School Press, 1996), chaps. 2 and 4.

Part **Five**

Evaluating Performance

CHAPTER 10   Evaluation and Control: Designing and
Implementing Strategic Control Systems

Evaluation and Control: Designing and Implementing Strategic Control Systems

CHAPTER OBJECTIVES

After reading this chapter, you should be able to:

- Define strategic control and describe its importance for strategic management

- Describe and discuss the components of a strategic control system

- Describe performance standards, identify the types of standards, and discuss the measurement mechanisms appropriate for those standards

- Match strategic control systems with the firm's strategy and structure

- Design control systems appropriate for a given strategy and organizational structure

Opening Case

Low fares and superior customer service are the cornerstones of Southwest Airlines's business-level strategy. Airline passengers are happy when they pay relatively low fares, when flights depart and arrive on time, and when ground personnel and flight crew are friendly and courteous. Several groups such as the pilots, flight attendants, gate agents, mechanics, caterers, and baggage handlers must coordinate their activities to ensure that planes depart and arrive on schedule and that passengers are taken care of. But, given the high level of uncertainty in the tasks performed by these groups, management cannot preplan the coordination of their work. Instead, it must be left to the groups themselves to coordinate their activities, based on day-to-day contingencies. Accordingly, Southwest Airlines uses a decentralized structure in which operations personnel are given freedom to perform their tasks as they think appropriate for realizing the firm's customer service goals.

Delegation of authority, by itself, does not guarantee that workers will complete the task according to plans. Appropriate control mechanisms are needed to make sure they do and, moreover, that they work responsibly with minimal supervision. Southwest employs several control mechanisms of a preventive nature—that is, measures that ensure worker behavior and output do not deviate from plans. Some of these mechanisms focus on employee selection so as to avoid hiring employees whose skills and personality traits are not a good match to the job. Others focus on the style of managerial supervision and the company atmosphere needed to promote a customer-driven work culture. Yet others focus on clearly specifying to employees the strategic goal of the firm and the level of performance expected of them.

Southwest attaches considerable importance to employee selection procedures. The firm focuses on selecting operational employees whose work values closely match the company's. The idea is that when employee and employer values are similar, employees will not need externally administered controls. They will exercise self-control—that is, they will set goals and voluntarily monitor their activities because they like their work. The firm also ensures that the employees selected are low on an attitude of superiority and high on team spirit. As mentioned earlier, this team spirit among airlines' operational personnel is essential to achieving a high level of customer service. Southwest augments these selection standards with job orientation and training that teaches all employees to voluntarily assume responsibility and work with customer need and comfort in mind.

Southwest's supervisory techniques and managerial culture are designed to create an atmosphere of learning and improvement—as opposed to one of blame and punishment. Southwest's managers are trained to do less supervisory evaluation and correction and, instead, to provide more constructive feedback, allowing employees greater opportunity for self-correction. The goal in supervision is to understand what went wrong rather than to find mistakes employees made and decide what penalties are appropriate. By positively reinforcing employee output that meets or exceeds company standards on customer service and by allowing employees to learn from mistakes, Southwest's managers not only prevent unsatisfactory performance from occurring but also enhance the quality of performance.

Airline passengers consistently rate Southwest's customer service the highest in the industry. Industry analysts say that Southwest's success can be explained by the fact that its coordination and control mechanisms are internally consistent and befit its strategy. By matching employee skills and attitude to the job, delegating authority to the employees, and motivating them through a learning approach, the firm has created an internal work environment conducive to providing superior customer service.[1]

Southwest Airlines's case illustrates the significance of strategic control to a firm's competitive performance. Formulation and implementation of strategies are necessary steps in the firm's journey toward its vision and long-term goals but not sufficient. A firm must additionally ensure that its strategies and structures are, in fact, delivering results—that is, that they are helping the firm move closer to its vision and goals. A firm may do this by continuously monitoring and adjusting its current activities, measuring long-term performance against vision, and taking corrective steps. Alternatively, like Southwest Airlines, it may employ preventive measures that inhibit deviations from goals or use motivational tools that positively influence goal achievement. Some firms may use a combination of preventive, corrective, and motivational techniques to achieve the desired organizational outcome. Collectively, these activities, aimed at ascertaining that the firm is making effective progress toward its vision and long-term goals, are called control, and they are the topic of this chapter.

We start this chapter with a brief description of how strategic control systems have evolved from a traditional focus on correcting deviations after the fact to a focus on preventing deviations and facilitating continuous improvement. We then define strategic control and its importance to strategic management, and describe the process involved in designing a strategic control system. We provide examples of standards that firms set to guide organizational performance and the mechanisms they use to measure performance. Our conclusion briefly describes organizational structure and control mechanisms that are appropriate for business-level, corporate-level, and international strategy choices.

What Is Strategic Control?

Control is a series of steps managers take to ensure that the firm is making progress toward its long-term goals. Its purpose is to alert managers to a potential problem before the problem becomes serious. Managers have traditionally achieved control by periodically comparing organizational output (that is, end results) to plans. In this approach, extreme variance between actual results and plans would indicate unsatisfactory progress toward goals. More importantly, it would indicate that the means employed to reach the goal were ineffective and that alternative means should be considered.[2] In this traditional sense, control is a post-strategy-implementation activity in which managers seek feedback about the effectiveness of the implementation mechanisms they used.[3] Based on the feedback, managers make remedial adjustments to strategy or structure, as the case may be. In the strict traditional view, therefore, control is the final step in a sequential process—plan and set goals, act, and compare output to goals—to verify whether the firm has made progress, whether strategies and structures have been effective, and, if not, what corrective actions must be undertaken.

Today, control still refers to managerial steps to monitor and verify the firm's progress toward long-term goals and to keep the firm functioning and on track. But the way managers achieve control has undergone significant transformation, for several reasons. First, with the business environment changing rapidly, managers now continuously monitor the firm's strategic performance. Waiting until activities have been completed to evaluate results can provide feedback too late to be useful. Strategy in Practice 10.1 describes how General Electric monitors the strategic performance of its various businesses in real time. Second, managers today employ preventive measures that can keep deviations from goals from occurring. Third, managers utilize facilitative measures that have the potential to positively influence performance. For these reasons, scholars presently view control as comprising a combination of preventive measures, positive enhancement, and remedial actions in the firm's efforts to achieve superior organizational performance.[4]

Defining Strategic Control

Based on our understanding of the term *control,* we define **strategic control** as a process in which managers continuously monitor the firm's strategic performance and evaluate progress toward strategic goals.[5] The purpose is to assess whether current strategies and structures are effective, whether they are helping the firm achieve its strategic goals, and if not, how strategies, structures, or goals should be modified. Included in the strategic control process are managerial actions to motivate employees,

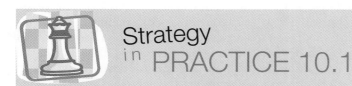

Strategy in PRACTICE 10.1

HOW GE MONITORS ITS STRATEGIC PERFORMANCE IN REAL TIME

General Electric Company (GE) is the world's biggest conglomerate, with over 300,000 employees and 2004 sales of $151 billion. The company manufactures thousands of related and unrelated products, from electric bulbs and dishwashers to plastics and aircraft engines, in company-owned factories situated across one hundred countries. Besides manufactured goods, GE also offers financial, insurance, and media services. For example, GE owns the National Broadcasting Corporation (NBC).

To effectively manage its vast and diverse product lines, GE has grouped them into eleven major business divisions, such as energy, transportation, consumer and industrial products, health care, and NBC Universal (broadcasting). Each division is headed by a general manager who is given sufficient authority to run the division independently in exchange for year-end profitable returns. Within divisions, operational units are allowed to set goals on the basis of top management guidelines and to monitor activities independently. They are rewarded when results meet or exceed expectations. Thus, by delegating authority to divisions and by rewarding good performance, GE has been able to effectively control the overall performance of its vast operations.

But GE does not wait until activities have been completed and business units have reported results to headquarters before it begins to evaluate company performance. It monitors from its corporate level both the operational performance of its business units (inventory levels, sales) and the strategic performance of the firm itself (overall competitiveness) on an ongoing basis. Many of GE's businesses compete in global markets that rapidly change due to changes in technology, government regulations, and consumer lifestyle. To respond to these changes speedily through strategy or structural adjustments, corporate managers must monitor business operations almost in real time. To help managers do that, the company has installed at its corporate headquarters in Fairfield, Connecticut, a computer system with a keyboard and a giant flat-screen monitor. The system displays real-time data on sales, costs, order rates, and inventory levels, allowing strategic managers to make mission-critical decisions quickly—as for example, moving resources from one division to another or, in extreme cases, restructuring the firm. In 2003, pursuant to feedback obtained through continuous monitoring at the corporate level, GE reorganized by reducing the number of its business divisions from thirteen to eleven.

Source: www.ge.com; D. Lindorff, "Case Study: General Electric and Real Time," *CIO Insight* (www.cioinsight.com), November 11, 2002.

prevent behaviors that will hinder goal achievement, and take remedial measures if needed.

Strategic control thus incorporates feed-forward, concurrent, and feedback mechanisms, along with tools that encourage behaviors conducive to desired organizational outcomes.[6] In **feed-forward control**, managers anticipate change that can adversely affect performance and take preventive measures through proper planning. In **concurrent control,** managers restrain deviations from expected performance through direct supervision. In **feedback control,** they assess performance after the fact and take corrective actions. To encourage performance-related behaviors, managers employ incentives and rewards and they create a positive work environment.

Strategic Goals as Evaluation Criteria

If strategic controls monitor and verify whether the firm is making progress toward strategic goals, what are strategic goals? Recall from Chapters 1 and 2 that **strategic goals** are the nonfinancial goals the firm seeks to realize—for example, a dominant industry position or industry reputation for product quality and innovativeness.[7] To be precise, Dell Computer's aim of "realizing superior processing efficiency in the PC industry" or Federal Express's aim to "deliver packages on time, all the time," are strategic goals. If you guessed from these examples that strategic goals are none other than a set of broad but enduring strategic advantages (either resource-based or positional) sought by a firm, you are absolutely correct. The fundamental aim in strategic management, as you may recall, is to seek and realize strategic goals—that is, advantages over competition. These advantages equip the firm with the potential or the ability to earn superior profits.

The logic of strategic management, then, is simple. A firm decides on the strategic goals it will pursue based on its vision. A single-business firm may pursue more than one strategic goal, and, certainly, a multibusiness firm will pursue several goals. A firm then chooses the strategies and structures it will adopt to realize its strategic goals and the control mechanisms it will employ to monitor and verify progress toward these goals. Continuous monitoring and adjustment, along with preventive and supportive measures, allow the firm to keep its strategic activities on track and moving toward desired strategic outcomes.

Why Not Use Financial Goals as Criteria?

We said that a firm evaluates the effectiveness of its strategy and structure by examining the progress it has made toward strategic goals. Can a firm assess how effective its strategy and structure have been by examining the current financial results, such as return on investment or equity? Of course, but current financial results provide feedback about past strategic decisions only; they offer no insight into the firm's potential for future performance. Strategic controls that use strategic goals as performance criteria, on the other hand, indicate to the firm its overall health and preparedness to earn profits now and in the future. Precisely stated, strategic controls that employ strategic goals as evaluation criteria examine how effective strategies and structures have been in preparing the firm for long-term good performance. Those firms that employ financial goals as performance criteria provide feedback on the effectiveness of past strategies and structures only.

Robert Kaplan and David Norton, while emphasizing the importance of using strategic goals as measurement criteria, suggest that both financial measures and strategic measures be employed when evaluating company performance.[8] Financial measures such as cash flow and return on equity indicate the effectiveness of strategies the firm employed in the past, allowing managers to decide whether those strategies should be continued, modified, or discarded. But, measuring a firm's performance only from such a single perspective, according to Kaplan and Norton, yields incomplete information. A balanced approach—the authors call it balanced scorecard—that evaluates performance from both financial and strategic perspectives offers a more effective assessment of performance because it enables the firm to track financial results while simultaneously monitoring progress toward the acquisition of capabilities the firm needs for future growth.[9] Kaplan and Norton suggest four different perspectives against which to measure a firm's performance—one financial and three strategic. These perspectives, their orientation, and sample measures that can be used within each of these perspectives are shown in Table 10.1.

Companies that employed the balanced scorecard have reported significant benefits because of it. After adopting it from 1993 to 1995, Mobil Oil (now Exxon-Mobil) leaped from last to first in profitability in its industry, a rank it maintained for the next four years. Cigna was losing $1 million a day in 1993, but within two years of adopting the balanced scorecard it was at the top quartile of profitability in its industry.[10] But a good number of firms have also reported that the balanced scorecard did not add much value to their performance.[11] Researchers suggest that this is because the balanced scorecard is incomplete since it excludes the effects of critical variables such as employees and suppliers on organizational performance.[12]

Incidentally, a point worth noting here is that the financial performance of a firm can, on occasion, result more from favorable industry conditions than from the strategies and structures employed by the firm. Consequently, reliance on current financial results alone to assess the effectiveness of a firm's strategy and structure can be misleading. A firm may solve this problem by assessing its progress on strategic

---

TABLE 10.1 **Strategic and Financial Controls—Balanced Scorecard Approach**

PERSPECTIVE	ORIENTATION	MEASUREMENT CRITERIA
Financial	Strategy for growth and profits from the shareholders' perspective	Cash flow Growth in sales and operating income Return on equity
Customer	Strategy for creating value from the customers' perspective	Customer order response time Customer satisfaction with product/ service quality Percentage of sales from new products
Internal business processes	Strategic priorities for internal business processes that create value for the customer and the shareholder	Processing efficiency—input/output ratio Asset utilization Design-manufacturing changeover time
Innovation and learning	Strategic priorities that create an internal environment conducive to innovation and growth	Number of patents registered Frequency of innovations compared to competition Enhancements in employee skills

goals and examining its financial performance on a long-term basis. Significantly superior profits, consistently earned, should indicate to the firm the effectiveness of its strategy and structure that is in addition to industry influences.

Importance of Strategic Control

Strategic management is based on the assumption that the strategy and structure chosen by the firm will lead it to the strategic goals it seeks. But goals may not materialize or the firm may be moving in the wrong direction, giving rise to the need for strategic control. Following are some of the benefits of strategic control:

- It provides managers with a basis on which to assess short- and long-term strategic performance to ensure that the firm is moving in the desired direction.

- Through continuous monitoring, it allows managers to intervene in strategic issues and problems in a timely manner. In a rapidly changing competitive environment, such timely interventions are imperative to avoid threats and ensure the firm's long-term success.

- Strategic control evaluates the firm's performance against its strategic goals, the enduring strengths that equip a firm for long-term success. By focusing managers' attention on measuring progress toward strategic strengths, strategic control prepares the firm for future performance.

- Managers are likely to be highly motivated when their performance is measured against strategic goals since realization of such goals indicates the competitive superiority of the firm. Because strategic goals are the criteria for measuring managerial performance, strategic control creates a motivating environment for managers.[13]

Designing a Strategic Control System

The purpose of a strategic control system is to continuously monitor and assess company performance against strategic plans so that corrective actions can be taken, if needed. These corrective actions may include changing the firm's strategy, its structure, or even its long-term goals. Several steps must be completed before evaluation of performance begins to develop an effective control system. Needless to say, these steps begin after a firm has determined its long-term goals, strategy, and structure.

Since what is to be measured is performance, the starting point for developing a control system is to define expected performance. This is done by setting *standards* for performance. **Standards** are models or benchmarks that specify an intended outcome. Tangible targets to be reached, rules to be followed, and behaviors to be learned are examples of standards. Standards thus provide a basis for actions against which actual results can be compared.. A firm generally sets standards in more than one area to strengthen the control process. For example, Southwest Airlines has set procedural standards in the areas of employee selection and managerial supervision to facilitate higher performance on customer service.

But standards are only one part of an effective strategic control system. A firm also needs tools to measure organizational performance in order to ascertain that performance conforms to predetermined standards. Some measurement tools are quantitative while others are qualitative, some provide feedback on past actions while others provide insight about future performance, and some provide direct evidence of performance while others provide indirect evidence. For example, Southwest Airlines can measure its performance on customer service by asking customers directly to provide feedback. Alternatively, the firm can infer performance effectiveness from an analysis of customer complaints. Generally, a firm measures its strategic performance from several perspectives: by examining market indicators and by analyzing organizational inputs, processes, and outputs.

Standards and measurement mechanisms are thus two important components of a strategic control system. With these in hand, we can briefly describe the steps in designing such a system. As we do, take a quick look at Figure 10.1, which illustrates the steps. We also suggest that you read Strategy in Practice 10.2 to understand the components of a control system and how they relate to each other. In later sections, we will describe standards and measurement mechanisms in detail.

Steps in Designing a Control System

1. *Set standards:* Standards are targets against which to measure the firm's performance. For example, "Maintain defect rate at 2 percent" or "Hold customer satisfaction levels at 98 percent" are targets. Standards can also be stated in nonnumeric terms, such as rules to be observed or behaviors to be learned and practiced. Standards are thus acceptable levels of organizational output or norms of behavior that emerge from the strategic goal of the firm. We identify four broad strategic competency areas within which most performance standards can be explained and understood: processing efficiency, processing speed, continuous value creation and innovation, and constituency relationship. We will explain these strategic competencies and the standards associated with them in the next section.

2. *Select tools to measure performance against standards:* Measurement tools are the mechanisms that indicate whether the firm is achieving its standards and targets. Mechanisms may focus on organizational output, process, or input or on market indicators to evaluate performance. For example, the input/output ratio (defined later) is an output-based measure that indicates efficiency in processing.

3. *Compare performance against standards:* By comparing actual performance to established standards, a firm learns whether its strategies and structures have been effective. Performance significantly higher or lower than the standard indicates that corrective action is needed.

4. *Take corrective action:* Performance significantly higher than the standard indicates that standards are too low and should be revised upward. Performance that is lower suggests that strategies and structures must be adjusted.

Types of Performance Standards

We have already defined a standard as a model or a norm. It serves as a tangible target for action or a guide for behavior against which performance will be measured. Another way to define a standard is as a specification describing a preferred skill,

FIGURE 10.1	Steps in the Strategic Control Process

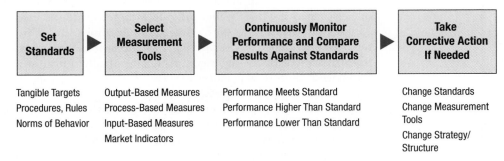

Set Standards	Select Measurement Tools	Continuously Monitor Performance and Compare Results Against Standards	Take Corrective Action If Needed
Tangible Targets	Output-Based Measures	Performance Meets Standard	Change Standards
Procedures, Rules	Process-Based Measures	Performance Higher Than Standard	Change Measurement Tools
Norms of Behavior	Input-Based Measures	Performance Lower Than Standard	Change Strategy/ Structure
	Market Indicators		

action, or outcome. A standard may thus specify the skills required for effectively completing the task. It may specify the procedures or steps employees must go through for task completion. Or, it may specify a certain output volume or quality level that must be reached at the end of a work cycle. Thus, standards may control the *input, processing,* or *output* stage of the work cycle to achieve a desired organizational outcome (see Figure 10.2).[14] We identify four broad strategic competency areas within which to explain and understand input, processing, and output standards: *processing efficiency, processing speed, continuous value creation and innovation,* and *constituency relationship.* Let's briefly describe these competency areas and the standards that firms set within them.

1. *Processing efficiency:* **Processing efficiency** is the ability of the firm to economically convert inputs into outputs. Although all firms are concerned about processing efficiency, cost leaders are especially concerned. A firm seeking a cost advantage must control variations across all stages of input-output conversion, from raw material input to product processing to finished output, to ensure that the overall cost of offering the product conforms to plans. Standards may specify the volume and frequency of raw material procurement, product design/variety, manufacturing lot sizes, inspection rate, and employee skill requirements to keep costs under control. For example, an output standard may call for the manufacture of each design in lot sizes of 25,000 units or more in order to minimize unit costs. A processing standard may be a procedure that states that purchasing must obtain and analyze quotations from at least three suppliers before placing orders for materials. Nucor, a low-cost steel manufacturer, specifies procedures and rules for selecting and locating plants as a way to achieve processing efficiency: plants should only be located in rural areas where mechanically inclined, cost-conscious labor will be plentifully

FIGURE 10.2	Input, Processing, and Output Standards

Input	Processing	Output
Specification of skills, behaviors, and other work inputs necessary for completing the task	Detailed procedures that specify how work should be completed	Targets that specify the characteristics of the expected output in qualitative or quantitative terms

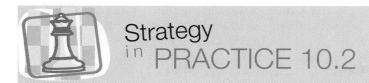

Strategy in PRACTICE 10.2

UNDERSTANDING CONTROL FROM A FAMILIAR EXAMPLE

Assume that I am obese and must lose weight to stay healthy. On the advice of my physician, I set a *goal* to reduce my weight by fifty pounds in the next six months. To make it manageable, I break this goal into six monthly goals of eight pounds each. Working with my physician, I evaluate three *alternatives* to reach my goal: joining a health spa, dieting, and running each day. I rule out the first alternative because it is beyond my budget and the second because it has potentially adverse side effects. I thus choose running as the alternative.

How many miles should I run each day to reach my goal? In consultation with my physician, I set four miles as my daily running *standard*. The local school's sports track offers me the venue for running and monitoring my daily four-mile performance requirement. A few weeks into my running routine, I am eager to know whether my running strategy in general, and the four-mile standard in particular, are delivering the desired results. To assess their effectiveness, I periodically *weigh myself on a scale and compare the reading to my goal*. I use additional indirect measures as supporting evidence: examining my face in the mirror, checking the looseness or tightness of my clothes, and noting comments by friends.

These assessments assure me that the running strategy is effective and that running four miles a day is an adequate performance standard. As a result, I decide that no additions or modifications to my strategy or performance standards are necessary.

available.[15] Finally, an input standard may specify the types of raw material or components that must be used in product design. Sony set an input standard for achieving processing efficiency: the total number of parts used in making all its products was to be reduced from 840,000 to 100,000 by the end of 2005.[16]

2. *Processing speed:* **Processing speed** is the rate at which the firm can design, make, and market products or serve customers. Firms that compete in industries where timely or fast delivery is critical for competitive success (e.g., overnight mail, fast food) are concerned about processing speed. Standards for such a firm would focus on preventing throughput delays and expediting the input-output conversion process to respond to customer demand rapidly. Firms use *cycle time*—the interval from the time customer orders are received to the time they are filled—to specify standards. An output standard may specify the time within which orders should be processed and customers served. Taco Bell, a fast-food chain, employs a customer responsiveness standard to monitor its competitive performance: a minimum of 95 percent of customers must be greeted within three minutes.[17] Dell Computer uses input standards to achieve processing speed: the number of parts used to mount the computer to the outer box should not be more than three.[18]

3. *Continuous value creation and innovation:* **Continuous value creation and innovation** is the ability of the firm to enhance the features and functionality of current products or develop and market new products. Product differentiators and firms that must frequently innovate because industry technology is undergoing constant change would set standards in this area. Standards may be tangible targets that focus on reducing defect rates or customer complaints about product functionality. Known for the number of new products it introduces, 3M's

standard for measuring its innovativeness is that one-third of its sales must come from products that are less than four years old. Most product differentiators and innovators focus on controlling organizational inputs and processes to ensure intended outcomes. For example, standards may specify the skills that potential managerial and nonmanagerial personnel must possess. Or, they may specify the cultivation of certain work values and norms that are likely to promote innovation.

4. *Constituency relationship:* **Constituency relationship** is the firm's ability to develop and maintain a cordial, transparent, and trusting relationship with its primary and secondary stakeholders. As we described in Chapter 2, today's business environment has become extremely complex, requiring firms to maintain an equitable balance in their relationship with diverse stakeholders. It has also become critical for firms to behave ethically and take responsibility for the social consequences of their actions. The goals in constituency management are, therefore, two-fold: (1) to build and sustain a healthy and cooperative work relationship with key primary stakeholders, such as suppliers, customers, and even competition;[19] and (2) to build the firm's positive public image and manage its reputation.[20] Firms that have successfully achieved these goals have been found to be high performing.[21] The standards that firms set in these areas may be the criteria for prestigious awards such as *Fortune*'s Most Admired Companies (for some reputation goals that firms aim to achieve, see Table 10.2). Or, they may be rules and procedures focusing on achieving a healthy level of cooperation with critical stakeholders.

TABLE 10.2   **Reputation Targets**

REPUTATION LIST	CONDUCTED BY	GROUPS SURVEYED	PRIMARY PURPOSE
100 Best Companies to Work for in America	Robert Levering, Milton Moskowitz, and Hewitt Associates	Fortune 100 companies' employees and top managers	Publication
America's Most Admired Companies	*Fortune* magazine and Clark, Martire & Bartolomeo	Company officers, directors, and analysts of Fortune 500 companies	Publication
Corporate Branding Index	Corporate Branding LLC	Vice president–level executives and above in the top 20 percent of U.S. businesses	Customized for clients
Corporate Reputation Index	Delahaye Medialink	Print and broadcast media	Sold as syndicated research
Maximizing Corporate Reputation	Burson-Marsteller	CEOs, executives, board members, financial community, government officials, business media, and consumers	Customized for clients
Reputation Quotient	Reputation Institute and Harris Interactive	General public	Customized for clients
World's Most Respected Companies	Pricewaterhouse Coopers	CEOs from 75 countries	Publication

Source: From *Business and Society* by McAlister, Ferrell, and Ferrell, p. 79. Copyright © 2003. Reprinted by permission of Houghton Mifflin Company.

Types of Measurement Tools

A firm may measure its performance by observing certain market indicators—that is, how the market is reacting to its decisions and actions. Or it may assess performance by analyzing input, processing, and output activities to determine how efficiently and effectively it is adding or creating value. A firm generally uses a combination of direct and indirect measures to ensure that the results are valid. As we mentioned earlier, Southwest Airlines may measure its performance on customer service by directly asking its customers to rate it. It may also use indirect measures such as the percentage of customer communications that are complaints or percentage of analysts' reviews that are positive. The exact measures a firm selects will depend on what is being measured.

Market-Based Measures

A firm may measure its strategic performance by examining certain market indicators. The ratio of new products to old, stakeholder perception of the firm, customer retention rate, performance reviews, and projections by industry analysts and the media—all are market measures of performance. While these measures provide feedback to all firms, they are especially important to those that pursue innovation and constituency relationship goals.

Output-Based Measures

For some businesses, strategic performance is best measured at the output stage. Output-based measures are those that focus on the outcome or end results of the input-output transformation process. Output measures are employed in instances where end results are tangible—for example, where they reduce unit costs or increase productivity rate relative to industry average. Output measures also apply when product processing is intricate and evaluation can only be undertaken after the process is complete and an output emerges.

Output measures indicate how efficiently and effectively the firm transformed inputs into outputs. A ratio of the value of the output to the cost of inputs and processing (commonly referred to as the input/output ratio) tells the firm how much value it added to the end product and how efficiently it added it.[22] A comparison of these data to industry rivals indicates the firm's competitive advantage in processing efficiency and product value additions. Thus, output-based measures are appropriate for cost leaders and, where feasible, for differentiators that compete on the basis of continuous value addition to the product.

Process-Based Measures

For some businesses, output may not be tangible, and competitive capabilities may lie in the processes employed in input-output conversion. Here strategic performance can be measured only by examining the procedures or techniques used to complete the task. For example, a hospital that wishes to be known as a leader in open-heart surgery will periodically evaluate its surgical techniques and procedures to determine whether they are state-of-the-art and use that as a basis for assessing its performance. A utility firm with the goal of effectively responding to catastrophes will periodically evaluate its response process against an ideal benchmark and use that as the basis on which to assess its performance.

Input-based measures assess performance based on the quality of the inputs used by the firm. Examples of inputs are people (skills/knowledge), systems, and capital investment. Professional organizations such as public accounting firms, consultancy service organizations, and research firms (in, for example, pharmaceutical research), and those that must continuously generate new scientific or technological information to develop new products, will use input-based measures. For these organizations, outputs are intangible and thus difficult to measure, and processes cannot be preplanned. Inputs are, therefore, the only viable measurement mechanisms. The organization assumes that by ensuring the quality of inputs needed to realize effective performance, it can ensure performance. For example, a biotechnology research firm would focus on quality research personnel and adequate funding for ensuring its performance.

Matching Strategic Control to Strategy

A firm selects a strategy and structure to attain its long-term goals. It selects a control system to measure progress toward goals and make corrective adjustments in strategy and structure, if needed. To be effective in its endeavors, a firm's strategy, structure, and control systems must be internally consistent—that is, they must fit with each other. In Chapter 9, we identified the structure that is appropriate for each strategy. In this section, we will briefly examine strategy, structure, and control systems collectively. In doing so, we certainly will be repeating ourselves somewhat but it is important that we look at them all together because it will help us to understand how to harmoniously match all three.

Recall that the cost leader's goal is to gain a cost advantage in the industry. A major portion of the cost for a firm stems from product design, production, and marketing activities. Hence, by controlling variations in these activities, a cost leader can expect to lower the overall cost. Accordingly, it standardizes the product's design (no variety), production process (set up for uniform output), and marketing techniques (no market segmentation), which allows it to standardize the entire operational sequence. To implement this strategy, the cost leader chooses a functional structure because it has congruent or matching features. A functional structure, as you may recall, narrowly divides tasks, groups them according to skills or knowledge, and sequentially integrates the output of each group. Narrow division of task permits skill and task standardization while sequential integration of tasks reduces process-related variations. Thus both allow the cost leader to effectively implement its strategy.

What control mechanisms would a cost leader choose? Output-based measures would most likely be its choice, for three important reasons. First, output measures are most congruent with a functional structure. A functional structure allows a firm to tightly monitor and evaluate the performance of each function based on quantifiable output—units produced, units sold, or cost incurred. Second, output-based measures are cheaper to implement. By defining the output and delegating authority to operations personnel, a firm eliminates the need for expensive layers of supervisory management. In addition, assessing performance based on output is easier. Third, output-based control allows the firm to implement incentive programs based on quantitative targets. Such programs are essential for a cost strategist, which must continuously increase its productivity to reduce cost.

Differentiation Strategy and Control

A differentiator, as you may remember, focuses on the product's features or the way it is offered as the primary means of gaining an advantage over rivals. The aim is for the product or the service surrounding it to be perceived by customers as unique and as satisfying their special needs. A differentiator, therefore, makes the product in several designs to appeal to individuals in distinct market segments. The focus is on customizing the product or service for each segment and continuously improving its features, not standardizing them. To implement this strategy, as we mentioned in Chapter 9, the differentiator would most likely choose a product- or market-based grouping that allows it to allocate separate engineering and marketing resources to each design (or brand). Product grouping also promotes the cross-functional cooperation needed to develop unique products because, in this structure, functional specialists focus on the success of the product, not their skill enhancement.

The control mechanisms suitable for the above-described structure are mostly input- and process-based and, to a limited extent, output-based. In a structure that emphasizes cross-functional cooperation, where teamwork is critical for competitive performance, the focus in measurement has to be on those factors that elicit the required cooperation. Output based measures, while not inappropriate, can be harder to implement. As a result, the firm relies on behavior control (as opposed to output control) and on promoting organizational values and norms that stimulate cross-functional cooperation and product innovation.

Focus Strategy and Control

As explained in Chapter 5, a focus strategist aims to gain cost or differentiation advantage within a narrow segment. The firm offers a single design or several designs that target a single customer or market segment. Because a niche segment is relatively smaller in size, and opportunities for scale economies do not exist, a focuser must be able to control costs. At the same time, if the firm is a differentiator, it must continuously invest in competencies on which the differentiation is based so as to sustain it. To implement this strategy, the focuser generally chooses a functional structure that not only is economical to adopt but also allows the development of product and marketing-related competencies. And as for control, the firm uses output control if it is a cost focuser because it is economical. If it is a differentiator, it uses input- and process-based controls because differentiation requires teamwork.

Vertical Integration and Diversification Strategies and Control

Corporate-level strategy expands the firm's scope of operations or the businesses in which it will compete. In vertical integration, the firm expands into distinct, sequentially related activities. In diversification, the firm expands into products and markets that share common resources but belong to different industries. As explained in Chapter 9, corporate-level strategies are complex and require complex structures to implement.

Vertical integration transfers material and semiprocessed units from one value chain stage to the next in a systematic and timely fashion. Diversification exploits technological or marketing/distribution resources by effectively sharing them across several products or business units. Thus, the focus in both vertical integration and diversification is on achieving coordination among distinct operations, products, or businesses. To achieve this, a firm uses a multidivisional structure, which provides for a corporate headquarters whose central authority brings about resource coordination and information sharing among distinct units. At the same time, this structure allows for the allocation of separate resources to each unit so that units can complete certain activities independently. By selectively centralizing some resources and decentralizing others, a multidivisional structure achieves interunit coordination without jeopardizing the autonomy of individual units.

What control mechanisms would be appropriate for corporate-level strategies? In vertical integration and related diversification, the emphasis is on sharing and transferring material and informational resources among divisions that require a high degree of cooperation to be successful. Input and process controls are, therefore, appropriate. In unrelated diversification, not only is cooperation among units unnecessary, but divisional autonomy is essential for success. Therefore, output controls in which divisions are evaluated on financial performance are appropriate.

International Strategies and Control

In this text, we discussed three international strategies that expand the firm's operations to international regions through direct foreign investment. We also identified the organizational structure that is appropriate for each strategy. They are as follows:

- A multidomestic strategy in which the firm customizes the product design and marketing features to match the unique needs of consumers in each region: to implement this strategy, the firm employs a product/market divisional structure in which it decentralizes control to the regional divisions.

- A global strategy in which the firm standardizes the design and marketing features so that its offering is perceived uniformly across all regions: to implement this strategy, the firm employs a global product division structure in which critical functional activities are centralized in advantageous international locations.

- A transnational strategy in which the firm standardizes some design and marketing features while customizing others: to implement this strategy, the firm uses a global matrix structure in which some functions are centralized while others are decentralized.

What control mechanisms are congruent with these strategies and structures? The international business environment generates complexities created by product/market scope; as a result, firms use a combination of input, process, and output controls. In general, almost all international strategy firms employ input controls, such as placing trustworthy personnel from headquarters in key divisional positions or fostering a certain organizational culture in which the expected performance-related behavior would automatically occur.[23] These measures are both economical and easy to implement. Firms also employ additional forms of control that are specific to the chosen strategy and structure.

In multidomestic strategy, because the authority to run the regional operations is delegated to division managers, a firm chooses output control. It thus sets tangible output goals (e.g., increase market share or ROI by x percent) and ensures that goals are achieved by providing rewards. In global strategy, since integration of value chain activities across regions is critical for performance, a firm employs process controls that specify rules and procedures for effective cross-functional coordination to occur. In transnational strategy, a firm employs both process and output controls. While output controls ensure that the task is completed at the division level according to plans, process controls ascertain that cross-divisional coordination occurs as expected.

Summary

A firm needs accurate information about the progress it is making toward its strategic goals. This information is necessary if the firm is to take corrective action—assuming any is needed. Such corrective action reallocates resources and organizational tasks that will better equip the firm to implement its strategy. Strategic control systems provide the feedback the firm needs in this regard. At the same time, they allow the firm to undertake measures that will prevent unsatisfactory performance and promote positive performance.

To measure performance, firms must set standards and choose measurement mechanisms. Four competency areas for setting standards and four types of measures were described in this chapter. The competency areas for setting standards are processing efficiency, processing speed, continuous value creation and innovation, and constituency building. The measures are market-based, output-based, process-based, and input-based. A firm may select a combination of these depending on how congruent they are with each other and with the firm's strategy and structure.

Chapter 10 Discussion Questions and Project

Discussion Questions

1. Use examples to distinguish strategic control from financial control. Discuss the importance of strategic control in strategic management.
2. From the information provided in this chapter's opening case, describe the strategic control system employed by Southwest Airlines. Discuss how it fits with Southwest's strategy and organizational structure.

Project

1. Design a control system for a savings bank (a bank that primarily serves the banking and credit needs of individuals) that aggressively pursues customer convenience as its strategic goal.

Continuing Case

Pepsi-Cola's Reorganization: Measuring Progress on Customer Responsiveness

Background

Early in 1988, Pepsi-Cola (a business unit of PepsiCo) radically reorganized from a functional structure that focused on job skills to a matrix structure that focused on job outcome. The purpose was to become a customer-responsive firm where work processes were built around the customer rather than around the product or predesigned job criteria. In other words, customer satisfaction would be the strategic goal that would guide organizational activities at Pepsi-Cola. Consolidation occurring in the supermarket segment of the food and beverage retail industry demanded that Pepsi-Cola achieve this transformation.

To assess the progress the company was making toward becoming a customer-responsive firm, and to prevent any deviations from it, Pepsi-Cola needed evaluation and control mechanisms. Specifically, the firm needed two things: (1) standards for performance against which progress could be measured, and (2) tools that would accurately measure performance and indicate whether progress was being made.

Standards for Performance

To develop the standards needed for becoming a customer-responsive firm, Pepsi-Cola invited input from employees, HR managers, and customers. It asked outstanding employees to describe the critical incidents that led to their outstanding work performance. It asked HR managers for insights on work processes that would facilitate customer responsiveness. It induced the customers (supermarkets) to share with the firm what they expected from a beverage supplier. With the information thus obtained, the company identified a set of work competencies and values that it needed to make Pepsi-Cola a highly customer responsive firm. For example, quality in customer transactions and effective communication were identified as critical worker competencies, ability to develop well-rounded employees was identified as an important managerial

competency, and teamwork and integrity were identified as crucial work values.

To realize these competencies and values, Pepsi-Cola designed standards to be used in employee selection and training, managerial training and development, and work processes and output. The focus in designing these standards was on creating and sustaining a customer-centered workforce. The company believed that by giving workers the identified skills and values, empowering them, and rewarding the expected behavior and output, it could create and retain such a workforce.

Measuring Performance

Pepsi-Cola measured its progress on the customer responsiveness goal by assessing employee satisfaction. The company reasoned that if employees were satisfied with their job and with the company in general, they would in turn satisfy the customer. Thus, employee satisfaction became the surrogate measure for assessing Pepsi-Cola's customer-responsiveness capability. Higher employee satisfaction was deemed to result when workers were given the right skills to respond to the customer, supported by management, empowered, and adequately rewarded when they delivered the expected performance.

Pepsi-Cola assessed employee satisfaction at regular intervals by asking employees to rate the firm on management quality, workplace quality, employee growth opportunities, compensation and rewards, and the like. Differences in employee satisfaction levels from year to year indicated to Pepsi-Cola the progress it was making toward becoming a customer-responsive firm and let the company know whether any modifications in structure or control mechanisms were necessary to reach the desired goal.

Discussion Questions

1. Describe the standards and performance measurement mechanisms that Pepsi-Cola designed

to assess its progress toward becoming a customer-responsive firm.

2. Do you think that employee satisfaction levels are a good indicator of Pepsi-Cola's progress toward becoming a customer-responsive firm? Can you suggest any other way by which this progress could be effectively measured?

Source: "Pepsi's Regeneration, 1990–93," Harvard Business School Case #9-395-048, March 19, 1996; "Using the FYI Guide to Build Coaching and Development Skills at Pepsi-Cola North America, http://www.lominger.com/71-1140.html, accessed on March 25, 2005.

Notes

Chapter 1

1. A. Serwer, "Kodak in the Noose," *Fortune*, February 4, 2002; G. Colvin, "Dinosaurs Rarely Escape Doom," *Wall Street Week with Fortune*, October 22, 2003; J. Bandler, "Kodak shifts focus from film, betting future on digital lines," *Wall Street Journal*, September 25, 2003; "Digital camera sales may reach 71.2 million in 2006," *The Detroit News*, December 11, 2003; "Has Kodak Missed the Moment ?" *The Economist*, December 30, 2003; D. Eisenberg, "Kodak's Photo Op," *Time*, April 30, 2001; A. Swasy, *Changing Focus* (New York: Times Books, 1997); P. Cary, S. J. Hedges, D. Hawkins, and S. Headden, "Loser Layoffs," *U.S. News & World Report*, November 25, 1996.

2. C. J. Loomis, "Dinosaurs?" *Fortune,* May 3, 1993, 36–42.

3. D. Welch and D. Beucke, "Why GM's Plans Won't Work," *Business Week*, May 9, 2005, 85–93.

4. G. Easterbrook, "What is Bad for GM is . . . ," *The New York Times*, June 12, 2005, C1; "How to Keep GM off the Disassembly Line," *Business Week* (Editorial), May 9, 2005, 116.

5. J. A. Byrne, "Strategic Planning," *Business Week*, August 26, 1996, 46–52; J. B. Barney, "Looking Inside for Competitive Advantage," *The Academy of Management Executive* 9, no. 4 (1995): 49–61.

6. C. L. Hays, "Kmart Takeover of Sears is Set," *The New York Times*, November 18, 2004, A1.

7. C. J. Loomis, "Dinosaurs?"

8. M. E. Porter, *Competitive Advantage* (New York: Free Press, 1985).

9. R. A. D'Aveni, *Hyper-Competition* (New York: The Free Press, 1994).

10. C. C. Markides, "Strategy as Balance: From Either-or to And," *Business Strategy Review* 12, no. 3 (2001): 1–10; C. C. Markides, "In Search of Strategy," *Sloan Management Review*, 40, no. 3, (1999), 6–7; J. B. Quinn, H. Mintzberg, and R. M. James, *The Strategy Process: Concepts, Contexts, and Cases* (New Jersey: Prentice Hall, 1988, p. 1).

11. H. Mintzberg and J. Lampel, "Reflecting on the Strategy Process," *Sloan Management Review* 40, no. 3 (1999): 21–30.

12. H. I. Ansoff, *Corporate Strategy* (New York: McGraw Hill, 1965).

13. K. Andrews, *The Concept of Corporate Strategy* (Homewood, Ill.: Dow-Jones Irwin, 1980).

14. H. Mintzberg, B. Ahlstrand, and J. Lampel, *Strategy Safari: A Guided Tour Through the Wilds of Strategic Management* (New York: The Free Press, 1998, p. 9).

15. H. Mintzberg, B. Ahlstrand, and J. Lampel, p. 9.

16. R. D. Sawyer, *Sun-tzu: The Art of War.* (New York: Barnes & Noble Books, 1994).

17. M. E. Porter, *Competitive Strategy* (New York: Free Press, 1980).

18. C. W. L. Hill and G. R. Jones, *Strategic Management Theory* (Boston: Houghton Mifflin, 2004), p. 3.

19. P. Ghemawat, *Strategy and the Business Landscape* (Reading, Mass.: Addison-Wesley, 1999), p. 20.

20. G. Saloner, A. Shepherd, and J. Podolny, *Strategic Management* (New York: John Wiley & Sons, 2001), p. 11.

21. R. Kaplan and D. P. Norton, "The Balanced Scorecard – Measures That Drive Performance," *Harvard Business Review,* 701, no. 1 (1992): 71–79.

22. R. Dobbs, K. Leslie, and L. T. Mendonca, "Building the Healthy Corporation," *The McKinsey Quarterly*, no. 3 (2005).

23. H. I. Ansoff, *Corporate Strategy*; K. Andrews, *The Concept of Corporate Strategy*.

24. H. Mintzberg, "Patterns in Strategy Formation," *Management Science*, 24, no. 9 (1978): 934–948.

25. J. C. Collins and J. I. Porras, "Organizational vision and visionary organizations," *California Management Review* 34, no. 1 (1991): 30–52.

26. M. E. Porter, *Competitive Strategy.*

27. G. Hamel and C. K. Prahalad, "Strategic Intent," *Harvard Business Review* 67, no. 3 (1989): 63–76.

28. G. Hamel and C. K. Prahalad, "Strategy as Stretch and Leverage," *Harvard Business Review* 71, no. 2 (March–April 1993): 75–84; See also, G. Hamel and C. K. Prahalad, *Competing for the Future* (Boston, Mass.: Harvard Business School Press, 1994).

29. G. Hamel and C. K. Prahalad, "Strategic Intent."

30. B. Wernerfelt, "A Resource-Based View of the Firm," *Strategic Management Journal* 5 (1994): 171–180.

31. C. Markides, "Strategy as Balance."

32. H. Mintzberg and A. McHugh, "Strategy Formation in an Adhocracy," *Administrative Science Quarterly*, 30 (1985): 160–197.

33. H. Mintzberg and F. Westley, "Decision-making: It Is Not What You Think," *Sloan Management Review*, 42, no. 3 (2001): 89–93.

34. R. M. Kanter, "Strategy as Improvisational Theater," *Sloan Management Review* 43, no. 2, (Winter 2002): 76–81.

35. C. Markides, "Strategy as Balance."; S. J. Wall, *On the Fly: Executing Strategy in a Changing World* (Hoboken, New Jersey: John Wiley & Sons, 2004): 3–26.

36. R. D. Ireland and M. A. Hitt, "Achieving and Maintaining Strategic Competitiveness in the 21st Century: The Role of Strategic Leadership," Academy of Management Executive, 13, no. 1 (1999): 43–57.

37. M. Hitt, R. D. Ireland, and R. E. Hoskisson, *Strategic Management* (Mason, Ohio: Southwestern Publishing, 2003), p. 385.

38. I. Bonn, "Developing Strategic Thinking as a Core Competency," *Management Decision* 39, no. 1 (2001): 63–71.

39. For some definitions of strategic leadership, see M. A. Hitt and R. D. Ireland, "The Essence of Strategic Leadership: Managing Human and Social Capital," *The Journal of Leadership and Organizational Studies*, 9, no. 1 (2002): 3–14; J. P. Kotter, "What Leaders Really Do," *Harvard Business Review* 79, no. 11 (2001): 85–90.

40. S. Finkelstein and D. C. Hambrick, *Strategic Leadership: Top Executive and Their Effects on Organizations* (St. Paul, Minn.: West Publishing, 1996); R. Charan and G. Colvin, "Why CEOs Fail" *Fortune*, June 21, 1999, 68–82.

Chapter 2

1. A. Serwer and K. Bonamici, "The Hottest Thing in the Sky," *Fortune*, February 23, 2004; E. Allenbaugh, *Deliberate Success: Realize Your Vision with Purpose, Passion, and Performance* (Lake Oswego, Ore.: Career Press, 2002); J. Huey and G. Colvin, "Staying Smart: The Jack and Herb Show," *Fortune,* January 11 (1999): 163–165; K. Freiberg and J. Freiberg, *NUTS! Southwest Airlines' Crazy Recipe for Business and Personal Success* (Austin, Tex.: Bard Press, 1996); Bureau of Transportation Statistics, U.S. Department of Transportation, Press releases dated March 10 and May 17, 2005, (www.bts.gov).

2. J. C. Collins and J. I. Porras, *Built to Last: Successful Habits of Visionary Companies* (New York: Harper Business, 1994).

3. R. A. Stone, "Mission Statements Revisited," *SAM Advanced Management Journal* 61, no. 1 (1996): 31–37.

4. F. R. David, "How Companies Define Their Mission," *Long Range Planning* 22 no. 1 (1989): 90–97.

5. C. A. Rarick and J. Vitton, "Mission Statements Make Cents," *Journal of Business Strategy* 16, no. 1 (1995): 1–12; A. Campbell and S. Yeung, "Creating a Sense of Mission," *Long Range Planning* 24, no. 4 (1991): 10–20.

6. L. Grossman and M. M. Jennings, *Building a Business Through Good Times and Bad* (Wesport, Conn.: Quorum Books, 2002).

7. R. D. Ireland and M. A. Hitt, "Mission Statements: Importance, Challenge, and Recommendations for Development," *Business Horizons*, May–June 1992, 34–42.

8. C. K. Bart, "Measuring the Mission Effect in Human Intellectual Capital," *Journal of Intellectual Capital* 2, no. 3 (2001): 320–330; M. C. Baetz and C. K. Bart, "Developing Mission Statements Which Work," *Long Range Planning* 29, no. 4 (1996): 526–533.

9. C. K. Bart, "Mission Matters," *The CPA Journal* 68, no. 8 (1998): 56–57.

10. C. K. Bart, N. Bontis, and S. Taggar, "A Model of the Impact of Mission Statements on Firm Performance," *Management Decision* 39, no. 1 (2001): 19–35; C. K. Bart and M. C. Baetz, "The Relationship Between Mission Statements and Firm Performance: An Exploratory Study," *Journal of Management Studies* 35, no. 6 (1998): 823–853.

11. J. C. Collins and J. I. Porras, "Organizational Vision and Visionary Organizations," *California Management Review* 34, no. 1 (1991): 30–52.

12. B. Bartkus, M. Glassman, and R. B. McAfee, "Mission Statements: Are They Smoke and Mirrors?" *Business Horizons* 43, no. 6 (2000): 23–28; P. Lencioni, "Make Your Values Mean Something," *Harvard Business Review* 80, no. 7 (2002): 113–117.

13. Bart and Baetz, "The Relationship Between Mission Statements and Firm Performance"; S. L. Oswald, K. W. Mossholder, and S. G. Harris, "Vision Salience and Strategic Involvement: Implications for Psychological Attachment to Organization and Job," *Strategic Management Journal* 15, no. 6 (1994): 477–489.

14. M. Klemm, S. Sanderson, and G. Luffman, "Mission Statements: Selling Corporate Values to Employees," *Long Range Planning* 24, no. 3 (1991): 73–78; Bart, Bontis, and Taggar, "A Model of the Impact of Mission Statements on Firm Performance."

15. David, "How Companies Define Their Mission."

16. A. Campbell, "The Power of Mission: Aligning Strategy and Culture," special issue, *Planning Review* (1993).

17. J. R. Latham, "Visioning: The Concept, Trilogy, and Process," *Quality Progress* 28, no. 4 (1995): 65–68.

18. G. Hamel and C. K. Prahalad, "Strategic Intent," *Harvard Business Review* 67, no. 3 (1989): 63–76.

19. J. C. Collins and J. I. Porras, *Built to Last.*

20. J. C. Collins and J. I. Porras, "Building Your Company's Vision," *Harvard Business Review* (September–October 1996): 65–77.

21. D. F. Abell, *Defining the Business: The Starting Point of Strategic Planning* (Englewood Cliffs, N.J.: Prentice-Hall, 1980), 17.

22. A. Campbell, "Mission Statements," *Long Range Planning* 30, no. 6: 931–932; Lencioni, "Make Your Values Mean Something."

23. Lencioni, "Make Your Values Mean Something"; Bartkus, Glassman, and McAfee, "Mission Statements: Are They Smoke and Mirrors?"

24. Bart, Bontis, and Taggar, "A Model of the Impact of Mission Statements on Firm Performance."

25. Collins and Porras, "Building Your Company's Vision."

26. T. M. Jones, "Instrumental Stakeholder Theory: A Synthesis of Ethics and Economics," *Academy of Management Review* 20, no. 2 (1995): 404–437.

27. E. R. Freeman, *Strategic Management: A Stakeholder Approach* (Boston: Pitman, 1984), 31–43.

28. A. B. Carroll, *Business and Society: Ethics and Stakeholder Management* (Cincinnati, Ohio: Southwestern Publishing, 1989); A. E. Clarkson, "A Stakeholder Framework for Analyzing and Evaluating Corporate Social Performance," *Academy of Management Review* 20, no. 1 (1995): 92–117.

29. R. Alsop, "Survey rates companies' reputation, and many are found wanting . . . ," The Wall Street Journal, February 7, 2001: B1; T. Forsman, "Firestone dealers still feel the heat," *Business Week Online*, January 12, 2001 (www.businessweek.com)

30. J. Dixon, "The fall of Kmart: Enriched ex-CEO left company struggling; new man in-charge vows full enquiry and says Kmart will rebound," *Detroit Free Press* (www.freep.com), July 2, 2002; K. Kerwin, "Creditors take on Kmart's frat boys," www.businessweekonline.com, November 21, 2003.

31. D. T. McAlister, O. C. Ferrell, and L. Ferrell, *Business and Society: A Strategic Approach to Corporate Citizenship* (Boston: Houghton Mifflin Company, 2003), 68–69.

32. Classification and discussion based on G. T. Savage, T. W. Nix, C. J. Whitehead, and J. D. Blair, "Strategies for Assessing and Managing Organizational Stakeholders," *Academy of Management Executive* 5, no. 2 (1991): 61–75.

33. Financial Times, London carried coverage of corporate governance from different aspects in a four-part weekly series starting May 10, 2005. It can be accessed through their website: www.ft.com/masteringcorporate governance.

34. M. C. Jensen and W. H. Meckling, "Theory of the Firm: Managerial Behavior, Agency Costs, and Ownership Structure" *Journal of Financial Economics* 3, (1976): 305–360.

35. J. H. Davis, F. D. Schoorman, and L. Donaldson, "Toward a Stewardship Theory of Management," *Academy of Management Review* 22, no. 1 (1997): 20–47.

36. C. Sundaramurthy and M. Lewis, "Control and Collaboration," *Academy of Management Review* 28, no. 3 (2003): 397–415.

37. J. L. Johnson, C. M. Daily, and A. E. Ellstrand, "Boards of Directors: A Review and Research Agenda," *Journal of Management* 22, no. 3 (1996): 409–438.

38. C. Bart and N. Bontis, "Distinguishing Between the Board and Management in Company Mission: Implications for Corporate Governance," *Journal of Intellectual Capital* 4, no. 3 (2003): 361–387.

39. D. A. Nadler, "Building Better Boards," *Harvard Business Review* 82, no. 5 (2004): 102–110.

40. E. M. Pillmore, "How We Are Fixing Up Tyco," *Harvard Business Review* 81, no. 12 (2003): 96–103; E. E. Lawler, D. Finegold, G. Benson, J. Conger, and P. T. Spiller, "Adding Value in the Boardroom," *Sloan Management Review* 43, no. 2: 92–95.

41. R. L. Martin, "The Virtue Matrix: Calculating the Return on Social Responsibility," *Harvard Business Review* (March 2002): 69–75.

42. J. S. McClenahen, "Defining Social Responsibility," *Industry Week*, Volume 254, 3, 2005, pp: 64–65.

43. S. B. Graves and S. A. Waddock, "Institutional Owners and Corporate Social Performance," *Academy of Management Journal* 37, no. 4 (1994): 1034–1046.

44. J. Hempel and L. Gard, "The Corporate Givers," *Business Week*, November 29, (2004): 101–104.

45. J. S. McClenahen, "Creating Value with Values" *Industry Week*, 254, no. 1 (2005): 22–25.

46. A. B. Carroll, "A Three Dimensional Conceptual Model of Corporate Performance," *Academy of Management Review* (October 1979): 497–505.

47. M. Friedman, "The Social Responsibility of Business Is to Increase Its Profits," *New York Times Magazine*, September 13, 1970, 30.

48. S. Waddock and N. Smith, "Corporate Social Responsibility Audits: Doing Well by Doing Good," *Sloan Management Review* 41, no. 2 (Winter 2000): 75–83.

49. T. M. Jones, "Instrumental Stakeholder Theory: A Synthesis of Ethics and Economics," *Academy of Management Review,* 20, no. 2 (1995): 404–437.

50. M. E. Porter and M. R. Kramer, "The Competitive Advantage of Corporate Philanthropy," *Harvard Business Review* (December 2002): 57–68.

Chapter 3

1. P. R. Lawrence and D. Dyer. *Renewing American Industry* (New York: Free Press, 1980), 17–54; "Autos: Heading into the Slow Lane," *Business Week,* January 13, 2003; "The Road Ahead for the U.S. Auto Industry." Office of Automotive Affairs, Machinery and International Trade Administration, U.S. Department of Commerce, April 2004; R. W. Crandall and C. Winston, "Auto Industry on the Line" *Detroit Free Press,* May 23, 2005.

2. "Detroit's Uphill Battle," *Time,* September 8, 1980, 48; J. Kraft, "Annals of Industry: The Downsizing Decision," *The New Yorker,* May 5, 1980, 134–162.

3. P. Chattopadhyay, W. H. Glick, and G. P. Huber, "Organizational Actions in Response to Threats and Opportunities," *Academy of Management Journal* 44, no. 5 (2001): 937–955.

4. U. C. Neisser, *Cognitive Psychology* (New York: Appleton-Century-Crofts, 1979).

5. J. E. Dutton and S. E. Jackson, "Categorizing Strategic Issues: Links to Organizational Action," *Academy of Management Review* 12, no. 1 (1987): 76–90.

6. D. Hambrick and P. A. Mason, "Upper Echelons: The Organization as a Reflection of Its Top Managers," *Academy of Management Review* 9, no. 2 (1984): 93–206.

7. M. Moritz. *The Little Kingdom: The Private Story of Apple Computer* (New York: William Morrow, 1984), 126.

8. V. Govindarajan and A. K. Gupta, *The Quest for Global Dominance* (San Francisco, Calif.: Jossey-Bass, 2001), 108.

9. L. J. Bourgeois, I. M. Duhaime, and J. L. Stimpert, *Strategic Management* (Fort Worth, Tex.: Harcourt College Publishers, 2001), 119.

10. A. Bianco, "The Vanishing Mass Market," *Business Week,* July 12, 2004, 61–68.

11. A. Doolittle, "Healthier eating spurs demand for organic foods," *Washington Times*, July 14, 2004.

12. "Corporate Scandals Hit Home," *Wall Street Journal,* February 19, 2004; "Easy to Lose," *Economist,* January 24, 2004.

13. J. A. Petrick, R. F. Scherer, J. D. Brodzinski, J. F. Quinn, and M. F. Ainina, "Global-Leadership Skills and Reputational Capital: Intangible Resources for Sustainable Competitive Advantage," *The Academy of Management Executive* 13, no. 1 (1999): 58–69.

14. P. W. Roberts and G. R. Dowling, "Corporate Reputation and Sustained Superior Financial Performance," *Strategic Management Journal* 23 (2002): 1077–1093.

15. P. Dussauge, S. Hart, and B. Ramanantsoa, *Strategic Technology Management* (West Sussex, England, 1992), 13.

16. K. Bradsher, "Economies Sickened by a Virus and Fear," *New York Times,* April 21, 2003, A1.

17. L. Fahey, "Strategic Management: The Challenge and the Opportunity," in *The New Portable MBA,* ed. E. G. C. Collins and M. A. Devanna (New York: John Wiley, 1994), 331.

18. To understand more about how firms scan and forecast the environment, read L. Fahey, W. R. King, and V. K. Narayanan, "Environmental Scanning and Forecasting in Strategic Planning—The State of the Art," *Long Range Planning* 14, no. 1 (1981): 32–39.

19. M. E. Porter, *Competitive Strategy* (New York: The Free Press, 1980).

20. P. Ghemawat, *Strategy and the Business Landscape* (Reading, Mass.: Addison-Wesley, 1999), 20.

21. M. E. Porter, *Competitive Advantage* (New York: The Free Press, 1985), 7.

22. Porter, *Competitive Strategy,* 1980, 5. See also, Porter, *Competitive Advantage,* 1985, 233.

23. K. J. Hatten and D. E. Schendel, "Heterogeneity Within an Industry: Firm Conduct in the U.S. Brewing Industry, 1952–71," *Journal of Industrial Economics* 26 (1977): 97–113; Porter, *Competitive Strategy,* 1980, 129–155.

24. S. M. Oster, *Modern Competitive Analysis* (New York: Oxford University Press, 1994), 80.

25. Porter, *Competitive Strategy,* 1980, 3–33.

26. D. F. Spulber, "Entry Barriers and Entry Strategies," *Journal of Strategic Management Education* 1, no. 1 (2003): 1–30.

27. Spulber, "Entry Barriers and Entry Strategies."

28. J. Curry and M. Kenney, "Beating the Clock: Corporate Responses to Rapid Change in the PC Industry," *California Management Review* 42, no. 1 (1999): 8–36.

29. H. Mintzberg, B. Ahlstrand, and J. Lampel, *Strategy Safari: A Guided Tour Through the Wilds of Strategic Management* (New York: The Free Press, 1998), 82.

30. R. D. D'Aveni, *Hyper-Competition* (New York: The Free Press, 1994), 1–36.

31. B. Wernerfelt, "A Resource-Based View of the Firm," *Strategic Management Journal* 5 (September–October 1984): 171–80; J. B. Barney, "*Gaining and Sustaining Competitive Advantage*" (Reading, Mass.: Addison-Wesley, 2002).

32. G. Hamel and C. K. Prahalad, "Strategy as Stretch and Leverage," *Harvard BusinessReview* 71, no. 2 (March–April 1993): 75–84.

Chapter 4

1. "EMI and The CT Scanner (A) and (B)" *Harvard Business School Case,* #383–194 and 383–195, 1994; D. J. Teece, "Profiting from Technological Innovation: Implications for Integration, Collaboration, Licensing, and Public Policy," *Research Policy* 15 (1986): 285–305; J. Stuckery and D. White, "When and When Not to Vertically Integrate," *The McKinsey Quarterly* 3 (1993): 3–27; H. Ma, "Of Competitive Advantage—Kinetic and Positional," *Business Horizons ,* 43, no. 1 (2000): 53.

2. M. E. Porter, *Competitive Advantage* (New York: The Free Press, 1985); D. J. Collis and C. A. Montgomery, "Competing on Resources: Strategy in the 1990s," *Harvard Business Review* (July–August 1995): 118–128; J. B. Barney, "Looking Inside for Competitive Advantage," *Academy of Management Executive* 9, no. 4, (1995): 49—61; Ma, "Of Competitive Advantage: Kinetic and Positional."

3. J. B. Barney, "*Gaining and Sustaining Competitive Advantage*" (Reading, Mass.: Addison-Wesley, 2002), 9.

4. D. Besanko, D. Dranove, and M. Shanley, "*Economics of Strategy* (New York: John Wiley, 2000), 389.

5. For a brief account of these two types of advantages in regard to their origin and viewpoints, see I. M. Cockburn, R. M. Henderson, and S. Stern, "Untangling the Origins of Competitive Advantage," *Strategic Management Journal* 21, no. 10–11 (2000): 1123–1145; J. Fahy, "The Resource-Based View of the Firm: Some Stumbling Blocks on the Road to Understanding Sustainable Competitive Advantage,"

Journal of European Industrial Training 24, no. 2–4 (2000): 94–104.

6. G. Saloner, A. Shepard, and J. Podolny, *Strategic Management* (New York: John Wiley, 2001), 43; G. T. Hult and D. Ketchen, "Does Market Orientation Matter? A Test of the Relationship Between Positional Advantages and Performance," *Strategic Management Journal* 22, no. 9 (2001): 899–906; N. Foss, "Strategy, Economics, and Michael Porter," *Journal of Management Studies* 33, no. 1 (1996): 1–24.

7. M. E. Porter, *Competitive Strategy* (New York: John Wiley, 1980). See also, A. McGahan and M. Porter, "How Much Does Industry Matter, Really?," special issue *Strategic Management Journal* 18 (1995): 15–30.

8. P. Ghemawat, *Strategy and the Business Landscape* (Reading, Mass.: Addison-Wesley, 1999), 20.

9. Saloner, Shepard, and Podolny, *Strategic Management,* 44–45.

10. G. Stalk and P. Evans-Clark, "Competing on Capabilities: The New Rules of Corporate Strategy," *Harvard Business Review* 70, no. 2 (1992): 54–65; R. M. Grant, "The Resource-Based Theory of Competitive Advantage: Implications for Strategy Formulation," *California Management Review* (Spring 1991); 114–135.

11. M. Makhija, "Comparing the Resource-Based and Market-Based Views of the Firm: Empirical Evidence from Czech Privatization," *Strategic Management Journal* 24, no. 5 (2003): 433–452; J. A. Black and K. B. Boal, "Strategic Resources: Traits, Configurations, and Paths to Sustainable Competitive Advantage," special issue, *Strategic Management Journal* 15 (1994): 131–148.

12. R. A. D'Aveni, "Strategic Supremacy Through Disruption and Dominance," *Sloan Management Review* 40, no. 3 (1999): 127–135.

13. B. Wernerfelt, "A Resource-Based View of the Firm," *Strategic Management Journal* 5 (September–October 1984): 171–180; Barney, "*Gaining and Sustaining Competitive Advantage.*"

14. D. J. Collis and C. A. Montgomery, "Competing on Resources: Strategy in the 1990s," *Harvard Business Review* (July–August 1995): 118–128; J. B. Barney, "Looking Inside for Competitive Advantage," *Academy of Management Executive* 9, no. 4 (1995): 49–61.

15. C. K. Prahalad and G. Hamel, "The Core Competence of the Corporation," *Harvard Business Review* 68, no. 3 (1990): 79–93.

16. R. Amit and P. J. H. Schoemaker, "Strategic Assets and Organizational Rent," *Strategic Management Journal* 14, no. 1 (1993): 33–46.

17. Amit and Schoemaker, "Strategic Assets and Organizational Rent."

18. R. R. Nelson and S. G. Winter, *An Evolutionary Theory of Economic Change* (Cambridge, Mass.: Belknap Press, 1982).

19. Amit and Schoemaker, "Strategic Asset and Organizational Rent."

20. W. G. Rowe, "Creating Wealth in Organizations: The Role of Strategic Leadership," *The Academy of Management Executive* 15, no. 1 (2001): 83–94.

21. D. F. Abell, "Competing Today While Preparing for Tomorrow," *Sloan Management Review* 40, no. 3 (Spring 1999): 73–81.

22. CNN Special Report, "Top 25: Influential Business Leaders," CNN.com, June 19, 2005 (accessed July 3, 2005).

23. B. Lev, "Sharpening the Intangibles Edge," *Harvard Business Review* (June 2004): 109–116; D. Ulrich and N. Smallwood, "Capitalizing on Capabilities," *Harvard Business Review* (June 2004): 119–127.

24. P. Selznick, *Leadership in Administration: A Sociological Interpretation* (New York: Harper and Row, 1957); C. C. Snow and L. G. Hrebiniak, "Strategy, Distinctive Competency, and Organizational Performance," *Administrative Science Quarterly* 25 (June1980): 317–336.

25. C. W. Hill and G. R. Jones, *Strategic Management Theory: An Integrated Approach* (Boston, Mass.: Houghton Mifflin, 2004), 82.

26. Barney, "Looking Inside for Competitive Advantage." 49–61.

27. Baney, "Looking Inside for Competitive Advantage."

28. Amit and Schoemaker, "Strategic Assets and Organizational Rent"; R. M. Grant, "The Resource-Based Theory of Competitive Advantage: Implications for Strategy Formulation," *California Management Review* (Spring 1991): 114–135.

29. P. Dussauge, S. Hart, and B. Ramanantsoa, *Strategic Technology Management* (Chichester, UK: John Wiley & Sons, 1987), 55.

30. C. A. Bartlett and U. Rangan, "Komatsu Ltd.," *Harvard Business School Case*, #9-385–277 (1985).

31. J. Schumpeter, *Capitalism, Socialism, and Democracy* (New York: Harper & Row, 1942); S. Oster, *Modern Competitive Analysis* (New York: Oxford University Press, 1994): 116.

32. G. Pinchot, *Intrapreneuring* (New York: Harper & Row, 1985). See also special issue, *Strategic Management Journal* 11 (1990).

33. For example, see T. Kidder, *The Soul of a New Machine* (New York: Avon Books, 1981), 12. See also A. C. Cooper and C. G. Smith, "How Established Firms Respond to Threatening Technologies," *The Academy of Management Executive* 6, no. 2 (1992): 55–70.

34. Ma, "Of Competitive Advantage—Kinetic and Positional."

35. S. A. Zahra, S. Nash, and D. J. Bickford, "Transforming Technological Pioneering into Competitive Advantage," *Academy of Management Executive* (February 1995), 17–31.

36. K. Belson, "Sony again turns to design to lift electronics," *New York Times,* February 2, 2003, Business sec., 4); M. Witzel, "Management A-to-Z: First Mover Advantage," *Financial Times,* www.ft.com, 2001.

37. U. C. Neisser, *Cognitive Psychology* (New York: Appleton-Century-Crofts, 1979).

38. Barney, "Looking Inside for Competitive Advantage," 49–61.

39. W. M. Cohen and D. A. Levinthal, "Absorptive Capacity: A New Perspective on Learning and Innovation," *Administrative Science Quarterly* 35 (1990): 128–152.

40. Porter, *Competitive Advantage*, 33–61.

41. R. A. D'Aveni, *Hyper Competition* (New York: The Free Press, 1994).

42. Saloner, Shepherd, and Podolny, *Strategic Management*, 51–55.

43. J. A. Pearce and R. B. Robinson, *Strategic Management* (New York: McGraw Hill, 2003), 136.

Chapter 5

1. "Wal-Mart Tops Fortune's List of America's Most Admired Companies," *Fortune,* February 18, 2003; S. Walton, *Made in America: My Story* (New York: Doubleday, 1992); D. B. Yoffie, "Wal-Mart in 2005," *Harvard Business School Case #9-705-460*, April 14, 2005; J. W. Camerius, "Wal-Mart Stores, Inc: Strategies for Dominance in the Millennium," in C. W. Hill and G. R. Jones, *Cases in Strategic Management*, 6th ed. (Boston, Mass.: Houghton Mifflin Company, 2004), C374–391; A. Bianco and W. Zellner, "Is Wal-Mart Too Powerful?," *Business Week*, October 6, 2003, cover story.

2. R. M. Grant, *Contemporary Strategy Analysis* (Cambridge, Mass: Basil Blackwell, 1995), 41–42.

3. C. Markides, "What Is Strategy and How Do You Know If You Have One?," *Business Strategy Review* 15, no. 2 (2004): 5–12; C. C. Markides, "In Search of Strategy," *Sloan Management Review* 40, 3 (1999): 6–7.

4. M. E. Porter, "Strategy and the Internet," *Harvard Business Review* 79, no. 3, (March 2001): 62–78.

5. M. E. Porter, *Competitive Advantage* (New York: Free Press, 1985), 12.

6. D. Miller, M. F. R. Kets de Vries, and J. M. Toulouse, "Top Executive Locus of Control and Its Relationship to Strategy-Making, Structure, and Environment," *Academy of Management Journal* 25, no. 2, (1982): 237–253.

7. K. M. Eisenhardt, "Strategy as Strategic Decision Making," *Sloan Management Review* (Spring 1999): 65–72; D. C. Hambrick and J. W. Fredrickson, "Are You Sure You Have a Strategy?" *Academy of Management Executive* 15, no. 4 (2001): 48–59.

8. M. E. Porter, *Competitive Strategy* (New York: Free Press, 1980), 34–46.

9. M. E. Porter, "Toward a Dynamic Theory of Strategy," special issue, *Strategic Management Journal* 12 (Winter 1991): 95–117.

10. Porter, "Strategy and the Internet,"62–78; M. E. Porter, "What Is Strategy?" *Harvard Business Review* (November–December 1996): 61–78; J. Kay, "The Structure of Strategy," *Business Strategy Review* 4, no. 2, (Summer 1993): 17–37.

11. M. E. Porter, *Competitive Advantage* (New York: Free Press, 1985): 12.

12. Porter, *Competitive Advantage*, 11.

13. C. W. Hill and G. R Jones, *Strategic Management Theory* (Boston, Mass.: Houghton Mifflin Company, 2004), 162.

14. M. M. Lele, *Creating Strategic Leverage* (New York: John Wiley, 1992), 98–99.

15. Lele, *Creating Strategic Leverage,* 99.

16. R. A. D'Aveni, *Hyper-Competition: Managing the Dynamics of Strategic Maneuvering* (New York: The Free Press, 1994); C. W. L. Hill, "Differentiation Versus Low Cost or Differentiation and Low Cost: A Contingency Framework," *Academy of Management Review* 13, no. 3 (1988): 401–412.; A. I. Murray, "A Contingency View of Porter's Generic Strategies," *Academy of Management Review* 13, no. 3 (1988): 390–400.

17. G. G. Dess and P. S. Davis, "Porter's (1980) Generic Strategies as Determinants of Strategic Group Membership and Organizational Performance," *Academy of Management Journal* 27, no. 3: 467–488; L. Kim and Y. Lim, "Environment, Generic Strategies, and Performance in a Rapidly Developing Country: A Taxonomic Approach," *Academy of Management Journal* 31, no. 4: 802–827; R. Parthasarthy and S. P. Sethi, "Relating Flexible Automation to Business Strategy and Organizational Structure: A Test of Fit and Performance Implications," *Strategic Management Journal* 14 (October 1993): 529–549.

18. A. Miller and G. G Dess, "Assessing Porter's (1980) Model in Terms of Its Generalizability, Accuracy, and Simplicity," *Journal of Management Studies* 30, no. 4, (1993): 553–585.

19. C. C. Markides, "A Dynamic View of Strategy," *Sloan Management Review* 40, no. 3, (1999): 55–63.

20. "Can Anything Stop Toyota?," *Business Week Online* (www.businessweek.com), November 17, 2003.

21. R. Parthasarthy and J. Yin, "Computer-Integrated Manufacturing and Competitive Performance," *Journal of Engineering and Technology Management* 13 (1996): 83–110.

22. R. E. Miles and C. C. Snow, *Organizational Strategy, Structure, and Process* (New York: McGraw Hill, 1978).

23. C. R. Anderson and C. P. Zeithaml, "Stage of the Product Life Cycle: Business Strategy and Business Performance, *Academy of Management Journal* 27 (1984), 5–24; C. W. Hofer and D. Schendel, *Strategy Formulation: Analytical Concepts* (St. Paul, Minn.: West Publishing, 1978), chap. 5.

Chapter 6

1. M. Walsh, *Making Connections: The Long Distance Bus Industry in the USA* (Aldershot, UK: Ashgate Publishing, 2000); C. Jackson, *Hounds of the Road: A History of the Greyhound Bus Company* (Bowling Green, Ohio: Bowling Green University Popular Press, 1984); O. Schisgall, *The Greyhound Story: From Hibbing to Everywhere* (Chicago, Ill.: J. C. Ferguson Publishing, 1985); G. R. Jones, "First Greyhound, Then Greyhound Dial, Then Dial: What Will Happen in 2002?" in *Cases in Strategic Management*, ed. C. W. Hill and G. R. Jones (Boston, Mass.: Houghton Mifflin Company, 2004), C634–647.

2. N. W. C. Harper and S. P. Viguerie, "Are You Too Focused?," special edition, *McKinsey Quarterly*, issue 2 (2002): 28–37; E. H. Bowman and C. E. Helfat, "Does Corporate Strategy Matter?," *Strategic Management Journal* 22, no. 1 (2001): 1–23.

3. A. D. Chandler, *Strategy and Structure: Chapters in the History of the Industrial Enterprise* (Cambridge, Mass.: MIT Press, 1962).

4. J. G. Matsusaka, "Corporate Diversification, Value Maximization, and Organizational Capabilities," *Journal of Business*, 74, no. 3 (July 2001): 409–432.

5. D. J. Collis and C. A. Montgomery, "Creating Corporate Advantage," *Harvard Business Review* (May–June 1998): 71–86.

6. Collis and Montgomery, "Creating Corporate Advantage."

7. R. M. Grant, *Contemporary Strategy Analysis*, (Cambridge, Mass.: Basil Blackwell, 1991), 402–403.

8. R. Gaitonde, "An analysis of HP's future strategy, post Carly Fiorina," www.osnews.com, February 24, 2005, accessed on April 9, 2005.

9. W. Comanor, "Vertical Mergers, Market Power, and Anti-trust Laws," *American Economic Review* 57, no. 2 (May 1967): 254–267.

10. O. E. Williamson, *Markets and Hierarchies: Analysis and Antitrust Implications*, (New York: The Free Press, 1975).

11. J. Stuckey and D. White, "When and When Not to Vertically Integrate," *Sloan Management Review* (Spring 1993): 71–83.

12. J. Yoshida, "Synergy plan in play at Sony", EETimes.com, March 11, 2005, accessed on April 9, 2005.

13. C. Malburg, "Vertical Integration: Grabbing More Links of the Value Chain Can Reduce Risk and Increase Control," *Industry Week*, 249, issue 20, (December 11, 2000): 17.

14. Malburg, "Vertical Integration."

15. M. Oster, *Modern Competitive Analysis* (New York: Oxford University Press, 1994), 181.

16. N. W. C. Harper and S. P. Viguerie, "Are You Too Focused?"

17. B. Einhorn, "Your Next TV," *Business Week*, April 4, 2005, 33–36.

18. E. T. Penrose, *The Theory of the Growth of the Firm* (Oxford: Basil Blackwell, 1959).

19. C. A. Montgomery, "Corporate Diversification," *Journal of Economic Perspectives* 8, no. 3 (1994): 163–179; C. W. L. Hill, "Diversified Growth and Competition: The Experience of 12 Large U.K. Firms," *Applied Economics* 17, no. 5 (October 1985): 827–848).

20. R. Biggadike, "The Risky Business of Diversification," *Harvard Business Review* 57, no. 3 (May–June 1979): 103–112.

21. P. G. Berger and E. Ofek, "Diversification's Effect on Firm Value," *Journal of Financial Economics* 37, no. 1 (1995): 39–65; L. E. Palich, L. B. Cardinal, and C. Chet Miller, "Curvilinearity in the Diversification-Performance Linkage: An Examination over Three Decades of Research," *Strategic Management Journal* 21 (2000): 155–174.

22. Montgomery, "Corporate Diversification."

23. B. D. Bernheim and M. D. Whinston, "Multi-Market Contact and Collusive Behavior," *RAND Journal of Economics* 21 (Spring 1990): 1–26.

24. Collis and Montgomery, "Creating Corporate Advantage."

25. C. K. Prahalad and G. Hamel, "The Core Competence of the Corporation," *Harvard Business Review* (May–June 1990): 79–91.

26. C. A. Montgomery and B. Wenerfelt, "Diversification, Ricardian Rent, and Tobin's Q," *RAND Journal of Economics* 19 (Winter 1988): 623–32; K. Palepu, "Diversification Strategy, Profit Performance, and the Entropy Measure," *Strategic Management Journal* 6, (July–September 1985): 239–255.

27. C. V. Bagli, "Snapple is just the latest case of mismatched reach and grasp," *New York Times*, March 29, 1997, business section; M. E. Porter, "From Competitive Advantage to Corporate Strategy," *Harvard Business Review* 65, no. 3 (1987): 43–59.

28. A. Shleifer and R. W. Vishny, "Management Entrenchment: The Case of Manager-Specific Investments," *Journal of Financial Economics* 25 (1989): 123–139; M. C. Jensen and K. J. Murphy, "Performance Pay and Top Management Incentives," *Journal of Political Economy* 98 (1990): 225–264.

29. R. Gibbons and K. J. Murphy, "Optimal Incentive Contracts in the Presence of Career Concerns: Theory and Evidence," *Journal of Political Economy* 100 (1992): 468–505; A. Khorana and M. Zenner, "Executive Compensation of Large Acquirers in the 1980s," *Journal of Corporate Finance* 4 (1998): 209–240.

30. L. E. Palich, L. B. Cardinal, and C. Chet Miller, "Curvilinearity in the Diversification-Performance Linkage: An Examination over Three Decades of

Research," *Strategic Management Journal* 21 (2000): 155–174; Harper and Viguerie, "Are You Too Focused?"

31. Prahalad and Hamel, "The Core Competence of the Corporation,"; C. K. Prahalad and R. A. Bettis, "The Dominant Logic: A New Linkage Between Diversity and Performance," *Strategic Management Journal* 10 (1986): 523–552.

32. M. A. Hitt, R. D. Ireland, and R. E. Hoskisson, *Strategic Management* (Ohio: Southwestern Publishing, 2003), 24.

33. M. A. Hitt, R. E. Hoskisson, R. A. Johnson, and D. D. Moesel, "The Market for Corporate Control and Firm Innovation," *Academy of Management Journal* 39, no. 5 (1996): 1084–1119.

34. A. Johnson, "Antecedents and Outcomes of Corporate Refocusing," special issue, *Journal of Management* 22, no. 3 (1996): 439–484.

35. C. Markides, "Corporate Refocusing," *Business Strategy Review* 4, no. 1 (Spring 1993): 1–15

36. D. C. Hambrick and I. C. Macmillan, "The Product Portfolio and Man's Best Friend," *California Management Review* 25, no. 1 (1982): 84–95.

37. A. Morrison and R. Wensley, "Boxing Up or Boxed In?: A Short History of the Boston Consulting Group Share/Growth Matrix," *Journal of Marketing Management* 7, no. 2 (1991): 105–129.

Chapter 7

1. R. J. Morris and A. T. Lawrence, "Nike's Dispute with the University of Oregon," in *Strategic Management,* ed. A. A. Thompson and A. J. Strickland (New York: McGraw-Hill Irwin, 2003), C759–775; S. Holmes, "The New Nike," *Business Week,* September 28, 2004, 79–86; S. Stevenson, "How to beat Nike," *New York Times Magazine,* January 5, 2003; R. M. Locke, "The Promise and Perils of Globalization: The Case of Nike," paper presented at the fiftieth anniversary celebration of the Sloan School of Management, Massachusetts Institute of Technology, October 2002.

2. P. Engardio, A. Bernstein, and M. Kripalani, "The New Global Job Shift," *Business Week,* February 3, 2003, 50–60.

3. D. Farrell, "Beyond Off-shoring: Assess Your Company's Global Potential," *Harvard Business Review* 82, no. 12 (2004): 82–90; "A New Goliath in Big Steel," *Business Week,* November 8, 2004, 47–48.

4. T. Levitt, "The Globalization of Markets," *Harvard Business Review* (May–June 1983): 92–102.

5. R. Veblen, "International Investment and International Trade in the Product Life Cycle," *Quarterly Journal of Economic,* 80, no. 1 (May 1966): 190–207.

6 T. Hout, M. E. Porter, and E. Rudden, "How Global Companies Win Out," *Harvard Business Review*; C. A.

Bartlett and S. Ghoshal, "Lessons from Late Movers," *Harvard Business Review* (March–April 2000): 133–142.

7. G. Hamel and C. K. Prahalad, "Do You Really Have a Global Strategy?," *Harvard Business Review* (July–August 1985): 139–148.

8. W. Kuemmerle and W. Kuemmerle, "Building Effective R&D Capabilities Abroad," *Harvard Business Review* 75, no. 2 (March–April 1997): 61–70.

9. C. A. Bartlett and S. Ghoshal, "Managing Across Borders: New Strategic Requirements," *Sloan Management Review* (Summer1987): 7–17.

10. P. Ghemawat, "Distance Still Matters: The Hard Reality of Global Expansion," *Harvard Business Review* 79, no. 8 (2001): 137–145.

11. V. Govindarajan and A. K. Gupta, "*The Quest for Global Dominance: Transforming Global Presence into Global Competitive Advantage*" (San Francisco, Calif.: Jossey-Bass, 2001), 4.

12. Levitt, "The Globalization of Markets," *Harvard Business Review.*

13. A. Morrison and K. Roth, "A Taxonomy of Business Level Strategies in Global Industries," *Strategic Management Journal* 13, no. 6 (1992): 399–418; M. E. Porter, "Changing Patterns of International Competition," *California Management Review* 28, no. 2 (1986): 9–40; Y. L. Doz, "Strategic Management in Multi-national Companies," *Sloan Management Review* 21, no. 2 (Winter 1980): 27–46.

14. Porter, *The Competitive Advantage of Nations,* 53.

15. J. H. Dunning, "Toward an Eclectic Theory of International Production: Some Empirical Tests," *Journal of International Business Studies* (Spring–Summer 1980): 9–31.

16. G. S. Yip, "Global Strategy: In a World of Nations?," *Sloan Management Review* 31, no. 1 (Fall 1989): 29–41.

17. Porter, "Changing Patterns of International Competition," *California Management Review.*

18. C. A. Bartlett and S. Ghoshal, *Managing Across Borders: The Transnational Solution* (Boston, Mass.: Harvard University Press, 1989).

19. S. Ghoshal and N. Nohria, "Horses for Courses: Organizational Forms for Multi-national Corporations," *Sloan Management Review* 34, no. 2 (Winter 1993): 23–35.

20. Porter, *Competitive Advantage of Nations.* 53.

21. M. V. Makhija, K. Kim, and S. D. Williamson, "Measuring Globalization of Industries Using a National Industry Approach: Empirical Evidence Across Five Continents and Over Time," *Journal of International Business Studies* 28, no. 4 (1997): 679–710; P. Ghemawat, "The Forgotten Strategy," *Harvard Business Review* 81, no. 11 (2003): 76–83.

22. S. P. Douglas and Y. Wind, "The Myth of Globalization," *Columbia Journal of World Business* 22, no. 4 (1987): 19–29.

23. A. Rugman and R. Hodgetts, "The End of Global Strategy," *European Management Journal* 19, no. 4 (2001): 333–343.

24. Bartlett and Ghoshal, *Managing Across Borders*; C. K. Prahalad and Y. L. Doz, *The Multinational Mission: Balancing Local Demands and Global Vision* (New York: The Free Press, 1987).

25. Bartlett and Ghoshal, *Managing Across Borders*.

26. H. V. Perlmutter, "The Tortuous Evolution of the Multinational Corporation," *Columbia Journal of World Business* 4, no. 1 (1969): 9–18.

27. Bartlett and Ghoshal, *Managing Across Borders*; A. Harzing, "An Empirical Analysis and Extension of the Bartlett and Ghoshal Typology of Multinational Companies," *Journal of International Business Studies* 31, no. 1 (2000): 101–120.

28. Perlmutter, "The Tortuous Evolution of the Multinational Corporation."

29. Bartlett and Ghoshal, *Managing Across Borders*; Harzing, "An Empirical Analysis and Extension of the Bartlett and Ghoshal Typology of Multinational Companies."

30. Bartlett and Ghoshal, *Managing Across Borders*.

31. Perlmutter, "The Tortuous Evolution of the Multinational Corporation,"

32. Goshal and Nohria, "Horses for Courses."

33. Porter, *The Competitive Advantage of Nations*.

34. F. Root, *Foreign Market Entry Strategies* (New York: AMACOM, 1982), 7.

35. Root, *Foreign Market Entry Strategies*.

36. Y. Pan and D. K. Tse, "The Hierarchical Model of Market Entry Modes," *Journal of International Business Studies* 31, no. 4 (2000): 535–554.

37. S. Agarwal and S. N. Ramaswami, "Choice of Foreign Market Entry Mode: Impact of Ownership, Location, and Internationalization Factors," *Journal of International Business Studies* 223, no. 1 (1992): 1–28.

38. A. Harzing, "Acquisitions Versus Greenfield Investments: International Strategy and Management of Entry," *Strategic Management Journal* 23, no. 3 (2002): 211–227.

Chapter 8

1. Amazon.com, *Annual Report 2004*; S. Krishnamoorthy, "Amazon.com: A Business History," in *E-Commerce Management: Text and Cases* (Case #1) (Mason, Ohio: South-Western, 2002); S. Kotha, "Amazon.com," in *Strategic Management,* ed. M. A. Hitt, R. D. Ireland, and R. E. Hoskisson (Mason, Ohio: South-Western Publishing, 2001), C83–103; "We Want to Be the Most Customer-Centric Company," *Business Week Online,* May 21, 1999; "Amazon.com: The Wild World of e-Commerce," *Business Week,* December 14, 1998.

2. P. R. Varadarajan and S. Jayachandran, "Marketing Strategy: An Assessment of the State of the Field and Outlook," *Journal of the Academy of Marketing Science* 27, no. 2 (1999): 120–143.

3. P. Kotler and G. Armstrong, *Principles of Marketing* (Englewood Cliffs, N.J.: Prentice Hall, 1991), 231.

4. Kotler and Armstrong, *Principles of Marketing,* 232–234.

5. A. Ries and J. Trout, "*Positioning: The Battle for Your Mind,*" (New York: Warner Books, 1986), 2.

6. R. J. E. Swan and D. R. Rink, "Fitting Market Strategy to Varying Product Life Cycles," *Business Horizons* 25, no. 1 (1982): 219–242.

7. E. Hutchinson, "Corporate Branding Unifies Product Lines," *American Marketing Association,* 2003, www.marketpower.com., accessed on April 27, 2005.

8. R. S. Russell and B. W. Taylor III, *Operations Management,* (Englewood Cliffs, N.J.: Prentice Hall, 2000): 5.

9. R. H. Hayes and S. C. Wheelwright, *Restoring Our Competitive Edge: Competing Through Manufacturing* (New York: John Wiley & Sones, 1984), 30.

10. W. Skinner, "The Focused Factory," *Harvard Business Review* 52, no. 3 (1974): 113–121; W. Skinner, *Manufacturing: The Formidable Competitive Weapon* (New York: John Wiley, 1985).

11. R. Parthasarthy and S. P. Sethi, "Relating Strategy and Structure to Flexible Automation: A Test of Fit and Performance Implication," *Strategic Management Journal* 14, no. 7 (1993): 529–549.

12. R. Parthasarthy and S. P. Sethi, "The Impact of Flexible Automation on Business Strategy and Organizational Structure," *Academy of Management Review* 17, no. 1 (1992): 86–111.

13. Parthasarthy and Sethi, "The Impact of Flexible Automation on Business Strategy and Organizational Structure."

14. J. D. Goldhar and M. Jelinek, "Plan for Economies of Scope," *Harvard Business Review* 61, no. 6 (1983): 141–148.

15. K. M. Eisenhardt and F. M. Santos, "Knowledge-Based View: A New Theory of Strategy?" in *Handbook of Strategy and Management,* ed. A. Pettigrew, H. Thomas, and R. Whittington (London: Sage Publications, 2002), 139–164.

16. P. Dussauge, S. Hart, and B. Ramanantsoa, *Strategic Technology Management* (Chichester, UK: John Wiley and Sons, 1992), 168.

17. J. Pfeffer, "Producing Sustainable Competitive Advantage Through the Effective Management of People," *Academy of Management Executive* 9, no. 1 (1995): 55–72.

18. J. B. Barney, "Looking Inside for Competitive Advantage," *Academy of Management Executive* 9, no. 4 (1995): 49–61; D. J. Collis and C. A. Montgomery, "Competing on Resources: Strategy in the 1990s," *Harvard Business Review* 73, no. 4 (July–August 1995): 118–128.

19. P. Bamberger and I. Meshoulam, *Human Resource Strategy* (Thousand Oaks, Calif.: Sage Publications, 2000), 67.

20. Bamberger and Meshoulam, *Human Resource Strategy*, 70.

21. R. E. Miles and C. C. Snow, "Designing Strategic Human Resource Systems," *Organizational Dynamics* 13, no. 1 (1984): 36–52; D. M. Rousseau and K. A. Wade-Benzoni, "Linking Strategy and Human Resource Practices: How Employee and Customer Contracts Are Created." *Human Resource Management* 33 (1994): 463–489.

22. Miles and Snow, "Designing Strategic Human Resource Systems"; Rousseau and Wade-Benzoni, "Linking Strategy and Human Resource Practices"

23. Bamberger and Meshoulam, *Human Resource Strategy*, 140.

24. R. Schuler and S. E. Jackson, "Linking Competitive Strategy with Human Resource Management Practices," *Academy of Management Executive* 1, no. 3 (1987): 207–219.

25. R. Kochhar and M. A. Hitt, "Research Notes and Comments Linking Corporate Strategy to Capital Structure: Diversification Strategy, Type, and Sources of Financing," *Strategic Management Journal* 19, no. 7 (1998): 601–610.

Chapter 9

1. J. H. Gittell, "Paradox of Coordination and Control," *California Management Review* 42, no. 3 (Spring 2000): 101–117; S. B. Donnelly, "One Airline's Magic," *Time*, October 28, 2002; G. Saloner, A. Shepard, and J. Podolny, *Strategic Management* (New York: John Wiley, 2001), 68–69; U. K. Bunz and J. D. Maes, "Learning Excellence: Southwest Airlines' Approach," *Managing Service Quality* 8, no. 3 (1998): 163–169.

2. R. R. Nelson , "Why Do Firms Differ, and How Does It Matter?," special issue, *Strategic Management Journal* 12 (Winter 1991): 61–74.

3. P. R. Lawrence and J. W. Lorsch, "Differentiation and Integration in Complex Organizations," *Administrative Science Quarterly* 12, no. 1, (1967): 1–47.

4. D. Miller and J. O. Whitney, "Beyond Strategy: Configuration as a Pillar of Competitive Advantage," *Business Horizons* (May–June 1999): 5–17; P. H. Fuchs, K. E. Mifflin, D. Miller, and J. O. Witney, "Strategic Integration: Competing in the Age of Capabilities," *California Management Review* 42, no. 3 (2000): 118–147.

5. Nelson, "Why Do Firms Differ, and How Does It Matter?"

6. A. D. Chandler, *Strategy and Structure* (Cambridge, Mass.: MIT Press, 1962).

7. R. P. Rumelt, *Strategy, Structure, and Economic Performance in Large American Industrial Corporations* (Boston, Mass.: Graduate School of Business Administration, Harvard University, 1974); J. M. Stopford, "Growth and Organizational Change in the Multinational Firm," D.B.A. dissertation, Harvard Business School, 1968.

8. R. R. Nelson and S. G. Winter, *An Evolutionary Theory of Economic Change* (Cambridge, Mass.: Harvard University Press, 1982); B. W. Keats and M. A. Hitt, "A Causal Model of Linkages Among Environmental Dimensions, Micro Organizational Characteristics, and Performance," *Academy of Management Journal* 31, no. 3 (1988): 570–598; J. W. Frederickson, "The Strategic Decision Process and Organizational Structure," *Academy of Management Review* 11 (1986): 280–297; R. Pitts, "The Strategy-Structure Relationship: An Exploration into Causality, paper presented at the *Academy of Management Annual Conference*, Detroit, 1980.

9. J. R. Galbraith, "Designing the Innovative Organization," *Organizational Dynamics* 10 (Winter 1982): 3–24.

10. R. M. Kanter, *The Change Masters* (New York: Simon and Schuster, 1983).

11. R. Parthasarthy and S. P. Sethi, "Relating Strategy and Structure to Flexible Automation: A Test of Fit and Performance Implications," *Strategic Management Journal* 14, no. 7 (1993): 529–549.

12. M. Weber, *The Theory of Social and Economic Organization*. trans. A. M. Henderson and T. Parsons (New York: Oxford University Press, 1947).

13. Chandler, *Strategy and Structure*.

14. "Dow draws its matrix again—and again, and again," *Economist,* August 5, 1989, 55–56.

15. C. Bartlett and S. Ghoshal, "Matrix Management: Not a Structure, a Frame of Mind," *Harvard Business Review* 68, no. 4 (1990): 138–145.

16. A. Schilling and H. K. Steensma, "The Use of Modular Organizational Forms: An Industry Level Analysis," *Academy of Management Journal* 44, no. 6 (2001): 1149–1168.

17. T. W. Malnight, "Emerging Structural Patterns Within Multinational Corporations: Toward Process-Based Structures," *Academy of Management Journal* 44, no. 6 (2001): 1187–2010.

18. A. Abbott, "From Causes to Events: Notes on Narrative Positivism," *Sociological Methods and Research* 20, no. 4 (1992).

19. J. R. Galbraith, "Organization Design: An Information Processing View," *Interfaces* 4, no. 3 (1974): 28–36.

20. Lawrence and Lorsch, *Organization and Environment*.

21. J. R. Galbraith, *Designing Complex Organizations* (Boston, Mass.; Addison-Wesley, 1973), 50.

22. Galbraith, *Designing Complex Organizations*.

23. J. B. Barney, "Organizational Culture: Can It Be a Source of Sustained Competitive Advantage," *Academy of Management Review* 11, no. 3 (1983): 656–665.

24. Eastman Kodak, *Annual Report 2004*. www.kodak.com.

Chapter 10

1. J. H. Gittell, "Paradox of Coordination and Control," *California Management Review* 42, no. 3 (2000): 11101–11117; A. C. Inkpen and V. DeGroot, "Southwest Airlines 1999," Case #A07-99-0030, The American Graduate School of International Management, Thunderbird University; A. A. Thompson and J. E. Gamble, "Southwest Airlines, Inc." in *Strategic Management* ed. A. A. Thompson and A. J. Strickland (New York: McGraw-Hill Irwin, 2003), C590–629.

2. P. Lorange and M. S. Scott, "A Framework for Management Control Systems," *Sloan Management Review* 16, no. 1 (Fall 1974): 41–56; G. B. Giglioni and G. Bedeian, "A Conspectus of Management Control Theory," *Academy of Management Journal* 17, no. 2 (1974): 292–305.

3. G. Schreyogg and H. Steinmann, "Strategic Control: A New Perspective," *Academy of Management Review* 12, no. 1 (1987): 91–103; J. C. Picken and G. G. Dess, "Out of (Strategic) Control," *Organizational Dynamics* (Summer 1997): 35–45.

4. G. Schreyogg and H. Steinmann, "Strategic Control: A New Perspective."

5. Several authors suggest that strategic controls must, first and foremost, measure the firm's strategic performance. See for example, C. D. Ittner and D. F. Larcker, "Innovations in Performance Measurement: Trends and Research Implications" *Journal of Management Accounting Research* 10 (1998): 205–238; R. D. Banker, G. Potter, and D. Srinivasan, "An Empirical Investigation of an Incentive Plan That Includes Non-financial Performance Measures," *Accounting Review* 75, no. 1 (2000): 65–92; M. Goold, "Strategic Control in the Decentralized Firm," *Sloan Management Review* 32, no. 2 (1991): 69–81.

6. J. S. Harrison, *Strategic Management* (New York: John Wiley & Sons, 2003), 317.

7. M. Goold, "Strategic Control in the Decentralized Firm," *Sloan Management Review* 32, no. 2 (Winter 1991): 69–81.

8. R. Kaplan and D. P. Norton, "Transforming the Balanced Scorecard from Performance Measurement to Strategic Management," *Accounting Horizons* 15, no. 1 (March 2001): 87–104; R. Kaplan and D. P Norton, "The Balanced Scorecard—Measures That Drive Performance," *Harvard Business Review* 70, no. 1 (1992): 71–79.

9. Kaplan and Norton, "The Balanced Scorecard—Measures That Drive Performance."

10. E. Berkman, "How to Use the Balanced Scorecard," *CIO Magazine* (May 15, 2002).

11. M. Bourne, "The Emperor's New Scorecard," *Financial World*, (August 2002): 48–50.

12. Bourne, "The Emperor's New Scorecard."

13. Goold, "Strategic Control in the Decentralized Firm."

14. H. Mintzberg, *The Structuring of Organizations* (Englewood Cliffs, N.J.: Prentice Hall, 1979), 5–7; Also, cf. T. L. C. M. Groot and K. A. Merchant, "Control of International Joint Ventures," *Accounting, Organizations, and Society* 25, no. 6 (2000): 579–607.

15. A. K. Gupta and V. Govindarajan, "Knowledge Management's Social Dimension: Lessons from Nucor Steel," *Sloan Management Review* 42, no. 1 (Fall 2000): 71–80.

16. "Confirming Sony's Position as a Leading Consumer Brand in the 21st Century," Sony Global press release, October 28, 2003.

17. R. W. Griffin, *Management* (Boston, Mass.: Houghton Mifflin Company, 2002), 622.

18. "Explaining Dell's Transformation," *HBS Working Knowledge*, June 8, 2003.

19. T. M. Jones, "Instrumental Stakeholder Theory: A Synthesis of Ethics and Economics," *Academy of Management Review* 20, no. 2 (1995): 404–437.

20. P. Nakra, "Corporate Reputation Management: CRM with a Strategic Twist," *Public Relations Quarterly* 45, no. 2 (2000): 35–42.

21. R. C. Vergin and M. W. Qoronfleh, "Corporate Reputation and the Stock Market," *Business Horizons* 41, no. 1 (1998): 19–26.

22. J. Kay, *Why Firms Succeed* (New York: Oxford University Press, 1995), 18.

23. B. R. Baliga, "Multinational Corporations: Control Systems and Delegation Issues," *Journal of International Business Studies* 15, no. 2 (984): 25–40.

Glossary

Above average profit Returns earned by a firm on its invested capital that are greater than the average earned by all firms in the industry.

Absorptive capacity The ability of the firm to absorb new information as a result of the previously stored information. (4)

Adaptation A process in which a firm continuously adjusts its resources and capabilities to match the demands of the external environment.

Advantageous market position A dominant market position or a secure market position (i.e., a niche) a firm enjoys that gives it an advantage over rivals. (3)

Analyzer A firm that competes by effectively serving current customers and seeking new opportunities, as well; prospector and defender combined. (1)

Applied research Focuses on the feasibility of transforming into products or processes the theoretical knowledge already obtained through basic research. (8)

At-risk pay A portion of the pay that employees receive when they reach or exceed a certain goal; it is a lump sum variable pay that is not part of the base pay and is paid contingent upon performance.

Audit committee of the board Comprising only outside directors, this committee reviews the firm's financial reports and evaluates the adequacy of internal control systems.

Backward integration A form of vertical integration in which the firm expands by moving toward raw material and component production stages. (6)

Balanced scorecard A model proposed by Robert Kaplan and David Norton that suggests that a firm evaluate its performance based on the progress made toward strategic and financial goals; the authors claim that such a balanced approach offers a more effective assessment of a firm's performance.

Basic research Fundamental or pure research; exploratory in nature. (8)

Board of directors A committee, elected by the shareholders of a company, to oversee the management of the company.

Brand loyalty Buyers' preference for an existing brand. (3)

Broad differentiator A firm that offers several designs to appeal to several niche segments. (5)

Broad division of task In which workers perform a family of related tasks; enhances worker understanding of the whole task, thereby increasing output quality and flexibility in worker's routines.

Bureaucratic costs Administrative costs; costs associated with running a company.

Business-level management Management consisting of the general manager of the business unit and functional managers. (1)

Business-level strategy Decisions and actions a firm takes to achieve competitive advantage or superiority in a particular business; specifies the advantage the firm will pursue in that business and how available resources will be deployed to acquire it; also referred to as business-unit strategy, competitive strategy.

Business-level strategy Focuses on gaining advantage in a single business (or business unit); also referred to as competitive strategy. (1)

Capability Refers to the firm's skills or knowledge in transforming inputs into outputs; an intangible resource. (1, 4)

Capital structure The balance between debt and equity in a firm's capital.

Cash cows Have high relative market share in a low growth industry. (6)

Centralization Concentration of authority at the top levels of the firm. (9)

Company infrastructure Comprises the organizational structure, administrative mechanisms, and the firm's culture or value system.

Compensation committee of the board Comprising mostly outside directors, this committee evaluates senior management performance and determines compensation.

Competency-based advantage The edge a firm has over rivals arising from its unique internal resources and capabilities.

Competitive advantage An edge or strength a firm has over rivals; a strategic measure of business success. (4)

Complementary product A product that is necessary for using another product.

Computer-aided manufacturing (CAM) A type of manufacturing automation technology that uses programmable robots and monitoring tools to ensure the consistency of output. (8)

Computer-integrated manufacturing (CIM) Operations technology that electronically integrates several value-chain activities: product design, component production, assembly, finished product storage.

Concentrated marketing A marketing strategy by which a firm focuses on a single segment within a large market (a niche) and aims for a high market share within that niche. (8)

Concentric diversification Diversifications based on the same core technology. (6)

Concurrent control Mechanisms managers employ at the time performance occurs so as to restrain deviations from expected output. (10)

Conglomerate acquisitions Buying a firm in another industry that is unrelated to the firm's current product or customers served.

Conglomerate diversification Diversifications that cannot be implemented with the firm's existing strategic assets; portfolio of businesses that do not have much in common, either in the technology used or markets served. (6)

Consolidated industry An industry with few large firms that dominate the industry, often referred to as an oligopoly. (3)

Constituency relationship The firm's ability to develop and maintain a cordial, transparent, and trusting relationship with its primary and secondary stakeholders. (10)

Continuous value creation and innovation The ability of the firm to enhance the features and functionality of current products or to develop and market new products. (10)

Core competency Something a firm does well relative to other internal activities. It is an activity in which the firm has deep knowledge. (4)

Corporate advantage Ability of a firm to integrate several products and businesses into a cohesive operation that creates more value than the sum of its parts. (6)

Corporate entrepreneur Also called intrapreneur, an established firm pursuing entrepreneurial activities.

Corporate governance Literally means directing the activities of the corporation. Corporate governance refers to all the systems, structures, and processes in place to ensure that managerial activities focus on the goals of the corporation and its owners. The board structure (composition, competency of the board members), monitoring mechanisms (rules of management supervision, reward structure), and monitoring process (steps in CEO evaluation) are all components of corporate governance. (2)

Corporate-level management Management consisting of the board of directors, the chief executive officer, and senior executives responsible for staff functions such as planning, finance, human resources, legal, and general administration. (1)

Corporate social responsibility Broadly includes, besides philanthropic activities, a firm's endeavors to be economically efficient, fair and just in dealings with customers, suppliers, employees, and competition, to obey the law, and be involved in socioeconomic projects, side-by-side with the government. (2)

Corporate-level strategies Decisions and actions a firm takes to gain advantage by expanding the product line, value-chain activities, or the range of businesses in which it will compete. (1, 6)

Cost focus A strategy in which the firm strives to outperform rivals by concentrating on a narrow product line or a narrow market segment and competing in it based on low cost.

Cost leadership strategy A strategy in which a firm aims for the lowest cost position, industry-wide, as a way to beat rivals. (5)

Cross-subsidization A tactic in which profits earned in a favorable market is used to support products or businesses competing in an unfavorable market. (6)

Cultural change Refers to changes in the customs, values, and beliefs of a society. They indicate products that a society may value, emerging patterns in consumption, and the overall trend in the attitude of people toward work and business practices.

Currency exchange rate The rate at which one currency exchanges for another; affects the price of goods in international markets.

Debt-to-equity ratio Borrowed funds as a ratio of owners' funds.

Decentralization Delegation of authority to lower levels in the organization.

Decline stage Demand for the product decreases reducing opportunities for incumbent firms; competition intensifies because industry capacity exceeds demand. (5)

Defender A firm that competes by effectively serving current customers and preventing competitor entry. (5)

Delegation of authority The distribution of power to the divided work units to make decisions. (9)

Deliberate strategy Strategy that was rigidly pursued.

Design flexibility The ability of the operating system and its set-up to efficiently and rapidly adjust to changes in the product's design. (8)

Design quality Quality of the product's design in regard to features and functionality. (8)

Development Activities that include designing, prototyping, testing, and verification of new products or processes.

Differentiated marketing A marketing strategy by which a firm targets several distinct segments by designing and offering the product differently for each. (8)

Differentiation strategy A strategy in which the firm positions its product, or the way it offers it, to be perceived industry-wide as distinct, thereby outperforming competition. (5)

Differentiation focus Similar to a cost focus, in this strategy a firm strives to outperform rivals by concentrating on a narrow product line or a narrow market segment but competes in it based on product/service differentiation.

Direct foreign investment Physical movement abroad of business capital to be invested in foreign plants and other business assets; firms engage in off-shore production of goods and compete side by side with host country sellers for a share of the local markets. (7)

Discretionary responsibility of the firm Voluntary obligations such as philanthropic contributions. (2)

Distinctive competency Also, distinctive capability; refers to the ability of a firm to perform competitively critical tasks relatively well. (4)

Diversification A strategy in which the firm offers a wide range of products and moves into new lines of business, creating a portfolio of products and businesses (a multi-business firm). (6)

Divestment The decisions and actions pertaining to restructuring that result in selective retrenchment and eventual re-composition of a firm's portfolio. (6)

Divestment strategy A strategy in which the firm adjusts its operational activities or business portfolio through restructuring and retrenchment. (6)

Dogs Have a low market share in a low-growth industry. (6)

Economic change Comprises changes occurring in employment levels, interest rate, and consumer spending. These changes indicate to managers the rate of growth in a nation's economy and opportunities emerging from it.

Economic forecasts Predict economic growth using trends in money supply, interest rates, employment data, growth in personal income, consumer sentiment, business investments in plant and equipment, and manufacturing inventories.

Economic responsibility of the firm Responsibility for production of goods and services, being of value to society, and operating efficiently so as to repay creditors and stockholders. (2)

Economic value added (EVA) Suggests that a firm must generate more cash than it raises from investors through stock and bond issues. (8)

Economies of scale Cost advantages that accrue due to an increase in the volume of output. Besides production, economies of scale can be derived in purchasing, distribution, advertising, and R&D, as well. (3)

Economies of scope Cost savings that arise when a critical resource (e.g., manufacturing tool, distribution system, skilled workforce, R&D facility) is shared by two or more products or business units. (6)

Emergence Formative stage of the industry; sellers are few in number, and growth in demand is uncertain. (5)

Emergent strategy An unplanned strategy that evolved during the course of implementing the intended strategy.

Employee-relations function Concerned with establishing, enforcing, and reinforcing the psychological contact between the employer and its employees in order to structure the work environment and the corporate culture.

Entrepreneurial competence Ability to recognize and seize emerging opportunities in a timely manner.

Entry barriers Factors that make it costly and difficult for new firms to enter an industry. (3)

Environmental awareness Cognizant of environmental trends: by continuously observing and interpreting the environmental events, managers stay well-informed about emerging trends.

Ethical responsibility of the firm The responsibility to conduct itself in ways that are generally deemed by society to be right.

Executive committee of the board Comprising both internal and external directors, this committee is responsible for formulation of corporate policies.

Exit barriers Factors that prevent a firm from exiting the industry even when demand is declining or profits are low. (3)

Experience-Curve effects Unit cost reductions occurring due to an accumulated experience in the making of a product. (3)

Extreme fragmentation Narrow or focused division of task in which each worker performs a part of the firm's task repetitively; creates work specialization, leading to low waste and high volume output.

Factor endowments Factors of production a nation is endowed with (e.g., skilled labor, infrastructure) that impact the competitive capabilities of firms situated in that nation.

Feedback control Mechanisms managers employ after performance has occurred that allows for corrective actions to take place, if necessary. (10)

Feed-forward control Mechanisms managers employ before performance begins so as to prevent likely deviations from expected output. (10)

Financial distress Occurs when the firm cannot make its payments on debt and runs the risk of bankruptcy.

Financial flexibility The ability of the firm to meet its obligations toward creditors and investors.

Financial function The role of the financial function is to raise and manage cash to meet the strategic needs of the firm and to create value for investors.

Financial goals Targets of financial performance (e.g., higher return on invested capital). (2)

First-mover-advantage Advantage a firm gains because it was the first to the market with a new product or service. (3)

Five forces model A framework developed by Michael Porter which focuses on five forces to assess an industry's attractiveness for profits: threat of entry posed by potential competitors; rivalry of incumbent firms; bargaining power of suppliers; bargaining power of buyers; threat of substitute products. (3)

Fixed automation Automation of the production line in which each machine performs a part of the main task repetitively; processing of units takes place incrementally in an assembly line fashion; also known as sequential automation. (8)

Flat structure Organizational structure with a few hierarchical levels, usually three or four.

Flexible automation Automation of the production line in which machines are programmed to perform discretely so that frequent design changes can be undertaken efficiently and speedily. (8)

Forward integration A form of vertical integration in which the firm expands by moving toward marketing and distribution stages of the end-product. (6)

Fragmented industry An industry with many small-to-medium size firms, each with a low market share. (3)

Franchising A form of licensing in which the franchiser grants the franchisee the right to use its trademark or trade secret within a specified market or geographic region for a fee and royalty payments. (7)

Functional-level management Management consisting of the functional heads or department supervisors to which subordinate management reports. (1)

Functional managers Managers in R&D, production, marketing, who are in-charge of specialized resources, and who assist the general manager in strategy formulation and implementation.

Functional-level strategy Decisions and actions a firm takes to achieve strengths in functional activities: manufacturing, marketing, research and development, human resource management, finance. (1, 8)

Functional structure A structure in which tasks are grouped based on knowledge or skills needed for task completion. (9)

General Agreement on Tariffs and Trade (GATT) In 1947, advanced nations of the world came together and signed an agreement giving birth to an organization bearing the same name. The purpose of GATT was to promote trade among member nations by providing each member with an opportunity to obtain from other members a "most favored trading partner" status.

General manager The president or the CEO of a corporation or one of its business units; is responsible for the overall performance of the entity he/she manages.

Geographic acquisitions Made to take the firm's current product to a new market or region.

Geographic structure A structure in which grouping of activities is based on the geographic region in which the firm competes.

Global change Refers to changes occurring in markets, economies, and political systems of the major regions of the world.

Global industry An industry that show signs of worldwide linkages in the movement of components, finished goods, know-how, and factors of production. (7)

Global strategy A strategy by which a firm designs a standard quality product, makes it in large volume in a few favorable international locations, and markets it uniformly for worldwide consumption. (7)

Globalization Refers to the cross-border integration presently occurring among national markets, resulting in their interdependence for goods, services, and factors of production. (7)

Goals and Objectives The targets and milestones the firm aims to reach in pursuit of its vision. (2)

Good governance Governance is deemed to be good when it epitomizes integrity, transparent actions, and accountability of results.

Greenfield investment Launching an entirely new operation from scratch; this is one way to establish a subsidiary in a foreign market.

Gross profit margin Operating profit, generally expressed as a ratio of sales, known as gross profit ratio or gross margin. Gross margin = (sales cost of goods sold) ÷ sales.

Grouping of tasks To achieve unity of effort, organizations must group divided tasks under common heads, into sections and departments.

Growth stage Industry is somewhat established; sellers are many in number but demand rapidly expands, keeping competition subdued; supplier and distribution segments fully emerge and the product's design undergoes incremental refinement. (5)

Hierarchical integration Coordination achieved through direct supervision.

Horizontal acquisitions (in diversification) Entail buying firms that make complementary products or serve the same customers; made to enter another segment of the same industry or a closely related industry.

Horizontal differentiation The degree to which a firm's task has been divided or fragmented into sub-tasks. (9)

Horizontal diversification Diversification that leverages a firm's current customer base or marketing assets. (6)

Horizontal integration The acquisition of direct competition.

Human resources Concerned with attracting, retaining, and motivating the right mix of people on the job.

Human resources function Is concerned with the development of policies and practices to attract, retain, motivate, and utilize competent organizational members.

Human resources strategy Decisions and actions managers take to acquire and effectively employ human resource capabilities in pursuit of the firm's business and corporate-level strategy goals.

Incumbent firms Firms already in operation in an industry. (3)

Industry A group of firms offering products or services that are similar or are close substitutes for each other. (3)

Industry environment Comprises supplier, buyer, and substitute segments, unique to each industry. Changes occurring in these segments impact firms belonging to that industry only.

Industry growth rate The percentage growth rate of the industry. (6)

Industry/product life cycle Stage-wise changes taking place in an industry or product over time. (5)

Input-based measures Measures that assess performance based on the quality of the inputs used by the firm; examples of inputs are people (skills/knowledge), systems, and capital investment. (10)

Intangible resources Not visible or easily quantifiable, such as employee skills, leadership and managerial capabilities, patents, brand name, and strategic partnerships.

Integration the means by which a firm coordinates the activities of the task-groups to achieve unity of effort.

Intended strategy Strategy selected through careful analysis.

Interactive process process in which information is continuously exchanged across individual stages to refine decisions and actions so as to enhance the quality of final outcome. (1)

Internal venturing Developing and commercializing new products through the firm's innovative capabilities. (6)

International strategy Focuses on gaining advantage through international expansion. (1)

International trade Exchange of goods in an international context through imports and exports; differs from direct foreign investment. (7)

Invested capital Stockholders' equity (or owners' funds) plus borrowed funds.

Joint venture Partnership between two or more firms that results in the creation of a third entity. (7)

Lateral integration Coordination achieved through lateral adjustments as opposed to supervisory intervention, for example, through cross-functional teams and liaison roles. (9)

Lead advantage Edge a firm enjoys because it is a pioneer; buyers associate the product with the firm's brand, endowing it with a high brand recognition and market leadership.

Legal responsibility of the firm The responsibility to obey all laws. (2)

Licensing A strategy by which a firm that owns a patented technology or design (the licensor) grants another firm (the licensee) the right to use its patent within a specified market or geographic region for a fee and royalty payments. (7)

Local responsiveness Making a dedicated investment in each geographical region to design, make, and market the product differently to suit local requirements.

Location advantages Advantages arising from locating value-chain operations in international regions most suitable for performing them.

Macro environment The broader environment comprising the economic, social, cultural, technological, political-legal, and global sectors; also known as the generic environment because the changes occurring within it impact all firms.

Managerial mindset Cognition resulting from the personal beliefs of managers and their understanding of the firm's vision and values.

Manufacturing quality How effectively each unit has been made, that is, whether the finished unit conforms to the specifications of the designed unit (also known as process quality). (8)

Market positioning Establishing the firm or its product in the market in a certain way; positioning creates in the minds of target customers a distinctive image of the firm and its products/services, relative to the competition. (4)

Market segmentation The classification of potential customers into distinct subgroups—groups with different needs, characteristics, or behavior. (8)

Market-based measures Measures that evaluate a firm's performance by examining certain market indicators, such as the ratio of new products to old, stakeholder perception, customer retention, and performance reviews by industry analysts.

Marketing Deals with the identification of customer segments, positioning the product in those segments, and delivering the message to the customer.

Marketing function Is concerned with the classification of market segments for the firm's product(s), selection of segments to target, and effectively positioning the firm or its products in the selected segment(s).

Matrix structure A structure that combines the features of functional and product structures.

Maturity stage Demand levels off and the industry is consolidated due to mergers and acquisitions; incumbent firms are well positioned in the industry with stable market share; competition intensifies. (5)

Mission statement A formal statement by the firm describing its current task or business and market position (what the firm presently is), its vision for the future (what it intends to become), and how it

plans to get to its future position (values and goals that will guide its actions toward the vision). (2)

Multidomestic industries Industries present in each nation in a distinct form; competition occurs locally and is not affected by competition in other regions of the world. (7)

Multidomestic strategy A strategy by which a firm customizes its product design and marketing to suit the unique needs of each international region. R&D, production, and marketing activities are thus undertaken in each region. (7)

Net profit margin Percentage of profit earned on sales (net income/sales).

Nominating committee of the board Comprising mostly outside directors, this committee is responsible for nominating candidates for the board and for senior management positions.

Operational competence Ability to develop, make, and market products of superior quality, at a relatively low cost, or in a timely manner.

Operational effectiveness The ability to execute similar activities more efficiently than rivals do.

Operations strategy Decisions and actions managers take to ensure that manufacturing capabilities are aligned with the firm's business strategy needs.

Opportunities Favorable conditions that, when effectively exploited, will lead a firm to its desired end. (1)

Organizational advantage An edge a firm has over rivals arising from its ability to integrate disparate organizational resources and process products more efficiently, speedily, or with unique features and attributes. (9)

Organizational culture Norms and values shared by organizational members that shape and control how they think and act.

Organizational design A framework for structuring the firm's tasks and allocating resources; it breeds and fosters the competencies the firm needs to implement its overall strategy. (9)

Output-based measures Measures that evaluate based on the outcome or end-results of the input-output transformation process.

Pay structure Refers to the relationship between different job types.

Pioneer A firm that develops a new technology and introduces it first. (4)

Political forecasts Predict government legislation likely to emerge using public opinion trends on matters of economic and social importance.

Political-legal change Refers to trends in the government's perspective toward business, resulting in increased or decreased governmental oversight of businesses.

Poor governance Opaque activities, unethical behavior, and self-dealing by company officials indicate poor governance.

Portfolio analysis Examines the potential for success for each product line or strategic business unit (SBU), given industry conditions.

Positional advantage The edge a firm has over rivals arising from a strong or a relatively secure market position (that is, a niche) it holds.

Potential competitors Firms not presently competing in an industry but have the ability to do so, if they choose to. (3)

Pricing advantage Ability to charge a higher price even when others are offering similar product at a lower price.

Primary activities Activities in the value chain directly related to the creation, making, and marketing of the product; also referred to as line activities.

Primary stakeholders Those that have an exchange relationship with the firm; provide valuable inputs to the firm's business in exchange for satisfaction of their own needs. (2)

Proactive environmental management A process in which a firm alters the environmental conditions in a way that matches its unique resources and capabilities.

Pro-business sentiment Creates a favorable climate for companies since they can operate without fear of antitrust or other accusations. Anti-business sentiment threatens operations as it increases the potential for conflict with the government.

Process design Deals with the layout and construction of the production process; also known as manufacturing engineering.

Process research Research that focuses on improving the production/operations process.

Process-based measures Measures that evaluate performance by examining the procedures or techniques used to complete the task.

Processing efficiency The ability of the firm to economically convert inputs into outputs. (10)

Processing speed The rate at which the firm can design, make, and market products or serve customers. (10)

Procurement and inbound logistics Deals with the purchasing of raw materials/components from vendors, storing them, and transferring them to production.

Product design Deals with features, functionality, and physical appearance of the product to be made; also known as product engineering.

Product research Research that focuses on improving the current product or developing a new product.

Product or Market structure A structure in which tasks are grouped based on the products made or markets (customers) served. (9)

Production/operations Deals with the processing of materials/components into finished goods.

Profitability A financial measure of business success.

Prospector A firm that competes by constantly exploring and exploiting new products or market opportunities. (5)

Question marks Businesses with a low market share in high-growth industries. (6)

Reactor A firm that has no consistent strategic approach; has no coherent plans, does not anticipate change, but reacts to environmental events as it deems fit. (5)

Realized strategy Strategy actually adopted in the end.

Related diversification Diversification that is implemented with the firm's existing strategic assets. (6)

Relative market share The ratio of the business unit's market share to the market share held by its largest rival in the industry. (6)

Research A scientific activity that focuses on identifying new information. (8)

Research and development (R&D) Combines two distinct, yet related, functions; research focuses on identifying scientific information needed to develop new products and processes or enhance current products and processes; developmental activities focus on the actual design of products and production processes. (8)

Resource-based view (RBV) The thinking that explains competitive advantage based on the firm's resources and capabilities. (4)

Resources The stockpile of assets held by a firm to be used as "inputs" in its business activities. (1, 4)

Rivalry The intensity of competition among incumbent firms. (3)

ROIC Percentage return that the firm has earned on financial capital contributed by investors.

Royalties Regular payment of commissions on sales.

Rules and procedures Planned mechanisms that integrate the activities of work groups.

Secondary stakeholders Those that do not have an exchange relationship with the firm but have the potential to harm the firm if the firm's actions harm them. (2)

Service Provides after-sales service such as product installation, parts delivery, maintenance and repairs, and technical assistance.

Single-business concentration A strategy in which the firm focuses on a single business only (e.g., beverage) by offering a range of products (e.g., cola, water, juice), either in one or several geographic locations. (6)

Situation analysis A continuous examination of company strengths and weaknesses against industry opportunities and threats.

Social change Comprises demographic and lifestyle trends. These trends indicate changes in consumer preferences and needs and opportunities arising from them.

Social forecasts Predict demographic and lifestyle changes using trends in population growth, life expectancies, education and training, family formation, and travel and leisure activities of people.

Sole venture A foreign business unit in which a firm has 100 percent stock ownership without a partner; also known as wholly-owned subsidiary. (7)

Staff specialists Experts with deep knowledge in specialized activities such as planning or general administration who act as advisors in strategy formulation and implementation.

Stakeholders Individuals or groups in the firm's environment that affect, or affected by, the firm's actions; have a stake in what the firm does and how well it performs. (2)

Standards Models or benchmarks that specify an intended outcome; tangible targets to be reached, rules to be followed, and behaviors to be learned are examples of standards. (10)

Stars Business units with a high market share in industries that have a high growth rate. (6)

Strategic alliance An agreement between two firms to cooperate in certain ways to achieve strategic benefits. (6, 7)

Strategic alliances, vertical Cooperative agreements among firms in the value chain sequence (suppliers, manufacturers, distributors) emphasizing reciprocal help.

Strategic business unit (SBU) Business unit of a diversified firm, grouped based on commonality of customers or competitors. (6)

Strategic Business Unit (SBU) structure Structure of a well-diversified firm that groups products based on the commonality of customers or competitors under a few manageable divisions (referred to as SBUs) to facilitate effective managerial control. (9)

Strategic control A process in which managers evaluate the firm's strategic performance, the progress it has made toward strategic goals. (1, 10)

Strategic goals Strategic or competitive advantages sought by a firm industry (e.g., technological leadership). (10)

Strategic groups Clusters of firms within an industry that pursue common or similar strategies. (3)

Strategic leadership Broadly refers to the ability of managers to conceive a vision and guide the firm toward that vision. Strategic management is successful when managers show leadership by not only articulating an inspiring vision, but also by making other choices that would give the firm the competency it needs to realize that vision. (1)

Strategic leadership Refers to the leadership capabilities of strategic managers in conceiving an inspiring vision and guiding the firm to its vision. The quality of leadership is assessed by the strategic choices managers make that endow the firm with the competitive advantages it needs for sustained good performance. (4)

Strategic management Comprises a series of long-term managerial decisions and actions in which a firm selects and implements strategies. The purpose of these strategies is to build the firm's strengths through market positioning and/or accumulation of internal resources that will give the firm an advantage over rivals. (1)

Strategy A set of decisions and actions that managers take to attain superior company performance relative to rivals.

Strategy implementation Focuses on the organizational choices a firm makes to achieve resource coordination necessary to effectively execute its strategy.

Stuck in the middle A situation in which a firm could not generate either a cost or differentiation advantage because it sought both.

Substitute products Products that satisfy the same consumer need as the subject firm's but competing in a different industry or market segment. (3)

Successful firm One that not only earns above average profits today but has the potential to earn similar profits in the future, as well, as evidenced by the competitive advantage it possesses.

Support activities Activities in the value chain that provide the expert help necessary for the primary activities to take place; also referred to as staff activities.

Sustained competitive advantage The ability of a firm to maintain its edge over rivals and earn superior profits for a long period of time.

Switching costs Costs the buyer must assume when switching from the product of an incumbent firm to the new entrant's. (3)

SWOT analysis A technique in which managers compare industry opportunities and threats to company strengths and weaknesses. (4)

Tall structure Organizational structure with many hierarchical levels, usually eight or nine.

Tangible resources Visible, quantifiable resources such as plants, facilities, equipment, and liquid funds.

Tapered integration Partial integration strategy in which the firm makes only part of the needed supplies in-house, buying the rest from outsiders, or sells its output through independent retailers in addition to company-owned outlets.

Target market Market segments that offer the greatest profit-making potential; target market selection is influenced by segment size, structure, and the firm's resources and capabilities.

Task What the firm currently does in terms of products offered and markets or customers served. (2)

Technological change Changes occurring in the technical knowledge used in transforming scientific information into commercial goods.

Technological forecasts Predict the types of technologies likely to emerge in the future using trends in private and public sector R&D investments, growth rate in categories of scientific personnel, patents awarded, and rate of technological obsolescence.

Technology Refers to engineering or technical know-how; commonly defined as the technique or process used in converting scientific information into commercial goods. (3)

Threats Unfavorable conditions that, when not effectively dealt with, can harm a firm's current business, profitability, and future plans.

Threats of entry Refers to the likelihood that new firms can easily enter the industry and carve inroads onto the profits of incumbent firms. (3)

Transaction costs Monies spent in the selection of a competitive vendor/distributor, contract negotiations, payment of legal fees, and inventory ordering. (6)

Transnational strategy Combination type strategy, mixing multinational and global features; competes through product standardization but also adapts through customization where necessary. (7)

Undifferentiated marketing A marketing strategy by which a firm ignores market segments and instead treats the market as a single, homogenous unit. (8)

Value chain Stages of activities during which value is added to the input at every stage; successive value-additions transform the input into a finished product. (4)

Value chain analysis An examination of the value-chain stages to determine whether the firm has strengths in operational areas relevant for competitive success.

Values and Beliefs The ideals the firm is committed to that will lead it to its vision. (2)

Vertical acquisitions Acquisitions along the value chain; made to meet the firm's supply or distribution needs.

Vertical differentiation The number of hierarchical levels in a structure. (9)

Vertical integration A strategy in which the firm expands the scope of its operations, allowing it to perform several value chain activities, in-house (for example, component production, product assembly, distribution, after-sales service). (6)

Vision What kind of business enterprise a firm aspires to become in the future. (1, 2)

Volume flexibility The ability of the operating system and its set-up to efficiently and rapidly adjust to volume changes when industry demand fluctuates. (8)

WACC Weighted average cost of capital; represents what investors require as a return on the capital they have invested.

Work systems The ways in which a firm structures jobs, allocates discretion, and exercises supervision.

World Trade Organization (WTO) In 1995, GATT was replaced by WTO which has a much broader mission in promoting trade among all nations, not just advanced nations. In 2005, there were about 150 nations as members of WTO.

Name Index

Abbott, A., 248n18
Abell, D. F., 240n21, 243n21
Agarwal, S., 247n37
Ahlstrand, B., 239n14–15, 242n29
Ainina, M. F., 242n13
Allenbaugh, E., 240n1
Alsop, R., 241n29
Amit, R., 243n16–17, 243n19, 243n28
Anderson, C. R., 244n23
Andrews, K., 239n13
Ansoff, H. I., 239n12, 239n23
Armstrong, G., 171n, 247n3–4

Baetz, M. C., 240n8, 240n10, 240n13
Baglli, C. V., 245n27
Baliga, B. R., 249n23
Bamberger, P., 248n19–20, 248n23
Bandler, J., 239n1
Banker, R. D., 249n5
Barney, J. B., 239n5, 242n2–3, 242n31,
    243n13–14, 243n26–27, 244n38, 247n18,
    248n23
Bart, C. K., 240n8–10, 240n13, 240n14,
    240n24, 241n38
Bartkus, B., 240n12, 240n23
Bartlett, C. A., 243n30, 246n6, 246n9, 246n18,
    247n24–25, 247n27, 247n29–30, 248n15
Bedeian, G., 249n2
Bell, A. G., 49
Belson, K., 243n36
Benson, G., 241n40
Berger, P. G., 245n21
Berkman, E., 249n10
Berner, R., 105n
Bernheim, B. D., 245n23
Bernstein, A., 246n2
Besanko, D., 242n4
Bettis, R. A., 246n31
Beucke, D., 239n3
Bianco, A., 242n10, 244n1
Bickford, D. J., 243n35

Biggadike, R., 245n20
Black, J. A., 243n11
Blair, J. D., 241n32
Boal, K. B., 243n11
Bonamici, K., 240n1
Bonn, I., 240n38
Bontis, N., 240n10, 240n14, 240n24, 241n38
Bourgeois, L. J., 242n9
Bourne, M., 249n12
Bowman, E. H., 245n2
Bradsher, K., 242n16
Brodzinski, J. D., 242n13
Bunz, U. K., 248n1
Byrne, J. A., 239n5

Camerius, J. W., 244n1
Campbell, A., 240n5, 240n16, 240n22
Cardinal, L. B., 245n21, 245n30
Carroll, A. B., 40–41, 241n28, 241n46
Cary, P., 239n1
Chandler, A. D., 195, 245n3, 248n6, 248n13
Charan, R., 240n40
Chattopadhyay, P., 241n3
Clarkson, A. E., 241n28
Cockburn, I. M., 242n5
Cohen, W. M., 244n39
Collins, E.G.C., 242n17
Collins, J. C., 239n25, 240n2, 240n11,
    240n19–20, 241n25
Collis, D. J., 242n2, 243n14, 245n5–6, 245n24,
    247n18
Colvin, G., 239n1, 240n1, 240n40
Comanor, W., 245n9
Conger, J., 241n40
Cooper, A. C., 243n33
Crandall, R. W., 241n1
Curry, J., 242n28

Daily, C. M., 241n37
D'Aveni, R. A., 239n9, 242n30, 243n12,
    244n16, 244n41

263

Subject Index